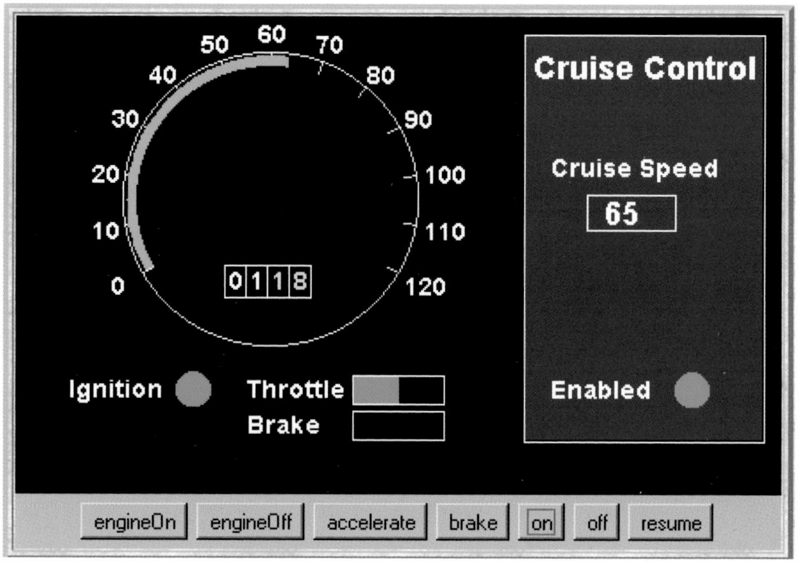

Cruise Control System Applet (Chapters 1 and 8)

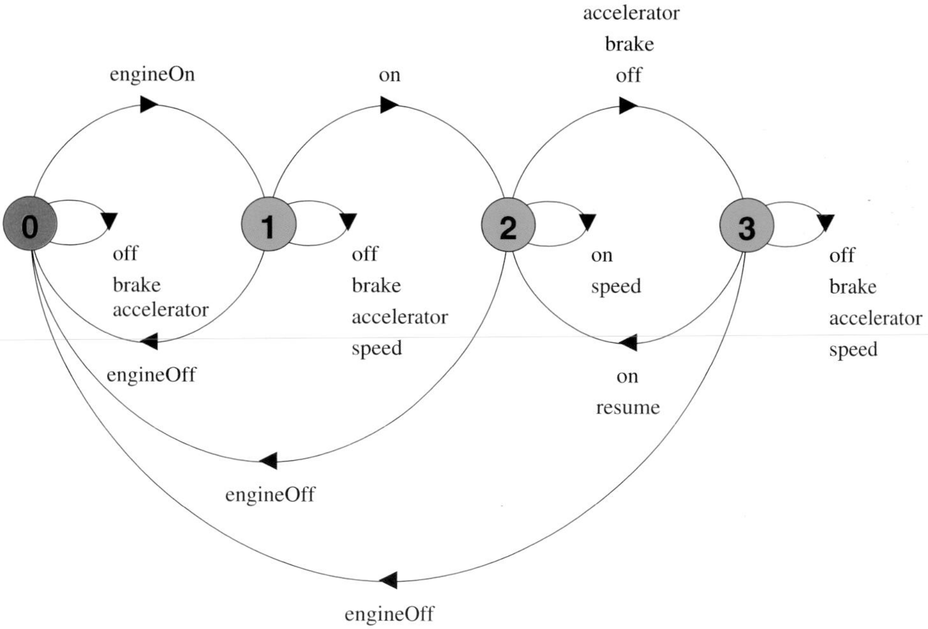

Labeled Transition System (LTS) for the Cruise Control System (Chapter 8)

Y. C. CHEN

CONCURRENCY

CONCURRENCY

STATE MODELS & JAVA PROGRAMS

JEFF MAGEE & JEFF KRAMER
Department of Computing, Imperial College London, UK

John Wiley & Sons, Ltd

Telephone (+44) 1243 779777

Email (for orders and customer service enquiries): cs-books@wiley.co.uk
Visit our Home Page on www.wiley.com

Other Wiley Editorial Offices

John Wiley & Sons Inc., 111 River Street, Hoboken, NJ 07030, USA

Jossey-Bass, 989 Market Street, San Francisco, CA 94103-1741, USA

Wiley-VCH Verlag GmbH, Boschstr. 12, D-69469 Weinheim, Germany

John Wiley & Sons Australia Ltd, 42 McDougall Street, Milton, Queensland 4064, Australia

John Wiley & Sons (Asia) Pte Ltd, 2 Clementi Loop #02-01, Jin Xing Distripark, Singapore 129809

John Wiley & Sons Canada Ltd, 22 Worcester Road, Etobicoke, Ontario, Canada M9W 1L1

Wiley also publishes its books in a variety of electronic formats. Some content that appears in print may not be available in electronic books.

Library of Congress Cataloging-in-Publication Data:

Magee, Jeff, 1952–
Concurrency : state models & Java programs / Jeff Magee & Jeff Kramer.
p. cm.
Includes bibliographical references and index.
ISBN-13 978-0-470-09355-9 (cloth : alk. paper)
ISBN-10 0-470-09355-2 (cloth : alk. paper)
1. Parallel programming (Computer science) 2. Java (Computer program language) I. Kramer, Jeff. II. Title.

QA76.642.M34 2006
005.2′75 – dc22

2006004540

British Library Cataloguing in Publication Data

A catalogue record for this book is available from the British Library

ISBN-13: 978-0-470-09356-6
ISBN-10: 0-470-09356-0

Typeset in 10/13pt Palatino by Laserwords Private Limited, Chennai, India
Printed and bound in Great Britain by Antony Rowe Ltd, Chippenham, Wiltshire
This book is printed on acid-free paper responsibly manufactured from sustainable forestry in which at least two trees are planted for each one used for paper production.

To Judith, Thomas and John

Jeff Magee

To Nitza, Lisa and Alon

Jeff Kramer

Contents

Preface

This book arose from concurrent programming courses taught by the authors at Imperial College London and from their experience with using concurrency in industrial applications. It was motivated by dissatisfaction with the lack of practical and accessible techniques that aid reasoning about designs for concurrent software.

Most courses and textbooks in this area are targeted at *either* the theory and formal methods aspects of concurrency *or* the practical aspects of concurrent programming and concurrency in operating systems. Due to the lack of a widely available concurrent programming language, textbooks had to resort to special purpose notations that could not easily be related by the reader to normal sequential programming practice. Two recent technical developments have made it possible to offer a practical and accessible approach to learning about concurrency and concurrent programming. First, model-checking tools have made the use of design models for concurrent behavior practical, informative and rewarding. Second, the availability and widespread use of Java has solved the problem of finding an accessible general purpose programming language with in-built concurrency constructs. As a result, this book offers a soundly-based systematic approach to the development of concurrent software which is supported by software tools, is interesting and fun to use, and can be used to develop practical concurrent programs.

What Can Readers Expect from this Book?

The book provides a comprehensive description and explanation of the important *concepts* and *techniques* in concurrent programming, the problems that arise and the means for ensuring that desirable properties are achieved and undesirable ones avoided. Readers will learn about concepts such as threads and interaction, gain an appreciation of how these lead to problems such as interference and deadlock, and learn how to use techniques such as exclusion and synchronization to good effect.

To ensure a thorough *understanding*, concurrency concepts, techniques and problems are presented in many forms: through informal descriptions and illustrative examples, abstractly in models and concretely in Java. The modeling techniques will enable readers to reason about the properties of their proposed designs and programs. As in other engineering disciplines, modeling is promoted as a means to gaining greater confidence in the proposed designs. Using Java, readers can turn their designs into programs.

Together with a knowledge and understanding of the principles of concurrency, readers can expect to aquire *experience* in its application. The book uses examples to illustrate concepts and techniques, and exercises for learning by doing. Use of the associated analysis tool provides practical experience of concurrency modeling, model animation, model property checking and model correction. Similarly, use of Java provides practical experience of programming concurrency.

Thus, the book provides:

- a systematic treatment of the concepts and issues in concurrency;
- a rigorous technique to specify and model concurrent behavior, with analysis tools for animation and verification;
- a wide range of Java examples to illustrate the concepts and issues in concurrent programming.

We hope that this will leave readers with the ability to use concurrency with confidence and expertise, recognizing when problems might arise and knowing how to avoid or solve them. Concurrency is a fascinating and challenging area of software design. The combination of *learning* and *doing* should make acquiring design skills in this area an interesting and enjoyable process. We hope that readers will find that concurrency can be both challenging and fun!

Intended Readership

The book is intended for students in Computer Science and for professional software engineers and programmers. We believe that it has much to offer for anyone interested in the concepts of concurrency, interaction and synchronization.

Readers are expected to have some background in sequential programming and an acquaintance with object-oriented concepts. Some knowledge of operating systems concepts is an advantage, but is not a prerequisite.

The material has been used by a variety of students: undergraduate students in the second year of three and four year computing, software engineering and combined computing/electrical engineering degree courses; and graduate students taking conversion courses in computing. In all cases, the material represented the students' first introduction to concurrent programming.

Chapters 1 to 8 are designed to provide a comprehensive and cohesive course on concurrency. They cover the main concepts of concurrency, including modeling, programming and the process of model-based design. Since each chapter builds on the preceding one, we recommend that these chapters be read sequentially from start to finish.

Chapters 9 to 14 provide more advanced material on dynamic systems, message passing, concurrent software architectures, timed systems, program verification and logical properties. Readers may pick and choose from these according to their interests.

Additional Resources

Accompanying this book are the following:

- Java examples and demonstration programs
- state models for the examples
- the Labeled Transition System Analyzer (*LTSA*) for concurrency modeling, model animation, and model property checking
- overhead slides for course presentation

These are provided at the following URL: http://www.wileyeurope.com/college/magee.

Second Edition

This second edition of the book provides the following main additions:

- Dynamic Systems.
  A new model and implementation for bounded dynamic resource allocation is presented and discussed in Chapter 9.
- A new chapter on Program Verification.
  The general approach used in the book is model-based design, where models are developed and analyzed before implementation. This chapter describes how concurrent implementations in Java can be modeled and verified. This is illustrated using examples from previous chapters.
- Sequential process composition.
  Processes are generally composed using parallel composition to model interaction and concurrency. Composition is extended to include sequential composition as well, thereby extending the ways in which models can be specified and analyzed.

- A new chapter on Logical Properties.
  The formalism used in the book is based on the identification and specification of events and actions rather than states. This chapter introduces the use of fluents and abstract states as a means of specifying logical, state-based properties in an event-based formalism. This extension supports property specification using Linear Temporal Logic (LTL). In addition to the provision of counterexamples in the case of property violations, witnesses can be provided to give examples of acceptable executions. This is illustrated using examples, both new and from previous chapters.
- Extensions to LTSA.
  Tool support for model analysis using *LTSA* has been extended to provide a number of additional features. These include a revised user interface, on-the-fly safety and progress analysis allowing complete analysis of much larger state spaces, approximate safety analysis using Holtzmann's SuperTrace algorithm for larger state spaces, support for sequential composition, support for graphic animation, no limit on potential statespace (previously 2**63), and Partial Order Reduction during composition and analysis.
- Java platform.
  The demonstration programs and examples have been updated to use the new Java version which includes generic classes.

Acknowledgments

We wish to thank our colleagues in the Distributed Software Engineering research section for many helpful discussions over the years, and for their contributions to the work on software architecture. In particular, we gratefully acknowledge the contributions of Shing Chi (SC) Cheung and Dimitra Giannakopoulou to the work on behavior analysis. SC had the insight to select LTS as an appropriate modeling formalism, provided much of the ground-work and was a prime contributor to our investigation of safety properties. Dimitra has contributed crucial work in the theory and analysis of safety, liveness and progress properties, and the semantics of FSP.

Our thanks are due to Steve Crane, Nat Pryce, Wolfgang Emmerich and the anonymous reviewers for their useful comments and suggestion, on early drafts of the book. Their encouragement, and the enthusiasm of our students, is greatly appreciated. We would like to thank Storm Thorgerson, the cover designer, who worked beyond the call of duty and even friendship to produce a cover worthy of a trainspotter extraordinaire.

We would like to thank our families for their tolerance during the writing of this book. Our children – Lisa, Alon, Thomas and John – were kind enough to feign enthusiam for the examples and demonstration applets. Let us hope that the delusion of future fortune, with which we placated our wives Nitza and Judith, is not revealed as such too soon.

We take this opportunity to thank those many readers who have offered us their encouragement and suggestions. In particular, we are indebted to David Holmes who provided the motivation for Chapter 13 to address the problem of verifying the Java implementations. We also thank Alexander Höher for his comments on the bounded allocator of Chapter 9, and Paul Stroop for his many useful comments and suggestions. Finally we would like to express our thanks to the more recent members of the Distributed Software Engineering research group for their comments and contributions. In particular, we gratefully acknowledge the further contribution of Dimitra Giannakopoulou on fluents, and of Sebastian Uchitel to the work on model synthesis.

Jeff Magee & Jeff Kramer
January 2006

1 Introduction

Between June 1985 and January 1987, a computerized radiation therapy machine called Therac-25 caused six known accidents involving massive overdoses with resultant deaths and serious injuries. Although most accidents are systemic involving complex interactions between various components and activities, and Therac-25 is not an exception in this respect, concurrent programming errors played an important part in these six accidents. Race conditions between different concurrent activities in the control program resulted in occasional erroneous control outputs. Furthermore, the sporadic nature of the errors caused by faulty concurrent programs contributed to the delay in recognizing that there was a problem. The designers of the Therac-25 software seemed largely unaware of the principles and practice of concurrent programming.

The wide acceptance of Java with its in-built concurrency constructs means that concurrent programming is no longer restricted to the minority of programmers involved in operating systems and embedded real-time applications. Concurrency is useful in a wide range of applications where responsiveness and throughput are issues. While most programmers are not engaged in the implementation of safety critical systems such as Therac-25, increasing numbers are using concurrent programming constructs in less esoteric applications. Errors in these applications and systems may not be directly life-threatening but they adversely affect our quality of life and may have severe financial implications. An understanding of the principles of concurrent programming and an appreciation of how it is practiced are an essential part of the education of computing science undergraduates and of the background of software engineering professionals. The pervasive nature of computing and the Internet makes it also an important topic for those whose primary activity may not be computing but who write programs none the less.

1.1 Concurrent Programs

Most complex systems and tasks that occur in the physical world can be broken down into a set of simpler activities. For example, the activities involved in building a house include bricklaying, carpentry, plumbing, electrical installation and roofing. These activities do not always occur strictly sequentially, one after the other, but can overlap and take place concurrently. For example, the plumbing and wiring in a new house can be installed at the same time. The activity described by a computer program can also be subdivided into simpler activities, each described by a subprogram. In traditional sequential programs, these subprograms or procedures are executed one after the other in a fixed order determined by the program and its input. The execution of one procedure does not overlap in time with another. In concurrent programs, computational activities are permitted to overlap in time and the subprogram executions describing these activities proceed concurrently.

The execution of a program (or subprogram) is termed a *process* and the execution of a concurrent program thus consists of multiple processes. As we see later, concurrent execution does not require multiple processors. Interleaving the instructions from multiple processes on a single processor can be used to simulate concurrency, giving the illusion of parallel execution. Of course, if a computer has multiple processors then the instructions of a concurrent program can actually be executed in parallel rather than being interleaved.

Structuring a program as a set of concurrent activities or processes has many advantages. For programs that interact with the environment to control some physical system, the parallelism and concurrency in that system can be reflected in the control program structure. Concurrency can be used to speed up response to user interaction by offloading time-consuming tasks to separate processes. Throughput can be improved by using multiple processes to manage communication and device latencies. These advantages are illustrated in detail in subsequent chapters. However, the advantages of concurrency may be offset by the increased complexity of concurrent programs. Managing this complexity and the principles and techniques necessary for the construction of well-behaved concurrent programs is the main subject matter of this book.

In order to illustrate the need for a rigorous approach to concurrent program design and implementation, let us consider an example.

Consider an automobile cruise control system that has the following requirements. It is controlled by three buttons: *resume, on* and *off* (Figure 1.1). When the engine is running and *on* is pressed, the cruise control system records the current speed and maintains the car at this speed. When the accelerator, brake or *off* is pressed, the cruise control system disengages but retains the speed setting. If *resume* is pressed, the system accelerates or de-accelerates the car back to the previously recorded speed.

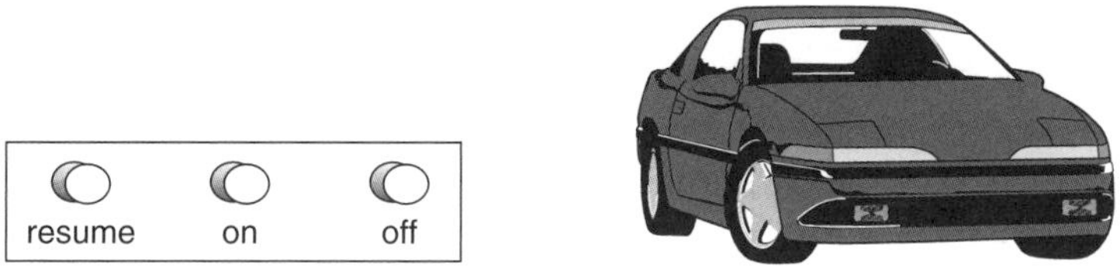

Figure 1.1 Cruise control system.

Our task is to provide a Java program that satisfies the specified requirements and behaves in a safe manner. How should we design such a program? What software processes should we construct and how should we structure them to form a program? How can we ensure that our program provides the behavior that we require while avoiding unsafe or undesirable behavior?

Given no guidance, we may be tempted simply to use previous design experience and construct the program as best as we can, using the appropriate Java concurrency constructs. To test the cruise control software, we could construct a simulation environment such as that illustrated in Figure 1.2. The website that accompanies this book contains this environment as an interactive Java applet for

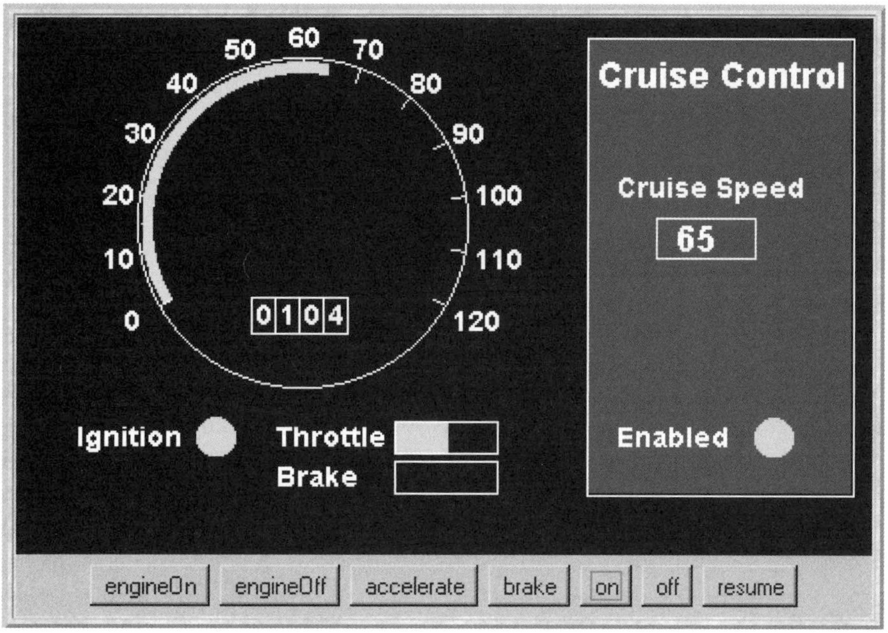

Figure 1.2 Simulation of the cruise control system.

use and experimentation (http://www.wileyeurope.com/college/magee). The buttons at the bottom of the display can be used to control the simulation: to switch the engine on or off; to *resume* or turn the cruise control system *on* or *off*; and to press the accelerator or brake (simulated by repeatedly pressing the relevant button).

The behavior of the system can be checked using particular scenarios such as the following:

- Is the cruise control system enabled after the engine is switched on and the *on* button is pressed?
- Is the cruise control system disabled when the brake is pressed?
- Is the cruise control system enabled when *resume* is then pressed?

However, testing such software is difficult, as there are many possible scenarios. How do we know when we have conducted a sufficient number of test scenarios?

For instance, what happens in the unlikely event that the engine is switched off while the cruise control system is still enabled? The system behaves as follows. It *retains the cruise control setting*, and, when the ignition is again switched on, the car accelerates so as to resume the previous speed setting!

Would testing have discovered that this dangerous behavior is present in the system? Perhaps, but in general testing is extremely difficult for concurrent programs as it relies on executing the particular sequence of events and actions that cause a problem. Since concurrent events may occur in any order, the problem sequences may never occur in the test environment, but may only show up in the deployed system, as with the Therac-25 machine.

There must be a better way to design, check and construct concurrent programs!

1.2 The Modeling Approach

A model is a simplified representation of the real world and, as such, includes only those aspects of the real-world system relevant to the problem at hand. For example, a model airplane, used in wind tunnel tests, models only the external shape of the airplane. The power of the airplane engines, the number of seats and its cargo capacity do not affect the plane's aerodynamic properties. Models are widely used in engineering since they can be used to focus on a particular aspect of a real-world system such as the aerodynamic properties of an airplane or the strength of a bridge. The reduction in scale and complexity achieved by modeling allows engineers to analyze properties such as the stress and strain on the structural components of a bridge. The earliest models used in engineering, such as airplane models for wind tunnels and ship models for drag tanks, were physical. Modern models tend to be mathematical in nature and as such can be analyzed using computers.

This book takes a modeling approach to the design of concurrent programs. Our models represent the behavior of real concurrent programs written in Java. The models abstract much of the detail of real programs concerned with data representation, resource allocation and user interaction. They let us focus on concurrency. We can animate these models to investigate the concurrent behavior of the intended program. More importantly, we can *mechanically* verify that a model satisfies particular safety and progress properties, which are required of the program when it is implemented. This mechanical or algorithmic verification is made possible by a model-checking tool *LTSA* (Labeled Transition System Analyzer). Exhaustive model checking using *LTSA* allows us to check for both desirable and undesirable properties for all possible sequences of events and actions. *LTSA* is available from the World Wide Web (http://www.wileyeurope.com/college/magee). As it has been implemented in Java, it runs on a wide range of platforms, either as an applet or as an application program.

The models introduced in the book are based on finite state machines. Finite state machines are familiar to many programmers and engineers. They are used to specify the dynamic behavior of objects in well-known object-oriented design methods such as Booch (1986), OMT (Object Modeling Technique) (Rumbaugh, Blaha, Premerlani, *et al.*, 1991) and, more recently, the all-encompassing UML (Unified Modeling Language) (Booch, Rumbaugh and Jacobson, 1998). They are also extensively used in the design of digital circuits – the original engineering use. For those not yet familiar with state machines, they have an intuitive, easily grasped semantics and a simple graphical representation. The state machines used in this book (technically, Labeled Transition Systems) have well-defined mathematical properties, which facilitate formal analysis and mechanical checking, thus avoiding the tedium (and error introduction) inherent in manual formal methods.

For instance, for the cruise control system described in section 1.1, we can model the various processes of the system as state machines. A state machine for the process responsible for obtaining the current speed is given in Figure 1.3. Starting from *state*(0), it indicates that once the engine is switched on, it transits to *state*(1) and can then repeatedly obtain a speed reading until the engine is switched off, when it returns to *state*(0). Other processes can be modeled similarly. We can compose the system from the constituent processes according to the proposed design structure, indicating the interactions between the processes. The advantage is that such models can be used to animate and check the behavior of the overall system *before* it is implemented. Figure 1.4 shows an animation of the model for the cruise control system. It clearly shows the problem encountered in our simulation: if the engine is switched off and on again when cruise control is enabled, the previous speed setting is resumed. Exhaustive analysis can be used to identify

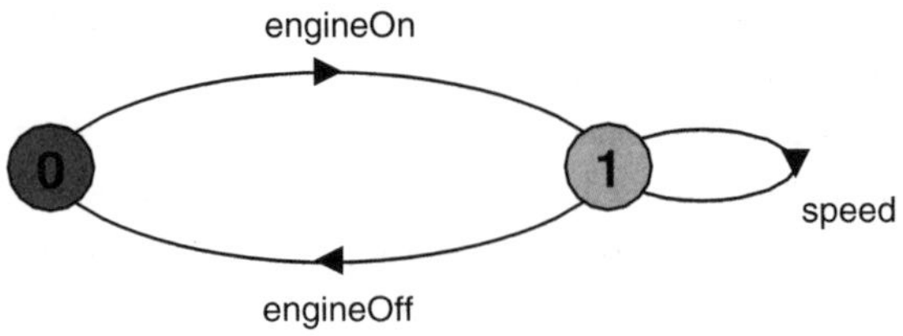

Figure 1.3 Speed input process.

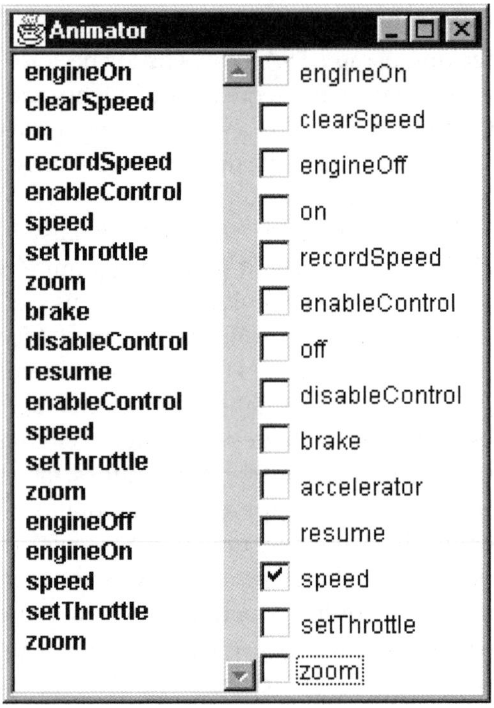

Figure 1.4 Animation of the cruise control system.

the problem under all possible situations. Furthermore, to help understand and correct the problem, the model checker produces the particular sequence of actions that led to it!

Later chapters describe and illustrate how to provide and use such models to gain confidence in the correctness and validity of a proposed design. We illustrate how premature and erroneous implementations can be avoided by careful modeling and analysis. Further, we indicate how such models can be systematically transformed into Java programs. The cruise control system is fully described, modeled and implemented in Chapter 8.

Note that representing state machines graphically severely limits the complexity of problems that can be addressed. Consequently, we use a textual notation (Finite State Processes, *FSP*) to describe our models. The *LTSA* tool associated with the book translates *FSP* descriptions to the equivalent graphical description. The book itself presents the initial models in both textual and graphical forms to enable the reader to become familiar with the meaning of *FSP* descriptions. Technically, *FSP* is a process calculus – one of a family of notations pioneered by Milner (1989), Calculus of Communicating Systems (CCS), and Hoare (1985), Communicating Sequential Processes (CSP), for concisely describing and reasoning about concurrent programs. The difference from these notations is largely syntactic: *FSP* is designed to be easily machine readable. Like CCS and CSP, *FSP* has algebraic properties; however, it is used in this book primarily as a concise way of describing Labeled Transition Systems.

1.3 Practice

Previous authors of concurrent programming textbooks have been hampered by the lack of a widely available and generally accepted programming language with concurrency features. Java meets the criteria of availability and acceptance and has the advantage of being a general-purpose language with concurrency rather than a special-purpose language of restricted applicability. Consequently, we use Java exclusively as the language for programming examples. The simplicity of the concurrency features in Java is an advantage since more complex concurrency abstractions can be constructed and packaged as classes.

The full source of the set of example programs presented in the book is provided with the book and is available on the Web. In addition, all of the example programs may be run as applets in Web browsers. We believe that the ability to execute the programs is a significant aid to understanding the issues involved. The controls embedded in most of the example programs enable different execution scenarios to be set up, facilitating "what if" questions to be asked of the programs. The satisfaction of seeing (and experiencing) rather than merely believing is important in sustaining both interest and comprehension. This is as true for self-study as it is for formally taught courses.

The availability of Java on a wide range of platforms means that most readers will be able to treat both the modeling and programming problems included in the book as implementation rather than purely pen-and-paper exercises. In many of the problems a graphical interface is already provided so that the reader can concentrate on the concurrent programming component of the problem.

We make no apologies for including in the set of examples and exercises those that are sometimes disparagingly referred to as "toy problems". Typical of this class of example is the Dining Philosophers problem. The authors regard these examples as being valuable in condensing and crystallizing particular concurrent programming problems. They let the reader concentrate on the concurrency issues without the burden of understanding the application context. These examples are widely used in the literature on concurrent programming as a means of comparing different concurrent programming languages and constructs.

1.4 Content Overview

The concepts of concurrency are presented in a careful, systematic manner. Each concept is introduced and explained, indicating how it is modeled and implemented. In this way, state models and Java programs are presented hand-in-hand throughout the book. Furthermore, every chapter uses examples to illustrate the concepts, models and programs.

The next two chapters introduce the basic concepts of concurrent programming. Chapter 2 introduces the concept of a process, for modeling a sequence of actions, and a thread, for implementing such a sequence in Java. Chapter 3 introduces concurrency, both in the form of models of concurrent processes and in the form of multi-threaded programs.

The following two chapters deal with some of the basic problems associated with concurrency and the means for dealing with them. Chapter 4 discusses shared objects and the associated problem of interference if concurrent activities are allowed free access to such objects. This leads to the need for mutually exclusive access to shared objects. Further requirements for synchronization and coordination are introduced in Chapter 5, manifested as guarded actions in the models and monitors in Java.

Concurrent programs must be checked to ensure that they satisfy the required properties. One of the general properties is the absence of deadlock, where the program stops and makes no further progress. Deadlock is discussed in Chapter 6. Properties are generally described as either safety properties, concerned with a program not reaching a bad state, or liveness properties, concerned with a program eventually reaching a good state. These are usually specific to the particular application required. The modeling and checking of safety and liveness properties for Java programs are discussed in Chapter 7.

Chapter 8 reiterates the design approach used implicitly in the previous chapters, that of model-based design of programs. The cruise control system, discussed above, is used as the example.

The last six chapters of the book deal with a number of more advanced topics of interest. Chapter 9 deals with dynamic systems of processes and threads.

Chapter 10 deals with systems that interact using message passing. Chapter 11 discusses various concurrent software architectures, modeling and implementing common structures and patterns of interaction. Chapter 12 discusses timed systems, indicating how time can be modeled and included in implementations of concurrent programs. Chapter 13 addresses the problem of verifying implementations by modeling the relevant program language constructs and analyzing the resultant models. Finally Chapter 14 introduces fluents as a means of specifying properties in a state-based manner and of checking properties specified using a temporal logic.

Summary

This chapter has introduced the area of concurrent programs and justified the need for a model-based approach to design and construction. In particular:

- Finite state models are used to represent concurrent behavior. These can be animated and analyzed to gain confidence in the correctness and validity of a proposed design.
- The Java programming language is used for constructing concurrent programs. Java is general-purpose and has concurrency features.
- Examples and exercises are used throughout the book to illustrate the concepts and provide the opportunity for experimentation and learning by experience.

Notes and Further Reading

A comprehensive description of the Therac-25 incident and investigation can be obtained from the paper, *An investigation of the Therac-25 accidents*, by Nancy Leveson and Clark Turner (1993).

The automobile cruise control system is a simplified version of a real system. The example is fully discussed in Chapter 8.

There are a number of existing books on concurrency and concurrent programming. A collection of original papers on the invention and origins of concurrent programming from the mid 1960s to the late 1970s is presented in the book by Per Brinch Hansen (2002), *The Origins of Concurrent Programming: From Semaphores to Remote Procedure Calls*. Ben-Ari (1990) provides a simple introduction to the area in his book, *Principles of Concurrent and Distributed Programming*. A comprehensive coverage of the area, with logical reasoning and many examples, is provided by Greg Andrews (1991) in his book, *Concurrent Programming: Principles and Practice*. A further readable text in the area is that by Burns and Davies (1993), *Concurrent Programming*. A formal, logic-based approach is provided by Fred Schneider

(1997) in his book, *On Concurrent Programming.* For more on the pragmatics of object-orientation and concurrent programming in Java, readers may consult the book by Doug Lea (1999), *Concurrent Programming in Java™: Design Principles and Patterns.* A recent comprehensive text is that by Vijay Garg (2004), *Concurrent and Distributed Computing in Java.*

2
Processes and Threads

In Chapter 1, we noted that in concurrent programs, computational activities are permitted to overlap in time and that the subprogram executions describing these activities proceed concurrently. The execution of a program (or subprogram) is termed a *process* and the execution of a concurrent program thus consists of multiple processes. In this chapter, we define how processes can be modeled as finite state machines. We then describe how processes can be programmed as *threads*, the form of process supported by Java.

2.1 Modeling Processes

A process is the execution of a sequential program. The state of a process at any point in time consists of the values of explicit variables, declared by the programmer, and implicit variables such as the program counter and contents of data/address registers. As a process executes, it transforms its state by executing statements. Each statement consists of a sequence of one or more *atomic actions* that make indivisible state changes. Examples of atomic actions are uninterruptible machine instructions that load and store registers. A more abstract model of a process, which ignores the details of state representation and machine instructions, is simply to consider a process as having a state modified by indivisible or atomic actions. Each action causes a transition from the current state to the next state. The order in which actions are allowed to occur is determined by a transition graph that is an abstract representation of the program. In other words, we can model processes as finite state machines.

Figure 2.1 depicts the state machine for a light switch that has the actions `on` and `off`. We use the following diagrammatic conventions. The initial state is always numbered *0* and transitions are always drawn in a clockwise direction. Thus in Figure 2.1, `on` causes a transition from *state*(0) to *state*(1) and `off` causes a transition from *state*(1) to *state*(0). This form of state machine description is known

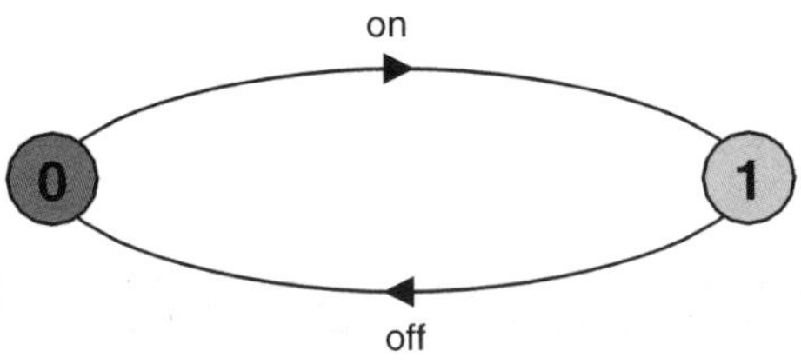

Figure 2.1 Light switch state machine.

as a Labeled Transition System (*LTS*), since transitions are labeled with action names. Diagrams of this form can be displayed in the *LTS* analysis tool, *LTSA*. Although this representation of a process is finite, the behavior described need not be finite. For example, the state machine of Figure 2.1 allows the following sequence of actions:

```
on→off→on→off→on→off→ ...
```

The graphical form of state machine description is excellent for simple processes; however, it becomes unmanageable (and unreadable) for large numbers of states and transitions. Consequently, we introduce a simple algebraic notation called *FSP* (Finite State Processes) to describe process models. Every *FSP* description has a corresponding state machine (*LTS*) description. In this chapter, we will introduce the action prefix and choice operators provided by *FSP*. The full language definition of *FSP* may be found in Appendix B.

2.1.1 Action Prefix

> If `x` is an action and `P` a process then the action prefix `(x->P)` describes a process that initially engages in the action `x` and then behaves exactly as described by `P`.

The action prefix operator "`->`" always has an action on its left and a process on its right. In *FSP*, identifiers beginning with a lowercase letter denote actions and identifiers beginning with an uppercase letter denote processes. The following example illustrates a process that engages in the action `once` and then stops:

```
ONESHOT = (once->STOP).
```

Figure 2.2 illustrates the equivalent *LTS* state machine description for ONESHOT. It shows that the action prefix in *FSP* describes a transition in the corresponding state machine description. STOP is a special predefined process that engages in no further actions, as is clear in Figure 2.2. Process definitions are terminated by ".".

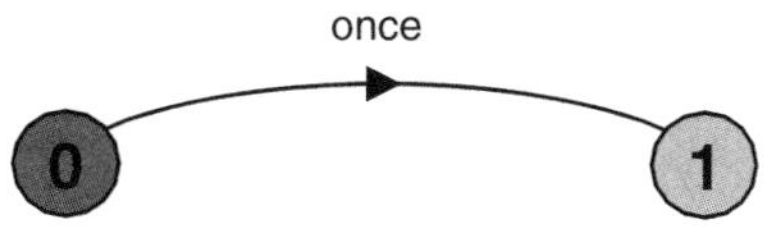

Figure 2.2 ONESHOT state machine.

Repetitive behavior is described in *FSP* using recursion. The following *FSP* process describes the light switch of Figure 2.1:

```
SWITCH = OFF,
OFF    = (on ->ON),
ON     = (off->OFF).
```

As indicated by the "," separators, the process definitions for ON and OFF are part of and local to the definition for SWITCH. It should be noted that these local process definitions correspond to states in Figure 2.1. OFF defines *state*(0) and ON defines *state*(1). A more succinct definition of SWITCH can be achieved by substituting the definition of ON in the definition of OFF:

```
SWITCH = OFF,
OFF    = (on ->(off->OFF)).
```

Finally, by substituting SWITCH for OFF, since they are defined to be equivalent, and dropping the internal parentheses we get:

```
SWITCH = (on->off->SWITCH).
```

These three definitions for SWITCH generate identical state machines (Figure 2.1). The reader can verify this using the *LTS* analysis tool, *LTSA*, to draw the state machine that corresponds to each *FSP* definition. The definitions may also be animated using the LTSA Animator to produce a sequence of actions. Figure 2.3 shows a screen shot of the LTSA Animator window. The animator lets the user control the actions offered by a model to its environment. Those actions that can be chosen for execution are ticked. In Figure 2.3, the previous sequence of actions, shown on the left, has put the SWITCH in a state where only the on action can occur next. We refer to the sequence of actions produced by the execution of a process (or set of processes) as a *trace*.

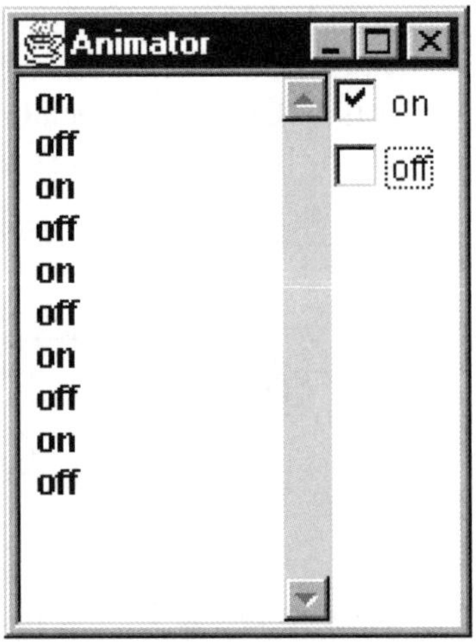

Figure 2.3 LTSA Animator window for SWITCH.

The process TRAFFICLIGHT is defined below with its equivalent state machine representation depicted in Figure 2.4.

```
TRAFFICLIGHT =
    (red->orange->green->orange->TRAFFICLIGHT).
```

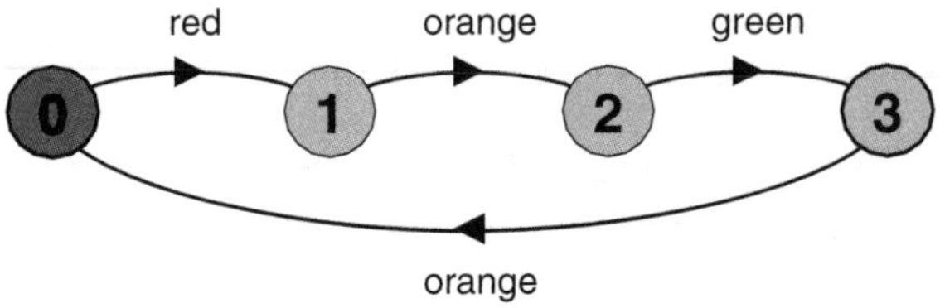

Figure 2.4 TRAFFICLIGHT.

In general, processes have many possible execution traces. However, the only possible trace of the execution of TRAFFICLIGHT is:

red→orange→green→orange→red→orange→green ...

To allow a process to describe more than a single execution trace, we introduce the choice operator.

2.1.2 Choice

> If x and y are actions then (x->P|y->Q) describes a process which initially engages in either of the actions x or y. After the first action has occurred, the subsequent behavior is described by P if the first action was x and Q if the first action was y.

The following example describes a drinks dispensing machine which dispenses hot coffee if the red button is pressed and iced tea if the blue button is pressed.

```
DRINKS = (red->coffee->DRINKS
         |blue->tea->DRINKS
         ).
```

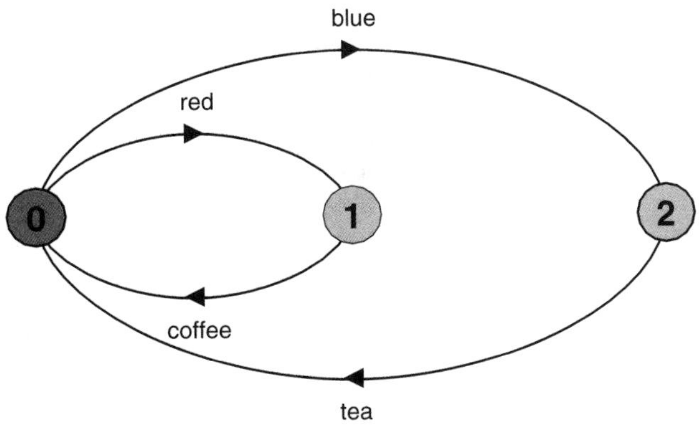

Figure 2.5 DRINKS state machine.

Figure 2.5 depicts the graphical state machine description of the drinks dispenser. Choice is represented as a state with more than one outgoing transition. The initial state has two possible outgoing transitions labeled `red` and `blue`. Who or what makes the choice as to which action is executed? In this example, the environment makes the choice – someone presses a button. We will see later that a choice may also be made internally within a process. The reader may also question at this point if there is a distinction between input and output actions. In fact, there is no semantic difference between an input action and an output action in the models we use. However, input actions are usually distinguished by forming part of a choice offered to the environment while outputs offer no choice. In the example, `red` and `blue` model input actions and `coffee` and `tea` model output actions. Possible traces of `DRINKS` include:

```
red→coffee→red→coffee→red→coffee......
blue→tea→blue→tea→blue→tea......
blue→tea→red→coffee→blue→tea→blue→tea......
```

As before, the LTSA Animator can be used to animate the model and produce a trace, as indicated in Figure 2.6. In this case, both `red` and `blue` actions are ticked as both are offered for selection.

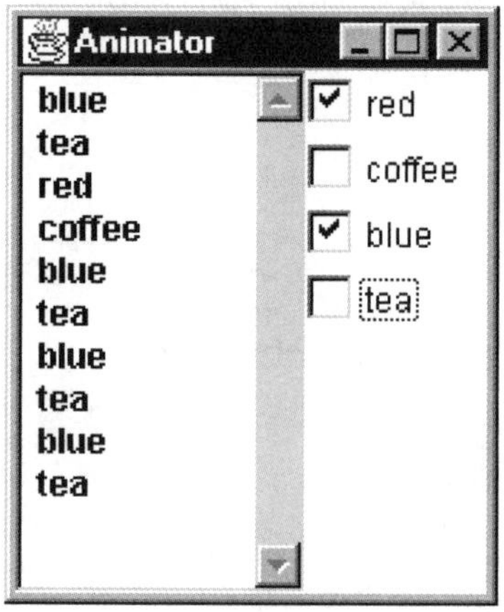

Figure 2.6 LTSA Animator window for `DRINKS`.

A state may have more than two outgoing transitions; hence the choice operator "|" can express a choice of more than two actions. For example, the following process describes a machine that has four colored buttons only one of which produces an output.

```
FAULTY = (red ->FAULTY
         |blue ->FAULTY
         |green->FAULTY
         |yellow->candy->FAULTY
         ).
```

The order of elements in the choice has no significance. The `FAULTY` process may be expressed more succinctly using a *set* of action labels. The set is interpreted as being a choice of one of its members. Both definitions of FAULTY generate exactly the same state machine graph as depicted in Figure 2.7. Note that red, blue and green label the same transition back to *state*(0).

```
FAULTY = ({red,blue,green}-> FAULTY
         |yellow -> candy -> FAULTY
         ).
```

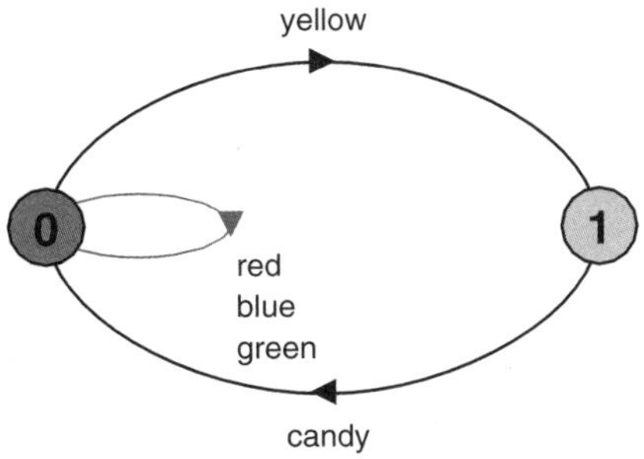

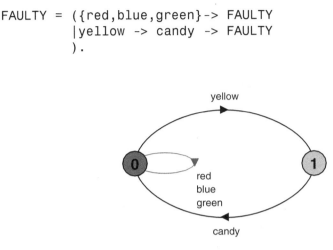

Figure 2.7 FAULTY.

Non-Deterministic Choice

The process (x->P|x->Q) is said to be *non-deterministic* since after the action x, it may behave as either P or Q. The COIN process defined below and drawn as a state machine in Figure 2.8 is an example of a non-deterministic process.

```
COIN = (toss -> heads -> COIN
       |toss -> tails -> COIN
       ).
```

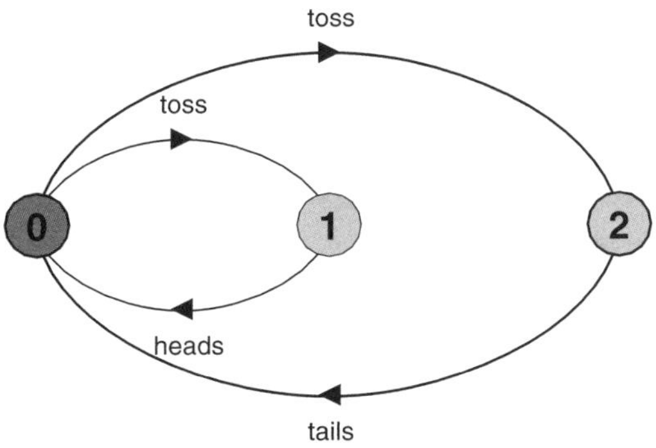

Figure 2.8 COIN.

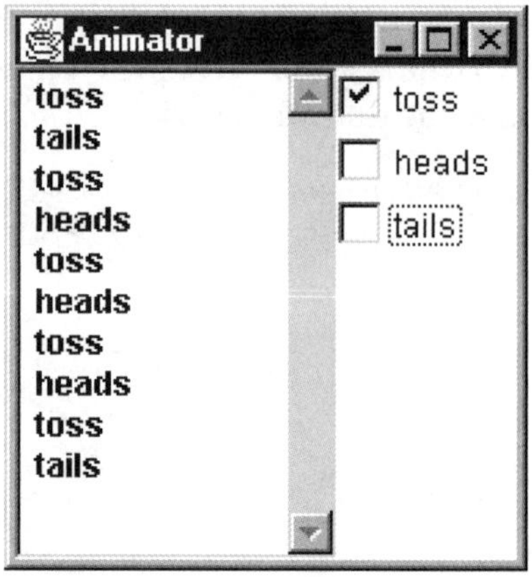

Figure 2.9 LTSA Animator window for `COIN`.

After a toss action, the next action may be either heads or tails. Figure 2.9 gives a sample trace for the `COIN` process.

2.1.3 Indexed Processes and Actions

In order to model processes and actions that can take multiple values, both local processes and action labels may be indexed in *FSP*. This greatly increases the expressive power of the notation. Indices always have a finite range of values that they can take. This ensures that the models we describe in *FSP* are finite and thus potentially mechanically analyzable. The process below is a buffer that can contain a single value – a single-slot buffer. It inputs a value in the range 0 to 3 and then outputs that value.

```
BUFF = (in[i:0..3]->out[i]-> BUFF).
```

The above process has an exactly equivalent definition in which the choice between input values is stated explicitly. The state machine for both of these definitions is depicted in Figure 2.10. Note that each index is translated into a dot notation "`.`" for the transition label, so that `in[0]` becomes `in.0`, and so on.

```
BUFF = (in[0]->out[0]->BUFF
       |in[1]->out[1]->BUFF
       |in[2]->out[2]->BUFF
       |in[3]->out[3]->BUFF
       ).
```

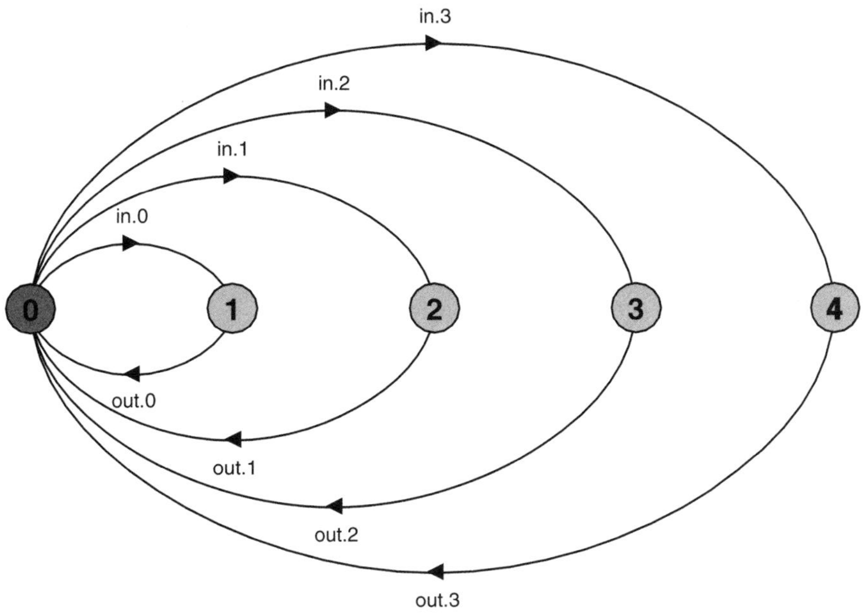

Figure 2.10 BUFF.

Another equivalent definition, which uses an indexed local process, is shown below. Since this uses two index variables with the same range, we declare a `range` type.

```
range T = 0..3

BUFF        = (in[i:T]->STORE[i]),
STORE[i:T]  = (out[i] ->BUFF).
```

The scope of a process index variable is the process definition. The scope of an action label index is the choice element in which it occurs. Consequently, the two definitions of the index variable `i` in `BUFF` above do not conflict. Both processes and action labels may have more than one index. The next example illustrates this for a process which inputs two values, `a` and `b`, and outputs their sum. Note that the usual arithmetic operations are supported on index variables.

```
const N = 1
range T = 0..N
range R = 0..2*N

SUM         = (in[a:T][b:T]->TOTAL[a+b]),
TOTAL[s:R]  = (out[s]->SUM).
```

We have chosen a small value for the constant N in the definition of SUM to ensure that the graphic representation of Figure 2.11 remains readable. The reader should generate the SUM state machine for larger values of N to see the limitation of graphic representation.

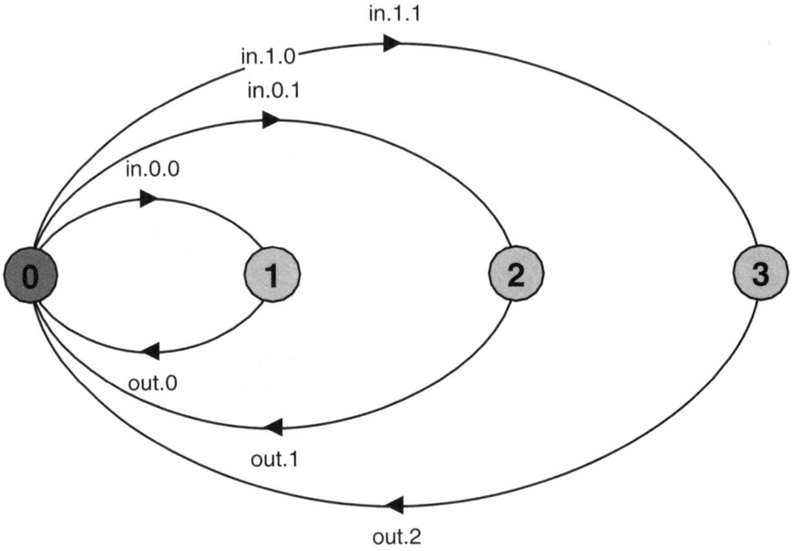

Figure 2.11 SUM.

2.1.4 Process Parameters

Processes may be parameterized so that they may be described in a general form and modeled for a particular parameter value. For instance, the single-slot buffer described in section 2.1.3 and illustrated in Figure 2.10 can be described as a parameterized process for values in the range 0 to N as follows:

```
BUFF(N=3) = (in[i:0..N]->out[i]-> BUFF).
```

Parameters must be given a default value and must start with an uppercase letter. The scope of the parameter is the process definition. Alternatively, N may be given a fixed, constant value. This may be more appropriate if N is to be used in more than one process description.

```
const N = 3
BUFF = (in[i:0..N]->out[i]-> BUFF).
```

2.1.5 Guarded Actions

It is often useful to define particular actions as conditional, depending on the current state of the machine. We use Boolean guards to indicate that a particular action can only be selected if its guard is satisfied.

> The choice (**when** B x ->P | y ->Q) means that when the guard B is true then the actions x and y are both eligible to be chosen, otherwise if B is false then the action x cannot be chosen.

The example below (with its state machine depicted in Figure 2.12) is a process that encapsulates a count variable. The count can be increased by `inc` operations and decreased by `dec` operations. The count is not allowed to exceed N or be less than zero.

```
COUNT (N=3)    = COUNT[0],
COUNT[i:0..N] = (when(i<N)  inc->COUNT[i+1]
                |when(i>0)  dec->COUNT[i-1]
                ).
```

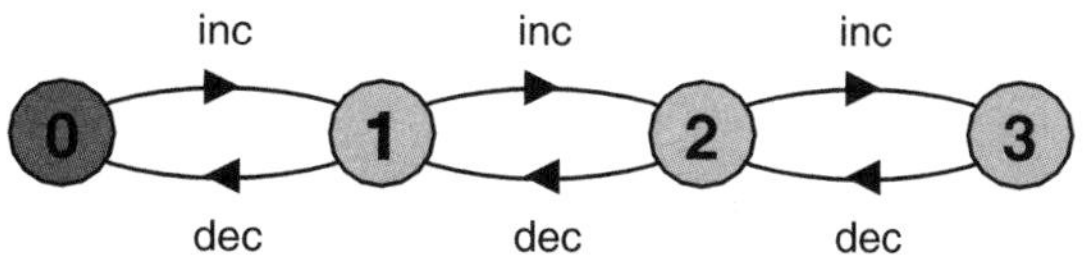

Figure 2.12 COUNT.

FSP supports only integer expressions; consequently, the value zero is used to represent false and any non-zero value represents true. Expression syntax is the same as C, C++ and Java.

In section 2.2, which describes how processes can be implemented in Java, we outline the implementation of a countdown timer. The timer, once started, outputs a tick sound each time it decrements the count and a beep when it reaches zero. At any point, the countdown may be aborted by a `stop` action. The model for the countdown timer is depicted below; the state machine is in Figure 2.13.

```
COUNTDOWN (N=3)    = (start-> COUNTDOWN[N]),
COUNTDOWN[i:0..N] = (when(i>0) tick-> COUNTDOWN[i-1]
                    |when(i==0) beep-> STOP
                    |stop-> STOP
                    ).
```

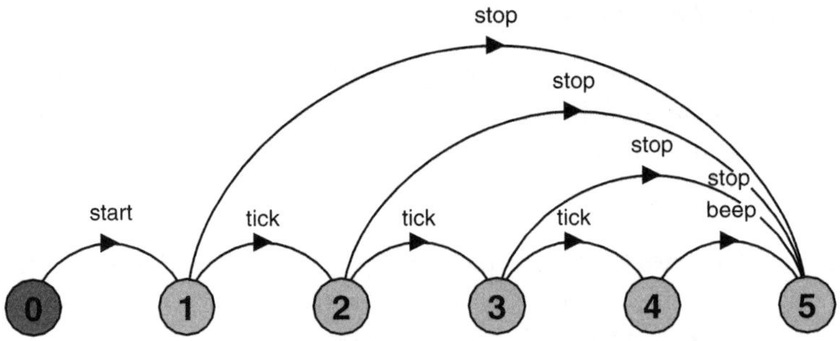

Figure 2.13 COUNTDOWN.

The set of possible traces of COUNTDOWN are as given below.

```
start→stop
start→tick→stop
start→tick→tick→stop
start→tick→tick→tick→stop
start→tick→tick→tick→beep
```

(Note that the LTSA Animator reports the STOP state as DEADLOCK. Deadlock is a more general situation where a system of processes can engage in no further actions. It is discussed later, in Chapter 6.)

2.1.6 Process Alphabets

> The alphabet of a process is the set of actions in which it can engage.

For example, the alphabet of the COUNTDOWN process of the previous section is `{start, stop, tick, beep}`. A process may only engage in the actions in its alphabet; however, it may have actions in its alphabet in which it never engages. For example, a process that writes to a store location may potentially write any 32-bit value to that location; however, it will usually write a more restricted set of values. In *FSP*, the alphabet of a process is determined implicitly by the set of actions referenced in its definition. We will see later in the book that it is important to be precise about the alphabet of a process.

How do we deal with the situation described above in which the set of actions in the alphabet is larger than the set of actions referenced in its definition? The answer is to use the alphabet extension construct provided by *FSP*. The process WRITER defined below uses the actions `write[1]` and `write[3]` in its definition but defines an alphabet extension "+{...}" of the actions `write[0..3]`. The alphabet of a process is the union of its implicit alphabet and any extension specified. Consequently, the alphabet of `WRITER` is `write[0..3]`.

```
WRITER = (write[1]->write[3]->WRITER)
         +{write[0..3]}.
```

It should be noted that where a process is defined using one or more local process definitions, the alphabet of each local process is exactly the same as that of the enclosing process. The alphabet of the enclosing process is simply the union of the set of actions referenced in all local definitions together with any explicitly specified alphabet extension.

2.2 Implementing Processes

At the beginning of this chapter, we introduced a process as being the execution of a program or subprogram. In the previous section, we described how a process could be modeled as a finite state machine. In this section, we will see how processes are represented in computing systems. In particular, we describe how processes are programmed in Java.

2.2.1 Operating System Processes

The term process, meaning the execution of a program, originates in the literature on the design of operating systems. A process in an operating system is a unit of resource allocation both for CPU time and for memory. A process is represented by its code, data and the state of the machine registers. The data of the process is divided into global variables and local variables organized as a stack. Generally, each process in an operating system has its own address space and some special action must be taken to allow different processes to access shared data. The execution of an application program in an operating system like Unix involves the following activities: allocating memory (global data and stack) for the process, loading some or all of its code into memory and running the code by loading the address of the initial instruction into the program counter register, the address of its stack into the stack pointer register and so on. The operating system maintains an internal data structure called a process descriptor which records details such as scheduling priority, allocated memory and the values of machine registers when the process is not running.

The above description does not conflict with our previous conception of a process, it is simply more concrete. This traditional operating system process has a single thread of control – it has no internal concurrency. With the advent of shared memory multiprocessors, operating system designers have catered for the requirement that a process might require internal concurrency by providing *lightweight processes* or *threads*. The name *thread* comes from the expression "thread of control". Modern operating systems like Windows NT permit an operating system process to have multiple threads of control.

The relationship between *heavyweight* operating system (OS) processes and lightweight processes or threads is depicted in Figure 2.14. The OS process has a data segment and a code segment; however, it has multiple stacks, one for each thread. The code for a thread is included in the OS process code segment and all the threads in a process can access the data segment. The Java Virtual Machine, which of course usually executes as a process under some operating system, supports multiple threads as depicted in Figure 2.14. Each Java thread has its own local variables organized as a stack and threads can access shared variables.

In the previous section, we modeled processes as state machines. Since threads are simply a particular implementation of the general idea of a process as an executing program, they too can be modeled as state machines. They have a state, which they transform by performing actions (executing instructions). To avoid confusion in the rest of the book, we will use the term *process* when referring to models of concurrent programs and the term *thread* when referring to implementations of processes in Java.

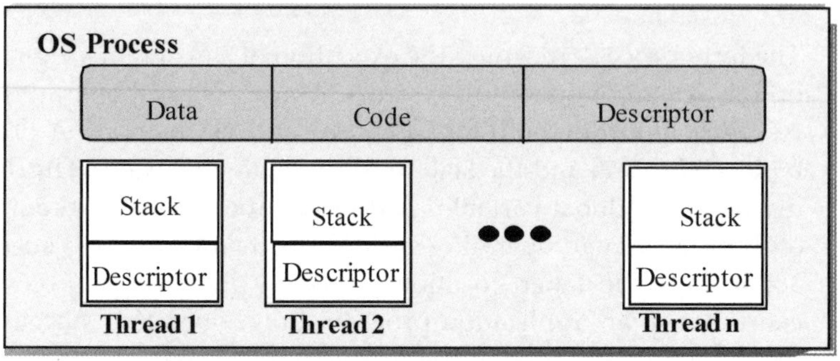

Figure 2.14 Operating system threads.

2.2.2 Threads in Java

The operations to create and initialize threads and to subsequently control their execution are provided by the Java class `Thread` in the package `java.lang`. The program code executed by a thread is provided by the method `run()`. The actual

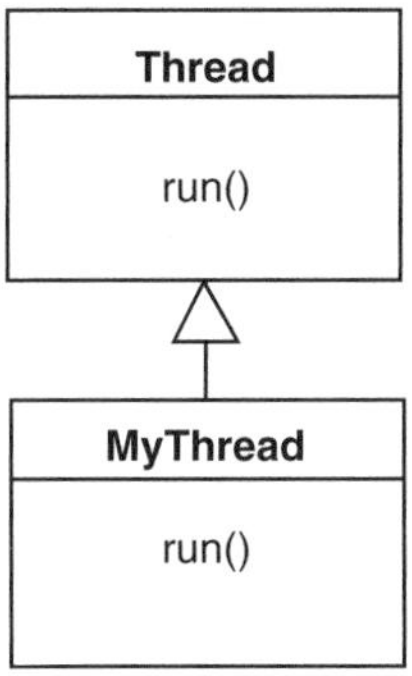

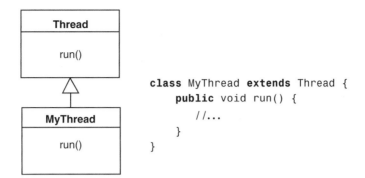

```
class MyThread extends Thread {
    public void run() {
        //...
    }
}
```

Figure 2.15 Implementing `run()` using inheritance.

code executed depends on the implementation provided for `run()` in a derived class, as depicted in the class diagram of Figure 2.15.

The class diagrams we use in this book are a subset of the Unified Modeling Language, UML (Fowler and Scott, 1997; Booch, Rumbaugh and Jacobson, 1998). For those unfamiliar with this notation, a key may be found in Appendix D.

Since Java does not permit multiple inheritance, it is sometimes more convenient to implement the `run()` method in a class not derived from `Thread` but from the interface `Runnable` as depicted in Figure 2.16.

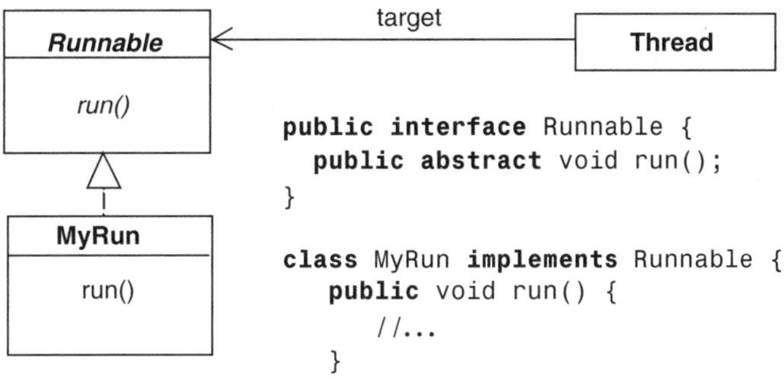


```
public interface Runnable {
  public abstract void run();
}

class MyRun implements Runnable {
   public void run() {
      //...
   }
}
```

Figure 2.16 Implementing `run()` using the `Runnable` interface.

2.2.3 Thread Life Cycle

A Java `Thread` object is created by a call to **`new`** in the same way that any other Java object is constructed. The two ways of creating a thread corresponding to Figures 2.15 and 2.16 respectively are:

```
Thread a = new MyThread();
Thread b = new Thread(new MyRun());
```

The thread constructor may optionally take a string argument to name the thread. This can be useful for debugging but has no other role. The following outlines the states (in *italics*) in which a thread may exist and the operations provided by the `Thread` class to control a thread.

- Once *created*, `start()` causes a thread to call its `run()` method and execute it as an independent activity, concurrent with the thread which called `start()`.
- A thread terminates when the `run()` method returns or when it is stopped by `stop()`. A *terminated* thread may not be restarted. A thread object is only garbage collected when there are no references to it and it has terminated.
- The predicate `isAlive()` returns true if a thread has been started but has not yet terminated.
- When started, a thread may be currently *running* on the processor, or it may be *runnable* but waiting to be scheduled. A running process may explicitly give up the processor using `yield()`.
- A thread may be *non-runnable* as a result of being suspended using `suspend()`. It can be made *runnable* again using `resume()`.
- `sleep()` causes a thread to be suspended (made *non-runnable*) for a given time (specified in milliseconds) and then automatically resume (be made *runnable*).

This is not a complete list of operations provided by the `Thread` class. For example, threads may be given a scheduling priority. We will introduce these extra operations later in the book, as they are required.

We can use *FSP* to give a concise description of the thread life cycle as shown below. The actions shown in *italics* are not methods from class `Thread`. Taking them in order of appearance: *end* represents the action of the `run()` method returning or exiting, *run* represents a set of application actions from the `run()` method and *dispatch* represents an action by the Java Virtual Machine to run a thread on the processor.

```
THREAD       = CREATED,
CREATED      = (start           ->RUNNABLE
               |stop            ->TERMINATED),
RUNNING      = ({suspend,sleep}->NON_RUNNABLE
               |yield           ->RUNNABLE
               |{stop, end}     ->TERMINATED
               | run            ->RUNNING),
RUNNABLE     = (suspend         ->NON_RUNNABLE
```

```
                   | dispatch      ->RUNNING
                   |stop           ->TERMINATED),
NON_RUNNABLE    = (resume         ->RUNNABLE
                   |stop           ->TERMINATED),
TERMINATED      = STOP.
```

The corresponding state machine is depicted in Figure 2.17. States 0 to 4 correspond to CREATED, TERMINATED, RUNNABLE, RUNNING and NON_RUNNABLE respectively.

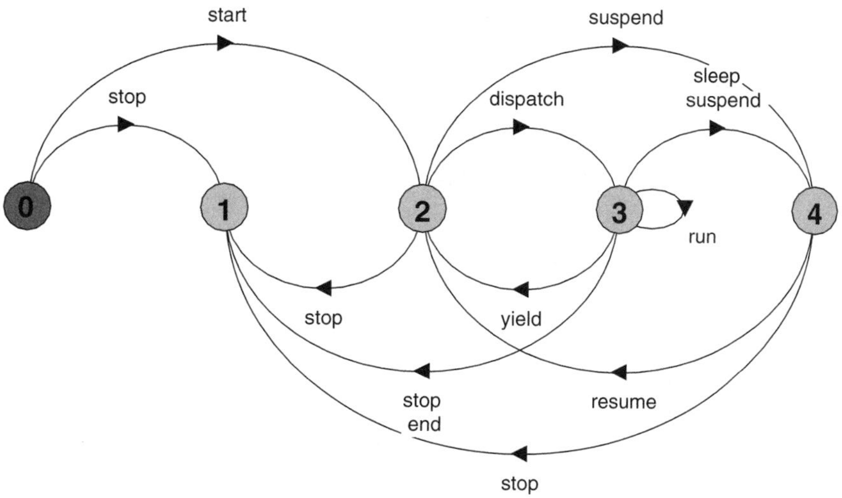

Figure 2.17 THREAD life cycle.

2.2.4 Countdown Timer Example

The model for a timer which counts down to zero and then beeps was described in section 2.1.5 (Figure 2.13). In this section, we describe the implementation of the countdown timer as a thread that is created by a Java applet. The class diagram for the timer is depicted in Figure 2.18.

NumberCanvas is a display canvas that paints an integer value on the screen. An outline of the class, describing the methods available to users, is presented in Program 2.1. It is the first of a set of display classes that will be used throughout the book. The full code for these classes can be found on the website that accompanies this book (http://www.wileyeurope.com/college/magee).

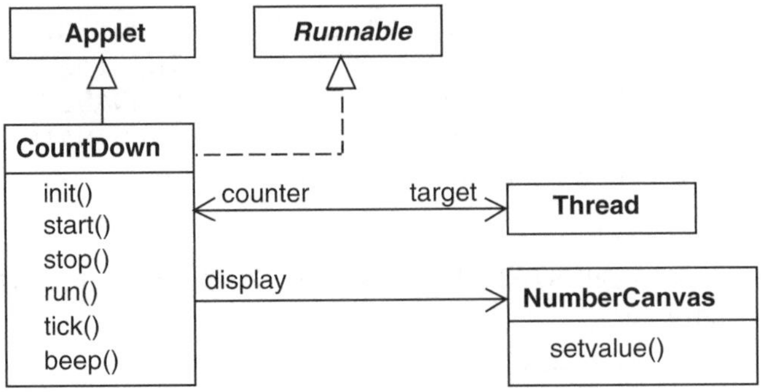

Figure 2.18 Countdown timer class diagram.

```
public class NumberCanvas extends Canvas {
  // create canvas with title and optionally set background color
  public NumberCanvas(String title) {...}
  public NumberCanvas(String title, Color c) {...}

  //set background color
  public void setcolor(Color c){...}

  //display newval on screen
  public void setvalue(int newval){...}
}
```

Program 2.1 `NumberCanvas` class.

The code for the `CountDown` applet is listed in Program 2.2.

```
public class CountDown extends Applet
                       implements Runnable {
  Thread counter; int i;
  final static int N = 10;
  AudioClip beepSound, tickSound;
  NumberCanvas display;

  public void init() {
    add(display=new NumberCanvas("CountDown"));
```

Program 2.2 `CountDown` applet class.

```
      display.resize(150,100);
      tickSound =
        getAudioClip(getDocumentBase(),"sound/tick.au");
      beepSound =
        getAudioClip(getDocumentBase(),"sound/beep.au");
    }

    public void start() {
      counter = new Thread(this);
      i = N; counter.start();
    }

    public void stop() {
      counter = null;
    }

    public void run() {
      while(true) {
        if (counter == null) return;
        if (i>0)  { tick(); --i; }
        if (i==0) { beep(); return;}
      }
    }

    private void tick(){
      display.setvalue(i); tickSound.play();
      try{ Thread.sleep(1000);}
      catch (InterruptedException e){}
    }

    private void beep(){
      display.setvalue(i); beepSound.play();
    }
  }
```

Program 2.2 (*Continued*).

The `counter` thread is created and started running by the `start()` method when the `CountDown` applet is started by the Web browser in which it executes. `CountDown` implements the `Runnable` interface by providing the method `run()` which defines the behavior of the thread. To permit easy comparison between the `COUNTDOWN` model and the behavior implemented by the `run()` method, the model is repeated below:

```
COUNTDOWN (N=3)    = (start-> COUNTDOWN[N]),
COUNTDOWN[i:0..N] = (when(i>0) tick-> COUNTDOWN[i-1]
                    |when(i==0) beep-> STOP
                    |stop-> STOP
                    ).
```

The thread `counter.start()` method causes the `run()` method to be invoked. Hence, just as the `start` action in the model is followed by `COUNTDOWN[i]`, so the `run()` method is an implementation of the `COUNTDOWN[i]` process. The index of the process `COUNTDOWN[i]` is represented by the integer field `i`. The recursion in the model is implemented as a Java **while** loop. Guarded choice in `COUNTDOWN[i]` is implemented by Java **if** statements. Note that we have reordered the conditions from the model, since in the implementation, they are evaluated sequentially. If the thread is stopped, it must not perform any further actions. In Chapters 4 and 5, we will see a different way of implementing choice when a model process is not implemented as a thread.

When `run()` returns the thread terminates – this corresponds to the model process `STOP`. This can happen for two reasons: either `i==0` or the thread reference `counter` becomes null. It can become null if the browser invokes the `stop()` method – usually as a result of a user requesting a change from the Web page in which the applet is active. The `stop()` method sets `counter` to null. This method of stopping a thread is preferable to using the `Thread.stop()` method since it allows a thread to terminate gracefully, performing cleanup actions if necessary. `Thread.stop()` terminates a thread whatever state it is in, giving it no opportunity to release resources. Melodramatically, we may think of `Thread.stop()` as killing the thread and the technique we have used as equivalent to requesting the thread to commit suicide! For these reasons, Sun have suggested that `Thread.stop()` be "deprecated". This means that it may not be supported by future Java releases.

The implementation of `tick()` displays the value of `i`, plays the tick sound and then delays the calling thread for 1000 milliseconds (one second) using `Thread.sleep()`. This is a class method since it always operates on the currently running thread. The method `sleep()` can terminate abnormally with an `InterruptedException`. The code of Program 2.2 simply provides an exception handler that does nothing.

The implementation of `beep()` displays `i` and plays the beep sound. The `tick()` and `beep()` methods correspond to the `tick` and `beep` actions of the model. An implementation must fill in the details that are abstracted in a model.

Summary

This chapter has introduced the concept of a process, explained how we model processes and described Java threads as implementations of processes. In particular:

- The execution of a program (or subprogram) is termed a *process*. Processes are the units of concurrent activity used in concurrent programming.
- A process can be modeled as a state machine in which the transitions are atomic or indivisible actions executed by the process. We use *LTS*, Labeled Transition Systems, to represent state machines.
- State machines are described concisely using *FSP*, a simple process algebra. The chapter introduced the action prefix, "-> ", and choice, "|", operators in addition to the use of recursion, index sets and guards.
- Our notations do not distinguish input actions from outputs. However, inputs usually form part of a choice offered to the environment of a process while outputs do not.
- We have used Java *threads* to show how processes are implemented and how they are used in programs. Java threads are an example of lightweight processes, in the terminology of operating systems.

Notes and Further Reading

The use of state machines as an abstract model for processes is widely used in the study of concurrent and distributed algorithms. For example, in her book *Distributed Algorithms,* Nancy Lynch (1996) uses I/O automata to describe and reason about concurrent and distributed programs. I/O automata are state machines in which input, output and internal actions are distinguished and in which input actions are always enabled (i.e., they are offered as a choice to the environment in all states). The interested reader will find an alternative approach to modeling concurrent systems in that book.

State machines are used as a diagrammatic aid (usually as State Transition Diagrams, STD) in most design methods to describe dynamic activity. They can be extended to cater for concurrency. An interesting and widely used form is statecharts (Harel, 1987), designed by David Harel and incorporated in the STATEMATE software tool (Harel, Lachover, Naamad, *et al.*, 1990) for the design of reactive systems. A form of this notation has been adopted in the Unified Modeling Language, UML, of Booch, Rumbaugh and Jacobson (1998). See http://www.uml.org/.

The association of state machines with process algebra is due to Robin Milner (1989) who gives an operational semantics for a Calculus of Communicating Systems (CCS) using Labeled Transition Systems in his inspirational book *Communication and Concurrency*. While we have adopted the CCS approach to semantics, the syntax of *FSP* owes more to C.A.R. Hoare's CSP presented in *Communicating Sequential Processes* (1985). The semantic differences between *FSP* and its antecedents, CCS and CSP, are documented and explained in succeeding chapters. The syntactic differences are largely due to the requirement that *FSP* be easily parsed by its support tool *LTSA*.

Process algebra has also been used in formal description languages such as LOTOS (ISO/IEC, 1988). LOTOS is an ISO standard language for the specification of distributed systems as interacting processes. As in *FSP*, process behavior is described using action prefix and choice operators, guards and recursion. However, unlike *FSP*, LOTOS includes facilities for defining abstract data types. Naive use of the data type part of LOTOS quickly leads to intractable models.

FSP was specifically designed to facilitate modeling of finite state processes as Labeled Transition Systems. *LTS* provides the well-defined mathematical properties that facilitate formal analysis. *LTSA* provides automated support for displaying and animating the examples in this chapter. Later in the book we will see how *LTSA* can be used for verifying properties using model checking.

The reader interested in more details on Java should consult the information on-line from JavaSoft. For more on the pragmatics of concurrent programming in Java, see Doug Lea's book *Concurrent Programming in Java™: Design Principles and Patterns* (1999).

Exercises

2.1 For each of the following processes, give the Finite State Process (*FSP*) description of the Labeled Transition System (*LTS*) graph. The *FSP* process descriptions may be checked by generating the corresponding state machines using the analysis tool, *LTSA*.

I. MEETING

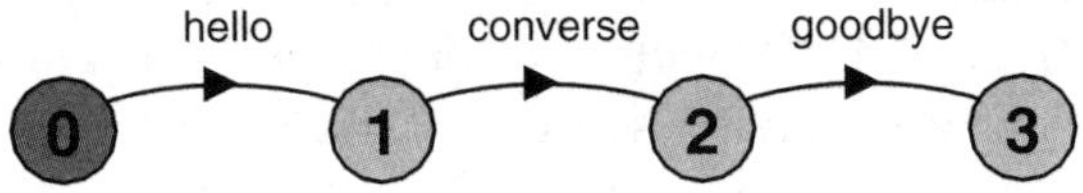

II. JOB

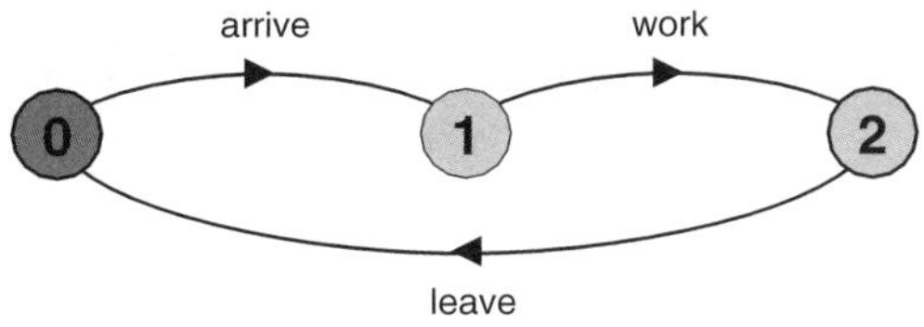

III. GAME

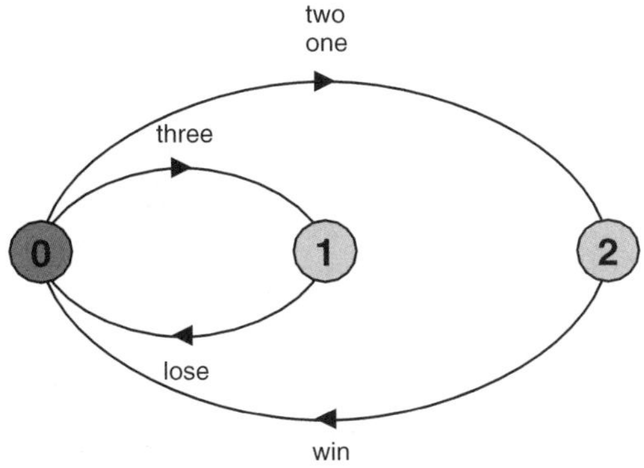

IV. MOVE

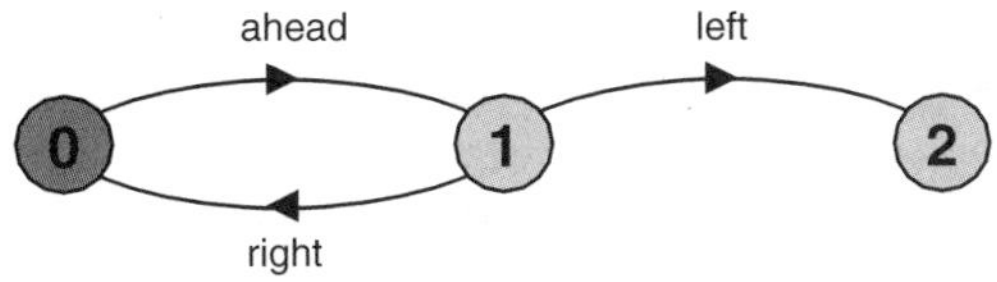

V. DOUBLE

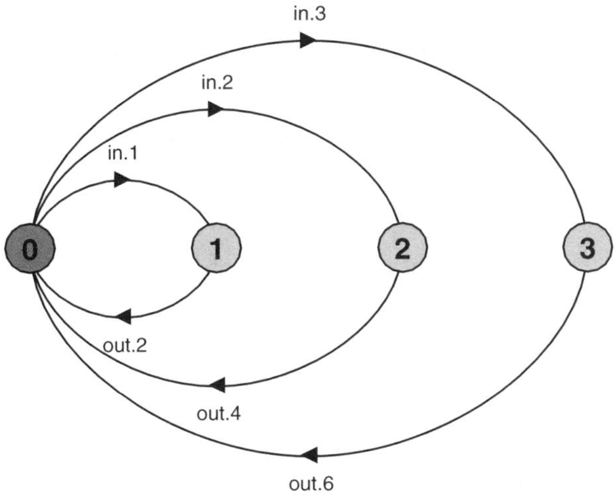

VI. FOURTICK

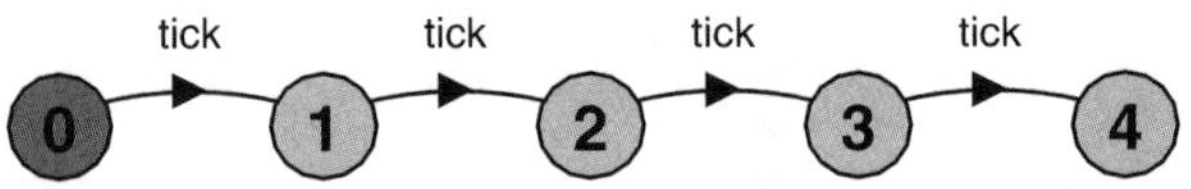

VII. PERSON

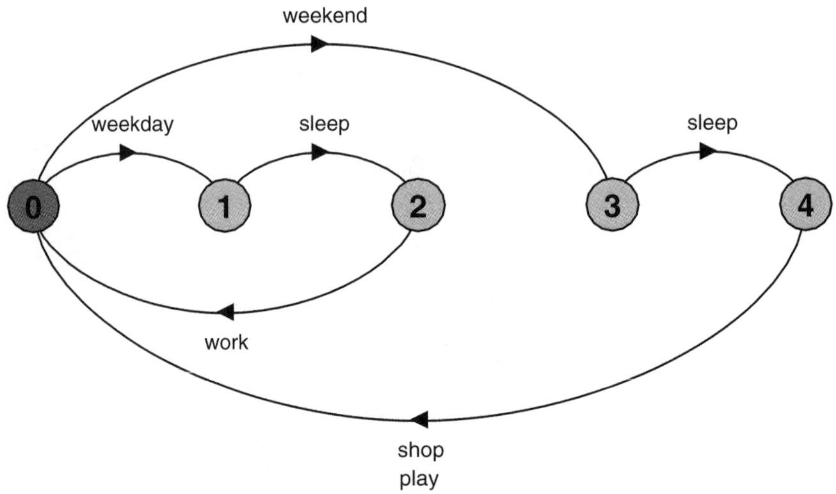

2.2 A variable stores values in the range 0..*N* and supports the actions *read* and *write*. Model the variable as a process, VARIABLE, using *FSP*.
For N=2, check that it can perform the actions given by the trace:

```
write.2→read.2→read.2→write.1→write.0→read.0
```

2.3 A bistable digital circuit receives a sequence of *trigger* inputs and alternately outputs 0 and 1. Model the process BISTABLE using *FSP*, and check that it produces the required output; i.e., it should perform the actions given by the trace:

```
trigger→1→trigger→0→trigger→1→trigger→0 ...
```

(*Hint*: The alphabet of **BISTABLE** is {[0],[1],trigger}.)

2.4 A sensor measures the water *level* of a tank. The level (initially 5) is measured in units 0..9. The sensor outputs a *low* signal if the level is less than 2 and a *high* signal if the level is greater than 8 otherwise it outputs *normal*. Model the sensor as an *FSP* process, **SENSOR**.
(*Hint*: The alphabet of **SENSOR** is {level[0..9], high, low, normal}.)

2.5 A drinks dispensing machine charges 15p for a can of Sugarola. The machine accepts coins with denominations 5p, 10p and 20p and gives change. Model the machine as an *FSP* process, **DRINKS**.

2.6 A miniature portable FM radio has three controls. An on/off switch turns the device on and off. Tuning is controlled by two buttons `scan` and `reset` which operate as follows. When the radio is turned on or `reset` is pressed, the radio is tuned to the top frequency of the FM band (108 MHz). When `scan` is pressed, the radio scans towards the bottom of the band (88 MHz). It stops scanning when it `locks` on to a station or it reaches the bottom (`end`). If the radio is currently tuned to a station and `scan` is pressed then it starts to scan from the frequency of that station towards the bottom. Similarly, when `reset` is pressed the receiver tunes to the top. Using the alphabet `{on, off, scan, reset, lock, end}`, model the FM radio as an *FSP* process, **`RADIO`**.

For each of the exercises 2.2 to 2.6, draw the state machine diagram that corresponds to your *FSP* specification and check that it can perform the required actions. The state machines may be drawn manually or generated using the analysis tool, *LTSA*. *LTSA* may also be used to animate (run) the specification to produce a trace.

2.7 Program the radio of exercise 2.6 in Java, complete with graphic display.

3 Concurrent Execution

The execution of a concurrent program consists of multiple processes active at the same time. As discussed in the last chapter, each process is the execution of a sequential program. A process progresses by submitting a sequence of instructions to a processor for execution. If the computer has multiple processors then instructions from a number of processes, equal to the number of physical processors, can be executed at the same time. This is sometimes referred to as parallel or *real* concurrent execution. However, it is usual to have more active processes than processors. In this case, the available processors are switched between processes. Figure 3.1 depicts this switching for the case of a single processor supporting three processes, *A*, *B* and *C*. The solid lines represent instructions from a process being executed on the processor. With a single processor, each process makes progress but, as depicted in Figure 3.1, instructions from only one process at a time can be executed.

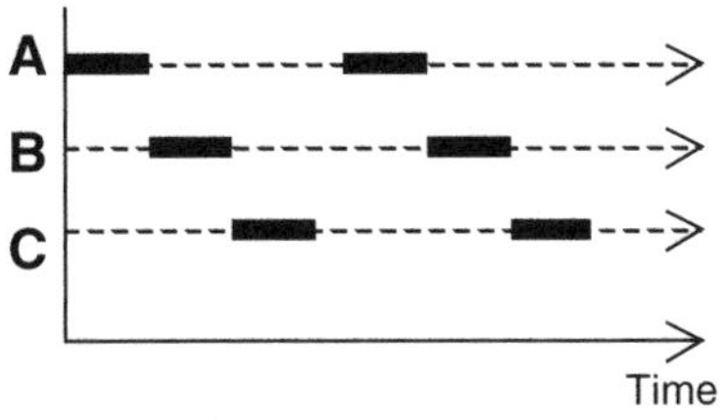

Figure 3.1 Process switching.

The switching between processes occurs voluntarily or in response to interrupts. Interrupts signal external events such as the completion of an I/O operation or a clock tick to the processor. As can be seen from Figure 3.1, processor switching does not affect the order of instructions executed by each process. The processor executes a sequence of instructions which is an *interleaving* of the instruction sequences from each individual process. This form of concurrent execution using interleaving is sometimes referred to as pseudo-concurrent execution since instructions from different processes are not executed at the same time but are interleaved. We use the terms *parallel* and *concurrent* interchangeably and usually do not distinguish between real and pseudo-concurrent execution since, in general, the same programming principles and techniques are applicable to both physically (real) concurrent and interleaved execution. In fact, we always model concurrent execution as interleaved whether or not implementations run on multiple processors.

This chapter describes how programs consisting of multiple processes are modeled and illustrates the correspondence between models and implementations of concurrent programs by a multi-threaded Java example.

3.1 Modeling Concurrency

In the previous chapter, we modeled a process abstractly as a state machine that proceeds by executing atomic actions, which transform its state. The execution of a process generates a sequence (trace) of atomic actions. We now examine how to model systems consisting of multiple processes.

The first issue to consider is how to model the speed at which one process executes relative to another. The relative speed at which a process proceeds depends on factors such as the number of processors and the scheduling strategy – how the operating system chooses the next process to execute. In fact, since we want to design concurrent programs which work correctly independently of the number of processors and the scheduling strategy, we choose not to model relative speed but state simply that processes execute at arbitrary relative speeds. This means that a process can take an arbitrarily long time to proceed from one action to the next. We abstract away from execution time. This has the disadvantage that we can say nothing about the real-time properties of programs but has the advantage that we can verify other properties independently of the particular configuration of the computer and its operating system. This independence is clearly important for the portability of concurrent programs.

The next issue is how to model concurrency or parallelism. Is it necessary to model the situation in which actions from different processes can be executed simultaneously by different processors in addition to the situation in which concurrency is simulated by interleaved execution? We choose always to model concurrency using interleaving. An action a is concurrent with another action b if a model permits the actions to occur in either the order $a \rightarrow b$ or the order $b \rightarrow a$. Since we do not represent time in the model, the fact that the event a actually occurs at the same time as event b does not affect the properties we can assert about concurrent executions.

Finally, having decided on an interleaved model of concurrent execution, what can we say about the relative order of actions from different processes in the interleaved action trace representing the concurrent program execution? We know that the actions from the same process are executed in order. However, since processes proceed at arbitrary relative speeds, actions from different processes are arbitrarily interleaved. Arbitrary interleaving turns out to be a good model of concurrent execution since it abstracts the way processors switch between processes as a result of external interrupts. The timing of interrupts relative to process execution cannot in general be predetermined since actions in the real world cannot be predicted exactly – we cannot foretell the future.

The concurrent execution model in which processes perform actions in an arbitrary order at arbitrary relative speeds is referred to as an *asynchronous* model of execution. It contrasts with the *synchronous* model in which processes perform actions in simultaneous execution steps, sometimes referred to as lock-step.

3.1.1 Parallel Composition

> If `P` and `Q` are processes then `(P||Q)` represents the concurrent execution of `P` and `Q`. The operator `||` is the parallel composition operator.

Parallel composition yields a process, which is represented as a state machine in the same way as any other process. The state machine representing the composition generates all possible interleavings of the traces of its constituent processes. For example, the process:

```
ITCH = (scratch->STOP).
```

has a single trace consisting of the action `scratch`. The process:

```
CONVERSE = (think->talk->STOP).
```

has the single trace `think→talk`. The composite process:

```
||CONVERSE_ITCH = (ITCH || CONVERSE).
```

has the following traces:

```
think→talk→scratch
think→scratch→talk
scratch→think→talk
```

The state machines corresponding to `ITCH`, `CONVERSE` and `CONVERSE_ITCH` are depicted in Figure 3.2. The state machine representing the composition is formed by the Cartesian product of its constituents. For example, if `ITCH` is in *state*(i) and `CONVERSE` is in *state*(j), then this combined state is represented by `CONVERSE_ITCH` in *state*($<i, j>$). So if `CONVERSE` has performed the `think` action and is in *state*(1) and `ITCH` performs its `scratch` action and is in *state*(1) then the state representing this in the composition is *state*($<1,1>$). This is depicted as *state*(4) of the composition. We do not manually compute the composite state machines in the rest of the book, since this would be tedious and error-prone. Compositions are computed by the *LTSA* tool and the interested reader may use it to verify that the compositions depicted in the text are in fact correct.

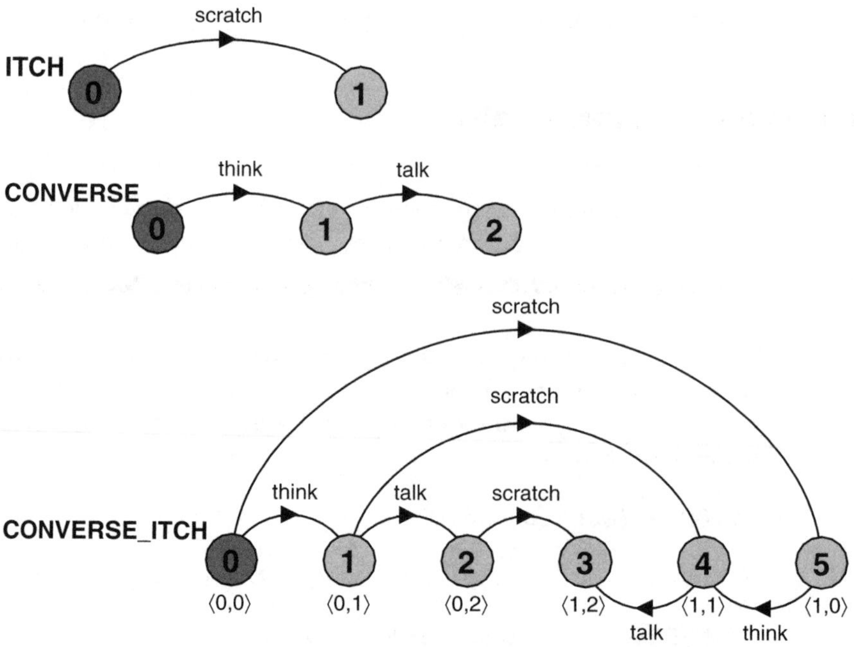

Figure 3.2 Composition `CONVERSE_ITCH`.

From Figure 3.2, it can be seen that the action `scratch` is concurrent with both `think` and `talk` as the model permits these actions to occur in any order while retaining the constraint that `think` must happen before `talk`. In other words, one must think before talking but one can scratch at any point!

Composite process definitions are always preceded by `||` to distinguish them from primitive process definitions. As described in the previous chapter, primitive processes are defined using action prefix and choice while composite processes are defined using only parallel composition. Maintaining this strict distinction between primitive and composite processes is required to ensure that the models described by *FSP* are finite.

As a further example, the following processes model a clock radio which incorporates two independent activities: a clock which ticks and a radio which can be switched on and off. The state machine for the composition is depicted in Figure 3.3.

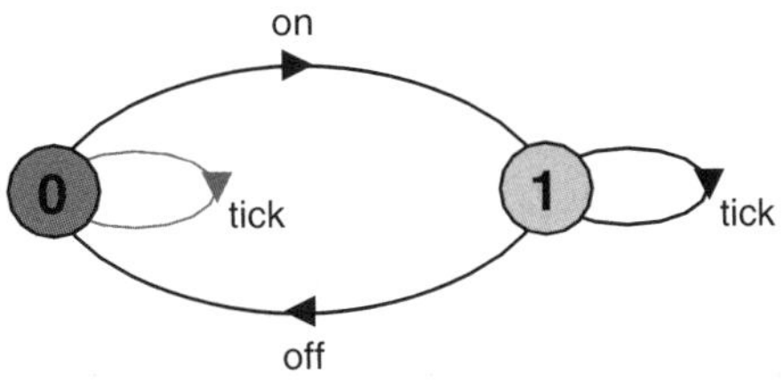

Figure 3.3 Composition CLOCK_RADIO.

```
CLOCK = (tick->CLOCK).
RADIO = (on->off->RADIO).

||CLOCK_RADIO = (CLOCK || RADIO).
```

Examples of traces generated by the state machine of Figure 3.3 are given below. The LTSA Animator can be used to generate such traces.

```
on→tick→tick→off→tick→tick→tick→on→off→...
tick→on→off→on→off→on→off→tick→on→tick→...
```

The parallel composition operator obeys some simple algebraic laws:

Commutative: `(P||Q) = (Q||P)`
Associative: `(P||(Q||R)) = ((P||Q)||R) = (P||Q||R).`

Taken together these mean that the brackets can be dispensed with and the order that processes appear in the composition is irrelevant.

3.1.2 Shared Actions

The examples in the previous section are all compositions of processes with disjoint alphabets. That is, the processes in a composition do not have any actions in common. If processes in a composition do have actions in common, these actions are said to be *shared*. Shared actions are the way that process interaction is modeled. While unshared actions may be arbitrarily interleaved, *a shared action must be executed at the same time by all the processes that participate in that shared action*. The following example is a composition of processes that share the action meet.

```
BILL = (play -> meet -> STOP).
BEN  = (work -> meet -> STOP).

||BILL_BEN = (BILL || BEN).
```

The possible execution traces of the composition are:

```
play→work→meet
work→play→meet
```

The unshared actions, play and work, are concurrent and thus may be executed in any order. However, both of these actions are constrained to happen before the shared action meet. The shared action *synchronizes* the execution of the processes BILL and BEN. The state machine for the composite process is depicted in Figure 3.4.

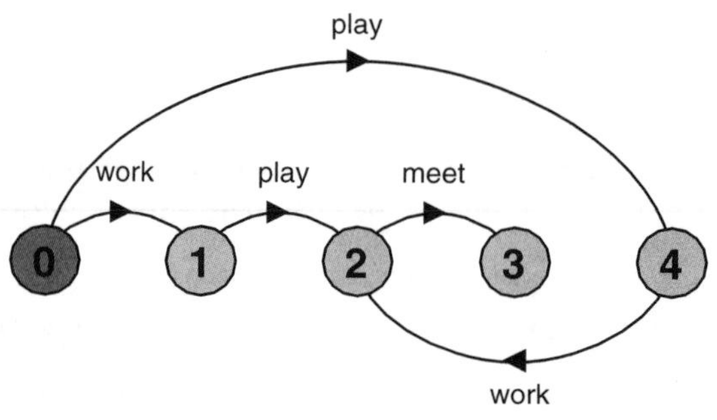

Figure 3.4 Composition BILL_BEN.

The next example consists of a process that manufactures an item and then signals that the item is ready for use by a shared ready action. A user can only use the item after the ready action occurs.

```
MAKER = (make->ready->MAKER).
USER  = (ready->use->USER).

||MAKER_USER = (MAKER || USER).
```

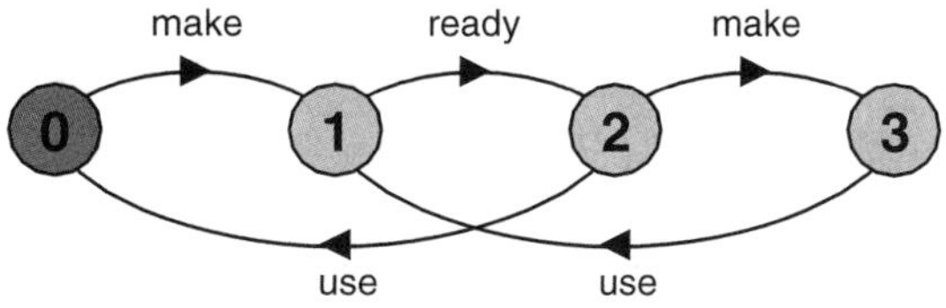

Figure 3.5 Composition MAKER_USER.

From Figure 3.5, it can be seen that the following are possible execution traces:

```
make→ready→use→make→ready→...
make→ready→make→use→ready→...
```

After the initial item is manufactured and becomes ready, manufacture and use can proceed in parallel since the actions make and use can occur in any order. However, it is always the case that an item is made before it is used since the first action is make in all traces. The second trace shows that two items can be made before the first is used. Suppose that this is undesirable behavior and we do not wish the MAKER process to get ahead in this way. The solution is to modify the model so that the user indicates that the item is used. This used action is shared with the MAKER who now cannot proceed to manufacture another item until the first is used. This second version is shown below and in Figure 3.6.

```
MAKERv2 = (make->ready->used->MAKERv2).
USERv2  = (ready->use->used->USERv2).

||MAKER_USERv2 = (MAKERv2 || USERv2).
```

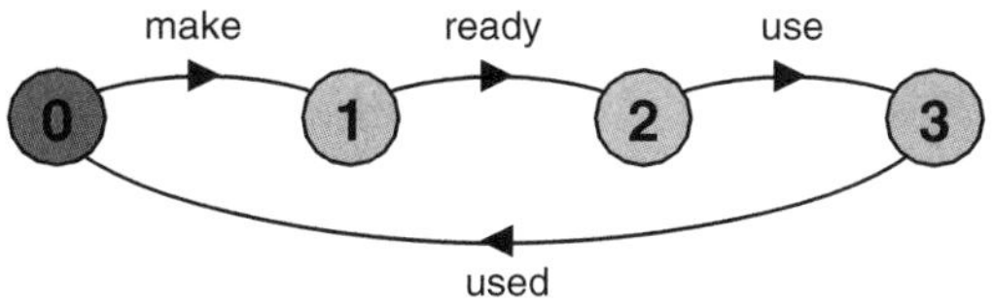

Figure 3.6 Composition MAKER_USERv2.

The interaction between MAKER and USER in this second version is an example of a *handshake*, an action which is acknowledged by another. As we see in the chapters to follow, handshake protocols are widely used to structure interactions between processes. Note that our model of interaction does not distinguish which process instigates a shared action even though it is natural to think of the MAKER process instigating the ready action and the USER process instigating the used action.

However, as noted previously, an output action instigated by a process does not usually form part of a choice while an input action may.

The examples of synchronization so far are between two processes; however, many processes can engage in a shared action. The next example illustrates the use of multi-party synchronization in a small manufacturing system which produces two different parts and assembles the parts into a product. Assembly cannot take place until both parts are ready. Again, makers are not permitted to get ahead of users. The state machine is depicted in Figure 3.7.

```
MAKE_A   = (makeA->ready->used->MAKE_A).
MAKE_B   = (makeB->ready->used->MAKE_B).
ASSEMBLE = (ready->assemble->used->ASSEMBLE).

||FACTORY = (MAKE_A || MAKE_B || ASSEMBLE).
```

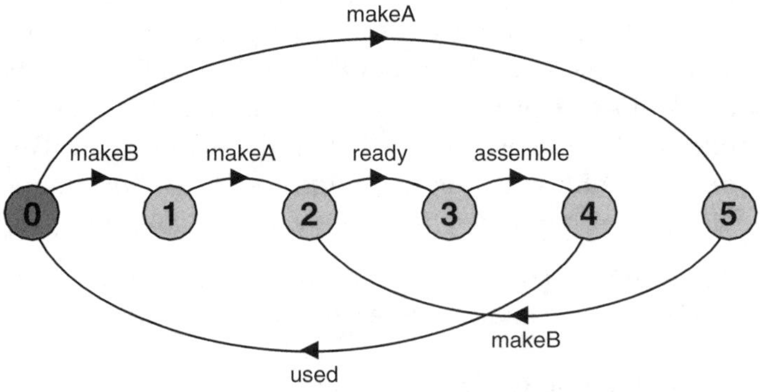

Figure 3.7 Composition FACTORY.

Since a parallel composition of processes is itself a process, called a composite process, it can be used in the definition of further compositions. We can restructure the previous example by creating a composite process from MAKE_A and MAKE_B as follows:

```
MAKE_A = (makeA->ready->used->MAKE_A).
MAKE_B = (makeB->ready->used->MAKE_B).

||MAKERS = (MAKE_A || MAKE_B).
```

The rest of the factory description now becomes:

```
ASSEMBLE = (ready->assemble->used->ASSEMBLE).

||FACTORY = (MAKERS || ASSEMBLE).
```

The state machine remains that depicted in Figure 3.7. Substituting the definition for MAKERS in FACTORY and applying the commutative and associative laws for parallel composition stated in the last section results in the original definition for FACTORY in terms of primitive processes. The *LTSA* tool can also be used to confirm that the same state machine results from the two descriptions.

3.1.3 Process Labeling

Given the definition of a process, we often want to use more than one copy of that process in a program or system model. For example, given the definition for a switch:

```
SWITCH = (on->off->SWITCH).
```

we may wish to describe a system that is the composition of two distinct switches. However, if we describe this system as (SWITCH||SWITCH), the composition is indistinguishable from a single switch since the two switch processes synchronize on their shared actions on and off. We must ensure that the actions of each SWITCH process are not shared, i.e. they must have disjoint labels. To do this we use the process labeling construct.

> a:P prefixes each action label in the alphabet of P with the label "a".

A system with two switches can now be defined as:

```
||TWO_SWITCH = (a:SWITCH || b:SWITCH).
```

The state machine representation for the processes a:SWITCH and b:SWITCH is given in Figure 3.8. It is clear that the alphabets of the two processes are disjoint, i.e. {a.on, a.off} and {b.on, b.off}.

Using a parameterized composite process, SWITCHES, we can describe an array of switches in *FSP* as follows:

```
||SWITCHES(N=3) =(forall[i:1..N] s[i]:SWITCH).
```

An equivalent but shorter definition is:

```
||SWITCHES(N=3) =(s[i:1..N]:SWITCH).
```

Processes may also be labeled by a set of prefix labels. The general form of this prefixing is as follows:

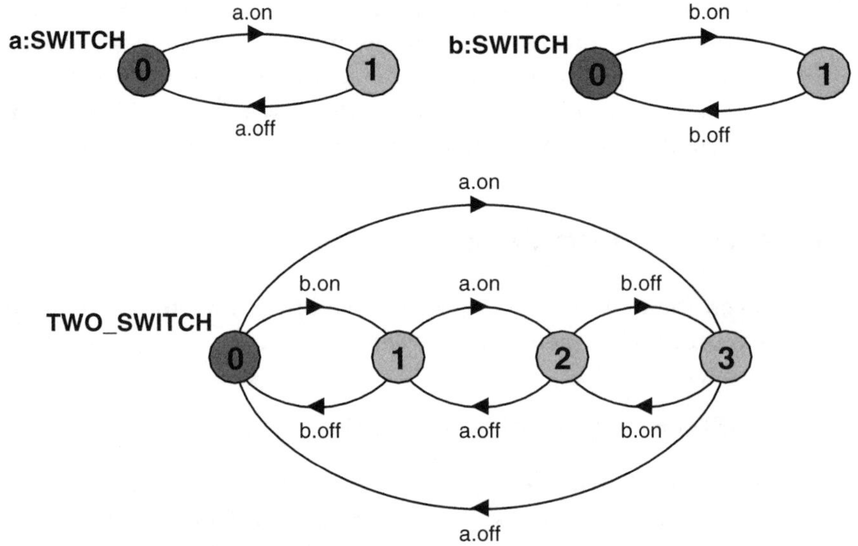

Figure 3.8 Process labeling in TWO_SWITCH.

> {a_1,..,a_x}::P replaces every action label n in the alphabet of P with the labels a_1.n,...,a_x.n. Further, every transition (n->Q) in the definition of P is replaced with the transitions ({a_1.n,...,a_x.n}->Q).

We explain the use of this facility in the following example. The control of a resource is modeled by the following process:

```
RESOURCE = (acquire->release->RESOURCE).
```

and users of the resource are modeled by the process:

```
USER = (acquire->use->release->USER).
```

We wish to model a system consisting of two users that share the resource such that only one user at a time may be using it (called "mutual exclusion"). The two users may be modeled using process labeling as a:USER and b:USER. This means that there are two distinct actions (a.acquire and b.acquire) to obtain the resource and similarly two actions to free it (a.release and b.release). Consequently, RESOURCE must be labeled with the set {a,b} to yield these transitions. The composition is described below.

```
||RESOURCE_SHARE =
      (a:USER || b:USER || {a,b}::RESOURCE).
```

The state machine representations of the processes in the RESOURCE_SHARE model are depicted in Figure 3.9. The effect of process labeling on RESOURCE can be clearly seen. The composite process graph shows that the desired result of allowing only one user to use the resource at a time has been achieved.

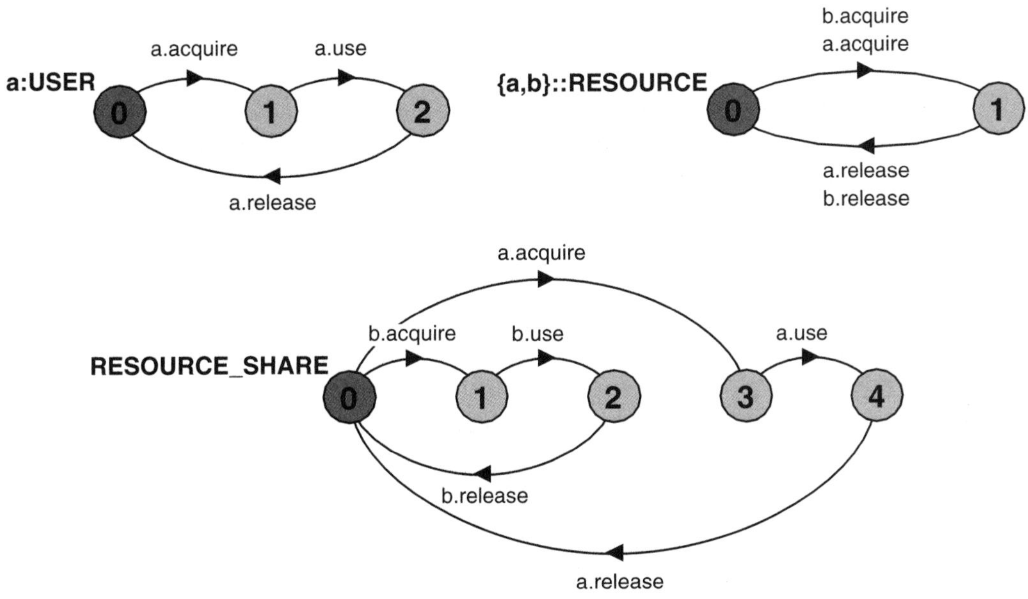

Figure 3.9 Process labeling in RESOURCE_SHARE.

A perceptive reader might notice that our model of the RESOURCE alone would permit one user to acquire the resource and the other to release it! For example, it would permit the following trace:

```
a.acquire →b.release →...
```

However, each of the USER processes cannot release the resource until it has succeeded in performing an acquire action. Hence, when the RESOURCE is composed with the USER processes, this composition ensures that only the same user that acquired the resource can release it. This is shown in the composite process RESOURCE_SHARE in Figure 3.9. This can also be confirmed using the LTSA Animator to run through the possible traces.

3.1.4 Relabeling

> Relabeling functions are applied to processes to change the names of action labels. The general form of the relabeling function is:
>
> /{*newlabel*_1/*oldlabel*_1, . . . *newlabel*_n/*oldlabel*_n}.

Relabeling is usually done to ensure that composite processes synchronize on the desired actions. A relabeling function can be applied to both primitive and composite processes. However, it is generally used more often in composition.

A server process that provides some service and a client process that invokes the service are described below:

```
CLIENT = (call->wait->continue->CLIENT).
SERVER = (request->service->reply->SERVER).
```

As described, the `CLIENT` and `SERVER` have disjoint alphabets and do not interact in any way. However, using relabeling, we can associate the `call` action of the `CLIENT` with the `request` action of the `SERVER` and similarly the `reply` and `wait` actions. The composition is defined below.

```
||CLIENT_SERVER = (CLIENT || SERVER)
                  /{call/request, reply/wait}.
```

The effect of applying the relabeling function can be seen in the state machine representations of Figure 3.10. The label `call` replaces `request` in the description of `SERVER` and `reply` replaces `wait` in the description of `CLIENT`.

An alternative formulation of the client–server system is described below using qualified or prefixed labels.

```
SERVERv2 = (accept.request
            ->service->accept.reply->SERVERv2).
CLIENTv2 = (call.request
            ->call.reply->continue->CLIENTv2).

||CLIENT_SERVERv2 = (CLIENTv2 || SERVERv2)
                    /{call/accept}.
```

The relabeling function `/{call/accept}` replaces any label prefixed by `accept` with the same label prefixed by `call`. Thus `accept.request` becomes `call.request` and `accept.reply` becomes `call.reply` in the composite

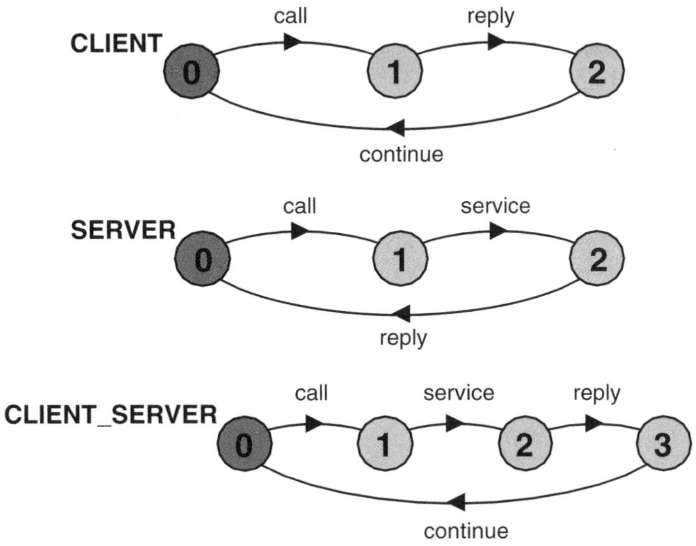

Figure 3.10 Relabeling in CLIENT_SERVER.

process CLIENT_SERVERv2. This relabeling by prefix is useful when a process has more than one interface. Each interface consists of a set of actions and can be related by having a common prefix. If required for composition, interfaces can be relabeled using this prefix as in the client–server example.

3.1.5 Hiding

> When applied to a process P, the hiding operator {a_1..a_x} removes the action names a_1..a_x from the alphabet of P and makes these concealed actions "silent". These silent actions are labeled tau. Silent actions in different processes are not shared.

The hidden actions become unobservable in that they cannot be shared with another process and so cannot affect the execution of another process. Hiding is essential in reducing the complexity of large systems for analysis purposes since, as we see later, it is possible to *minimize* the size of state machines to remove tauactions. Hiding can be applied to both primitive and composite processes but is generally used in defining composite processes. Sometimes it is more convenient to state the set of action labels which are visible and hide all other labels.

When applied to a process P, the interface operator @{a_1..a_x} hides all actions in the alphabet of P not labeled in the set a_1..a_x.

The following definitions lead to the state machine depicted in Figure 3.11:

```
USER = (acquire->use->release->USER)
       \{use}.

USER = (acquire->use->release->USER)
       @{acquire,release}.
```

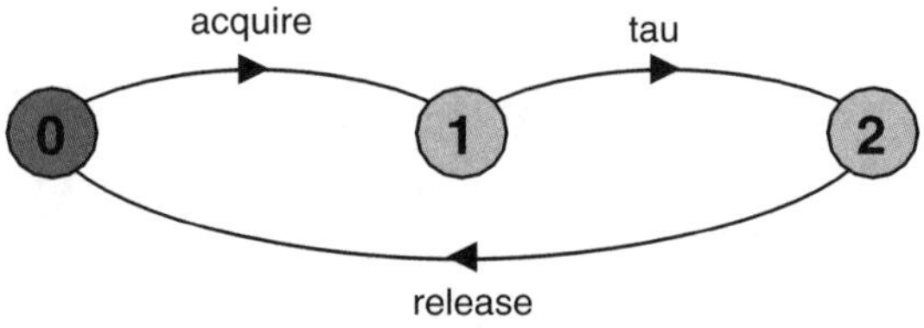

Figure 3.11 Hiding applied to USER.

Minimization of USER removes the hidden tau action to produce a state machine with equivalent observable behavior, but fewer states and transitions (Figure 3.12). *LTSA* can be used to confirm this.

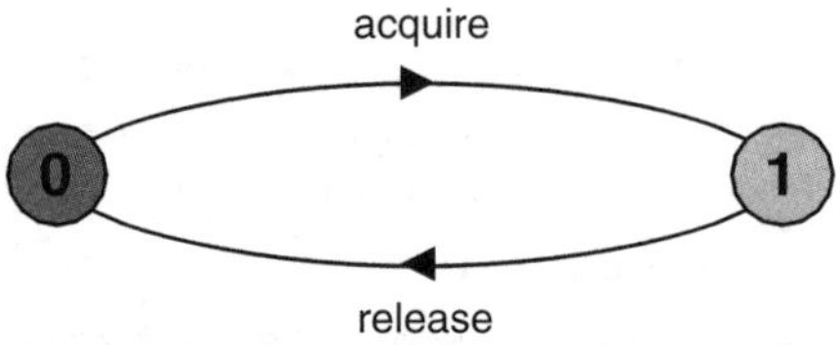

Figure 3.12 Minimized *LTS* for USER.

3.1.6 Structure Diagrams

We have used state machine diagrams to depict the dynamic behavior of processes. State machine diagrams represent the dynamic process operators, action prefix and choice. However, these diagrams do not capture the static structure of a model. While the result of applying parallel composition can be described as a

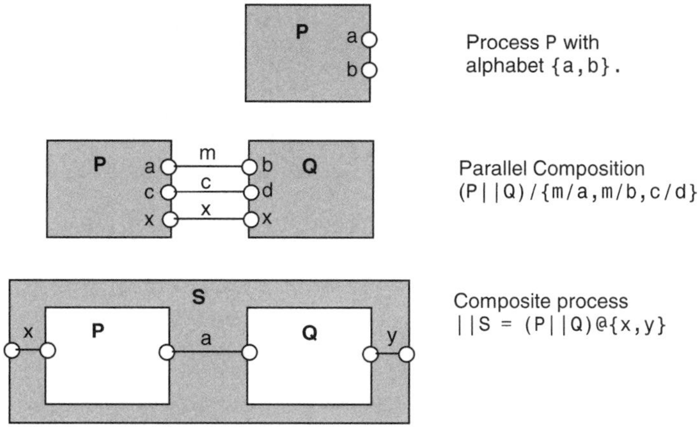

Figure 3.13 Structure diagram conventions.

state machine (since it is a process), the parallel composition expression itself is not represented. Parallel composition, relabeling and hiding are static operators that describe the structure of a model in terms of primitive processes and their interactions. Composition expressions can be represented graphically as shown in Figure 3.13.

A process is represented as a box with visible actions shown as circles on the perimeter. A shared action is depicted as a line connecting two action circles, with relabeling if necessary. A line joining two actions with the same name indicates only a shared action since relabeling is not required. A composite process is the box enclosing a set of process boxes. The alphabet of the composite is again indicated by action circles on the perimeter. Lines joining these circles to internal action circles show how the composite's actions are defined by primitive processes. These lines may also indicate relabeling functions if the composite name for an action differs from the internal name. Those actions that appear internally, but are not joined to a composite action circle, are hidden. This is the case for action a inside S in Figure 3.13. The processes inside a composite may, of course, themselves be composite and have structure diagram descriptions.

We sometimes use a line in a structure diagram to represent a set of shared actions that have a common prefix label. The line is labeled with the prefix rather than explicitly by the actions. The example in Figure 3.14 uses the single-slot buffer of section 2.1.3 to construct a buffer that can store two values. A definition of the single-slot buffer is given below.

```
range T = 0..3
BUFF = (in[i:T]->out[i]->BUFF).
```

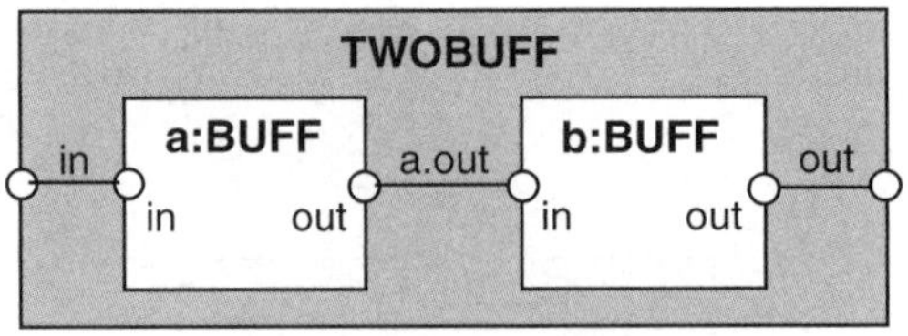


```
||TWOBUF =(a:BUFF||b:BUFF)
          /{in/a.in,
            a.out/b.in,
            out/b.out}
          @{in,out}.
```

Figure 3.14 Two-slot buffer TWOBUF.

Each of the labels in the diagram of Figure 3.14 – `in`, `out` and `a.out` – represents the set of labels `in[i:T]`, `out[i:T]` and `a.out[i:T]`, respectively.

Sometimes we omit the label on a connection line where it does not matter how relabeling is done since the label does not appear in the alphabet (interface) of the composite. For example, in Figure 3.14, it would not matter if we omitted the label `a.out` and used `b.in/a.out` instead of `a.out/b.in` as shown. We also omit labels where all the labels are the same, i.e. no relabeling function is required.

Lastly, we use a diagrammatic convention to depict the common situation of resource sharing as described in section 3.1.3. The resource-sharing model is repeated in Figure 3.15 together with its structure diagram representation. The resource is not anonymous as before; it is named `printer`. Sharing is indicated by enclosing a process in a rounded rectangle. Processes, which share the enclosed process, are connected to it by thick lines. The lines in Figure 3.15 could be labeled `a.printer` and `b.printer`; however these labels are omitted as a relabeling function is not required.

3.2 Multi-Threaded Programs

Concurrency occurs in Java programs when more than one thread is alive. Remember from Chapter 2 that a thread is alive if it has started but has not yet terminated. In this section, we present an example of a simple Java multi-threaded program that has two concurrently active threads in addition to the main thread of execution present in every Java program. The threads in the example program do not interact directly. The topic of how threads interact is left to succeeding chapters.

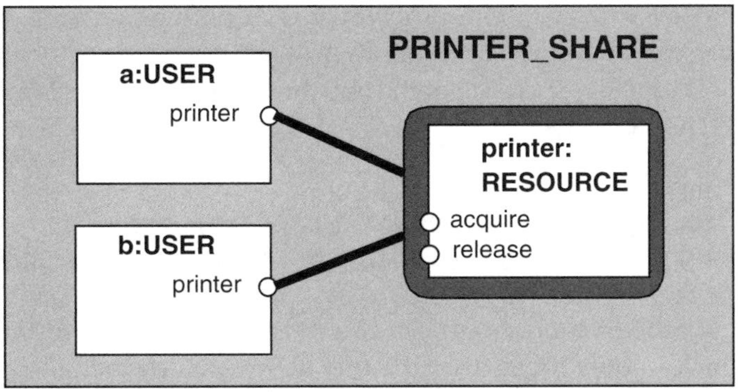

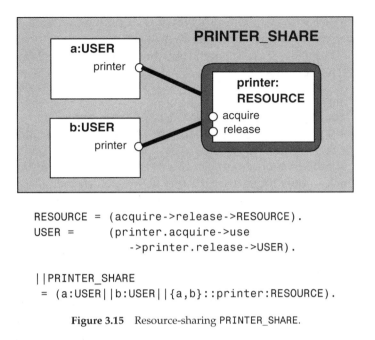

```
RESOURCE = (acquire->release->RESOURCE).
USER =     (printer.acquire->use
              ->printer.release->USER).

||PRINTER_SHARE
 = (a:USER||b:USER||{a,b}::printer:RESOURCE).
```

Figure 3.15 Resource-sharing PRINTER_SHARE.

3.2.1 ThreadDemo Example - Model

The example program drives the display depicted in Figure 3.16. Each of the threads, A and B, can be run and paused by pressing the appropriate button. When a thread is run, the display associated with it rotates. Rotation stops when the thread is paused. When a thread is paused, its background color is set to red and when it is running, the background color is set to green. The threads do not

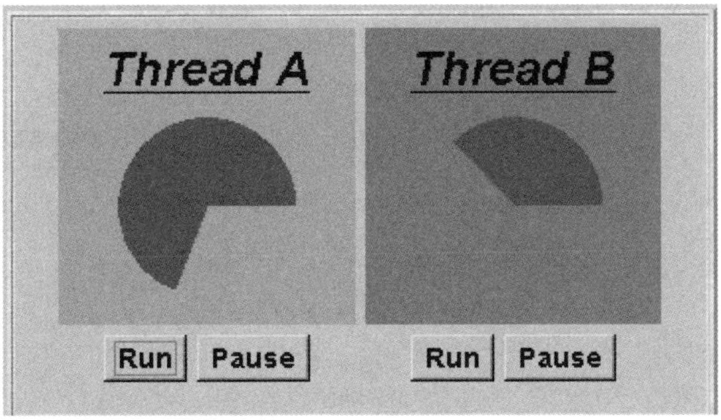

Figure 3.16 ThreadDemo display.

interact with each other; however they do interact with the Java main thread of execution when the buttons are pressed.

The behavior of each of the two threads in the applet is modeled by the following ROTATOR process:

```
ROTATOR = PAUSED,
PAUSED  = (run->RUN | pause->PAUSED),
RUN     = (pause->PAUSED |{run,rotate}->RUN).
```

The process cannot perform the `rotate` action until it moves into the RUN state. This can only occur after the `run` action, which models pushing the **Run** button. When the `pause` action occurs – modeling the **Pause** button – the process moves back to the PAUSED state in which the `rotate` action cannot take place. The model implies that the implementation of ROTATOR runs forever – there is no way of stopping it. It is not good practice to program threads which run forever; they should terminate in an orderly manner when, for example, the `Applet.stop()` method is called by a browser. As we discussed in the previous chapter, the designers of Java do not recommend using `Thread.stop()` to terminate the execution of a thread. Instead, they suggest the use of `Thread.interrupt()` which raises the `InterruptedException` that allows a thread to clean up before terminating. We can include termination in the ROTATOR process as shown below. The corresponding *LTS* is depicted in Figure 3.17.

```
ROTATOR = PAUSED,
PAUSED  = (run->RUN |pause->PAUSED
          |interrupt->STOP),
RUN     = (pause->PAUSED |{run,rotate}->RUN
          |interrupt->STOP).
```

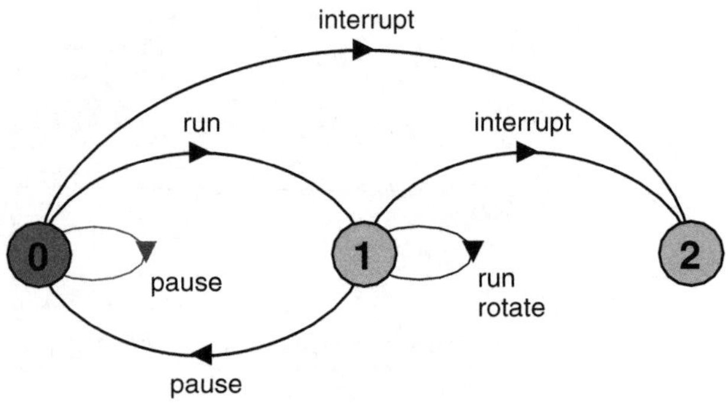

Figure 3.17 ROTATOR.

This revised model includes the effect of an interrupt action. Whether the ROTATOR process is in the paused or running state, the interrupt takes it into a final state in which no further actions are possible, i.e. it is terminated. The model for the ThreadDemo program consisting of two copies or instances of the ROTATOR thread is shown in Figure 3.18.

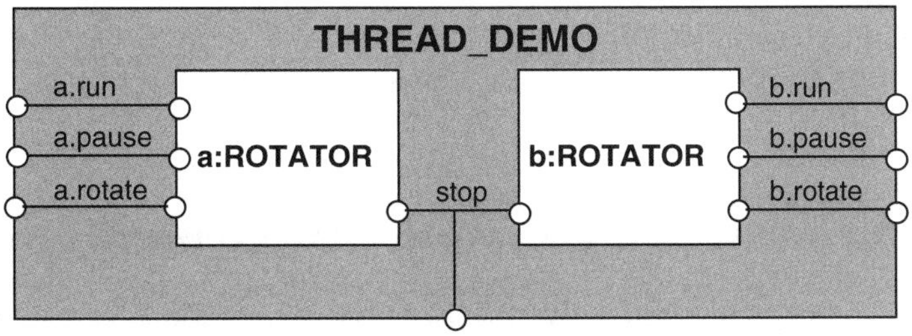


```
||THREAD_DEMO = (a:ROTATOR || b:ROTATOR)
                /{stop/{a,b}.interrupt}.
```

Figure 3.18 ThreadDemo model.

We have relabeled the a.interrupt and b.interrupt actions to be the same action stop, indicating that we always interrupt both threads at the same time, when the browser calls Applet.stop(). Having constructed the model, we can animate it using the *LTSA* tool to check that its behavior corresponds to the behavior we expect of the ThreadDemo applet. Figure 3.19 shows a screen shot of the LTSA Animator window. As described in Chapter 2, those actions that can be chosen for execution are ticked. In the figure, the action a.run has put process a in the state where a.rotate actions can occur while process b cannot perform its b.rotate action since b.run has not occurred.

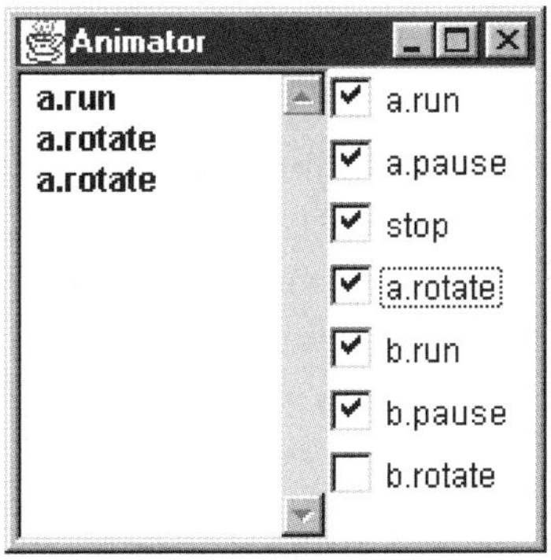

Figure 3.19 LTSA Animator window for THREAD_DEMO.

In fact, in the implementation, the environment is provided by the main thread of execution of the Java program. We can of course also model this main thread as a process that shares the actions. The display can rotate at any time and the buttons can be pushed at any time. Consequently, this main thread can be modeled as:

```
MAIN = ({a.rotate,a.run,a.pause,stop,
         b.rotate,b.run,b.pause}->MAIN).
```

Composing `MAIN` with `THREAD_DEMO` does not modify the behavior of `THREAD_DEMO` since it does not provide any additional ordering constraints on the actions.

3.2.2 ThreadDemo Example - Implementation

The implementation for the process is provided by the `Rotator` class, which implements the `Runnable` interface as shown in Program 3.1. The `run()` method simply finishes if an `InterruptedException` raised by `Thread.interrupt()` occurs. As described in the previous chapter, when the `run()` method exits, the thread which is executing it terminates.

```
class Rotator implements Runnable {

  public void run() {
     try {
       while(true) ThreadPanel.rotate();
     } catch(InterruptedException e) {}
  }
}
```

Program 3.1 `Rotator` class.

The details of suspending and resuming threads when buttons are pressed are encapsulated in the `ThreadPanel` class. The `run()` method simply calls `ThreadPanel.rotate()` to move the display. If the **Pause** button has been pressed, this method suspends a calling thread until **Run** is pressed. We use the `ThreadPanel` class extensively in programs throughout the book. The methods offered by this class relevant to the current example are listed in Program 3.2.

The `ThreadPanel` class manages the display and control buttons for the thread that is created by a call to the `start()` method. The thread is created from the class `DisplayThread` which is derived from `Thread`. The implemention of `start()` is given below:

```
public class ThreadPanel extends Panel {

   // construct display with title and segment color c
   public ThreadPanel(String title, Color c) {...}

   // rotate display of currently running thread 6 degrees
   // return value not used in this example
   public static boolean rotate()
          throws InterruptedException {...}

   // create a new thread with target r and start it running
   public void start(Runnable r) {...}

   // stop the thread using Thread.interrupt()
   public void stop() {...}
}
```

Program 3.2 ThreadPanel class.

```
public void start(Runnable r) {
     thread = new DisplayThread(canvas,r,...);
     thread.start();
}
```

where canvas is the display used to draw the rotating segment. The thread is terminated by the stop() method using Thread.interrupt() as shown below:

```
public void stop() {thread.interrupt();}
```

ThreadPanel delegates calls to rotate() to DisplayThread. The relationship between these classes, the applet and the Rotator class is depicted in the class diagram of Figure 3.20. Note that rotate() is a static method which determines the particular thread instance to which it applies by calling the method Thread.currentThread(). This returns a reference to the currently running thread, which, of course, is the only thread which can have called the method.

The Applet class ThreadDemo creates the two ThreadPanel displays when it is initialized and the two threads when it is started. The class is listed in Program 3.3.

In section 2.2.3, we saw that Java provides a standard set of operations on threads including suspend() and resume() which the reader might surmise have been used to suspend and resume the execution of the threads in response to pushing the buttons. In fact, we cannot use the operations directly in the implementation of the

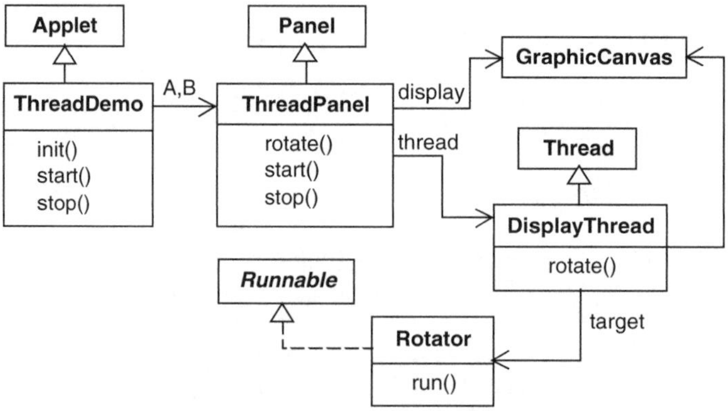

Figure 3.20 `ThreadDemo` class diagram.

```
public class ThreadDemo extends Applet {
  ThreadPanel A;
  ThreadPanel B;

  public void init() {
    A = new ThreadPanel("Thread A",Color.blue);
    B = new ThreadPanel("Thread B",Color.blue);
    add(A);
    add(B);
  }

  public void start() {
    A.start(new Rotator());
    B.start(new Rotator());
  }

  public void stop() {
    A.stop();
    B.stop();
  }
}
```

Program 3.3 `ThreadDemo` applet class.

`ThreadDemo` program for the following reason. The `rotate()` method acquires and releases resources from the graphical interface provided by the browser in which the applet runs. If we used `suspend()`, a thread could be suspended at some arbitrary time when **Pause** was pressed. In particular, it could be suspended while it was holding on to display resources. This can cause some browsers to hang or deadlock[1]. Consequently, the threads in the program are suspended using the methods `Object.wait()` and `Object.notify()`. We defer an explanation of how these work until Chapter 5 and consider the problem of deadlock in Chapter 6.

Summary

This chapter has introduced the concept of *interleaving* both as a way of executing multiple processes on a single processor and as a way of modeling concurrent execution. The chapter has dealt mainly with modeling concurrency:

- The model of concurrency is interleaved and asynchronous. By asynchronous we mean that processes proceed at arbitrary relative speeds and consequently their actions can be arbitrarily interleaved.
- The parallel composition of two or more processes modeled as finite state processes results in a finite state process that can generate all possible interleavings of the execution traces of the constituent processes.
- Process interaction is modeled by shared actions, where a shared action is executed at the same time by all the processes that share the action. A shared action can only occur when all the processes that have the action in their alphabets are ready to participate in it – they must all have the action as an eligible choice.
- Process labeling, relabeling and hiding are all ways of describing and controlling the actions shared between processes. Minimization can be used to help reduce the complexity of systems with hidden actions.
- Parallel composition and the labeling operator describe the static structure of a model. This structure can be represented diagrammatically by structure diagrams.
- Concurrent execution in Java is programmed simply by creating and starting multiple threads.

Notes and Further Reading

The parallel composition operator used here is from CSP (Hoare, 1985). It is also used in the ISO specification language LOTOS (ISO/IEC, 1988). We have chosen to use explicit process labeling as the sole means of creating multiple copies of a process definition. LOTOS and CSP introduce the interleaving operator "|||"

[1] For just this reason, `stop ()`, `suspend ()` and `resume ()` are now deprecated.

which interleaves all actions even if they have the same name. We have found that explicit process labeling clarifies trace information from the *LTSA* tool. Further, having a single composition operator rather than the three provided by LOTOS is a worthwhile notational simplification. The simple rule that actions with the same name synchronize and those that are different interleave is intuitive for users to grasp.

Most process calculi have an underlying interleaved model of concurrent execution. The reader should look at the extensive literature on Petri Nets (Peterson, J.L., 1981) for a model that permits simultaneous execution of concurrent actions.

Forms of action relabeling and hiding are provided in both CSP (Hoare, 1985) and CCS (Milner, 1989). The *FSP* approach is based on that of CCS, from which the concepts of the silent `tau` action and observational equivalence also come. Techniques for equivalence testing and minimization can be found in the paper by Kanellakis and Smolka (1990).

The structure diagrams presented in this chapter are a simplified form of the graphical representation of Darwin (Magee, Dulay and Kramer, 1994; Magee, Dulay, Eisenbach *et al.*, 1995), a language for describing Software Architectures. The Darwin toolset includes a translator from Darwin to *FSP* composition expressions (Magee, Kramer and Giannakopoulou, 1997).

Exercises

Exercises 3.1 to 3.6 are more instructive and interesting if the *FSP* models are developed using the analyzer tool *LTSA*.

3.1 Show that `S1` and `S2` describe the same behavior:

```
P = (a->b->P).
Q = (c->b->Q).
||S1 = (P||Q).

S2 =(a->c->b->S2| c->a->b->S2).
```

3.2 `ELEMENT=(up->down->ELEMENT)` accepts an `up` action and then a `down` action. Using parallel composition and the `ELEMENT` process describe a model that can accept up to four `up` actions before a `down` action. Draw a structure diagram for your solution.

3.3 Extend the model of the client–server system described in section 3.1.4 such that more than one client can use the server.

3.4 Modify the model of the client–server system in exercise 3.3 such that the call may terminate with a timeout action rather than a response from the server. What happens to the server in this situation?

3.5 A roller-coaster control system only permits its car to depart when it is full. Passengers arriving at the departure platform are registered with the roller-coaster controller by a turnstile. The controller signals the car to depart when there are enough passengers on the platform to fill the car to its maximum capacity of *M* passengers. The car goes around the roller-coaster track and then waits for another *M* passengers. A maximum of *M* passengers may occupy the platform. Ignore the synchronization detail of passengers embarking from the platform and car departure. The roller coaster consists of three processes: `TURNSTILE`, `CONTROL` and `CAR`. `TURNSTILE` and `CONTROL` interact by the shared action `passenger` indicating an arrival and `CONTROL` and `CAR` interact by the shared action `depart` signaling car departure. Draw the structure diagram for the system and provide *FSP* descriptions for each process and the overall composition.

3.6 A museum allows visitors to enter through the east entrance and leave through its west exit. Arrivals and departures are signaled to the museum controller by the turnstiles at the entrance and exit. At opening time, the museum director signals the controller that the museum is open and then the controller permits both arrivals and departures. At closing time, the director signals that the museum is closed, at which point only departures are permitted by the controller. Given that it consists of the four processes `EAST`, `WEST`, `CONTROL` and `DIRECTOR`, draw the structure diagram for the museum. Now provide an *FSP* description for each of the processes and the overall composition.

3.7 Modify the example Java program of section 3.2.2 such that it consists of three rotating displays.

4

Shared Objects and Mutual Exclusion

In the last chapter, we discussed the execution of multiple processes on one or more processors, modeling concurrent execution by interleaving and executing multiple concurrent threads in a Java program. We explained how process interaction is modeled using shared atomic actions, but not how real processes or threads interact. In this chapter, we turn to the issues involved in constructing concurrent programs in which threads interact to communicate and cooperate.

The simplest way for two or more threads in a Java program to interact is via an object whose methods can be invoked by the set of threads. This *shared* object's state can of course be observed and modified by its methods. Consequently, two threads can communicate by one thread writing the state of the shared object and the other thread reading that state. Similarly, a set of threads may cooperate to update some information encapsulated in a shared object. Unfortunately, as we will explain, this simple scheme of interaction does not work.

4.1 Interference

We have seen that the execution of the instructions from a set of threads can be interleaved in an arbitrary fashion. This interleaving can result in incorrect updates to the state of a shared object. The phenomenon is known as *interference.* The problem of interference, and how to deal with it, is the main topic of this chapter.

4.1.1 Ornamental Garden Problem

To focus on the issues of thread interaction, we use an example known as the problem of the Ornamental Garden, due to Alan Burns and Geoff Davies (1993).

The problem is stated as follows. A large ornamental garden is open to members of the public who can enter through either of two turnstiles as depicted in Figure 4.1. The management wants to determine how many people there are in the garden at any one time. They require a computer system to provide this information.

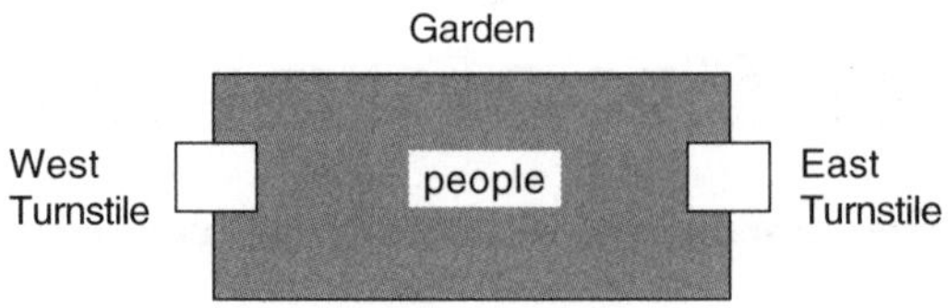

Figure 4.1 Ornamental Garden.

To simplify the problem further, we consider a garden that people are allowed to enter but never leave! The concurrent program to implement the population count required by the management of the ornamental garden consists of two concurrent threads and a shared counter object. Each thread controls a turnstile and increments the shared counter when a person passes through the turnstile. The class diagram for the program is depicted in Figure 4.2.

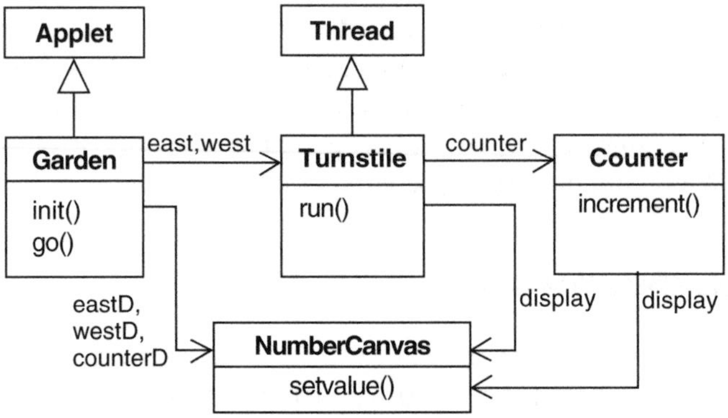

Figure 4.2 Ornamental Garden class diagram.

The `Counter` object and `Turnstile` threads are created by the `go()` method of the `Garden` applet shown below in which `eastD`, `westD` and `counterD` are objects of the same `NumberCanvas` class that we used in Chapter 2.

```
private void go() {
  counter = new Counter(counterD);
  west = new Turnstile(westD,counter);
  east = new Turnstile(eastD,counter);
  west.start();
  east.start();
}
```

The `Turnstile` thread shown in Program 4.1 simulates the periodic arrival of a visitor to the garden by sleeping for half a second and then invoking the `increment()` method of the counter. After the arrival of `Garden.MAX` visitors, the `run()` method exits and consequently, the thread terminates.

```
class Turnstile extends Thread {
  NumberCanvas display;
  Counter people;

  Turnstile(NumberCanvas n,Counter c)
    { display = n; people = c; }

  public void run() {
    try{
      display.setvalue(0);
      for (int i=1;i<=Garden.MAX;i++){
        Thread.sleep(500); //0.5 second between arrivals
        display.setvalue(i);
        people.increment();
      }
    } catch (InterruptedException e) {}
  }
}
```

Program 4.1 `Turnstile` class.

The remaining class `Counter` is more complex than is strictly necessary. The additional complexity is to ensure that the program demonstrates the effects of interference independently of any particular implementation of Java. To ensure that the program demonstrates the desired effect, Program 4.2 ensures that arbitrary interleaving occurs.

```
class Counter {
  int value=0;
  NumberCanvas display;

  Counter(NumberCanvas n) {
    display=n;
    display.setvalue(value);
  }

  void increment() {
    int temp = value;     //read value
    Simulate.HWinterrupt();
    value=temp+1;          //write value
    display.setvalue(value);
  }
}
```

Program 4.2 `Counter` class.

It does this by using the class `Simulate` which provides the method `HWinterrupt()`. The method, when called, sometimes causes a thread switch by calling `Thread.yield()` and sometimes omits the call leaving the current thread running. The idea is to simulate a hardware interrupt which can occur at arbitrary times between reading and writing to the shared `Counter` when performing an increment. Thus thread switches can occur at arbitrary times as discussed at the beginning of the last chapter. The `Simulate` class is defined by the following code:

```
class Simulate {
    public static void HWinterrupt() {
        if (Math.random()< 0.5) Thread.yield();
    }
}
```

The problem with the Ornamental Garden program is illustrated by the screen shot of the running applet in Figure 4.3. When the **Go** button is pressed, the `Garden.go()` method is invoked to create a `Counter` object and the two `Turnstile` threads. Each thread then increments the counter exactly `Garden.MAX` times and then terminates. The value of the constant `Garden.MAX` has been set to 20, consequently, when both `Turnstile` threads terminate, the counter display should register that 40 people have entered the garden. In fact, as can be seen from Figure 4.3, the counter registers only 31. Where have the missing people

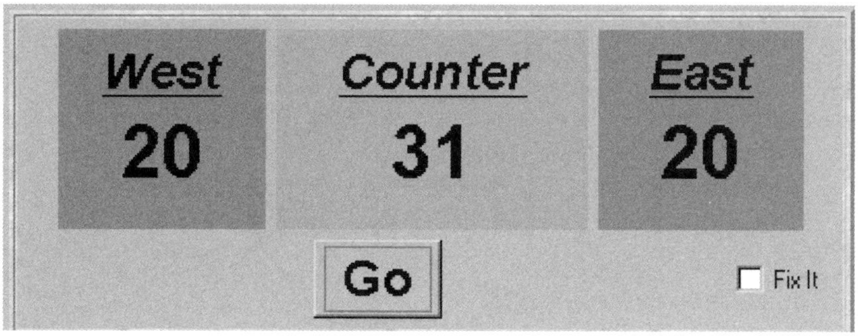

Figure 4.3 `Garden` display.

gone? Why have nine increments to the counter been lost? To investigate why, we develop a model of the Ornamental Garden problem.

4.1.2 Ornamental Garden Model

In the remainder of the book, we generally model each object or set of objects as an *FSP* process. However, to find out why the Ornamental Garden program operates incorrectly, we must model it at the level of store accesses. Consequently, the model includes a `VAR` process that describes the read and write accesses to a store location. This store location is the `value` variable encapsulated by the `people` instance of the `Counter` class (Program 4.2). The complete model is described in Figure 4.4. The reader may be surprised that there is no explicit mention of an increment action. Instead, increment is modeled using `read` and `write` actions by the definition `INCREMENT` inside `TURNSTILE`. Each thread object, `east` and `west`, has its own copy of the `read` and `write` actions that make up the increment operation or procedure. This models what happens in the actual Java program since methods are re-entrant and thus the instructions which constitute a method may be interleaved on behalf of the threads executing the method concurrently. In other words, method activations are not atomic actions. The *LTS* for the `TURNSTILE` is given in Figure 4.5.

The alphabet of the process `VAR` has been declared explicitly as the **set** in Figure 4.4. We have not used set constants before. A set constant can be used wherever we previously declared sets of action labels explicitly. Sets are simply a way of abbreviating model descriptions. `VarAlpha` is declared as follows:

```
set VarAlpha = {value.{read[T],write[T]} }
```

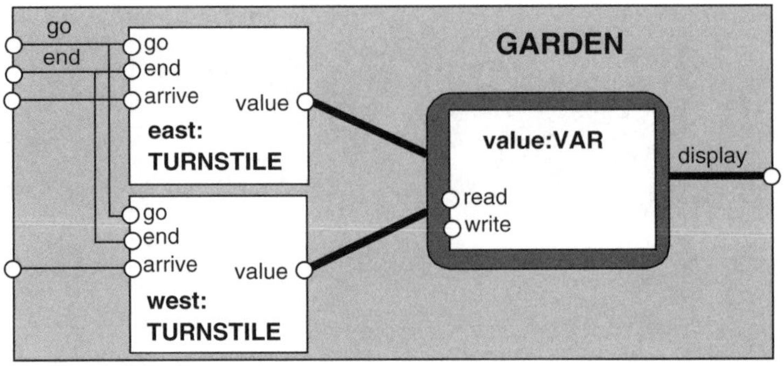


```
const N = 4
range T = 0..N
set   VarAlpha = {value.{read[T],write[T]}}

VAR       = VAR[0],
VAR[u:T] = (read[u]    ->VAR[u]
           |write[v:T]->VAR[v]).

TURNSTILE = (go     -> RUN),
RUN       = (arrive-> INCREMENT
            |end    -> TURNSTILE),
INCREMENT = (value.read[x:T]
             -> value.write[x+1]->RUN
            )+VarAlpha.

||GARDEN = (east:TURNSTILE || west:TURNSTILE
           || {east,west,display}::value:VAR)
            /{go /{east,west}.go,
              end/{ east,west}.end}.
```

Figure 4.4 Ornamental Garden model.

The alphabet for the TURNSTILE process is extended with this set using the alphabet extension construct +{...}. This is to ensure that there are no unintended free actions. For example, if a VAR write of a particular value is not shared with another process then it can occur autonomously. A TURNSTILE process never engages in the action value.write[0] since it always increments the value it reads. However, since this action is included in the alphabet extension of TURNSTILE, although it is not used in the process definition, it is prevented from occurring autonomously. The TURNSTILE process is slightly different from its Java implementation in that it does not run for a fixed number of arrivals but may end at any point. However, it cannot end in the middle of updating the shared variable value. The end action is only accepted as an alternative to an

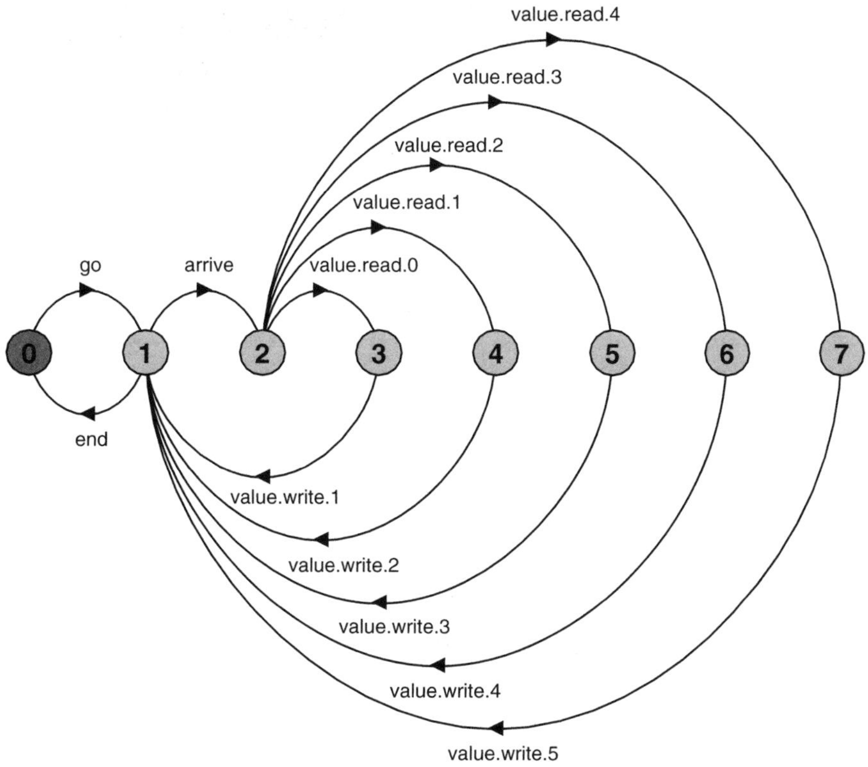

Figure 4.5 *LTS* for TURNSTILE.

arrive action. Furthermore, TURNSTILE is defined as recursive so that analysis (discussed below) will not report spurious deadlocks as would be the case if we had used STOP after the action end. Note that the shared variable VAR is not only shared by the turnstiles east and west, but also by display which is used for checking purposes.

Having developed a model of the Ornamental Garden program, in some detail, what can we do with it? Well, we can animate the model using the *LTSA* tool to produce action traces for particular input scenarios. For example, the trace in Figure 4.6 illustrates the case where there is an east arrival and a west arrival and then end occurs.

The trace is correct in that after two arrivals the counter has a value of two. However, we might try many input scenarios before finding out what is wrong with the program. To automate the search for the error, we combine a TEST process with the existing model that signals when an erroneous action trace occurs. The process is defined below:

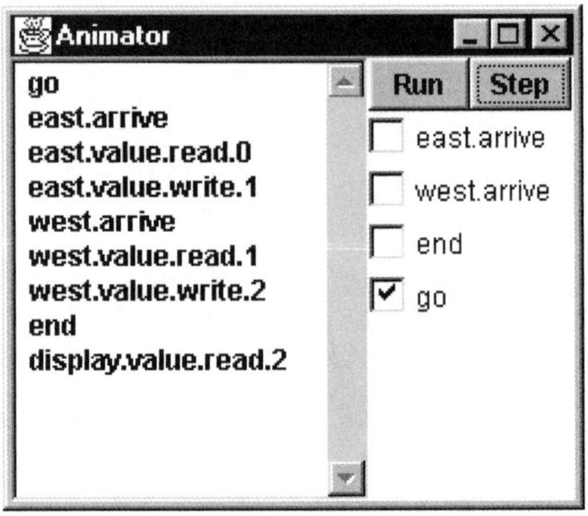

Figure 4.6 An Animator trace for the Ornamental Garden.

```
TEST       = TEST[0],
TEST[v:T]  =
     (when (v<N){east.arrive,west.arrive}->TEST[v+1]
     |end->CHECK[v]
     ),
CHECK[v:T] =
    (display.value.read[u:T] ->
       (when (u==v) right -> TEST[v]
       |when (u!=v) wrong -> ERROR
       )
    )+{display.VarAlpha}.
```

The process counts the total number of `east.arrive` and `west.arrive` actions. When an `end` action occurs, and consequently the shared variable updates are complete, it checks that the value stored is the same as the total number of arrival events. If not, an error is declared by moving into the `ERROR` state. `ERROR` (like `STOP`) is a predefined *FSP* local process (or state). It is always numbered -1 in the equivalent *LTS*. Again, alphabet extension is used to ensure that no actions prefixed by `display` can occur autonomously.

The `TEST` process is combined with the existing model as follows:

```
||TESTGARDEN = (GARDEN || TEST).
```

We can now request the *LTSA* analysis tool to perform an exhaustive search to see if the `ERROR` state in `TEST` can be reached and if so to produce an example trace. The trace produced is:

```
Trace to property violation in TEST:
     go
     east.arrive
     east.value.read.0
     west.arrive
     west.value.read.0
     east.value.write.1
     west.value.write.1
     end
     display.value.read.1
     wrong
```

This trace clearly indicates the problem with the original Java program. Increments are lost because the shared variable is not updated atomically. Thus both east and west turnstiles read the value 0 and write 1. If the east increment finished before the west increment started or vice versa, then the result would be two (as in the previous trace).

> Destructive update, caused by the arbitrary interleaving of `read` and `write` actions, is termed *interference*.

In real concurrent programs, interference bugs are extremely difficult to locate. They occur infrequently, perhaps due to some specific combination of device interrupts and application I/O requests. They may not be found even after extensive testing. We had to include a simulated interrupt in the example program to demonstrate the error. Without the simulated interrupt, the program is still incorrect, although the erroneous behavior may not manifest itself on all systems.

The general solution to the problem of interference is to give methods that access a shared object *mutually exclusive* access to that object. This ensures that an update is not interrupted by concurrent updates. As we see in the following sections, methods with mutually exclusive access can be modeled as atomic actions.

4.2 Mutual Exclusion in Java

> Concurrent activations of a method in Java can be made mutually exclusive by prefixing the method with the keyword **synchronized**.

The `Counter` class from the Ornamental Garden program can be corrected by deriving a `SynchronizedCounter` class from `Counter` and making the increment method in the subclass **synchronized** as shown in Program 4.3.

```
class SynchronizedCounter extends Counter {

  SynchronizedCounter(NumberCanvas n)
     {super(n);}

  synchronized void increment() {
       super.increment();
  }
}
```

Program 4.3 Corrected `Counter` class.

Java associates a lock with every object. The Java compiler inserts code to acquire the lock before executing the body of a synchronized method and code to release the lock before the method returns. Concurrent threads are blocked until the lock is released. Since only one thread at a time may hold the lock, only one thread may be executing the synchronized method. If this is the only method, as in the example, mutual exclusion to the shared object is ensured. If an object has more than one method, to ensure mutually exclusive access to the state of the object, all the methods should be synchronized.

Access to an object may also be made mutually exclusive by using the synchronized statement:

`synchronized` (*object*) { *statements* }

This acquires the referenced object's lock before executing the bracketed statement block and releases it on exiting the block. For example, an alternative (but less elegant) way to correct the example would be to modify the `Turnstile.run()` method to use:

```
synchronized(people) {people.increment();}
```

This is less elegant as the user of the shared object has the responsibility for imposing the lock, rather than embedding it in the shared object itself. Since not all users of the object may act responsibly, it may also be less secure against interference.

Figure 4.7 Corrected `Garden` display.

The output from the corrected Ornamental Garden program is depicted in Figure 4.7. The only change is to use the class defined in Program 4.3 rather than the original `Counter` class. This change is made by clicking the **Fix It** check box before pressing **Go**.

Once a thread has acquired the lock on an object by executing a synchronized method, that method may itself call another synchronized method from the same object (directly or indirectly) without having to wait to acquire the lock again. The lock counts how many times it has been acquired by the same thread and does not allow another thread to access the object until there has been an equivalent number of releases. This locking strategy is sometimes termed *recursive* locking since it permits recursive synchronized methods. For example:

```
public synchronized void increment(int n) {
   if (n>0) {
       ++value;
       increment(n-1);
   } else return;
}
```

This is a rather unlikely recursive version of a method which increments `value` by `n`. If locking in Java was not recursive, it would cause a calling thread to be blocked forever, waiting to acquire a lock which it already holds!

4.3 Modeling Mutual Exclusion

The simplest way to correct the model of the Ornamental Garden program listed in Figure 4.4 is to add locking in exactly the same way as it was added to the

Java program. For simplicity, we ignore the detail that Java locks are recursive since whether or not the lock is recursive has no impact on this problem. A (non-recursive) lock can be modeled by the process:

```
LOCK = (acquire->release->LOCK).
```

The composition LOCKVAR associates a lock with a variable. It is substituted for VAR in the definition of GARDEN.

```
||LOCKVAR = (LOCK || VAR).
```

The alphabet VarAlpha is modified as follows to include the additional locking actions:

```
set VarAlpha = {value.{read[T],write[T],
                          acquire, release}}
```

Finally, the definition of TURNSTILE must be modified to acquire the lock before accessing the variable and to release it afterwards:

```
TURNSTILE = (go     -> RUN),
RUN       = (arrive-> INCREMENT
            |end    -> TURNSTILE),
INCREMENT = (value.acquire
             -> value.read[x:T]->value.write[x+1]
             -> value.release->RUN
            )+VarAlpha.
```

We can check this model in exactly the same way as before using TEST. An exhaustive search does not find any errors. Consequently, we have mechanically verified that this new version of the model satisfies the property that the count value is equal to the total number of arrivals when stop is pressed. A sample execution trace of the new model is shown below:

```
go
east.arrive
east.value.acquire
east.value.read.0
east.value.write.1
east.value.release
west.arrive
west.value.acquire
west.value.read.1
west.value.write.2
```

```
west.value.release
end
display.value.read.2
right
```

Now that we have shown that we can make shared actions indivisible or atomic using locks, we can abstract the details of variables and locks and model shared objects directly in terms of their synchronized methods. We can perform abstraction mechanically by hiding actions. For example, we can describe the behavior of the `SynchronizedCounter` class (over a finite integer range) by:

```
const N = 4
range T = 0..N

VAR = VAR[0],
VAR[u:T] = ( read[u]->VAR[u]
           | write[v:T]->VAR[v]).

LOCK = (acquire->release->LOCK).

INCREMENT = (acquire->read[x:T]
             -> (when (x<N) write[x+1]
                 ->release->increment->INCREMENT
                )
             )+{read[T],write[T]}.

||COUNTER = (INCREMENT||LOCK||VAR)@{increment}.
```

The definition of `INCREMENT` has been slightly modified from that used previously. The **`when`** clause ensures that the `increment` action can only occur when the value stored is less than `N`. In other words, `increment` is not allowed to overflow the range `T`. The alphabet declaration `@{increment}` means that `read`, `write`, `acquire` and `release` become internal actions (`tau`) of `COUNTER`. The *LTS* which results from minimizing `COUNTER` is depicted in Figure 4.8.

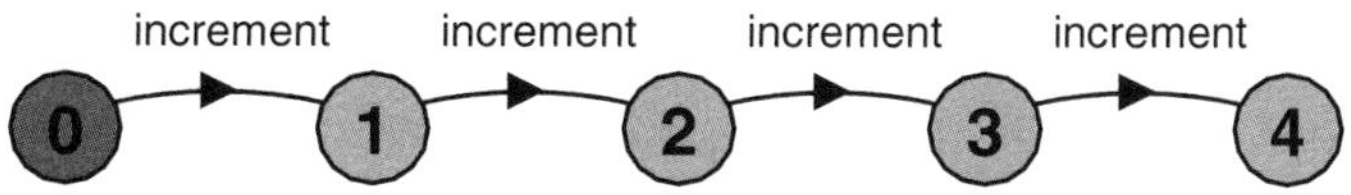

Figure 4.8 Minimized *LTS* for `COUNTER`.

We can describe a single process that generates exactly the same *LTS*:

```
COUNTER = COUNTER[0],
COUNTER[v:T] = (when (v<N) increment->COUNTER[v+1]).
```

This is a much more abstract and consequently simpler model of the shared `Counter` object with its synchronized `increment` method. We have demonstrated above (by *LTSA* minimization) that it has exactly the same observable behavior as the more complex definition. A display action to read the value of the counter can be added as shown below:

```
DISPLAY_COUNTER = COUNTER[0],
COUNTER[v:T] = (when (v<N) increment->COUNTER[v+1]
               |display[v] -> COUNTER[v]).
```

The *LTS* which results from minimizing `DISPLAY_COUNTER` is depicted in Figure 4.9.

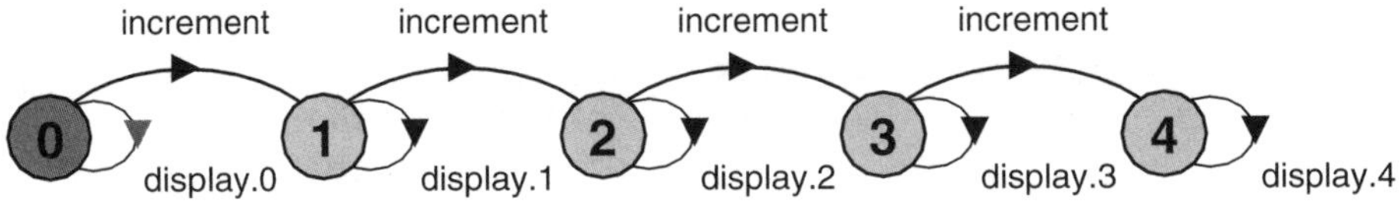

Figure 4.9 Minimized *LTS* for `DISPLAY_COUNTER`.

To implement this action in the Java class, we would simply add the synchronized method:

```
public synchronized int display() {
    return value;
}
```

In the following chapters, we usually model shared objects at this level of abstraction, ignoring the details of locks and mutual exclusion (as provided by the use of synchronized methods in Java). Each shared object is modeled as an *FSP* process, in addition to modeling each Java thread as an *FSP* process. The model of a program does not distinguish active entities (threads) from passive entities (shared objects). They are both modeled as finite state machines. This uniform treatment facilitates analysis.

Summary

In this chapter, we have discussed thread interaction via shared objects. The Ornamental Garden example served to demonstrate that uncontrolled interleaving of method instructions leads to destructive update of the state of the shared object. This is termed *interference*. Interference can be avoided by giving each concurrent method activation mutually exclusive access to the shared state. In Java, this is achieved by making such methods **synchronized**. Synchronized methods acquire a lock associated with the object before accessing the object state and release the lock after access. Since only one thread at a time can acquire the lock, synchronized methods obtain mutually exclusive access to the object state.

Interference bugs in real concurrent programs are notoriously difficult to find. They can be found by analyzing program models as we demonstrated. However, this requires detailed modeling at the level of store accesses to variables. Such models quickly become too large to analyze. The answer is to ensure systematically that all the methods of objects shared between threads are synchronized. They can then be treated as atomic actions for modeling purposes.

Notes and Further Reading

We have dealt with the problem of access to shared objects encapsulating variables. However, access to any resource must be made mutually exclusive if the resource cannot be concurrently shared. These resources are sometimes termed serially reusable since they can be used by many processes at different times but not shared by many processes at the same time. For example, a printer can only produce the output from one print job at a time. The solution of using locks to ensure mutual exclusion is a general one that can be applied to controlling access to a printer in the same way as to shared variables.

A solution to the mutual exclusion problem was first proposed by Dijkstra (1965). All operating systems and concurrent programming textbooks deal with mutual exclusion. Usually, great emphasis is placed on the concept of a *critical section*. A critical section is simply the section of code belonging to a thread or process which accesses the shared variables. To ensure correct behavior, this critical section must be given mutually exclusive access by acquiring a lock before the critical section and releasing it afterwards. We have not used the term critical section since, in an object-oriented language such as Java, shared variables are encapsulated in objects and accessed via methods. In other words, synchronized methods are critical sections. The synchronized statement is another way of making a section of code a critical section in Java. However, it is usually the case in well-designed concurrent object-oriented programs that critical sections are methods.

Exercises

4.1 Modify the uncorrected version of the Ornamental Garden program such that `Turnstile` threads can sleep for different times. Is it possible to choose these sleep times such that interference does not occur?

4.2 Given the following declarations:

```
const N = 3
range P = 1..2 //thread identities
range C = 0..N //counter range for lock
```

Model a Java recursive lock as the *FSP* process `RECURSIVE_LOCK` with the alphabet `{acquire[p:P],release[p:P]}`. The action `acquire[p]` acquires the lock for thread `p`.

4.3 A central computer connected to remote terminals via communication links is used to automate seat reservations for a concert hall. A booking clerk can display the current state of reservations on the terminal screen. To book a seat, a client chooses a free seat and the clerk enters the number of the chosen seat at the terminal and issues a ticket. A system is required which avoids double-booking of the same seat while allowing clients free choice of the available seats. Construct a model of the system and demonstrate that your model does not permit double-bookings. (*Hint*: It is only necessary to model a few terminals and a few seats. Remember, a seat can appear to be free although it is booked or being booked by another clerk.)

4.4 Write a Java program that implements the seat reservation system of exercise 4.3.

5 Monitors and Condition Synchronization

Monitors are language features for concurrent programming. A monitor encapsulates data, which can only be observed and modified by monitor access procedures. Only a single access procedure may be active at a time. An access procedure thus has mutually exclusive access to the data variables encapsulated in the monitor. Monitors should sound familiar since we have already seen the monitor concept in the last chapter, though explained using different terminology. An object satisfies the data access requirement of a monitor since it encapsulates data which, if declared **`private`**, can be accessed only by the object's methods. These methods can be **`synchronized`** to provide mutually exclusive access. Thus, a monitor is simply represented in Java as a class that has synchronized methods.

Monitors support *condition synchronization* in addition to ensuring that access to the data they encapsulate is mutually exclusive. Condition synchronization, as the term suggests, permits a monitor to block threads until a particular condition holds, such as a count becoming non-zero, a buffer becoming empty or new input becoming available. This chapter describes how condition synchronization in monitors is modeled and how it is implemented in Java.

5.1 Condition Synchronization

We illustrate condition synchronization using a simple example. A controller is required for a car park, which only permits cars to enter when the car park is not full and, for consistency, does not permit cars to leave when there are no cars in the car park. A snapshot of our Java simulation of the car park is given in Figure 5.1. It depicts the situation in which the car park is full, the barrier is down and no further cars are permitted to enter. Car arrivals and departures are simulated by separate threads. In Figure 5.1, the departures thread has been stopped to allow

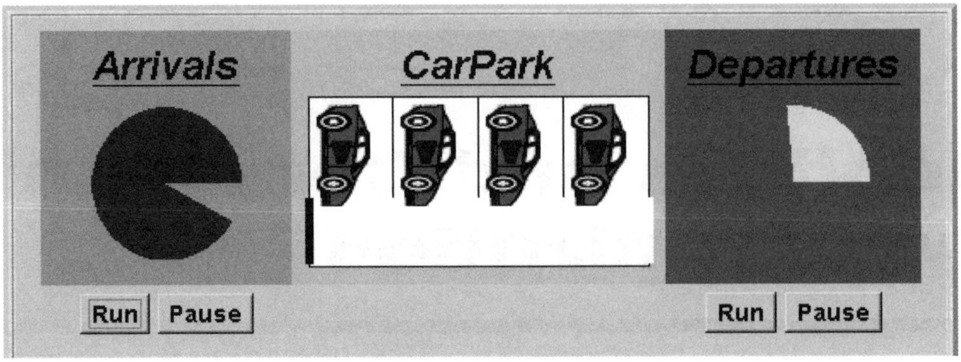

Figure 5.1 Car park display.

the car park to become full. The arrivals thread is therefore blocked from further progress.

5.1.1 Car Park Model

The first step in modeling a system is to decide which events or actions are of interest. In the car park system, we can abstract details such as display panel rotation and the starting and stopping of the display threads. We thus omit the actions concerned with running, rotation, pausing and terminating threads that we modeled in section 3.2.1. Instead, we concern ourselves with only two actions: car arrival at the car park and car departure from the car park. These actions are named *arrive* and *depart* respectively. The next step is to identify the processes. These are the arrivals process, the departures process and the process that controls access to the car park. Both the arrivals process and the departures process are trivial. They attempt to generate, respectively, a sequence of arrival actions and a sequence of departure actions. The car park control must only permit arrival actions to occur *when* there is space in the car park and departures to occur *when* there are cars in the car park. This expresses the synchronization conditions that must be satisfied by the other processes when interacting with the car park.

The car park model is given in Figure 5.2. The `CARPARKCONTROL` process uses the indexed state `SPACES` to record the number of available spaces in the car park. The control requirements described above have been modeled using the *FSP* guarded action construct (see section 2.1.5). Thus in state `SPACES[0]`, `arrive` actions are not accepted and in state `SPACES[N]`, `depart` actions are not accepted.

The behavior of the car park system is depicted as an *LTS* in Figure 5.3. The *LTS* has been generated directly from the model of Figure 5.2. It clearly shows that a

```
CARPARKCONTROL(N=4) = SPACES[N],
SPACES[i:0..N] = (when(i>0) arrive->SPACES[i-1]
                 |when(i<N) depart->SPACES[i+1]
                 ).

ARRIVALS   = (arrive->ARRIVALS).
DEPARTURES = (depart->DEPARTURES).

||CARPARK =
      (ARRIVALS||CARPARKCONTROL(4)||DEPARTURES).
```

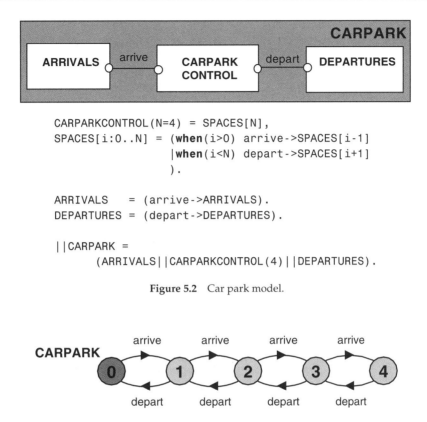

Figure 5.2 Car park model.

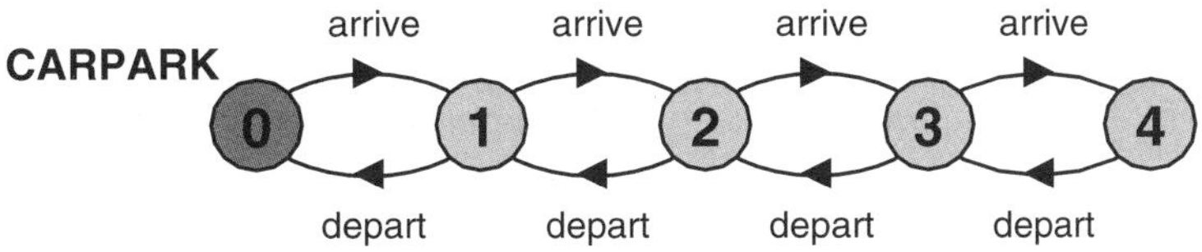

Figure 5.3 Car park *LTS*.

maximum of four `arrive` actions can be accepted before a `depart` action must occur.

5.1.2 Car Park Program

Our models of concurrent systems represent all the entities in a system as processes. In implementing the behavior of a model as a Java program, we must decide which entities are active and which are passive. By *active*, we mean an entity that initiates actions; this is implemented as a *thread*. By *passive*, we mean an entity that responds to actions; this is implemented as a *monitor*. As we will see in subsequent examples, the decision as to which processes in a model become threads in the implementation and which become monitors is not always clear-cut. However, in the car park example, the decision is clear. The processes `ARRIVALS` and `DEPARTURES`, which initiate `arrive` and `depart` actions, should

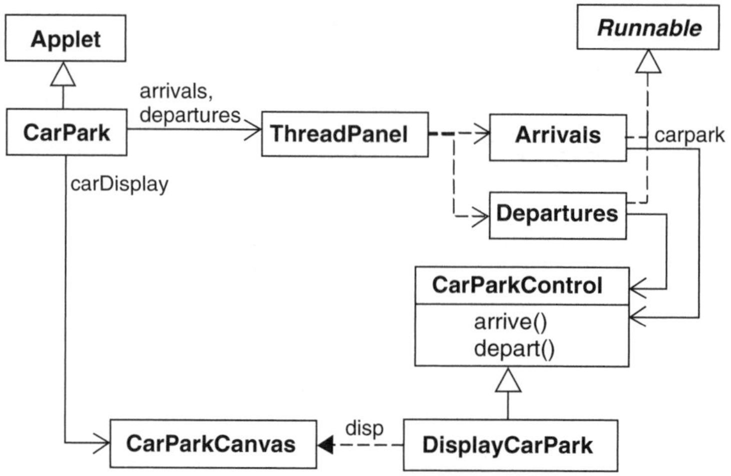

Figure 5.4 Car park class diagram.

be implemented as threads. The `CARPARKCONTROL` process, which responds to `arrive` and `depart` actions, should be a monitor. The class structure of the car park program is depicted in Figure 5.4.

We have omitted the `DisplayThread` and `GraphicCanvas` threads managed by `ThreadPanel` to simplify Figure 5.4. These are organized in exactly the same way as depicted in the class diagram for `ThreadDemo` in Chapter 3. The classes that are relevant to the concurrent execution of the program are the two `Runnable` classes, `Arrivals` and `Departures`, and the `CarParkControl` class, which controls arrivals and departures. Instances of these classes are created by the `CarPark` applet `start()` method:

```
public void start() {
  CarParkControl c =
     new DisplayCarPark(carDisplay,Places);
     arrivals.start(new Arrivals(c));
     departures.start(new Departures(c));
}
```

`Arrivals` and `Departures` are instances of the `ThreadPanel` class and `carDisplay` is an instance of `CarParkCanvas` as shown in the class diagram.

The code for the `Arrivals` and `Departures` classes is listed in Program 5.1. These classes use a `ThreadPanel.rotate()` method which takes as its parameter the number of degrees the rotating display segment is moved. The `CarParkControl` class must block the activation of `arrive()` by the arrivals thread if the car

```
class Arrivals implements Runnable {
  CarParkControl carpark;

  Arrivals(CarParkControl c) {carpark = c;}

  public void run() {
    try {
      while(true) {
        ThreadPanel.rotate(330);
        carpark.arrive();
        ThreadPanel.rotate(30);
      }
    } catch (InterruptedException e){}
  }
}

class Departures implements Runnable {
  CarParkControl carpark;

  Departures(CarParkControl c) {carpark = c;}

  public void run() {
    try {
      while(true) {
        ThreadPanel.rotate(180);
        carpark.depart();
        ThreadPanel.rotate(180);
      }
    } catch (InterruptedException e){}
  }
}
```

Program 5.1 `Arrivals` and `Departures` classes.

park is full and block the activation of `depart()` by the departures thread if the car park is empty. How do we implement this in Java?

5.1.3 Condition Synchronization in Java

Java provides a thread wait set per monitor; actually, per object, since any object may have a monitor synchronization lock associated with it. The following methods are provided by **`class Object`** from which all other classes are derived.

`public final void notify()`
Wakes up a single thread that is waiting on this object's wait set.

`public final void notifyAll()`
Wakes up all threads that are waiting on this object's wait set.

`public final void wait() throws InterruptedException`
Waits to be notified by another thread. The waiting thread releases the synchronization lock associated with the monitor. When notified, the thread must wait to reacquire the monitor before resuming execution.

The operations fail if called by a thread that does not currently "own" the monitor (i.e. one that has not previously acquired the synchronization lock by executing a synchronized method or statement). We refer to a thread *entering* a monitor when it acquires the mutual exclusion lock associated with the monitor and *exiting* the monitor when it releases the lock. From the above definitions, it can be seen that a thread calling `wait()` exits the monitor. This allows other threads to enter the monitor and, when the appropriate condition is satisfied, to call `notify()` or `notifyAll()` to awake waiting threads. The operation of `wait()` and `notify()` is depicted in Figure 5.5.

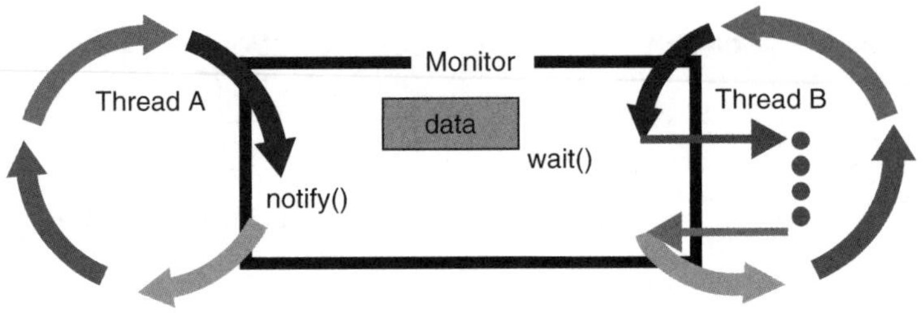

Figure 5.5 Monitor `wait()` and `notify()`.

The basic format for modeling a guarded action for some condition *`cond`* and action *`act`* using *FSP* is shown below:

```
FSP:   when cond act -> NEWSTAT
```

The corresponding format for implementing the guarded action for condition *`cond`* and action *`act`* using Java is as follows:

```
Java: public synchronized void act()
              throws InterruptedException
      {
        while (!cond) wait();
        // modify monitor data
        notifyAll()
      }
```

The **while** loop is necessary to ensure that `cond` is indeed satisfied when a thread re-enters the monitor. Although the thread invoking `wait()` may have been notified that `cond` is satisfied, thereby releasing it from the monitor wait set, `cond` may be invalidated by another thread that runs between the time that the waiting thread is awakened and the time it re-enters the monitor (by acquiring the lock).

If an action modifies the data of the monitor, it can call `notifyAll()` to awaken all other threads that may be waiting for a particular condition to hold with respect to this data. If it is not certain that only a single thread needs to be awakened, it is safer to call `notifyAll()` than `notify()` to make sure that threads are not kept waiting unnecessarily.

Returning to the car park example, the implementation of the `CarParkControl` monitor is given in Program 5.2. Since either the `ARRIVALS` thread is blocked waiting space or the `DEPARTURES` thread is blocked waiting cars and these conditions are exclusive, only a single thread may be waiting on the monitor queue at any one time. Consequently, we can use `notify()` rather than `notifyAll()`. Note that we have made the `spaces` and `capacity` variables **protected** rather than **private** so that they can be accessed by the display class that is derived from `CarParkControl`.

The general rules for guiding the translation of the process model into a Java monitor are as follows:

> Each guarded action in the model of a monitor is implemented as a **synchronized** method which uses a **while** loop and `wait()` to implement the guard. The **while** loop condition is the negation of the model guard condition.

and

> Changes in the state of the monitor are signaled to waiting threads using `notify()` or `notifyAll()`.

```
class CarParkControl {
  protected int spaces;
  protected int capacity;

  CarParkControl(n)
    {capacity = spaces = n;}

  synchronized void arrive()
      throws InterruptedException {
    while (spaces==0) wait();
    --spaces;
    notify();
  }

  synchronized void depart()
     throws InterruptedException{
    while (spaces==capacity) wait();
    ++spaces;
    notify();
  }
}
```

Program 5.2 `CarParkControl` monitor.

Thus in the car park model:

```
FSP: when(i>0) arrive->SPACES[i-1]
```

becomes

```
Java: while (spaces==0) wait(); --spaces;
```

and

```
FSP: when(i<N) depart->SPACES[i+1]
```

becomes

```
Java: while (spaces==N) wait(); ++spaces;
```

The state of the car park monitor is the integer variable `spaces`. Each method modifies `spaces` and consequently, the change is signaled by `notify()` at the end of each method.

5.2 Semaphores

Semaphores, introduced by Dijkstra (1968a), were one of the first mechanisms proposed to deal with inter-process synchronization problems. A semaphore *s* is an integer variable that can take only non-negative values. Once *s* has been given an initial value, the only operations permitted on *s* are *up(s)* and *down(s)* defined as follows:

down(s): **when** $s>0$ **do** decrement *s*;

up(s): increment *s*

In Dijkstra's original proposal, the *down* operation was called *P* (for the first letter in the Dutch word *passeren*, which means "to pass"). The *up* operation was called *V* (for the first letter of the Dutch word *vrijgeven*, which means "to release"). Semaphores are implemented in the kernels of many operating systems and real-time executives. The above definition of semaphores seems to imply some sort of busy wait by *down(s)* until *s* becomes non-zero. In fact, in the kernel of an operating system, semaphores are usually implemented by a blocking wait as shown below:

down(s): **if** $s>0$ **then**
        decrement *s*
    else
        block execution of the calling process

up(s): **if** processes blocked on *s* **then**
        awaken one of them
    else
        increment *s*

Implementations of semaphores usually manage processes, blocked on a semaphore by *down*, as a first-in-first-out (FIFO) queue. The *up* operation awakens the process at the head of the queue. FIFO queuing should not be relied on in reasoning about the correctness of semaphore programs.

In the following, we describe how semaphores are modeled and how they can be implemented using Java monitors. However, it should be realized that semaphores are a low-level mechanism sometimes used in implementing the higher-level monitor construct, rather than vice versa as presented here for pedagogic reasons.

5.2.1 Modeling Semaphores

The models of concurrent systems that we can describe in *FSP* are finite, to ensure they can be analyzed. Consequently, we can only model semaphores that take a finite range of values. If the range is exceeded then this is regarded as an error in the model as described below:

```
const Max = 3
range Int = 0..Max

SEMAPHORE(N=0)  = SEMA[N],
SEMA[v:Int]     = (up->SEMA[v+1]
                  |when(v>0) down->SEMA[v-1]
                  ),
SEMA[Max+1]     = ERROR.
```

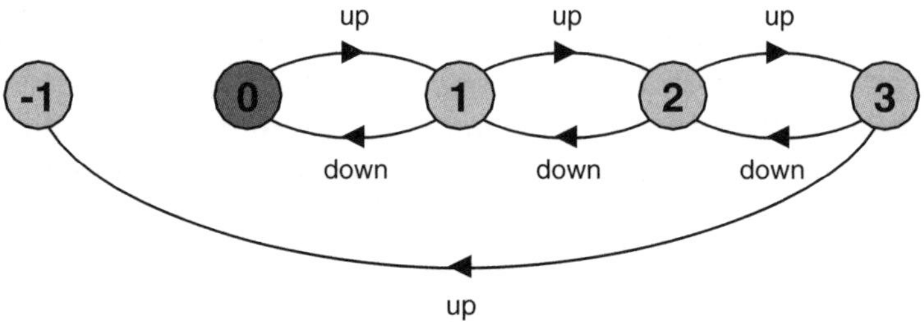

Figure 5.6 Semaphore *LTS*.

The behavior of the semaphore is depicted in Figure 5.6, with the ERROR state indicated by *state*(−1). In fact, since the *FSP* compiler automatically maps undefined states to the ERROR state, we can omit the last line of the description and model a semaphore more succinctly as:

```
SEMAPHORE(N=0)  = SEMA[N],
SEMA[v:Int]     = (up->SEMA[v+1]
                  |when(v>0) down->SEMA[v-1]
                  ).
```

The model follows directly from the first definition for a semaphore in the previous section. The action down is only accepted when the value v of the SEMAPHORE is greater than zero. The action up is not guarded. SEMAPHORE can take values in the range 0..Max and has an initial value N. If an up action causes Max to be exceeded then SEMAPHORE moves to the ERROR state. When SEMAPHORE is used in a larger model, we must ensure that this ERROR state does not occur. As an example, we model the use of semaphores to provide mutual exclusion.

Figure 5.7 depicts a model in which three processes p[1..3] use a shared semaphore mutex to ensure mutually exclusive access to some resource. Each process performs the action mutex.down to get exclusive access and mutex.up to release it. Access to the resource is modeled as the action critical (for the

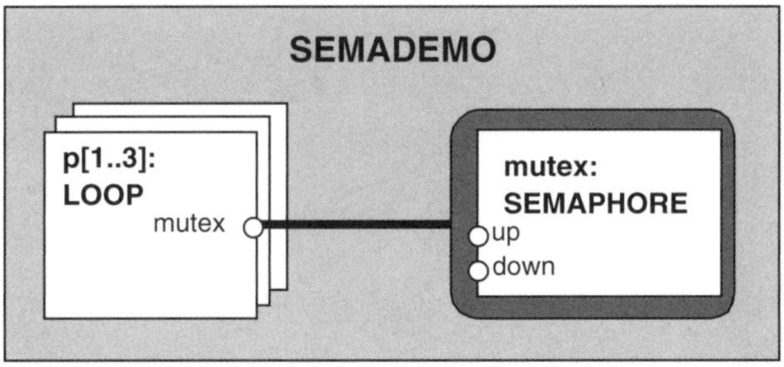

Figure 5.7 Semaphore mutual exclusion model.

critical section of code used to access the shared resource). The model for each of the processes is as shown below:

```
LOOP = (mutex.down->critical->mutex.up->LOOP).
```

The composite process SEMADEMO, which combines processes and semaphore and which is depicted graphically in Figure 5.7, is defined as:

```
||SEMADEMO = (p[1..3]:LOOP
             ||{p[1..3]}::mutex:SEMAPHORE(1)).
```

Note that for mutual exclusion, the semaphore must be given the initial value one. The first process that tries to execute its `critical` action, performs a `mutex.down` action making the value of `mutex` zero. No further process can perform `mutex.down` until the original process releases exclusion by `mutex.up`. This can be seen clearly from the SEMADEMO labeled transition system in Figure 5.8.

It should also be clear from Figure 5.8 that no ERROR state is reachable in SEMADEMO since it does not appear in the *LTS*. In fact, the value of the semaphore does not exceed one (from the *LTS*, we can see that a trace of two consecutive `mutex.up` actions without an intermediate `mutex.down` cannot occur). For mutual exclusion, it is sufficient to use a *binary* semaphore which takes the values 0 or 1. We have already seen in the previous chapter that we can use the analysis tool to check mechanically for errors. We will see in subsequent chapters that we do not have to rely on visual inspection of the *LTS* to assert properties concerning sequences of actions. Of course, in this example, we can quickly check if `mutex` ever goes above 1 by setting `Max` to 1 and searching for errors.

5.2.2 Semaphores in Java

Semaphores are passive objects that react to `up` and `down` actions; they do not initiate actions. Consequently, we implement a semaphore in Java as a monitor

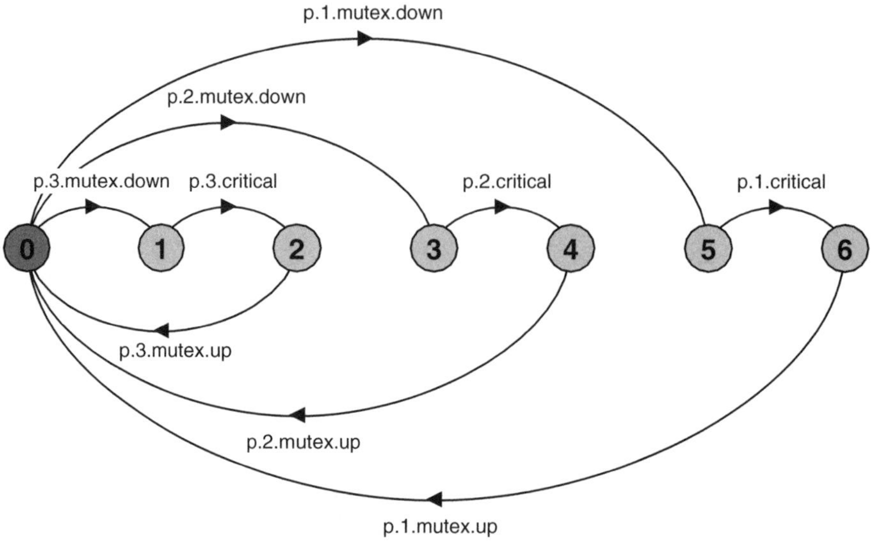

Figure 5.8 SEMADEMO *LTS*.

```
public class Semaphore {
  private int value;

  public Semaphore (int initial)
    {value = initial;}

  synchronized public void up() {
     ++value;
     notify();
  }

  synchronized public void down()
      throws InterruptedException {
    while (value== 0) wait();
    --value;
  }
}
```

Program 5.3 `Semaphore` class.

class. The actions `up` and `down` become synchronized methods. The guard on the `down` action in the model is implemented using condition synchronization as we saw in section 5.1. The class that implements semaphores is listed in Program 5.3.

Even though the `down()` method in Program 5.3 changes the state of the monitor by decrementing `value`, we do not use `notify()` to signal the change in state. This is because threads only wait for the value of the semaphore to be incremented, they do not wait for the value to be decremented. The semaphore implementation does not check for overflow on increment. This is usually the case in semaphores implemented by operating systems. It is the responsibility of the programmer to ensure, during design, that overflow cannot occur. We advocate the use of analyzable models to check such properties.

Figure 5.9 depicts the display of the semaphore demonstration program modeled in the previous section. A thread executing in its critical section is indicated by a lighter-colored segment. Each thread display rotates counter-clockwise. In Figure 5.9, Thread 1 is executing in its critical section, Thread 2 is blocked waiting to enter its critical section and Thread 3 has finished its critical section and is executing non-critical actions. The sliders underneath each thread adjust the time a thread spends executing critical, as opposed to non-critical, actions. If the total time spent in critical sections by all three threads is less than a full rotation then it is possible to get all three threads to execute concurrently. In other words, there need be no conflict for access to the critical resource. This is often the case in real systems. Mechanisms for mutual exclusion only take effect when there is conflicting access to a shared resource. In real systems, it is therefore advisable to keep the time spent in critical sections as short as possible so as to reduce the likelihood of conflict.

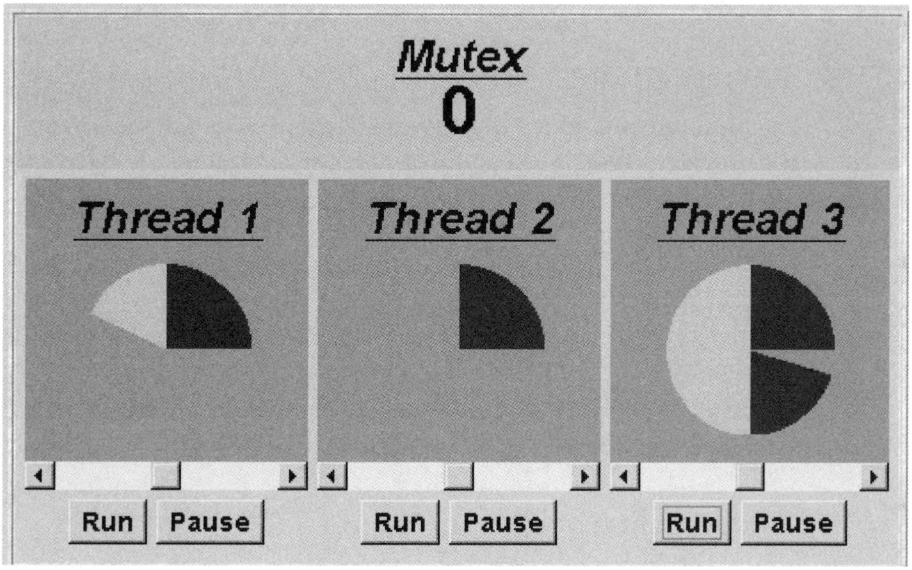

Figure 5.9 SEMADEMO display.

```
public class ThreadPanel extends Panel {

  // construct display with title and rotating arc color c
  public ThreadPanel(String title, Color c) {...}

  // hasSlider == true creates panel with slider
  public ThreadPanel
  (String title, Color c, boolean hasSlider) {...}

  // rotate display of currently running thread 6 degrees
  // return false when in initial color
  // return true when in second color
  public static boolean rotate()
         throws InterruptedException {...}

  // rotate display of currently running thread by degrees
  public static void rotate(int degrees)
         throws InterruptedException {...}

  // create a new thread with target r and start it running
  public void start(Runnable r) {...}

  // stop the thread using Thread.interrupt()
  public void stop() {...}
}
```

Program 5.4 Extended version of `ThreadPanel` class.

The program behind the display of Figure 5.9 uses the same `ThreadPanel` class as before; however, it uses a different constructor to create the display with multi-colored segments. The interface offered by the class, extended with the methods used in this chapter, is shown in Program 5.4.

The `MutexLoop` class, which provides the `run()` method for each thread, is listed in Program 5.5. The critical (mutually exclusive) actions are the `rotate()` actions which are executed when the segment changes to the lighter color. This is indicated by the `rotate()` method returning false when the rotating arc is dark-colored and true when light-colored.

The threads and semaphore are created in the usual way by the applet `start()` method:

```
public void start() {
     Semaphore mutex =
        new DisplaySemaphore(semaDisplay,1);
```

```
class MutexLoop implements Runnable {
  Semaphore mutex;

  MutexLoop (Semaphore sema) {mutex=sema;}

  public void run() {
    try {
      while(true) {
        while(!ThreadPanel.rotate());
        mutex.down(); // get mutual exclusion
        while(ThreadPanel.rotate()); //critical actions
        mutex.up(); //release mutual exclusion
      }
    } catch(InterruptedException e){}
  }
}
```

Program 5.5 MutexLoop class.

```
      thread1.start(new MutexLoop(mutex));
      thread2.start(new MutexLoop(mutex));
      thread3.start(new MutexLoop(mutex));
  }
```

where `thread1`, `thread2` and `thread3` are `ThreadPanel` instances and `semaDisplay` is an instance of `NumberCanvas`.

5.3 Bounded Buffers

Buffers are frequently used in concurrent systems to smooth out information transfer rates between the producers of data and the consumers of that data. Consider, for example, a keyboard device driver that is supplying characters typed at a keyboard to an editor program. The editor can consume characters at a much faster rate, on average, than a person can type at a keyboard. However, some characters can take longer than others to process, for example a character that causes the screen to scroll or a keyboard command that invokes a formatting command. When the editor is processing a character that takes a long time to process, it is necessary to buffer characters from the keyboard, otherwise they would be lost. This buffer is sometimes referred to as the *type-ahead* buffer. It is an example of the sort of buffer that we describe in the following.

In this section we model and program a bounded buffer, which consists of a fixed number of slots. Items are put into the buffer by a *producer* process and

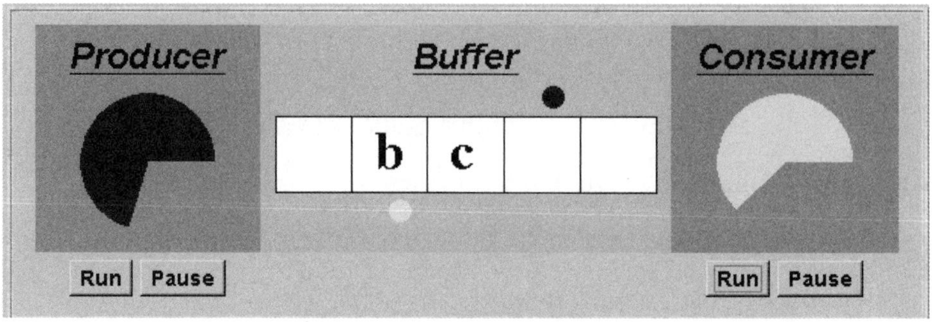

Figure 5.10 Bounded buffer display.

removed by a *consumer* process. The buffer is organized so that the first item put into it will be the first item out (FIFO).

Figure 5.10 depicts the display of our example system in which a producer process communicates characters to a consumer process via a five-slot buffer. The small circle above the buffer indicates the next free slot into which the producer process can place a character. The circle below the buffer indicates the next slot from which the consumer process can take a character. The reader may note the similarity between this example and the initial car park example in section 5.1. In fact, the synchronization requirements are the same. The producer is only allowed to put a character into the buffer when there is a free slot and the consumer process can only get a character when there is at least one in the buffer. These are exactly the requirements for the car park, if we substitute space for slot and car for character. What is different between the two examples is the FIFO discipline enforced by the buffer, in contrast to the car park where cars can occupy any free space and need not leave in arrival order.

5.3.1 Bounded Buffer Model

The producer–consumer system with a bounded buffer is an example of a program that handles data items without altering them. In addition, the behavior of the producer, the consumer and the buffer itself are not affected by the value of the items they handle. In other words, they do not test the value of these data items. The behavior is said to be *data-independent*. If data independence can be established then models can be simplified by omitting the detailed representation of parameters and data structures. This leads to much smaller and more tractable models. The `get` and `put` operations in Figure 5.11 are simple actions that do not have parameters. The *LTS* for the bounded buffer system, depicted in Figure 5.12,

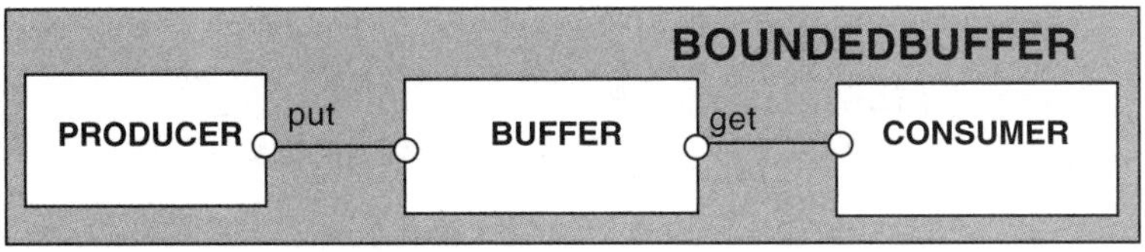

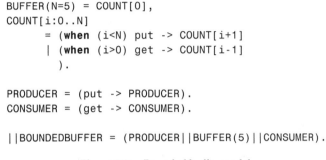

```
BUFFER(N=5) = COUNT[0],
COUNT[i:0..N]
      = (when (i<N) put -> COUNT[i+1]
      | (when (i>0) get -> COUNT[i-1]
        ).

PRODUCER = (put -> PRODUCER).
CONSUMER = (get -> CONSUMER).

||BOUNDEDBUFFER = (PRODUCER||BUFFER(5)||CONSUMER).
```

Figure 5.11 Bounded buffer model.

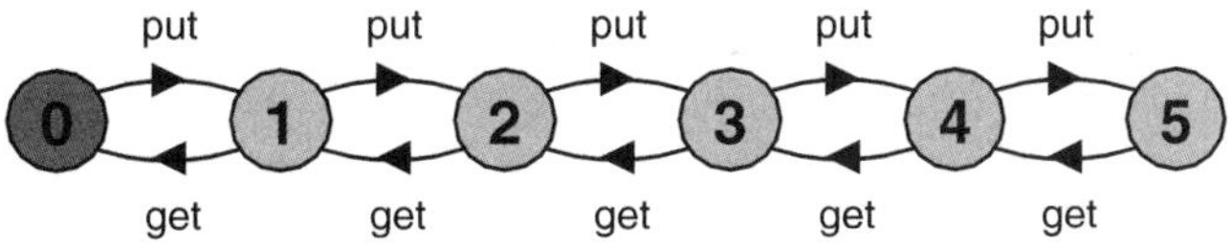

Figure 5.12 Bounded buffer *LTS*.

should be compared with the car park *LTS* of Figure 5.3 to see the similarity between the synchronization behavior of the two systems.

5.3.2 Bounded Buffer Program

The `BUFFER` of the model becomes a monitor in the Java implementation, with synchronized methods `put` and `get` (Program 5.6). We have separated the interface of the buffer from its implementation since we will provide an alternative implementation in the next section.

The buffer has been implemented as a general-purpose class that can buffer any type of Java object. The buffer data structure is a fixed size array `buf`, indexed by `in` which points to the next free slot and `out` which points to the next slot to be emptied. These indexes are incremented modulo the size of the buffer. The code for the producer and consumer programs is listed in Program 5.7.

```
public interface Buffer<E> {
  public void put(E o)
    throws InterruptedException; //put object into buffer
  public E get()
    throws InterruptedException; //get object from buffer
}

public class BufferImpl<E> implements Buffer<E> {
  protected E[] buf;
  protected int in = 0;
  protected int out= 0;
  protected int count= 0;
  protected int size;

  public BufferImpl(int size) {
    this.size = size;
    buf = (E[])new Object[size];
  }

  public synchronized void put(E o)
            throws InterruptedException {
    while (count==size) wait();
    buf[in] = o;
    ++count;
    in=(in+1) % size;
    notifyAll();
  }

  public synchronized E get()
           throws InterruptedException {
    while (count==0) wait();
    E o = buf[out];
    buf[out]=null;
    --count;
    out=(out+1) % size;
    notifyAll();
    return (o);
  }
}
```

Program 5.6 `Buffer` interface and `BufferImpl` class.

```
class Producer implements Runnable {
  Buffer<Character> buf;
  String alphabet= "abcdefghijklmnopqrstuvwxyz";

  Producer(Buffer<Character> b) {buf = b;}

  public void run() {
    try {
      int ai = 0;
      while(true) {
        ThreadPanel.rotate(12);
        buf.put(alphabet.charAt(ai));
        ai=(ai+1) % alphabet.length();
        ThreadPanel.rotate(348);
      }
    } catch (InterruptedException e){}
  }
}

class Consumer implements Runnable {
  Buffer<Character> buf;

  Consumer(Buffer<Character> b) {buf = b;}

  public void run() {
    try {
      while(true) {
        ThreadPanel.rotate(180);
        Character c = buf.get();
        ThreadPanel.rotate(180);
      }
    } catch(InterruptedException e ){}
  }
}
```

Program 5.7 `Producer` and `Consumer` classes.

5.4 Nested Monitors

Suppose that we did not wish to use condition synchronization directly in the implementation of the buffer monitor class but instead we decided to use two semaphores `full` and `empty` to reflect the state of the buffer. The semaphore `empty` counts the number of spaces and is decremented during a `put` operation. The `put` is, of course, blocked if the value of `empty` is zero. Similarly, `full` counts the number of items in the buffer and is decremented by a `get` operation. The

```
class SemaBuffer<E> implements Buffer<E> {
  protected E[] buf;
  protected int in = 0;
  protected int out= 0;
  protected int count= 0;
  protected int size;

  Semaphore full; //counts number of items
  Semaphore empty; //counts number of spaces

  SemaBuffer(int size) {
    this.size = size; buf = (E[])new Object[size];
    full = new Semaphore(0);
    empty= new Semaphore(size);
  }

  synchronized public void put(E o)
            throws InterruptedException {
    empty.down();
    buf[in] = o;
    ++count;
    in=(in+1) % size;
    full.up();
  }

  synchronized public E get()
             throws InterruptedException{
    full.down();
    E o =buf[out];
    buf[out]=null;
    --count;
    out=(out+1) % size;
    empty.up();
    return (o);
  }
}
```

Program 5.8 `Buffer` `class` using semaphores.

`get` is therefore blocked if the value of `full` is zero. The modified buffer class is shown in Program 5.8.

The semaphores of Program 5.8 replace the `count` variable in the original implementation, the conditional waits on the value of count and the notification of changes in its value. An updated model to reflect the changes in the buffer implementation is shown below:

```
const Max = 5
range Int = 0..Max

SEMAPHORE(I=0) = SEMA[I],
SEMA[v:Int]    = (up->SEMA[v+1]
                 |when(v>0) down->SEMA[v-1]
                 ).

BUFFER = (put -> empty.down ->full.up ->BUFFER
         |get -> full.down ->empty.up ->BUFFER
         ).

PRODUCER = (put -> PRODUCER).
CONSUMER = (get -> CONSUMER).

||BOUNDEDBUFFER = (PRODUCER|| BUFFER || CONSUMER
                  ||empty:SEMAPHORE(5)
                  ||full:SEMAPHORE(0))@{put,get}.
```

A problem occurs when we check this model using the analyzer tool *LTSA* and find that it reports a potential deadlock together with a trace of actions to that deadlock:

```
Composing
 potential DEADLOCK
States Composed: 28 Transitions: 32 in 60ms
Trace to DEADLOCK:
     get
```

We discuss deadlock in more detail in the next chapter. However, in essence, it means that a system can make no further progress since there are no further actions it can take. The deadlock in the model can be seen in the demonstration version of the program by starting the consumer and letting it block, waiting to get a character from the empty buffer. When the producer is started, it cannot put a character into the buffer. Why? The reason is to do with the use of two levels of synchronization lock: the first gives mutually exclusive access to the buffer monitor and the second gives mutually exclusive access to the semaphores.

When the consumer calls `get`, it acquires the `Buffer` monitor lock and then acquires the monitor lock for the `full` semaphore by calling `full.down()` to check if there is something in the buffer. Since initially the buffer is empty, the call to `full.down()` blocks the consumer thread (using `wait()`) and releases the monitor lock for the `full` semaphore. However, it does not release the monitor lock for `Buffer`. Consequently, the producer cannot enter the monitor to put a

```
class FixedSemaBuffer<E> implements Buffer<E> {
  protected E[] buf;
  protected int in = 0;
  protected int out= 0;
  protected int count= 0; //only used for display purposes
  protected int size;

  Semaphore full;  //counts number of items
  Semaphore empty; //counts number of spaces

  FixedSemaBuffer(int size) {
    this.size = size; buf = (E[])new Object[size];
    full = new Semaphore(0);
    empty= new Semaphore(size);
  }

  public void put(E o)
             throws InterruptedException {
    empty.down();
    synchronized(this){
      buf[in] = o; ++count; in=(in+1)%size;
    }
    full.up();
  }

  public E get()
          throws InterruptedException{
    full.down(); E o;
    synchronized(this){
      o =buf[out]; buf[out]=null;
      --count; out=(out+1)%size;
    }
    empty.up();
    return (o);
  }
}
```

Program 5.9 Fixed bounded buffer using semaphores.

character into the buffer and so no progress can be made by either producer or consumer – hence the deadlock. The situation described above is known as the *nested monitor problem*. The only way to avoid it in Java is by careful design. In our example, the deadlock can be removed by ensuring that the monitor lock for the buffer is not acquired until after semaphores are decremented (Program 5.9).

As mentioned before, in this book we advocate the use of the model and analysis to aid in the process of "careful design". Those parts of the model which need to be revised to take into account the changes to the buffer, documented in Program 5.9, are shown below:

```
BUFFER = (put -> BUFFER
         |get -> BUFFER
         ).

PRODUCER = (empty.down->put ->full.up ->PRODUCER).
CONSUMER = (full.down ->get ->empty.up->CONSUMER).
```

Moving the semaphore actions from the buffer process to the producer and consumer processes reflects the change in the implementation where the semaphore actions are performed outside the monitor (i.e. before acquiring the monitor lock). If this modified model is composed and minimized, it generates an identical *LTS* to that depicted in Figure 5.12 for the original model. This gives us confidence that our revised semaphore implementation of the bounded buffer is equivalent to the original one which used `wait()` and `notify()` directly.

5.5 Monitor Invariants

An invariant for a monitor is an assertion concerning the variables it encapsulates. This assertion must hold whenever there is no thread executing inside the monitor. Consequently, the invariant must be true at any point that a thread releases the monitor lock – when a thread returns from a synchronized method call and when a thread is blocked by a `wait()`. A formal proof of the correctness of a monitor can be achieved by demonstrating that the constructor for a monitor establishes the invariant and that the invariant holds after the execution of each access method and just before a `wait()` is executed. Such an approach requires a programming logic, a formal logical system that facilitates making precise statements about program execution. Greg Andrews (1991) uses this approach in his book. Similarly, Fred Schneider (1997) discusses formal derivation and reasoning about concurrent programs in his book.

Instead, for the reasons outlined at length in Chapter 1, we have chosen to use a model-based approach amenable to mechanical proof. The disadvantage is that our mechanical proofs only apply to specific cases or models while the manual proof-theoretic approach used by Andrews permits correctness proofs for the general case. For example, a proof method could establish monitor correctness for all sizes of a bounded buffer rather than just a specific size. However, it is usually the case that if a model for a specific case is shown to be correct, the general case can be inferred by induction.

Although we do not use invariants in formal correctness proofs, they are useful program documentation that aid informal correctness reasoning. The invariants for the monitor programs developed in this chapter are:

CarParkControl Invariant: $0 \le spaces \le N$

The invariant for the car park controller simply states that the number of spaces available must always be greater than or equal to zero and less than or equal to the maximum size of the car park (*N*).

Semaphore Invariant: $0 \le value$

The semaphore invariant simply asserts that the value of a semaphore must always be a non-negative value.

Buffer Invariant: $0 \le count \le size$
and $0 \le in < size$
and $0 \le out < size$
and $in = (out + count)$ modulo $size$

The bounded buffer invariant asserts that the number of items in the buffer must lie in the range zero to `size` and that the indexes `in` and `out` must lie in the range zero to `size`-1. It states that the `in` index must always be `count` items "ahead" of the `out` index where ahead means addition modulo `size`.

Invariants are also used to reason about the correctness of classes in sequential object-oriented programs. The invariant is required to hold after each method execution. The difference in concurrent programs is the additional responsibility to establish that the invariant holds at any point where the object's monitor lock is released. These additional points are where a `wait()` can be executed.

Summary

In this chapter, we introduced condition synchronization, which in combination with the mutual exclusion provided by **synchronized** methods, supports the concept of a monitor in Java. Condition synchronization is implemented using the `wait()`, `notify()` and `notifyAll()` primitives which operate on a waiting queue which can be associated with any Java object. Operation `wait()` suspends the calling thread on the wait queue, `notify()` unblocks one of the threads on the wait queue and `notifyAll()` unblocks all the threads on the wait queue. When a thread suspends itself by calling `wait()`, the monitor mutual exclusion lock is released. Use of these primitives causes an exception if the invoking thread does not currently hold the monitor lock.

Model processes that react to actions rather than instigate them are usually translated into monitors in the program that implements the model. Each guarded action in the model of a monitor is implemented as a **synchronized** method which uses a **`while`** loop and `wait()` to implement the guard. The **`while`** loop condition is the negation of the model guard condition. Changes in the state of the monitor are signaled to waiting threads using `notify()` or `notifyAll()`.

Nested monitor calls should be used with great care as they can cause a program to deadlock. This can occur since a thread that waits in a monitor releases only its lock, not the lock of any monitor from which it may have been called.

Notes and Further Reading

The idea of associating data encapsulation with mutual exclusion, which is the essence of the monitor concept, is jointly due to Edsger W. Dijkstra (1972b), Per Brinch-Hansen (1972) and C.A.R. Hoare (1974). The monitors in C.A.R. Hoare's classic paper differ in a number of respects from the way monitors appear in Java. Condition wait queues are declared explicitly in the original proposal and more than one can be declared in a monitor. This contrasts with the Java monitor, which permits only a single implicit condition queue. Multiple queues allow less rescheduling and thread-awakening if multiple threads are waiting on different conditions. In Java, all threads must be awakened to re-test their waiting conditions. If a thread's condition does not hold, it blocks again. In practice, threads waiting on different conditions usually wait at different times and consequently there is no extra thread-activation cost. Even when it does occur, the extra scheduling does not usually cause a problem.

Another difference is the semantics of `notify()`. The Java semantic for `notify()` is known as *signal and continue*. This means that the notified thread is taken off the wait queue and put into the scheduler's ready queue. However, the thread invoking the `notify` operation does not necessarily give up the processor and can continue running. Conditions in Java are thus always re-tested when the notified thread regains the monitor, since the condition may have been invalidated between the time it was notified and the time the monitor lock is re-acquired. In contrast, the `notify` operation of the original proposal had *signal and urgent wait* semantics. `Notify` would cause the notified thread to be executed immediately and the notifying thread to be suspended. However, the notifying thread would regain the monitor lock before new entries. Signal and urgent wait has the advantage that wait conditions do not need to be re-tested. The disadvantages are additional implementation complexity and, in a Java context, the fact that the semantics do not fit well with having a single wait queue. An extensive discussion of the different semantics possible for condition synchronization may be found in Greg Andrews' book (1991).

The development of monitors was inspired by the class concept of SIMULA-67 (Birtwistle, Dahl, Myhrhaug, *et al.*, 1973). Monitors have been included in a wide range of early concurrent programming languages. Concurrent Pascal (Brinch-Hansen, 1975) was the first concurrent programming language to include monitors. Subsequent influential concurrent programming languages with monitors include Modula (Wirth, 1977), Mesa (Lampson and Redell, 1980), Pascal Plus (Welsh and Bustard, 1979), Concurrent Euclid (Holt, 1983) and Turing Plus (Holt and Cordy, 1988). The problem of nested monitor calls was raised by Andrew Lister (1977). Java has brought the development of monitors full circle by including the concept in an object-oriented programming language.

Exercises

5.1 A single-slot buffer may be modeled by:

```
ONEBUF = (put->get->ONEBUF).
```

Program a Java class, `OneBuf`, that implements this one-slot buffer as a monitor.

5.2 Replace the condition synchronization in your implementation of the one-slot buffer by using semaphores. Given that Java defines assignment to scalar types (with the exception of long and double) and reference types to be atomic, does your revised implementation require the use of the monitor's mutual exclusion lock?

5.3 In the museum example (Chapter 3, exercise 3.6), identify which of the processes, `EAST`, `WEST`, `CONTROL` and `DIRECTOR`, should be threads and which should be monitors. Provide an implementation of the monitors.

5.4 *The Dining Savages:* A tribe of savages eats communal dinners from a large pot that can hold *M* servings of stewed missionary. When a savage wants to eat, he helps himself from the pot unless it is empty in which case he waits for the pot to be filled. If the pot is empty, the cook refills the pot with *M* servings. The behavior of the savages and the cook is described by:

```
SAVAGE = (getserving -> SAVAGE).
COOK   = (fillpot -> COOK).
```

Model the behavior of the pot as an *FSP* process and then implement it as a Java monitor.

5.5 *FSP* allows multiple processes to synchronize on a single action. A set of processes with the action `sync` in their alphabets must all perform this action before any of them can proceed. Implement a monitor called `Barrier` in Java with a `sync` method that ensures that all of *N* threads must call `sync` before any of them can proceed.

5.6 *The Savings Account Problem:* A savings account is shared by several people. Each person may deposit or withdraw funds from the account subject to the constraint that the balance of the account must never become negative. Develop a model for the problem and from the model derive a Java implementation of a monitor for the savings account.

6
Deadlock

Deadlock occurs in a system when all its constituent processes are blocked. Another way of saying this is that the system is deadlocked because there are no eligible actions that it can perform. We have already seen an example of deadlock in the nested monitor example of the last chapter. There, neither producer nor consumer process could make further progress since the consumer was blocked waiting for characters from the producer and the producer was blocked waiting for the monitor lock held by the consumer. In other words, each process was blocked waiting for a resource held by the other, sometimes referred to as a "deadly embrace". Coffman, Elphick and Shoshani (1971) identified four necessary and sufficient conditions for the occurrence of deadlock:

- *Serially reusable resources*: *the processes involved share resources which they use under mutual exclusion.*
  For example, monitors encapsulate resources which are accessed using mutual exclusion (i.e. synchronized methods).
- *Incremental acquisition*: *processes hold on to resources already allocated to them while waiting to acquire additional resources.*
  This is exactly the situation in the nested monitor deadlock where the consumer holds the monitor lock while waiting for the producer to put a character into the buffer.
- *No preemption*: *once acquired by a process, resources cannot be preempted (forcibly withdrawn) but are only released voluntarily.*
  Again, the relevance of this to the nested monitor deadlock can easily be seen since if the consumer thread could be forced to release the monitor lock then execution of the producer could proceed.
- *Wait-for cycle*: *a circular chain (or cycle) of processes exists such that each process holds a resource which its successor in the cycle is waiting to acquire.*

The nested monitor deadlock is a specific example of this with a chain of length two. The consumer holds the monitor lock for which the producer is waiting and the producer has a character for which the consumer is waiting.

Strategies for dealing with deadlock involve ensuring that one of these four conditions does not hold. For example, consider a system which allows deadlocked cycles of processes to occur but then detects these cycles and aborts the deadlocked processes, perhaps by operator action. Such a system is denying the third condition (no preemption), since the aborted processes are forced to release the resources they hold. The system implements *deadlock detection and recovery*.

In this chapter, we are concerned with an alternative strategy. Our aim is to design programs such that deadlock cannot occur. We describe how to analyze models for deadlock and how to show that a model is free from deadlock. Finally, both the model and implementation of a classic concurrent programming problem, the Dining Philosophers, is presented.

6.1 Deadlock Analysis

In the finite state model of a process, a deadlocked state is, simply, a state with no outgoing transitions. A process in such a state can engage in no further actions. In *FSP* this deadlocked state is represented by the local process `STOP`. An example of a process which can lead to a deadlocked state is depicted in Figure 6.1.

The `MOVE` process of Figure 6.1 can engage in alternating `north` and `south` actions. However, an action sequence of `north` followed by `north` leads to a deadlocked state in which no further actions are possible. This can be seen using the Animator. We can ask the *LTSA* analyzer tool to find deadlock states and to produce a sample trace of how these states can be reached from the start state. By performing a breadth-first search of the *LTS* graph, the *LTSA* tool guarantees that the sample trace is the shortest trace to the deadlock state. In the example of Figure 6.1, *LTSA* produces the following output:

```
Trace to DEADLOCK:
     north
     north
```

In general, the deadlocks which interest us are not those that are declared explicitly in primitive processes using `STOP` as above, but those that arise from the parallel composition of a number of interacting primitive processes. The deadlock check that the analyzer performs for composite processes is, of course, the same as the

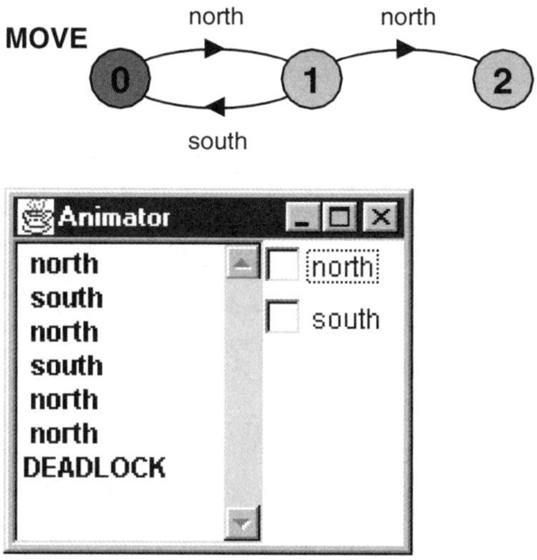

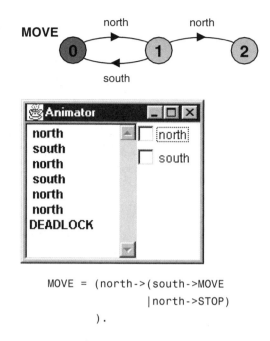

```
MOVE = (north->(south->MOVE
               |north->STOP)
       ).
```

Figure 6.1 MOVE process.

check it performs for primitive processes since a composition is also described by an *LTS* graph. The check remains a search for states with no outgoing transitions.

The example of Figure 6.2 is a system in which two processes, P and Q, perform the same task, that of scanning a document and printing it, by using a shared printer and shared scanner. Each process acquires both the printer and the scanner, performs the scanning and printing and then releases the scanner and printer resources. The *LTS* diagrams for process P and for the shared `printer` are given in Figures 6.3 and 6.4 respectively.

The only difference between the processes P and Q is that P acquires the printer first and Q acquires the scanner first. This system satisfies the four necessary and sufficient conditions for deadlock which were outlined in the introduction to this chapter: the scanner and printer resources are serially reused; each process holds on to either the scanner or printer while waiting to get the second resource it requires; these resources are not preempted; and the wait-for cycle is apparent from the following deadlock discovered by *LTSA*:

```
Trace to DEADLOCK:
     p.printer.get
     q.scanner.get
```

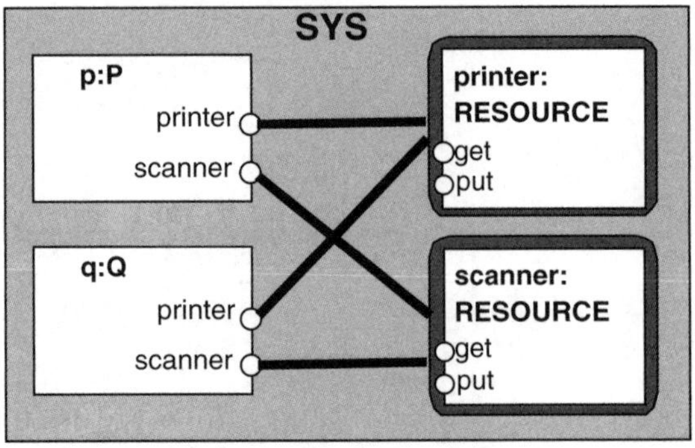


```
RESOURCE = (get -> put -> RESOURCE).

P = (printer.get -> scanner.get -> copy
        -> printer.put -> scanner.put -> P).

Q = (scanner.get -> printer.get -> copy
        -> printer.put -> scanner.put -> Q).

||SYS = (p:P || q:Q
        || {p,q}::printer:RESOURCE
        || {p,q}::scanner:RESOURCE
        ).
```

Figure 6.2 Printer–scanner system.

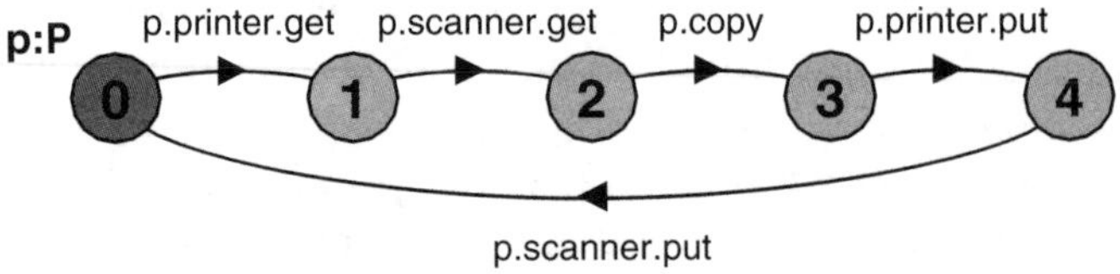

Figure 6.3 *LTS* for process P.

This is the situation in which the process P has the printer and is waiting for the scanner and the process Q has the scanner and is waiting for the printer. The deadlock is easily fixed in the example by ensuring that both processes ask for the printer and the scanner in the same order. (The reader should verify, using *LTSA*, that if the model of Figure 6.1 is modified in this way, deadlock no longer occurs.) In fact, where processes share different classes of resources, such as printers and scanners, a general-purpose strategy for avoiding deadlock is to *order* the resource

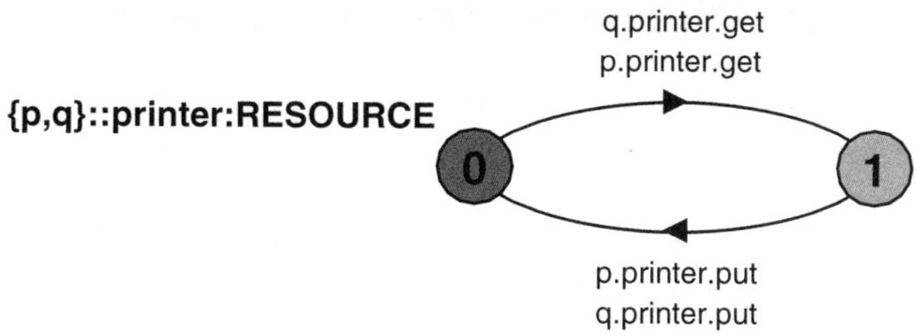

Figure 6.4 *LTS* for the shared `printer` process.

classes; i.e. if processes use resources from different classes, all processes acquire these resources in the same order. For our example, this can be achieved by, for example, always requesting printers before scanners.

Another solution to avoiding deadlock, in this example, is to set a timeout on waiting for the second resource. If the resource has not been acquired within the timeout period then the first resource is released and the process starts afresh as shown below:

```
P          = (printer.get-> GETSCANNER),
GETSCANNER = (scanner.get->copy->printer.put
                          ->scanner.put->P
             |timeout -> printer.put->P
             ).
Q          = (scanner.get-> GETPRINTER),
GETPRINTER = (printer.get->copy->printer.put
                          ->scanner.put->Q
             |timeout -> scanner.put->Q
             ).
```

This denies the second deadlock condition of incremental acquisition. The solution can be implemented in Java using a timed wait. However, it is not a good solution as both processes can continually acquire the first resource, time out and then repeat this cycle without making any progress towards accomplishing the copy action. *LTSA* detects this progress problem, returning the following:

```
Progress violation for actions:
{p.scanner.get, p.copy, p.scanner.put,
q.printer.get, q.copy, q.printer.put}
```

We deal with this class of problems in the next chapter.

6.2 Dining Philosophers Problem

The Dining Philosophers problem (Dijkstra, 1968a) is a classic concurrent-programming problem in which the deadlock is not quite so apparent as in the previous examples. We develop both the model and Java implementation. The problem is stated as follows: five philosophers share a circular table (as depicted in Figure 6.5) at which they have allotted seats. Each philosopher spends his life alternately thinking and eating. In the center of the table is a large plate of tangled spaghetti. A philosopher needs two forks to eat a helping of spaghetti. Unfortunately, as philosophy is not as well paid as computing, the philosophers can only afford five forks. One fork is placed between each pair of philosophers and they agree that each will only use the forks to his immediate right and left.

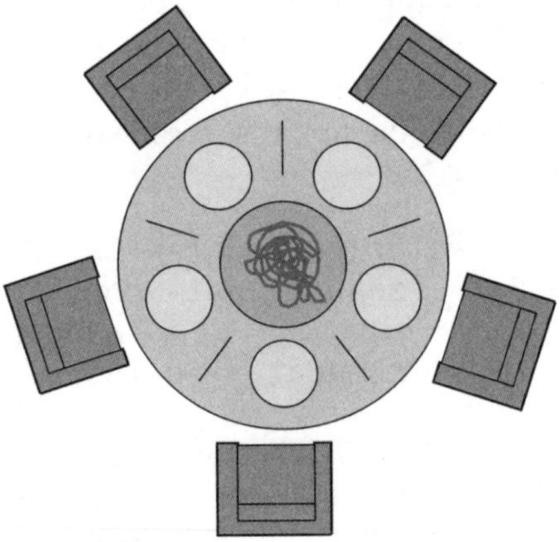

Figure 6.5 The Dining Philosophers table.

The resources in this system are the forks shared between the philosophers. We model a fork in the same way that we modeled the scanner and printer resources in the previous section:

```
FORK = (get -> put -> FORK).
```

To use a fork, a philosopher must first pick up (`get`) that fork and when finished with the fork, the philosopher puts it down (`put`). Each philosopher is modeled by the process:

```
PHIL = (sitdown->right.get->left.get
          ->eat->left.put->right.put
          ->arise->PHIL).
```

In other words, when a philosopher becomes hungry, he (or she) sits down at the table, picks up the fork to his right, if it is free, and then picks up the fork to his left, if it is free. The philosopher can then eat. When finished eating, the philosopher releases the forks and leaves the table. The Dining Philosophers system can now be described by the composition of five fork processes and five philosopher processes as depicted in Figure 6.6.

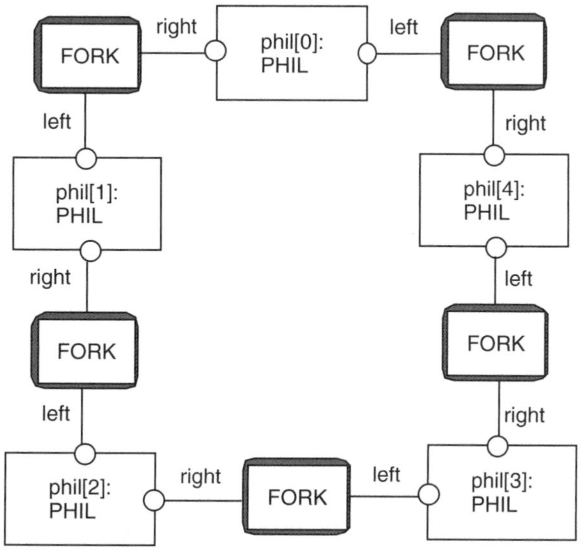

Figure 6.6 Dining Philosophers composite model.

The diagram of Figure 6.6 can be expressed concisely as the composite process:

```
||DINERS(N=5)=
   forall [i:0..N-1]
   (phil[i]:PHIL
   || {phil[i].left,phil[((i-1)+N)%N].right}::FORK).
```

The expression `((i-1)+N)%N` is subtraction modulo `N` so that, for example, a fork is shared between `phil[0]` and `phil[4]`. Analysis of this system reveals the following deadlock:

```
Trace to DEADLOCK:
     phil.0.sitdown
     phil.0.right.get
     phil.1.sitdown
```

```
phil.1.right.get
phil.2.sitdown
phil.2.right.get
phil.3.sitdown
phil.3.right.get
phil.4.sitdown
phil.4.right.get
```

This is the situation where all the philosophers become hungry at the same time, sit down at the table and then each philosopher picks up the fork to his (or her) right. The system can make no further progress since each philosopher is waiting for a fork held by his neighbor. In other words, a wait-for cycle exists, as described in the introduction.

6.2.1 Dining Philosophers Implementation

It is generally not a good idea to implement an erroneous model. However, in this section, our objective is to show that, while deadlock can be detected easily in a model, it is not so apparent in the running program which corresponds to that model. In translating the Dining Philosophers model into an implementation, we must consider which processes in the model will be represented by passive objects (monitors) and which by active objects (threads), as outlined in the previous chapter. The decision is reasonably obvious; forks are the passive entities and philosophers are the active entities in this system.

The relationships between the various classes involved in the Dining Philosophers program is shown in the class diagram of Figure 6.7.

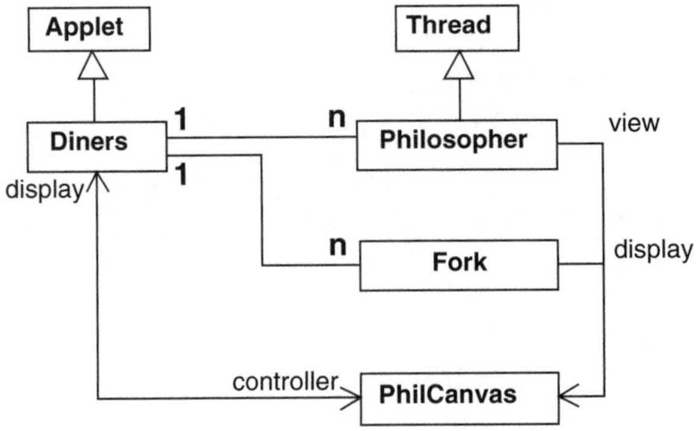

Figure 6.7 Dining Philosophers class diagram.

```
class PhilCanvas extends Canvas {

  // set state of philosopher id to display state s,
  // method blocks calling thread if display is frozen
  synchronized void setPhil(int id,int s)
        throws java.lang.InterruptedException{}

  // "freeze" display
  synchronized void freeze(){}

  // "un-freeze" display
  synchronized void thaw() {}

  // set state of fork id  to taken
  synchronized void setFork(int id, boolean taken){}
}
```

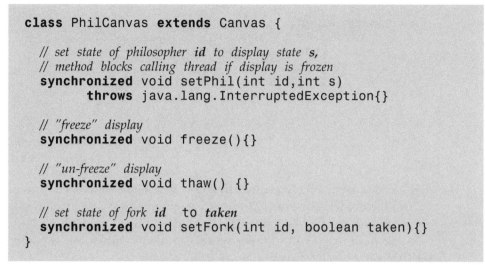

Program 6.1 Outline of `PhilCanvas` class.

The display is implemented by the `PhilCanvas` class. The interface offered by this class is given in Program 6.1.

The Java implementation of the `Fork` monitor is listed in Program 6.2. The boolean variable, `taken`, encodes the state of the fork. When the fork is on the table, `taken` is false. When the fork has been picked up by a philosopher, `taken` is true.

```
class Fork {
  private boolean taken=false;
  private PhilCanvas display;
  private int identity;

  Fork(PhilCanvas disp, int id)
    { display = disp; identity = id;}

  synchronized void put() {
    taken=false;
    display.setFork(identity,taken);
    notify();
  }
```

Program 6.2 `Fork` monitor.

```
  synchronized void get()
     throws java.lang.InterruptedException {
    while (taken) wait();
    taken=true;
    display.setFork(identity,taken);
  }
}
```

Program 6.2 (*Continued*).

The code for the `Philosopher` thread is listed in Program 6.3. It follows directly from the model. The detail of the philosopher sitting down and leaving the table has been omitted; philosophers think while sitting at the table.

The time that a philosopher spends thinking and eating is controlled by the slider in the applet display (Figure 6.8).

```
class Philosopher extends Thread {
  private int identity;
  private PhilCanvas view;
  private Diners controller;
  private Fork left;
  private Fork right;

  Philosopher(Diners ctr,int id,Fork l,Fork r){
    controller = ctr; view = ctr.display;
    identity = id; left = l; right = r;
  }

  public void run() {
    try {
      while (true) {
        // thinking
        view.setPhil(identity,view.THINKING);
        sleep(controller.sleepTime());
        // hungry
        view.setPhil(identity,view.HUNGRY);
        right.get();
        // gotright fork
        view.setPhil(identity,view.GOTRIGHT);
        sleep(500);
        left.get();
```

Program 6.3 `Philosopher` thread class.

```
            // eating
            view.setPhil(identity,view.EATING);
            sleep(controller.eatTime());
            right.put();
            left.put();
          }
        } catch (java.lang.InterruptedException e){}
      }
    }
```

Program 6.3 *(Continued)*.

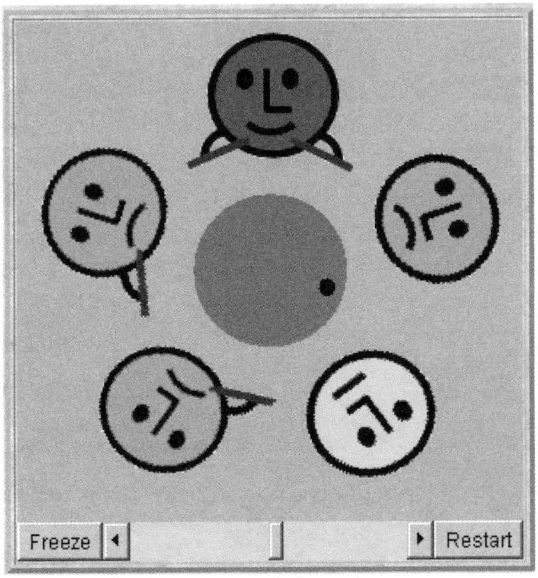

Figure 6.8 Dining Philosophers applet – executing.

The code to create the `Philosopher` threads and `Fork` monitors is:

```
for (int i =0; i<N; ++i)
  fork[i] = new Fork(display,i);
for (int i =0; i<N; ++i){
  phil[i] =
    new Philosopher(this,i,fork[(i-1+N)%N],fork[i]);
  phil[i].start();
}
```

Figure 6.8 depicts the Dining Philosophers applet running. The applet may run for a long time before deadlock occurs. To ensure deadlock occurs eventually, the slider control may be moved to the left. This reduces the time philosophers spend thinking and eating and this "speedup" increases the probability of deadlock occurring. Figure 6.9 depicts the applet when deadlock occurs. It is clear that each philosopher is holding on to the fork on his right.

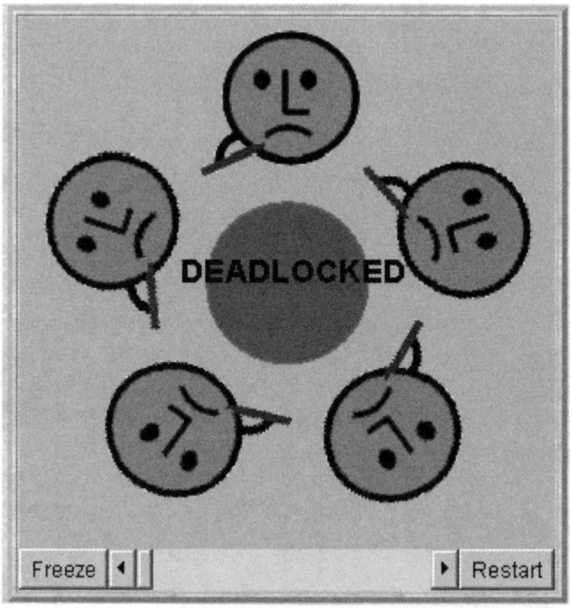

Figure 6.9 Dining Philosophers applet – deadlocked.

6.2.2 Deadlock-Free Philosophers

There are many different solutions to the Dining Philosophers problem. Some of these are referenced in *Notes and Further Reading* at the end of this chapter. All of the solutions involve denying one of the four necessary and sufficient conditions for deadlock identified at the beginning of the chapter. The solution we outline here depends on ensuring that a *wait-for* cycle cannot exist. To do this, we introduce some asymmetry into the definition of a philosopher. Up to now, each philosopher has had an identical definition. We make odd-numbered philosophers get the right fork first and even-numbered philosophers get the left fork first. The revised model is listed below:

```
FORK = (get -> put -> FORK).

PHIL(I=0)
    = (when (I%2==0) sitdown
          ->left.get->right.get
          ->eat->left.put->right.put->arise->PHIL
      |when (I%2==1) sitdown
          ->right.get->left.get
          ->eat->left.put->right.put->arise->PHIL
      ).

||DINERS(N=5)=
   forall [i:0..N-1]
   (phil[i]:PHIL(i)
   || {phil[i].left,phil[((i-1)+N)%N].right}::FORK).
```

This specification for the Dining Philosophers is deadlock-free since it is no longer possible for the wait-for cycle to exist, in which each philosopher holds the right fork. The reader should verify using *LTSA* that the above model is in fact deadlock-free. The same change can of course be made to the Java implementation and the result is a deadlock-free program.

Summary

In this chapter, we have seen that deadlock is a system state in which all of the processes in a system are blocked and the system can consequently make no further progress. Deadlock is modeled by a state with no outgoing transitions. Deadlock analysis of a model involves performing an exhaustive search of the labeled transition system for such states. If none are found, the model is shown to be deadlock-free.

We identified four necessary and sufficient conditions for deadlock. Strategies for dealing with deadlock involve ensuring that at least one of these conditions does not hold. The conditions are:

- *Serially reusable resources: the processes involved share resources which they use under mutual exclusion.*
- *Incremental acquisition: processes hold on to resources already allocated to them while waiting to acquire additional resources.*

- *No preemption: once acquired by a process, resources cannot be preempted (forcibly withdrawn) but are only released voluntarily.*
- *Wait-for cycle: a circular chain (or cycle) of processes exists such that each process holds a resource which its successor in the cycle is waiting to acquire.*

The Dining Philosophers problem was used to illustrate the point that while deadlocks are easily found in models, they are not so readily apparent in programs. Indeed, the reason for modeling is to remove problems such as deadlock during design.

Notes and Further Reading

The Dining Philosophers problem has been widely used to compare both process synchronization primitives and strategies for dealing with deadlock. The problem was introduced by Dijkstra (1968a) in a paper which shows how to use semaphores to solve a variety of synchronization problems. We have used asymmetry to avoid deadlock. A second way to avoid deadlock is to allow at most four philosophers to sit down together at the table. Another approach is to ensure that the act of picking up both forks is atomic. Chandy and Misra (1984) proposed a fully distributed solution which passes tokens between philosophers. All of these approaches to the Dining Philosophers problem are deterministic: each process takes a predetermined set of actions. Lehman and Rabin (1981) showed that any deterministic solution has to be asymmetric or use an outside agent (such as the butler in exercise 6.2). They also presented a probabilistic solution to the problem which is perfectly symmetric. Philosophers toss a coin to determine the order of picking up forks and defer to a neighbor if it has used the fork less recently.

Exercises

6.1 The figure below depicts a maze. Write a description of the maze in *FSP* which, using deadlock analysis, finds the shortest path out of the maze starting at any square.

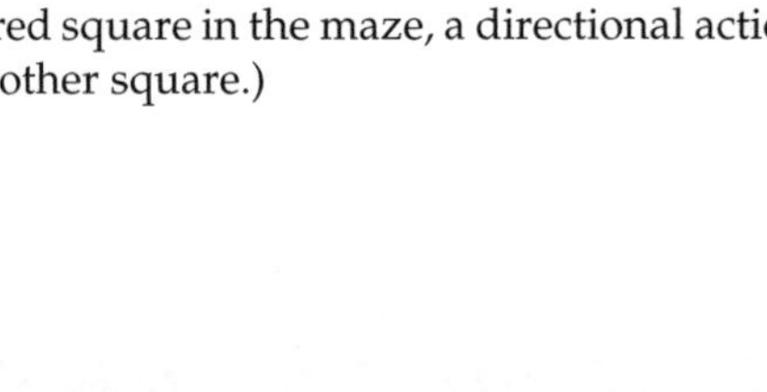

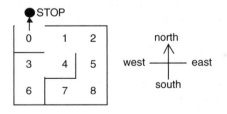

(*Hint*: At each numbered square in the maze, a directional action can be used to indicate an allowed path to another square.)

6.2 One solution to the Dining Philosophers problem permits only four philosophers to sit down at the table at the same time. Specify a `BUTLER` process which, when composed with the model of section 6.2, permits a maximum of four philosophers to engage in the `sitdown` action before an `arise` action occurs. Show that this system is deadlock-free.

6.3 Using the Java timed wait primitive:

```
public final void wait(long timeout)
                  throws InterruptedException
```

modify the `Fork` monitor such that after a wait of 1 second, the call to `get` times out and returns the result false. The `Philosopher` should release the other fork, if it holds it, and try again. Observe the behavior of the resulting system.

6.4 It is possible for the following system to deadlock. Explain how this deadlock occurs and relate it to one of the four necessary and sufficient conditions for deadlock to occur.

```
Alice = (call.bob -> wait.chris -> Alice).
Bob   = (call.chris -> wait.alice -> Bob).
Chris = (call.alice -> wait.bob -> Chris).

||S = (Alice || Bob || Chris) /{call/wait}.
```

The following model attempts to fix the problem by allowing Alice, Bob and Chris to time out from a call attempt. Is a deadlock still possible? If so, describe how the deadlock can occur and give an execution trace leading to the deadlock.

```
Alice = (call.bob -> wait.chris -> Alice
        | timeout.alice -> wait.chris ->Alice).
Bob   = (call.chris -> wait.alice -> Bob
        | timeout.bob -> wait.alice ->Bob).
Chris = (call.alice -> wait.bob -> Chris
        | timeout.chris -> wait.bob ->Chris).

||S = (Alice || Bob || Chris) /{call/wait}.
```

7 Safety and Liveness Properties

A property is an attribute of a program that is true for every possible execution of that program. Properties of interest for concurrent programs fall into two categories: *safety* and *liveness*. A safety property asserts that nothing bad happens during execution. A liveness property asserts that something good eventually happens. Another way of putting this is that safety is concerned with a program not reaching a bad state and that liveness is concerned with a program eventually reaching a good state.

In sequential programs, the most important safety property is that the final state is correct. We have already seen that for concurrent programs, important safety properties are mutual exclusion and the absence of deadlock. In the previous chapter, we determined that deadlock is generally a bad state from which no further actions can be executed. In Chapter 4, we saw that allowing more than one process to access a shared variable resulted in interference and thus incorrect or bad states.

The most important liveness property for a sequential program is that it eventually terminates. However, in concurrent programming, we are frequently concerned with systems that do not terminate. In this chapter, we primarily deal with liveness issues relating to resource access: are process requests for shared resources eventually granted? We will see that liveness properties are affected by the scheduling policy that determines which of a set of eligible actions are chosen for execution.

This chapter explains how we can analyze the finite state models of concurrent systems for both safety and liveness problems. The example of cars crossing a single-lane bridge is used to focus discussion. We then analyze a number of implementations of read/write locks. Read/write locks allow many processes to access a shared resource at the same time for read access, but require write access to be mutually exclusive. They occur in many concurrent programs.

7.1 Safety

In the previous chapter, we saw that the *LTSA* analysis tool performs deadlock analysis using a breadth-first search on the labeled transition system corresponding to an *FSP* model. The "bad" states that are the objective of this search are those states with no outgoing transitions, i.e. deadlock states. In addition to deadlock states, the search is looking for ERROR states. These are distinguished in the *LTS* by having a unique identity (−1). So far in the book, we have used the ERROR state explicitly denoted by the local process ERROR. In Chapter 4, we specified a test process that explicitly caused a transition to ERROR when it detected erroneous behavior. In Chapter 5, the ERROR state was used to detect when a finite range was exceeded. The example given in Figure 7.1 is an actuator that must not receive a second command before it has responded to the first.

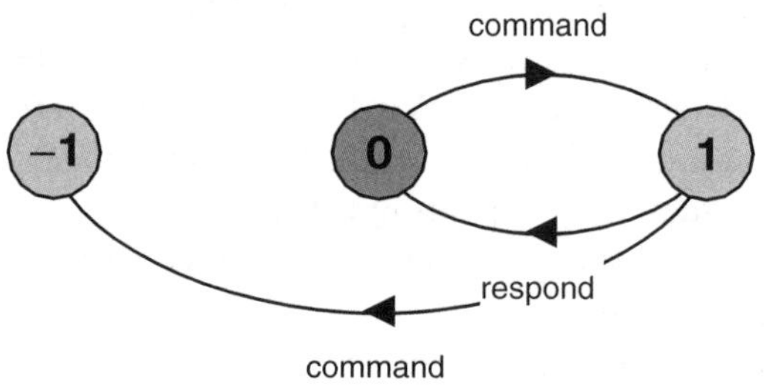

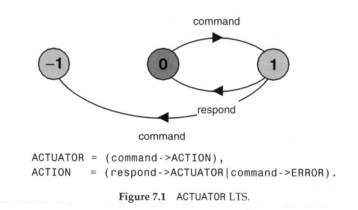

```
ACTUATOR = (command->ACTION),
ACTION   = (respond->ACTUATOR|command->ERROR).
```

Figure 7.1 ACTUATOR LTS.

With no control system to ensure that the actuator does not receive multiple unacknowledged commands, *safety* analysis performed by *LTSA* produces the following trace:

```
Trace to property violation in ACTUATOR:
     command
     command
```

In the test process of Chapter 4, the range excess of Chapter 5 and the actuator example of Figure 7.1, we have specified the situations regarded as errors rather than directly expressing the required safety property that we wish to preserve. In the actuator example, the safety property is that a command action must always be followed by a respond action without an intervening command. In complex systems it is usually better to specify safety properties by stating directly what *is* required rather than stating what is *not* required. In this way, we can concentrate on the desired behavior of a system rather than trying to enumerate all the possible undesirable behaviors.

7.1.1 Safety Properties

Safety properties are specified in *FSP* by property processes. Syntactically, these are simply *FSP* processes prefixed by the keyword **property**. They are composed with a target system to ensure that the specified property holds for that system. The example of Figure 7.2 specifies the property that it is polite to knock before entering a room.

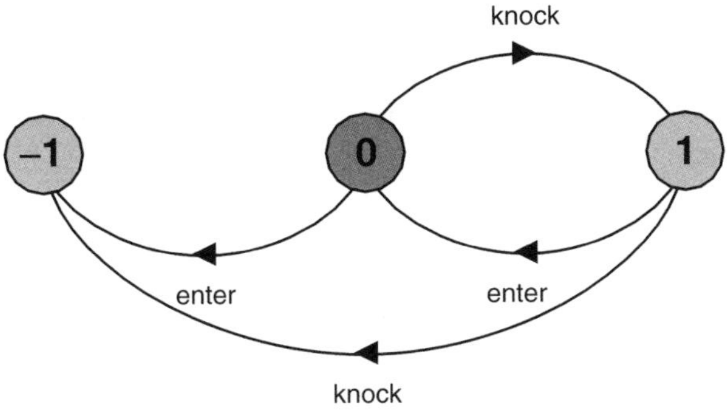


```
property POLITE = (knock->enter->POLITE).
```

Figure 7.2 property POLITE.

The *LTS* diagram of Figure 7.2 reveals that in translating a property process, the compiler automatically generates the transitions to the ERROR state. It is easily seen that an enter action before a knock action causes a transition to the ERROR state. In addition, knocking twice is a violation of the POLITE property. It should be noted that in every state of the property process of Figure 7.2, all the actions in its alphabet (enter,knock) are eligible choices. Those that are not part of the behavior allowed by the safety property are transitions to the ERROR state. This is true of all property processes.

The property to check the correct operation of the ACTUATOR of Figure 7.1 is simply:

```
property SAFE_ACTUATOR
      =(command->respond->SAFE_ACTUATOR).
```

Property processes may be composed with a system without affecting the correct behavior of that system. In other words, composing a property process with a set of processes does not affect their normal operation. However, if behavior can occur which violates the safety property, then a transition to the ERROR state results. To preserve this *transparency* of safety properties, property processes must be deterministic. That is they must not contain non-deterministic choices. Experience has shown that this is rarely a restriction in practice.

> A safety **property** P defines a deterministic process that asserts that any trace including actions in the alphabet of P, is accepted by P.

Thus, if P is composed with S, then traces of actions that are in the alphabet of S and the alphabet of P, must also be valid traces of P, otherwise ERROR is reachable. We can specify that an action or a set of actions should never happen by using alphabet extension. The example of Figure 7.3 asserts that disaster should never happen.

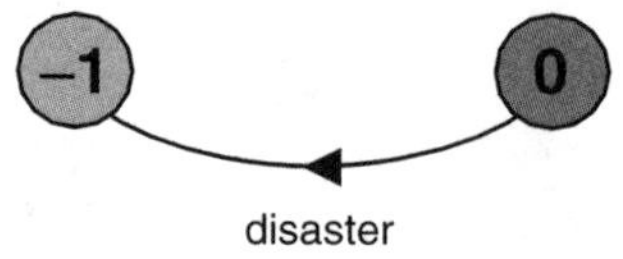

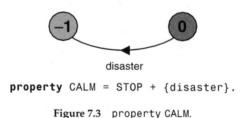

```
property CALM = STOP + {disaster}.
```

Figure 7.3 property CALM.

7.1.2 Safety Property for Mutual Exclusion

Listed below is a slightly modified version of the SEMADEMO model used in section 5.2.1 to show how semaphores are used to ensure mutual exclusion. The modification is to replace the single action critical with the actions enter and exit which model the entry and exit to the critical section in which mutually exclusive access to a shared resource is required.

```
LOOP =
    (mutex.down->enter->exit->mutex.up->LOOP).

||SEMADEMO = (p[1..3]:LOOP
             ||{p[1..3]}::mutex:SEMAPHORE(1)).
```

To verify that this system does in fact ensure mutual exclusion, we can specify a mutual exclusion property and compose it with the system as follows:

```
property MUTEX =
      (p[i:1..3].enter->p[i].exit->MUTEX).

||CHECK = (SEMADEMO || MUTEX).
```

The safety property MUTEX specifies that when a process enters the critical section (p[i].enter), the same process must exit the critical section (p[i].exit) before another process can enter. The property is not violated in the system as it stands; however, if we change the value with which the semaphore is initialized from one to two (i.e. SEMAPHORE(2)) then safety analysis using *LTSA* produces the following trace:

```
Trace to property violation in MUTEX:
     p.1.mutex.down
     p.1.enter
     p.2.mutex.down
     p.2.enter
```

The trace is clearly a violation of mutual exclusion since two processes have entered the critical section.

7.2 Single-Lane Bridge Problem

The problem is depicted in Figure 7.4. A bridge over a river is only wide enough to permit a single lane of traffic. Consequently, cars can only move concurrently if they are moving in the same direction. A safety violation occurs if two cars moving in different directions enter the bridge at the same time.

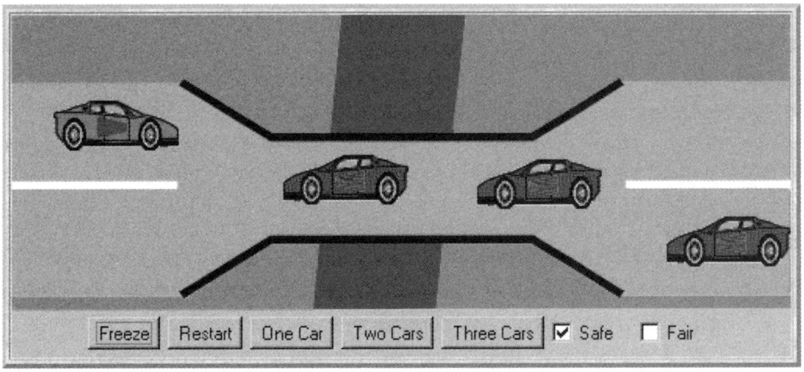

Figure 7.4 Single-lane bridge.

To clarify the discussion, we refer to cars moving from left to right as red cars and cars moving from right to left as blue cars (see demonstration applet). In our concurrent-programming model, each car is a process and the problem is to ensure that cars moving in different directions cannot concurrently access the shared resource that is the bridge. To make the simulation more realistic, we must also ensure that cars moving in the same direction cannot pass each other.

In the following section, we develop a model of the system and a Java implementation that corresponds to the model. In this section, we are concerned primarily with the safety properties of the problem. Later in the chapter, we will address liveness issues.

7.2.1 Single-Lane Bridge Model

In modeling the single-lane bridge, we use the following constant and range definitions:

```
const N = 3     // number of each type of car
range T = 0..N  // type of car count
range ID= 1..N  // car identities
```

The essence of the problem is access to the bridge, so the only events of interest in which a car participates are entering the bridge and leaving the bridge. Consequently, a car is modeled by a process that repeatedly enters and leaves the bridge:

```
CAR = (enter->exit->CAR).
```

To model the fact that cars cannot pass each other on the bridge, we require the following processes which constrain the order of the `enter` and `exit` actions respectively:

```
NOPASS1   = C[1], //preserves entry order
C[i:ID]   = ([i].enter->C[i%N+1]).

NOPASS2   = C[1], //preserves exit order
C[i:ID]   = ([i].exit->C[i%N+1]).

||CONVOY  = ([ID]:CAR||NOPASS1||NOPASS2).
```

The `CONVOY` process models a set of cars traveling in the same direction that enter the bridge one after the other and leave the bridge one after the other. However, it does not stop one car exiting the bridge before the next car enters. The behavior of all cars is captured by the following composition:

```
||CARS = (red:CONVOY || blue:CONVOY).
```

The remaining entity that must be modeled is the bridge itself. This must constrain CARS so that although one or more cars moving in the same direction may be on the bridge concurrently, cars moving in different directions may not. To enforce this, the bridge maintains a count of blue cars on the bridge and of red cars on the bridge. Red cars are only allowed to enter when the blue count is zero and vice versa. The BRIDGE process is listed below:

```
BRIDGE = BRIDGE[0][0], // initially empty
BRIDGE[nr:T][nb:T] =   //nr is the red count, nb the blue
      (when (nb==0)
         red[ID].enter -> BRIDGE[nr+1][nb]
      |red[ID].exit    -> BRIDGE[nr-1][nb]
      |when (nr==0)
         blue[ID].enter-> BRIDGE[nr][nb+1]
      |blue[ID].exit   -> BRIDGE[nr][nb-1]
      ).
```

Note that the exit actions of the bridge permit the car counts, nr and nb, to be decremented even though their value is 0. As described in Chapter 5, the *FSP* compiler in the *LTSA* tool will automatically map these undefined states to the ERROR state, indicating this by issuing warnings:

```
Warning - BRIDGE.-1.0 defined to be ERROR
Warning - BRIDGE.0.-1 defined to be ERROR
...
```

In fact, when BRIDGE is composed with CARS, their behavior prevents cars which have not entered from exiting and the ERROR state is unreachable.

Before describing the overall system composition, we need to specify a safety property to compose with the system that verifies that cars do not collide on the bridge. The required property is listed below. It specifies that while red cars are on the bridge only red cars can enter and while blue cars are on the bridge only blue cars can enter. When the bridge is empty, either a red car or a blue car may enter. The index i is used to count the red (or blue) cars currently on the bridge.

```
property ONEWAY =(red[ID].enter   -> RED[1]
                 |blue[ID].enter -> BLUE[1]
                 ),
RED[i:ID] = (red[ID].enter -> RED[i+1]
            |when(i==1)red[ID].exit -> ONEWAY
            |when(i>1) red[ID].exit -> RED[i-1]
            ),
```

```
BLUE[i:ID]= (blue[ID].enter -> BLUE[i+1]
            |when(i==1)blue[ID].exit -> ONEWAY
            |when(i>1) blue[ID].exit -> BLUE[i-1]
            ).
```

The entire system can now be modeled by the composite process specified in Figure 7.5.

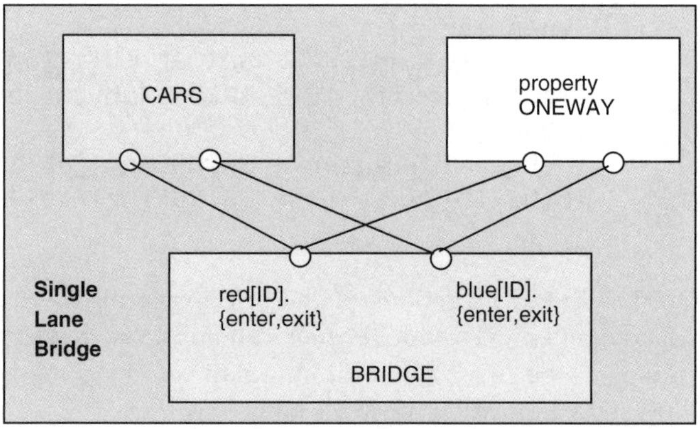

`||SingleLaneBridge = (CARS||BRIDGE||ONEWAY).`

Figure 7.5 `SingleLaneBridge` model.

Safety analysis using *LTSA* verifies that the `ONEWAY` safety property is not violated.

However, without the constraints provided by the `BRIDGE`, the composition `(CARS||ONEWAY)` yields the following safety violation:

```
Trace to property violation in ONEWAY:
     red.1.enter
     blue.1.enter
```

7.2.2 Single-Lane Bridge Implementation

In the single-lane bridge problem, it is reasonably clear which are the active entities and which are the passive entities. Cars are implemented as Java threads and the bridge as a monitor. This leaves the model entities `NOPASS1` and `NOPASS2` concerned with constraining overtaking. These have no explicit representation in the implementation. The overtaking constraint is dealt with in the `BridgeCanvas` class which displays car movement. Figure 7.6 depicts the class diagram for the program.

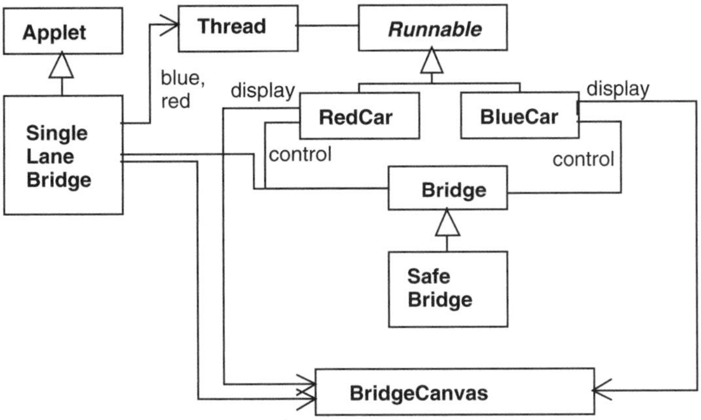

Figure 7.6 Single-lane bridge class diagram.

An instance of the `BridgeCanvas` class is created by the `SingleLaneBridge` applet. A reference to it is passed to each newly created `RedCar` and `BlueCar` object. The methods provided by the `BridgeCanvas` class are listed in Program 7.1.

```
class BridgeCanvas extends Canvas {

  public void init(int ncars) {...}     //set number of cars

  //move red car with the identity i a step
  //returns true for the period from just before,
  // until just after car on bridge
  public boolean moveRed(int i)
         throws InterruptedException{...}

  //move blue car with the identity i a step
  //returns true for the period from just before,
  //until just after car on bridge
  public boolean moveBlue(int i)
         throws InterruptedException{...}

  public synchronized void freeze(){...} //freeze display
  public synchronized void thaw(){...}   //unfreeze display
}
```

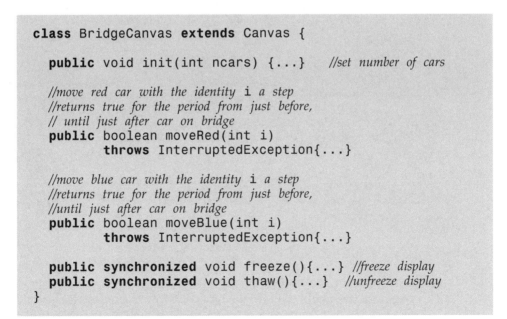

Program 7.1 `BridgeCanvas` class.

```
class RedCar implements Runnable {

  BridgeCanvas display; Bridge control; int id;

  RedCar(Bridge b, BridgeCanvas d, int id) {
    display = d; this.id = id; control = b;
  }

  public void run() {
    try {
      while(true) {
        while (!display.moveRed(id));           // not on bridge
        control.redEnter();               // request access to bridge
        while (display.moveRed(id));           // move over bridge
        control.redExit();                // release access to bridge
      }
    } catch (InterruptedException e) {}
  }
}

class BlueCar implements Runnable {

  BridgeCanvas display; Bridge control; int id;

  BlueCar(Bridge b, BridgeCanvas d, int id) {
    display = d; this.id = id; control = b;
  }

  public void run() {
    try {
      while (true) {
        while (!display.moveBlue(id));          // not on bridge
        control.blueEnter();              // request access to bridge
        while (display.moveBlue(id));           // move over bridge
        control.blueExit();               // release access to bridge
      }
    } catch (InterruptedException e) {}
  }
}
```

Program 7.2 `RedCar` and `BlueCar` classes.

The code for the two classes representing cars is listed in Program 7.2. Each car moves until it is about to enter the bridge. It then requests access to the bridge by invoking `control.redEnter()` if it is a red car and `control.blueEnter()` if it is blue. When a car has crossed the bridge, it invokes the appropriate `Exit` method.

```
class Bridge {
  synchronized void redEnter()
   throws InterruptedException {}
  synchronized void redExit()  {}
  synchronized void blueEnter()
   throws InterruptedException {}
  synchronized void blueExit() {}
}
```

Program 7.3 `Bridge` class.

The entry and exit bridge access methods are provided by an instance of the class `Bridge` or a class derived from `Bridge`. Class `Bridge` provides a null implementation as listed in Program 7.3. This enables us to view the results of an unsafe bridge implementation.

The `SingleLaneBridge` applet class creates one, two or three of each of the red and blue cars depending on which button is clicked. In addition, the check boxes select an implementation of the bridge monitor. Figure 7.7 depicts the consequences of using the null implementation of Program 7.3.

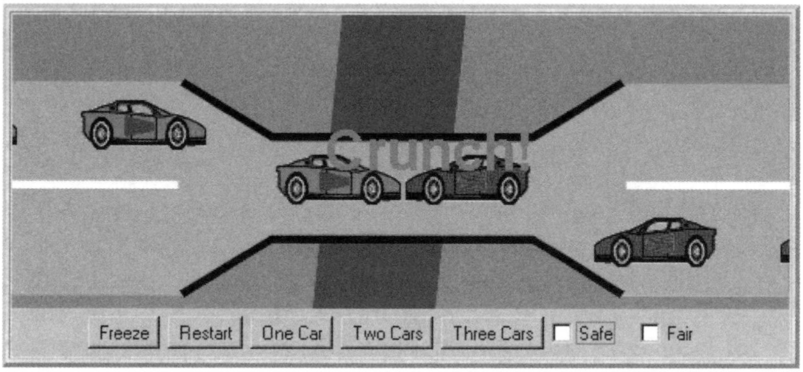

Figure 7.7 Single-lane bridge display using `Bridge` class.

Clicking the **Safe** check box creates a system that avoids the collisions of Figure 7.7. It uses the class `SafeBridge` which is a direct translation of the `BRIDGE` process from the model. Each of the guarded actions from the model becomes a conditionally synchronized method. Since this has been modeled and shown to preserve

```
class SafeBridge extends Bridge {

  private int nred  = 0; //number of red cars on bridge
  private int nblue = 0; //number of blue cars on bridge

  //Monitor Invariant:   nred≥0 and nblue≥0 and
  //              not (nred>0 and nblue>0)

 synchronized void redEnter()
      throws InterruptedException {
    while (nblue>0) wait();
    ++nred;
  }

 synchronized void redExit(){
    --nred; if (nred==0)notifyAll();
  }

 synchronized void blueEnter()
      throws InterruptedException {
    while (nred>0) wait();
    ++nblue;
  }

 synchronized void blueExit(){
    --nblue; if (nblue==0)notifyAll();
  }
}
```

Program 7.4 SafeBridge class.

the ONEWAY safety property, we can be reasonably confident in the safety of the SafeBridge implementation. The code for the class is listed in Program 7.4.

The implementation of SafeBridge uses conditional notification. We only wake up waiting threads when the number of cars on the bridge – either red or blue – is decremented to zero. This avoids unnecessary thread switches since otherwise, blue cars would be woken up every time a red car leaves the bridge and vice versa. It is only the last car of a particular color to leave the bridge that should wake up waiting car threads.

SafeBridge ensures that cars do not collide on the bridge; however, it does not ensure that cars eventually get the opportunity to cross the bridge. With three cars of each color, if a red car crosses the bridge first there is always a red car on the bridge and consequently, blue cars never get to cross. This situation is called *starvation*: a form of liveness property discussed in the next section.

7.3 Liveness

A liveness property asserts that something good eventually happens. A reasonable liveness property for the single-lane bridge would be that all red and blue cars eventually get to cross the bridge. As we have seen, the program developed in the previous section does not satisfy this property in the situation where there are three cars of each type. In this section, we see how models can be analyzed for liveness. Like deadlock and other safety properties, the objective is to solve liveness problems at the modeling stage so that they do not occur in the implemented program.

A completely general treatment of liveness is rather involved and requires the use of a temporal logic to specify the required liveness properties. Rather than burden the reader with another formalism, we deal with a restricted class of liveness properties which we term *progress*. A progress property asserts that whatever state a system is in, it is always the case that a specified action will eventually be executed. Progress is the opposite of *starvation*, the name given to a concurrent-programming situation in which an action is never executed. Progress properties are simple to specify and are sufficiently powerful to capture a wide range of liveness problems in concurrent programs.

7.3.1 Progress Properties

To illustrate the notion of progress, we use a simple example, that of tossing a coin. The model is depicted in Figure 7.8.

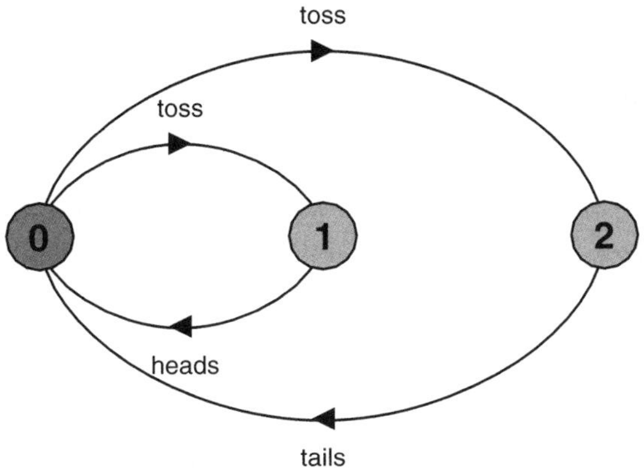


```
COIN = (toss->heads->COIN|toss->tails->COIN).
```

Figure 7.8 COIN model.

If the coin were tossed an infinite number of times, we would expect that heads would be chosen infinitely often and that tails would be chosen infinitely often. In fact, this depends on the scheduling policy used to decide on which transition from the set of eligible transitions should be executed. If the policy is not *fair* then we could always choose the `toss` transition leading to `heads`. We assume that the scheduling policy for choice is fair as defined in the following:

> **Fair Choice:** If a choice over a set of transitions is executed infinitely often, then every transition in the set will be executed infinitely often.

If the transition (or transitions) of an action occurs infinitely often in a system, we can say that it is always the case at any stage of the execution that the action will eventually occur. With the assumption of fair choice then the coin-tossing system should eventually choose heads and eventually choose tails. We can assert this with progress properties specified in *FSP*. A progress property is defined by:

> **`progress`** `P = {`a_1`,`a_2`..`a_n`}` defines a progress property `P` which asserts that in an infinite execution of a target system, at least one of the actions a_1`,`a_2`..`a_n will be executed infinitely often.

In other words, a progress property asserts that at any stage of execution one of the actions in the progress set will eventually occur. The liveness requirement for coin tossing can now be expressed as:

```
progress HEADS = {heads}
progress TAILS = {tails}
```

The `COIN` system we have defined so far satisfies these properties. We now examine a system that does not. Suppose that the agent which tosses the coin first picks one of two coins: a normal coin with a head and a tail as defined in Figure 7.8 and a trick coin which has a head on both sides. The outcome of tossing the trick coin must always be heads. This system is modeled in Figure 7.9.

Progress analysis of the `TWOCOIN` system against the progress properties `HEADS` and `TAILS` produces the following output:

```
Progress violation: TAILS
Path to terminal set of states:
```

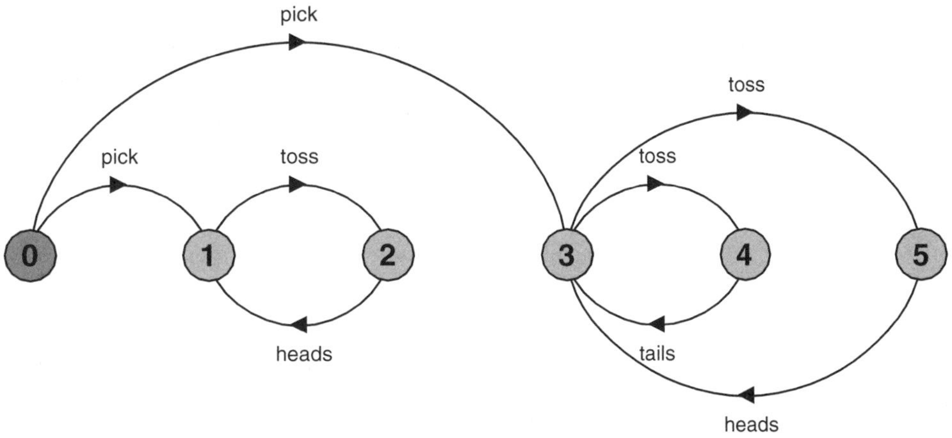

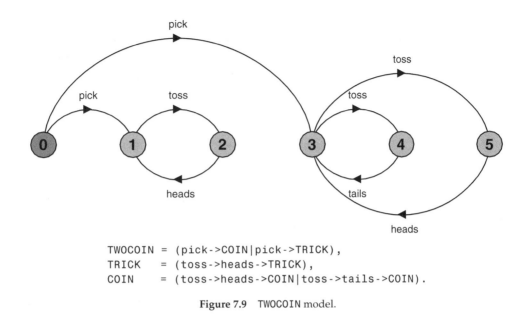

```
TWOCOIN = (pick->COIN|pick->TRICK),
TRICK   = (toss->heads->TRICK),
COIN    = (toss->heads->COIN|toss->tails->COIN).
```

Figure 7.9 TWOCOIN model.

```
    pick
Actions in terminal set:
{toss, heads}
```

This confirms the expected result: if the agent picks the trick coin then the action `tails` will never occur. This is of course a violation of the `TAILS` progress property, which asserts that in an infinite execution, tails must occur infinitely often. The reader should note that the system of Figure 7.9 does not violate the progress property:

```
progress HEADSorTAILS = {heads,tails}
```

Property `HEADSorTAILS` is not violated since only one of the actions in the progress set need be executed infinitely often to satisfy the property.

7.3.2 Progress Analysis

Progress analysis involves first performing a search for terminal sets of states.

> A terminal set of states is one in which every state is reachable from every other state in the set via one or more transitions and there is no transition from within the set to any state outside the set.

In graph theory, this is known as a strongly connected component, which has no path to any nodes outside the set of nodes in the component. For example, the labeled transition system of Figure 7.9 has two terminal sets of states, {1, 2}, which are the states relating to the trick coin, and {3, 4, 5}, which are the states relating to the normal coin.

An execution of a system represented by a finite set of states can only be infinite if some of the states are visited infinitely often. The states that are visited infinitely often in an execution must form a terminal set. Given fair choice, each terminal set of states represents an execution in which each transition in the set is executed infinitely often. Since there is no transition out of a terminal set, any action that is not used in all terminal sets cannot occur infinitely often in all executions of the system. Checking that a progress property holds is now simply checking that in each terminal set, at least one of the actions in the progress set occurs as a transition. Conversely, a progress property is violated if analysis finds a terminal set of states in which none of the progress set actions appear. For the `TAILS` property, this terminal set is the set of states {1, 2} in which the action `tails` does not occur. The output gives the shortest execution path to the root of the terminal set and lists the actions that do appear in the set.

If no progress properties are specified, *LTSA* performs progress analysis using a *default property*. This property asserts that for every action in the alphabet of the target system, given fair choice, that action will be executed infinitely often. This is equivalent to specifying a separate progress property for every action. For the `TWOCOIN` system, this default analysis produces the following output:

```
Progress violation for actions:
{pick}
Path to terminal set of states:
     pick
Actions in terminal set:
{toss, heads, tails}

Progress violation for actions:
{pick, tails}
Path to terminal set of states:
     pick
Actions in terminal set:
{toss, heads}
```

The analysis produces two progress violations since the action `pick` is not executed infinitely often in either terminal set. The value of this default property is that if it is not violated, then no specified progress properties can be violated. In other words, if the default property holds, then every other progress property, specified in terms of subsets of the action alphabet of a target system, must also hold. This is true since the default property asserts that every action is executed infinitely often. All systems in which the states occur inside a single terminal set satisfy the default progress property.

7.3.3 Action Priority

If default progress analysis is applied to the single-lane bridge model then no violations are detected. However, we know from the implementation that it is possible for progress violations to occur. Either the blue cars or the red cars may wait forever to cross the bridge. Why do we not detect these progress problems?

The answer lies in the fair choice assumption underlying the progress test. This means that every possible execution of the system will eventually happen including those in which cars do not starve. To detect progress problems we must superimpose some scheduling policy for actions, which models the situation in which the bridge is heavily used, i.e. we need to impose adverse conditions which "stress-test" the system. We use action priority expressions to describe these scheduling policies. Action priority is specified in *FSP* with respect to process compositions.

High Priority Operator ("<<")

> ||C = (P||Q) <<{$a_1,\ldots,a_n$} specifies a composition in which the actions $a_1,\ldots,a_n$ have higher priority than any other action in the alphabet of P||Q including the silent action `tau`. In any choice in this system which has one or more of the actions $a_1,\ldots,a_n$ labeling a transition, the transitions labeled with lower priority actions are discarded.

Low Priority Operator (">>")

> ||C = (P||Q)>>{$a_1,\ldots,a_n$} specifies a composition in which the actions $a_1,\ldots,a_n$ have lower priority than any other action in the alphabet of P||Q including the silent action `tau`. In any choice in this system which has one or more transitions not labeled by $a_1,\ldots,a_n$, the transitions labeled by $a_1,\ldots,a_n$ are discarded.

Action priority operators simplify the composite processes by discarding particular transitions. Figure 7.10 illustrates the effect for a simple example. When `work` is

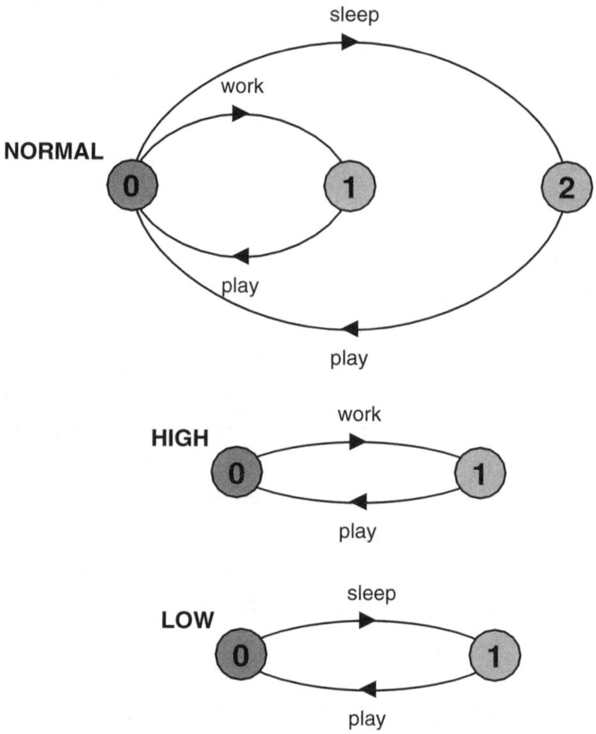

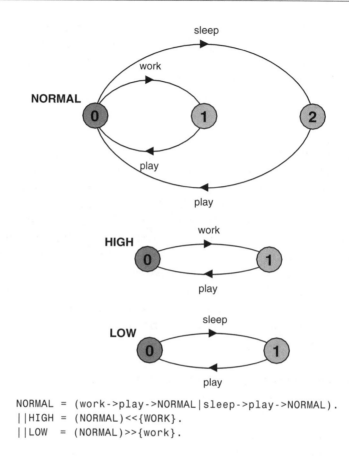

```
NORMAL = (work->play->NORMAL|sleep->play->NORMAL).
||HIGH = (NORMAL)<<{WORK}.
||LOW  = (NORMAL)>>{work}.
```

Figure 7.10 Action priority.

specified to be a high priority action in the composition `HIGH`, the `sleep` transition disappears since it is lower priority and consequently in a choice between `sleep` and `work`, `work` will always be chosen. When `work` is specified to be a low priority action in the composition `LOW`, the `work` transition disappears since it is lower priority and consequently in a choice between `sleep` and `work`, `sleep` will always be chosen.

7.4 Liveness of the Single-Lane Bridge

Using progress properties and action priorities, we are now in a position to investigate the liveness problems of the single-lane bridge. In particular, we are interested in the following two progress properties when the bridge is heavily loaded or congested.

```
progress BLUECROSS = {blue[ID].enter}
progress REDCROSS =  {red[ID].enter}
```

BLUECROSS asserts that it is always the case that one of the blue cars will be able to enter the bridge; REDCROSS asserts the same for red cars. This leaves the problem of how to model congestion using action priority. If we give all the actions related to red cars priority over blue cars we get the situation where BLUECROSS is violated and similarly if we give blue cars priority REDCROSS is violated. Neither of these scheduling policies is a good model of the program. Neither red nor blue cars have priority in the implementation. Instead, we give car exit from the bridge low priority. This models the situation where the bridge is congested since in any choice between another car entering the bridge and a car leaving the bridge, we choose to let a car enter. The congested bridge is modeled by:

```
||CongestedBridge = (SingleLaneBridge)
                    >>{red[ID].exit,blue[ID].exit}.
```

Progress analysis of this system against the properties BLUECROSS and REDCROSS produces the following output:

```
Progress violation: BLUECROSS
Path to terminal set of states:
     red.1.enter
     red.2.enter
Actions in terminal set:
{red.1.enter, red1.exit, red.2.enter,
red.2.exit, red.3.enter, red.3.exit}
Progress violation: REDCROSS
Path to terminal set of states:
     blue.1.enter
     blue.2.enter
Actions in terminal set:
{blue.1.enter, blue.1.exit, blue.2.enter,
blue.2.exit, blue.3.enter, blue.3.exit}
```

The output corresponds with observations of the program. When there are three cars and a red car enters first then the bridge is continuously occupied by red cars and blue cars never cross. Similarly, red cars never cross if a blue car enters first. However, the model abstracts from a number of program details such as the length of the bridge and consequently, the number of cars needed to continuously occupy it. As a result, the model detects lack of progress when there are only two cars moving in each direction. The terminal sets of states for this scenario can clearly be seen in the transition system depicted in Figure 7.11.

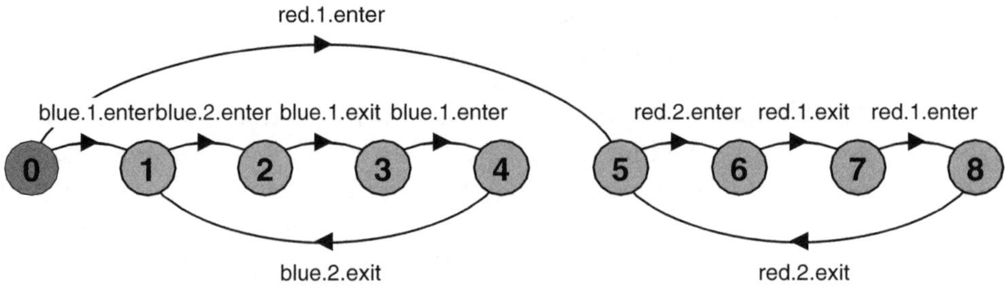

Figure 7.11 `CongestedBridge` model with two cars.

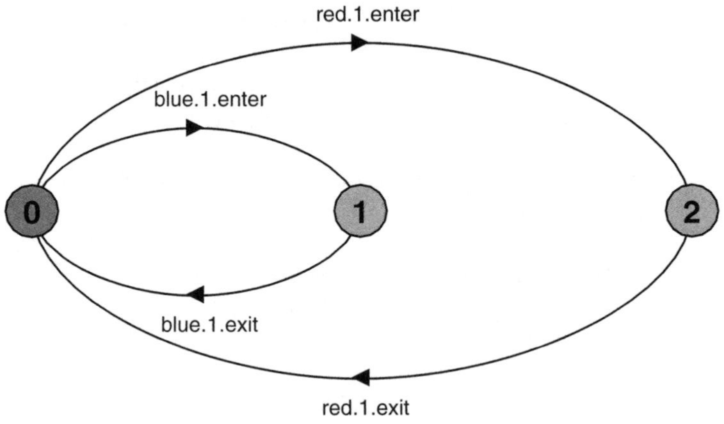

Figure 7.12 `CongestedBridge` model with one car.

When there is only one car moving in each direction, the bridge does not become congested and both red and blue cars make progress. The transition system for the one car scenario is depicted in Figure 7.12.

Will we receive the same progress results if we instead model congestion by giving car *entry* to the bridge *high* priority? The interested reader should check that this is indeed the case.

What we must now do is devise a model which does not exhibit progress problems when there is more than one car moving in each direction.

7.4.1 Revised Single-Lane Bridge Model

A bridge which decides dynamically at any given point whether to admit blue cars or red cars needs to have more information about the state of cars than is currently available in the model. In particular, the bridge needs to know whether cars are waiting to cross. To this end, the model for a car is modified so that it requests access to the bridge before attempting to enter. The revised model for a car is:

```
CAR = (request->enter->exit->CAR).
```

The bridge model can now count the number of cars waiting at each end. The count is incremented when a car requests access and decremented when the car enters the bridge. Our first attempt at a revised BRIDGE process uses this count of waiting cars as follows. Red cars are only allowed to enter the bridge if there are no blue cars on the bridge and there are no blue cars waiting. Blue cars are only allowed to enter the bridge if there are no red cars on the bridge and no red cars waiting to enter the bridge. The revised BRIDGE process is as follows:

```
/* nr - number of red cars on the bridge
   nb - number of blue cars on the bridge
   wr - number of red cars waiting to enter
   wb - number of blue cars waiting to enter
*/
BRIDGE = BRIDGE[0][0][0][0],
BRIDGE[nr:T][nb:T][wr:T][wb:T] =
  (red[ID].request   -> BRIDGE[nr][nb][wr+1][wb]
  |when (nb==0 && wb==0)
    red[ID].enter    -> BRIDGE[nr+1][nb][wr-1][wb]
  |red[ID].exit      -> BRIDGE[nr-1][nb][wr][wb]
  |blue[ID].request  -> BRIDGE[nr][nb][wr][wb+1]
  |when (nr==0 && wr==0)
    blue[ID].enter   -> BRIDGE[nr][nb+1][wr][wb-1]
  |blue[ID].exit     -> BRIDGE[nr][nb-1][wr][wb]
  ).
```

The problem with this model is that when we check the safety properties of the new SingleLaneBridge system, a deadlock is reported:

```
Trace to DEADLOCK:
      red.1.request
      red.2.request
      red.3.request
      blue.1.request
      blue.2.request
      blue.3.request
```

The trace is the scenario in which there are cars waiting at both ends, and consequently, the bridge does not allow either red or blue cars to enter. To solve this problem, we must introduce some *asymmetry* into the problem (as was done for the Dining Philosophers in Chapter 6). This takes the form of a boolean variable (`bt`) which indicates whether it is the turn of blue cars or red cars to enter the bridge. Initially, `bt` is set to true indicating it is blue's turn. As soon as a blue car exits the bridge, `bt` is set to false. When a red car exits, `bt` is set to true again. The `BRIDGE` process becomes:

```
const True = 1
const False = 0
range B = False..True
/* nr - number of red cars on the bridge
   nb - number of blue cars on the bridge
   wr - number of red cars waiting to enter
   wb - number of blue cars waiting to enter
   bt - true indicates blue turn,
        false indicates red turn
*/
BRIDGE = BRIDGE[0][0][0][0][True],
BRIDGE[nr:T][nb:T][wr:T][wb:T][bt:B] =
  (red[ID].request ->BRIDGE[nr][nb][wr+1][wb][bt]
  |when (nb==0 && (wb==0||!bt))
    red[ID].enter  ->BRIDGE[nr+1][nb][wr-1][wb][bt]
  |red[ID].exit    ->BRIDGE[nr-1][nb][wr][wb][True]
  |blue[ID].request->BRIDGE[nr][nb][wr][wb+1][bt]
  |when (nr==0 && (wr==0||bt))
    blue[ID].enter ->BRIDGE[nr][nb+1][wr][wb-1][bt]
  |blue[ID].exit   ->BRIDGE[nr][nb-1][wr][wb][False]
  ).
```

The condition under which the bridge permits a red car to enter is that there are no blue cars on the bridge and either there are no blue cars waiting or it is not blue's turn: `nb==0 &&(wb==0 || !bt)`. The condition for a blue car to enter is that there are no red cars on the bridge and either there are no red cars waiting or it is blue's turn: `nr==0 &&(wr==0 || bt)`.

This corrected model no longer deadlocks. Further, a progress analysis reports that `BLUECROSS` and `REDCROSS` properties are not violated.

7.4.2 Revised Single-Lane Bridge Implementation

The revision to the program involves a new version of the bridge monitor which implements precisely the `BRIDGE` process from the model developed in the last section. In fact, we do not need to introduce a new monitor method to implement the `request` action made by cars. The existing `enter` methods can be modified to increment a wait count before testing whether or not the caller can access the bridge. As before, the tests are simply the negation of the guards in the model `BRIDGE` process. The new implementation is listed in Program 7.5.

In the demonstration applet, this implementation of the monitor is used when the **Fair** check box is clicked.

```
class FairBridge extends Bridge {
  private int nred = 0; //count of red cars on the bridge
  private int nblue = 0; //count of blue cars on the bridge
  private int waitblue = 0;  //count of waiting blue cars
  private int waitred = 0;   //count of waiting red cars
  private boolean blueturn = true;

  synchronized void redEnter()
      throws InterruptedException {
    ++waitred;
    while (nblue>0||(waitblue>0 && blueturn)) wait();
    --waitred;
    ++nred;
  }

  synchronized void redExit(){
    --nred;
    blueturn = true;
    if (nred==0)notifyAll();
  }

  synchronized void blueEnter(){
      throws InterruptedException {
    ++waitblue;
    while (nred>0||(waitred>0 && !blueturn)) wait();
    --waitblue;
    ++nblue;
  }

  synchronized void blueExit(){
    --nblue;
    blueturn = false;
    if (nblue==0) notifyAll();
  }
}
```

Program 7.5 `FairBridge` class.

7.5 Readers-Writers Problem

The Readers–Writers problem is concerned with access to a shared database by two kinds of processes. Readers execute transactions that examine the database while Writers both examine and update the database. For the database to be updated correctly, Writers must have exclusive access to the database while they are updating it. If no Writer is accessing the database, any number of Readers may concurrently access it. In this section, we develop a solution to the problem. As usual, we construct a model of the problem to examine its safety and liveness properties before proceeding to an implementation.

7.5.1 Readers-Writers Model

In modeling the problem, the first step is to decide on the actions of interest. These are acquiring and releasing read access to the shared database and acquiring and releasing write access. The actions are declared below as the set `Actions`:

```
set Actions = {acquireRead,releaseRead,
               acquireWrite,releaseWrite}
```

As for the Ornamental Garden model in section 4.1.2, we use a set constant simply as a way of abbreviating the model description. The processes that model Readers and Writers are:

```
READER =
  (acquireRead->examine->releaseRead->READER)
  +Actions
  \ {examine}.

WRITER =
  (acquireWrite->modify->releaseWrite->WRITER)
  +Actions
  \ {modify}.
```

A `READER` process must acquire read access before examining the database and a `WRITER` must acquire write access before modifying the database. The alphabets of both processes have been defined to be the full set of access actions by the alphabet extension `+Actions`. This ensures that while a `READER` only engages in the `acquireRead` and `releaseRead` actions, the `acquireWrite` and `releaseWrite` actions cannot occur freely for any prefixed instance of the process. Similarly, for `WRITER` processes, the `acquireRead` and `releaseRead` actions cannot occur freely. The `examine` and `modify` actions are hidden since they are irrelevant to the problem of synchronizing access to the shared database.

Access to the shared database is controlled by a read/write lock. The lock accepts `acquireRead` actions when it has not been acquired for write access by `acquireWrite`. It permits only a single write access when it has not been acquired for read access. The lock is modeled by the `RW_LOCK` process:

```
const False = 0   const True = 1
range Bool  = False..True
const Nread = 2             // Maximum readers
const Nwrite= 2             // Maximum writers

RW_LOCK = RW[0][False],
RW[readers:0..Nread][writing:Bool] =
      (when (!writing)
         acquireRead  ->RW[readers+1][writing]
      |releaseRead    ->RW[readers-1][writing]
      |when (readers==0 && !writing)
         acquireWrite->RW[readers][True]
      |releaseWrite   ->RW[readers][False]
      ).
```

The `RW_LOCK` process maintains a count of the number of concurrent read accesses (`readers`) and a boolean (`writing`) which is set to true when the lock is acquired for write access. The action to acquire read access is only accepted when `writing` is false and the action to acquire write access is only accepted when `readers==0` and `writing` is false.

Safety Property

To check that the lock behaves as desired, we define a safety property, `RW_SAFE`, as follows:

```
property SAFE_RW
  = (acquireRead->READING[1]
    |acquireWrite->WRITING
    ),
READING[i:1..Nread]
  = (acquireRead->READING[i+1]
    |when(i>1) releaseRead  ->READING[i-1]
    |when(i==1)releaseRead  ->SAFE_RW
    ),
WRITING = (releaseWrite->SAFE_RW).
```

The property asserts that initially either an `acquireRead` action or a `acquireWrite` action can be accepted. In other words when the lock is free, it can be acquired for either read or write access. When acquired for read access (`READING`), further `acquireRead` actions are permitted but no `acquireWrite` actions. The lock does not become free until all the `releaseRead` actions which correspond to the `acquireRead` actions have happened. When the lock has been acquired for write access (`WRITING`), only the `releaseWrite` action should occur. To check that the lock implementation `RW_LOCK` satisfies the property, the lock is composed with the property as follows:

```
||READWRITELOCK = (RW_LOCK || SAFE_RW).
```

The resulting *LTS* is depicted in Figure 7.13.

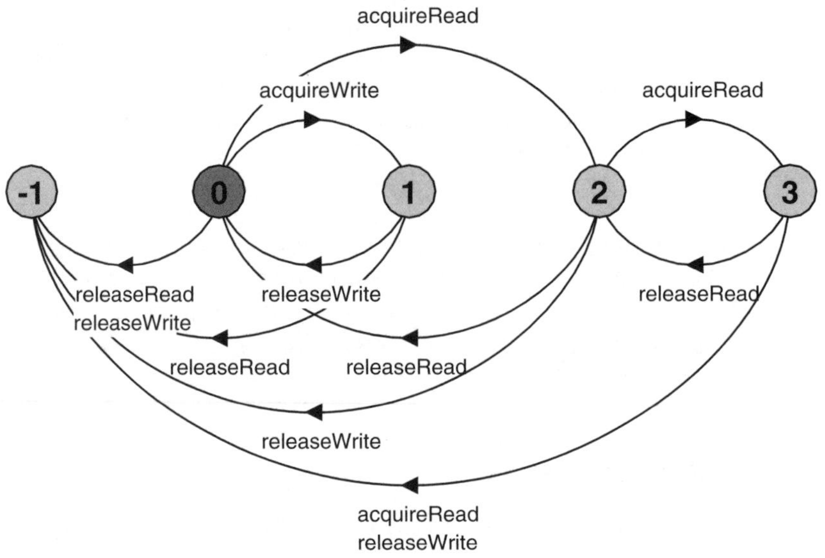

Figure 7.13 `READWRITELOCK` *LTS*.

The transitions to the `ERROR` state in Figure 7.13 occur if a Reader or Writer is badly behaved. For example, if a Reader performs a `releaseRead` without previously having performed an `acquireRead` then a safety violation will occur. A violation will also occur if more than two `acquireRead` requests are made.

The composition of `READER` and `WRITER` processes with the read/write lock is described in Figure 7.14. Analysis of this system reveals no deadlocks or safety violations. The addition of well-behaved `READER` and `WRITER` processes ensures that the error transitions of Figure 7.13 cannot occur.

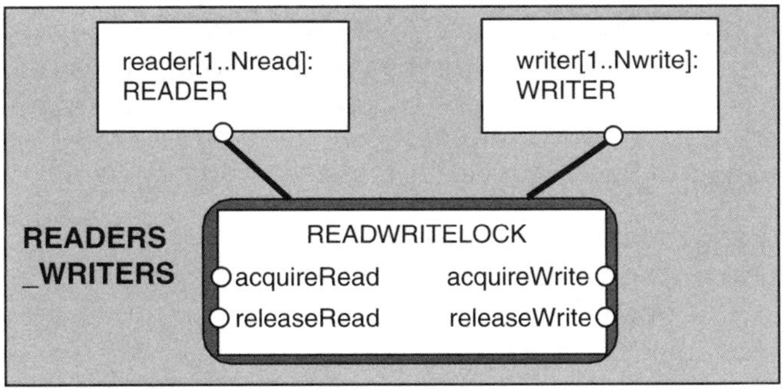


```
||READERS_WRITERS
   = (reader[1..Nread]:READER
     ||writer[1..Nwrite]:WRITER
     ||{reader[1..Nread],
        writer[1..Nwrite]}::READWRITELOCK).
```

Figure 7.14 READERS_WRITERS model.

Progress Property

The progress properties that are important in the Readers–Writers system are that both Readers and Writers should eventually acquire access to the shared database. We can express the required progress properties as follows:

```
progress WRITE = {writer[1..Nwrite].acquireWrite}
progress READ  = {reader[1..Nread].acquireRead}
```

The WRITE property asserts that it should always be the case that at least one of the WRITER processes can perform an acquireWrite action. Since WRITER s are completely symmetric, we can reasonably expect that if one can acquireWrite then so can the others. READ specifies the same property for READER processes and acquireRead. A progress check reports no violations of these properties in the system specified by READERS_WRITERS. Because of the fair choice assumption, progress problems only occur in complete system models that are erroneous. To find how the system performs when loaded or "stressed", we must specify adverse scheduling conditions using action priority. This is exactly the procedure we adopted to find the progress problems in the single-lane bridge model. Indeed, the adverse conditions are similar to those used in the bridge problem. To model a heavily loaded system, we give lower priority to release actions in the same way we gave lower priority to exit actions in the bridge problem. (Alternatively, we could give higher priority to the acquire actions.) The system model used for progress analysis is described by:

```
||RW_PROGRESS = READERS_WRITERS
               >>{reader[1..Nread].releaseRead,
                  writer[1..Nread].releaseWrite}.
```

Analysis of this system leads to the violation:

```
Progress violation: WRITE
Path to terminal set of states:
     reader.1.acquireRead
Actions in terminal set:
{reader.1.acquireRead, reader.1.releaseRead,
 reader.2.acquireRead, reader.2.releaseRead}
```

The violation describes the scenario in which Writers cannot access the shared database because a Reader always has read access. In other words, the number of Readers never drops to zero and consequently, the read/write lock denies access to Writers. The terminal set of states that describes this behavior can clearly be seen in Figure 7.15. It contains the states numbered 3, 4 and 5. Before exploring solutions to this progress problem, we translate the existing model into an implementation in the next section.

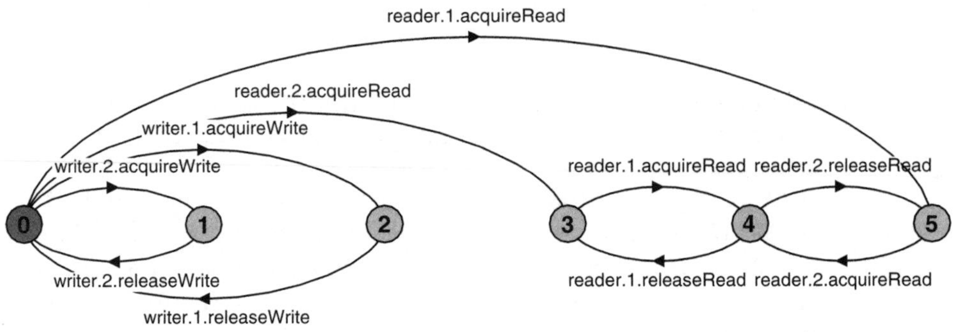

Figure 7.15 RW_PROGRESS *LTS.*

7.5.2 Readers-Writers Implementation

In the interests of brevity, we describe only the monitor that synchronizes the accesses of Readers and Writers to a shared database. This synchronization is the essence of the problem. In the same way that we defined the set of actions of interest in the Readers–Writers model, we define an interface that identifies the monitor methods that must be implemented. In the sections that follow, we

```
interface ReadWrite {
     public void acquireRead()
         throws InterruptedException;
     public void releaseRead();
     public void acquireWrite()
        throws InterruptedException;
    public void releaseWrite();
}
```

Program 7.6 ReadWrite interface.

develop a number of alternative implementations of this interface. The interface is listed in Program 7.6.

Each method in the ReadWrite interface corresponds directly to the action of the same name in the model. Our first implementation of ReadWrite, which corresponds exactly to the RW_LOCK process from the model, is listed in Program 7.7.

The guarded actions from the model become synchronized methods containing waits. However, in the implementation, we must decide on notification to awake threads blocked in waits. The simple solution, as discussed in Chapter 5, is to include a call to notifyAll() in every monitor method that modifies the state of the monitor. However, this can lead to unnecessary thread switches. In the ReadWriteSafe monitor, notification is required only when the last Reader has relinquished access and when a Writer releases. When the last Reader calls

```
class ReadWriteSafe implements ReadWrite {
  private int readers =0;
  private boolean writing = false;

  public synchronized void acquireRead()
             throws InterruptedException {
    while (writing) wait();
    ++readers;
  }

  public synchronized void releaseRead() {
    --readers;
    if(readers==0) notify();
  }
```

Program 7.7 ReadWriteSafe class.

```
  public synchronized void acquireWrite()
            throws InterruptedException {
    while (readers>0 || writing) wait();
    writing = true;
  }

  public synchronized void releaseWrite() {
    writing = false;
    notifyAll();
  }
}
```

Program 7.7 (*Continued*).

`releaseRead()` (i.e. `readers==0`), `notify()` rather than `notifyAll()` can be used since only Writers can be waiting and it is only necessary to unblock a single Writer. When a Writer is finished it calls `releaseWrite()` which then calls `notifyAll()`. This is because it may be necessary to unblock either one or more Readers or a Writer.

The implementation suffers from the progress problem detected in the model. If the number of Readers accessing the shared database never drops to zero, then Writers can never gain access. This behavior can be seen in the demonstration applet when the two Reader threads are started such that there is always one holding the lock. The applet display is depicted in Figure 7.16.

Figure 7.16 Readers–Writers applet display.

7.5.3 Revised Readers-Writers Model and Implementation

To address the progress problem discovered with our first model and implementation of the Readers–Writers problem, we adopt an approach in which Readers are denied access if there are Writers waiting to acquire access. This should give Writers priority in acquiring the lock and avoid the situation in which they wait forever for access. To detect that a Writer is waiting for access, we must add another action to its repertoire. A Writer must request access before attempting to acquire it. This is exactly the same solution we adopted in the single-lane bridge solution to detect whether cars were waiting. The additional action is `requestWrite` and the revised `WRITER` process is shown below:

```
set Actions = {acquireRead,releaseRead,
      acquireWrite,releaseWrite,requestWrite}

WRITER =
   (requestWrite->acquireWrite->modify
               ->releaseWrite->WRITER
   )+Actions\{modify}.
```

The `READER` process remains unchanged. `RW_LOCK` is modified to maintain a count of waiting Writers (`waitingW`). The count is incremented when a Writer requests access and decremented when it actually acquires access. Readers are only allowed to acquire the lock when the number of waiting Writers is zero. The revised lock process is listed below:

```
RW_LOCK = RW[0][False][0],
RW[readers:0..Nread]
  [writing:Bool]
  [waitingW:0..Nwrite] =
  (when (!writing && waitingW==0)
     acquireRead -> RW[readers+1][writing][waitingW]
  |releaseRead   -> RW[readers-1][writing][waitingW]
  |when (readers==0 && !writing)
     acquireWrite-> RW[readers][True][waitingW-1]
  |releaseWrite  -> RW[readers][False][waitingW]
  |requestWrite  -> RW[readers][writing][waitingW+1]
  ).
```

This definition of `RW_LOCK` still satisfies the `RW_SAFE` property. Note that we have not had to change the definition of the safety property. The `request` action (`requestWrite`) is not relevant to the safe operation of the lock and so does not appear in the alphabet of the safety property. Safety is determined only by the correct sequencing of `acquire` and `release` actions.

A progress analysis of RW_PROGRESS now produces the output:

```
Progress violation: READ
Path to terminal set of states:
     writer.1.requestWrite
     writer.2.requestWrite
Actions in terminal set:
{writer.1.requestWrite, writer.1.acquireWrite,
 writer.1.releaseWrite, writer.2.requestWrite,
 writer.2.acquireWrite, writer.2.releaseWrite}
```

We no longer have a violation of the WRITE property, demonstrating that in this Writers priority system, Writers can always access the shared database. However, we now have a READ progress violation. This occurs since, if there is always a Writer waiting to acquire the lock, then Readers will never gain access. However, in the practical application of read/write locks, the Writers priority solution is often satisfactory since there are usually many more read accesses to a database than write accesses. In addition, it may be important that Readers get the most up-to-date information. The implementation of a Writers priority lock is listed in Program 7.8. It follows directly from the revised definition of RW_LOCK.

A version of the read/write lock that satisfies both the READ and WRITE properties involves the addition of a boolean which indicates whether it is the Readers' turn or the Writers' turn. Readers only defer to waiting Writers when it is not their turn to acquire the lock. This turn variable plays exactly the same role in the Readers–Writers problem as the turn variable in the single-lane bridge. The final version of the read/write lock model is listed below. The implementation is left as an exercise.

```
RW_LOCK = RW[0][False][0][False],
RW[readers:0..Nread]
  [writing:Bool]
  [waitingW:0..Nwrite]
  [readersturn:Bool] =
(when (!writing && (waitingW==0||readersturn))
      acquireRead  ->RW[readers+1][writing][waitingW][readersturn]
  |releaseRead     ->RW[readers-1][writing][waitingW][False]
  |when (readers==0 && !writing)
     acquireWrite   ->RW[readers][True][waitingW-1][readersturn]
  |releaseWrite     ->RW[readers][False][waitingW][True]
  |requestWrite     ->RW[readers][writing][waitingW+1][readersturn]
).
```

```
class ReadWritePriority implements ReadWrite{
  private int readers =0;
  private boolean writing = false;
  private int waitingW = 0; // no of waiting Writers.

  public synchronized void acquireRead()
             throws InterruptedException {
    while (writing || waitingW>0) wait();
    ++readers;
  }

  public synchronized void releaseRead() {
    --readers;
    if (readers==0) notifyAll();
  }

  public synchronized void acquireWrite()
             throws InterruptedException {
    ++waitingW;
    while (readers>0 || writing) wait();
    --waitingW;
    writing = true;
  }

  public synchronized void releaseWrite() {
    writing = false;
    notifyAll();
  }
}
```

Program 7.8 `ReadWritePriority` class.

Summary

A *safety* property asserts that nothing bad happens during the execution of a program and a *liveness* property asserts that something good eventually happens. In this chapter, we described how *FSP* models can be checked for both safety and liveness properties.

A safety property is defined by a deterministic process **property** P. This asserts that any trace including actions in the alphabet of P is accepted by P. When the property P is composed with a system S, traces of actions that are in the alphabet of S and the alphabet of P must also be valid traces of P, otherwise the ERROR state is reachable. Consequently, if safety analysis does not detect an ERROR state, we know that the property holds for the system.

We defined a subset of liveness properties which we termed *progress* properties. A progress property is defined by a **progress** set of action labels. It asserts that in any infinite execution of a system, one of the actions in the progress set must happen infinitely often. In asserting progress, it is necessary to make some scheduling assumptions as to which transitions are chosen for execution. We assume fair choice for a set of transitions such that if the set is executed infinitely often, then every transition in the set will be executed infinitely often. To investigate the liveness problems that occurred in our example programs, we introduced a way of specifying action priority that let us superimpose a specific scheduling policy on fair choice. This enabled us to model adverse situations in which processes compete for scarce resources.

The example programs developed in this chapter had a fixed set of threads competing for a resource. In Chapter 9, we examine systems in which the size of the set varies as threads are dynamically created and terminated.

Notes and Further Reading

The terms *safety* and *liveness* applied to concurrent programs were first introduced by Lamport (1977). In this book, we have adopted a modeling approach to reasoning about concurrent programs and consequently a model-checking approach to verifying properties. As discussed at the end of Chapter 5, an alternative approach is to reason about safety properties of concurrent programs using assertions and invariants specified in predicate logic. The reader should consult Greg Andrews' book (1991) for an extensive exposition of this approach.

The mechanisms used in this chapter for checking safety and progress properties have been developed by the authors and their colleagues. The safety property technique is due to Cheung and Kramer (1999). Progress checking as described here is due to Giannakopoulou, Magee and Kramer (1999) and is a simplified form of a more general technique for checking that properties specified in Linear Temporal Logic (LTL) hold for a system. The property that our approach checks is that an action always eventually occurs. As an LTL formula, this is specified as $\Box\Diamond$ **a**, where $\Box$ means always and $\Diamond$ means eventually. The general technique involves translating the LTL formula into Büchi automata and then composing the Büchi automata with the target system and performing a connected component analysis of the resulting automata (Gribomont and Wolper, 1989). Technically, this is a check that the system is a valid model of the formula – the origin of the term *model checking*, which we have used in the looser sense to refer to any technique for analyzing models. Büchi automata are a form of finite state automata which recognize infinite sequences of actions. The interested reader should look at Holzmann's SPIN model checker (Holzmann, 1991, 1997) which uses this approach. The pioneering work on model checking is due to Clarke, Emerson and

Sistla (1986). Fred Schneider (1997) provides an introduction to temporal logic and discusses derivation and reasoning about concurrent programs.

Chapter 14 provides more details on the use of LTL for property checking, and introduces *fluents* to *FSP* as a means of specifying state-based properties in an event-based formalism such as *LTS*. Fairness and the use of Büchi automata are also discussed and supported by *LTSA* for property checking.

The topic of fairness in concurrent programs has an extensive literature. We have used a strong form of fair choice. For an extensive discussion on the different classes of fairness, see the book by Francez (1986).

Exercises

7.1 What action trace violates the following safety property?

```
property PS = (a->(b->PS|a->PS)|b->a->PS).
```

7.2 A lift has a maximum capacity of ten people. In the model of the lift control system, passengers entering a lift are signaled by an `enter` action and passengers leaving the lift are signaled by an `exit` action. Specify a safety property in *FSP* which when composed with the lift will check that the system never allows the lift that it controls to have more than ten occupants.

7.3 Specify a safety property for the car park problem of Chapter 5, which asserts that the car park does not overflow. Specify a progress property which asserts that cars eventually enter the car park. If car departure is lower priority than car arrival, does starvation occur?

7.4 In an operating system, a binary semaphore is used to control access to the console. The console is used by user processes and system processes. Construct a model of this system and investigate the scheduling conditions under which user processes may be denied access to the console.

7.5 Implement the system modeled in exercise 7.4 in Java using the `ThreadPanel` and `NumberCanvas` classes for display. Can you induce starvation in a user thread by giving it a lower scheduling priority using `Thread.setPriority()`? If not, can you explain why starvation does not occur?

7.6 Two warring neighbors are separated by a field with wild berries. They agree to permit each other to enter the field to pick berries, but also need to ensure that only one of them is ever in the field at a time. After negotiation, they agree to the following protocol.

When one neighbor wants to enter the field, he raises a flag. If he sees his neighbor's flag, he does not enter but lowers his flag and tries again. If he does not see his neighbor's flag, he enters the field and picks berries. He lowers his flag after leaving the field.

Model this algorithm for two neighbors, `n1` and `n2`. Specify the required *safety* property for the field and check that it does indeed ensure mutually exclusive access. Specify the required *progress* properties for the neighbors such that they both get to pick berries given a fair scheduling strategy. Are there any adverse circumstances in which neighbors would not make progress? What if the neighbors are greedy?

(*Hint*: The following *FSP* can be used to model the flags.)

```
const True = 1    const False = 0
range Bool = False..True
set BoolActions =
     {setTrue,setFalse,[False],[True]}

BOOLVAR = VAL[False],
VAL[v:Bool] = ( setTrue -> VAL[True]
              | setFalse -> VAL[False]
              | [v] -> VAL[v]
              ).

||FLAGS = (flag1:BOOLVAR||flag2:BOOLVAR).
```

7.7 Peterson's Algorithm for two processes (Peterson, G.L., 1981)

Fortunately for the neighbors in exercise 7.6, Gary Peterson visits one day and explains his algorithm to them. He explains that, in addition to the flags, the neighbors must share a *turn* indicator which can take the values 1 or 2. This is used to avoid potential deadlock.

When one neighbor wants to enter the field, he raises his flag and sets the turn indicator to indicate his neighbor. If he sees his neighbor's flag and it is his neighbor's turn, he may not enter but must try again later. Otherwise, he can enter the field and pick berries and must lower his flag after leaving the field.

For instance, neighbor `n1` behaves as shown below, and neighbor `n2` behaves symmetrically.

```
while (true) {
      flag1 = true; turn = 2;
      while (flag2 and turn==2) {};
      enterField; pickBerries;
       flag1 = false;
}
```

Model Peterson's Algorithm for the two neighbors. Check that it does indeed avoid deadlock and satisfy the mutual exclusion (safety) and berry-picking (progress) properties.

(*Hint*: The following *FSP* can be used to model the turn indicator.)

```
set CardActions = {set1,set2,[1],[2]}

CARDVAR = VAL[1],
VAL[i:Card] = ( set1 -> VAL[1]
              | set2 -> VAL[2]
              | [i] -> VAL[i]
              ).
```

7.8 Implement Peterson's Algorithm as modeled in exercise 7.7.

8
Model-Based Design

Modeling is widely used in engineering design. Models are simplified representations of the real world, designed to include only those aspects relevant to the problem at hand. The reduction in scale and complexity achieved by modeling enables design engineers to analyze their designs to check the properties of interest.

For instance, a structural engineer may build a mathematical model of a particular bridge design to investigate its strength. Using different model parameters to represent differing situations and materials, the engineer analyzes the stresses and strains on the structural components of the proposed bridge, thereby assessing its strength. The engineer uses data from past experience and knowledge and skill to design and tailor the model such that it accurately reflects the behavior of a real bridge. This is essential if the faults found in the model are to be true indications of faults that could occur in the real bridge, and conversely that the lack of faults indicates a sound design for a fault-free bridge. Thus the engineer interprets the model behavior in order to infer behavior of the real bridge. Of course, the engineer may need to modify the design and corresponding model until, satisfied with the results, he or she can continue with confidence on the path to bridge construction.

As illustrated in the preceding chapters, this book takes a modeling approach to the design of concurrent programs. Our models represent the concurrent behavior of real concurrent programs written in Java. We abstract much of the detail of the real programs, neglecting aspects concerned with data representation, resource usage and user interaction. Instead, we focus on actions, interactions and concurrency. For instance, in our model of the bridge for the single-lane bridge problem in the previous chapter, we are only concerned with the `enter` and `exit` actions of a car. We therefore restrict our model to these actions. We model the constraints imposed on these actions by the cars and the bridge, and investigate the particular safety and progress properties of interest. Adjustments, such as action priorities, are made to the model to ''stress-test'' it and to ensure continuing correspondence between the model and the desired program. Safety and progress violations, and the associated trace and path information, require interpretation to understand the circumstances of the violation and the implications for the program. The model provides a sound basis for proceeding towards program construction with greater confidence, insight and understanding.

This chapter recapitulates and consolidates the concepts presented in previous chapters. It carefully and systematically describes the process of moving from system requirements through modeling to programming. No particular design method is imposed, since different designers may choose to use different techniques according to their own particular training or experience, or according to the particular system application. The intention is to emphasize the role and utility of modeling in association with any design method. Modeling and program design go hand-in-hand when designing any software, but it is particularly important when constructing concurrent programs. The example of a cruise control system for a car is used to illustrate the description. This was briefly introduced in Chapter 1; for convenience, we repeat the description and deal with it in detail in this chapter.

8.1 From Requirements to Models

The *requirements specification* of a system states the goals that the system is expected to satisfy. These are couched in application domain terms, describing the desired behavior of the proposed system in the context of its environment. It is the responsibility of the requirements engineers to elicit the requirements from the system stakeholders and to produce the requirements specification. Even at this stage, models are essential to facilitate understanding and analysis. For instance, the different scenarios that the system should support can be captured as use case models using the Unified Modeling Language (UML). These provide a description of the various actors that interact with the system and the typical interactions. Use case scenarios can also be useful later in examining traces in the design model and test cases in the implemented system. Furthermore, the requirements specification should identify the particular properties of interest. This can help to articulate the safety and progress properties which must hold for the system.

The process of design is required to decompose the requirements into a *design architecture*. This describes the gross organization and global structure of the system in terms of its constituent components. In order to cope with complexity, hierarchical composition is employed. Quite simply, this means that the architecture is composed from components such that each component may be composite, constructed from simpler components.

The *components* of a design architecture have a state, exhibit some well-defined behavior, and have a unique identity. The identity distinguishes it from all other components; the behavior represents its outwardly visible and testable activity;

and the state of a component represents the cumulative results of its behavior. Design architectures and components satisfy the basic three principles underlying object-oriented approaches:

- *Abstraction* – this is the removal or neglecting of unnecessary detail. Levels of abstraction are supported by moving up and down the hierarchy of composed components.
- *Encapsulation* – components encapsulate local behavior and information, and only expose activity at their interfaces. Components thereby provide information-hiding facilities.
- *Modularity* – the architecture provides an organizing structure of components which dictates the component compositions and interactions.

Any design approach which produces a decomposition into components may be used to provide an outline design architecture. The main activities are as follows:

- Identify the main actions and interactions of the system.
- Identify the main components of the system.
- Structure the components into an architecture.

The aim is to produce an outline architecture that can be used to informally check that all the required system functionality is satisfied. This would include informal checks that the use case scenarios are supported and that the properties of interest are satisfied.

However, in order to check the adequacy and validity of a proposed design in a more rigorous manner, it is necessary to model the system behavior more precisely. A structure diagram model can be used as a precise form of design architecture for a system. Structure diagrams were introduced in Chapter 3 and have been used in subsequent chapters to describe the structure of the models in terms of processes and their interactions. Processes model components and composite processes model composite components. Action hiding, relabeling and sharing are used to model component encapsulation and interaction respectively.

8.1.1 A Cruise Control System

An automobile cruise control system has the following requirements. It is controlled by three buttons: *resume*, *on* and *off* (Figure 8.1). When the engine is running and *on* is pressed, the cruise control system records the current speed and maintains the car at this speed. When the accelerator, brake or *off* is pressed, the cruise control system disengages but retains the speed setting. If *resume* is pressed, the system accelerates or de-accelerates the car back to the previously-recorded speed.

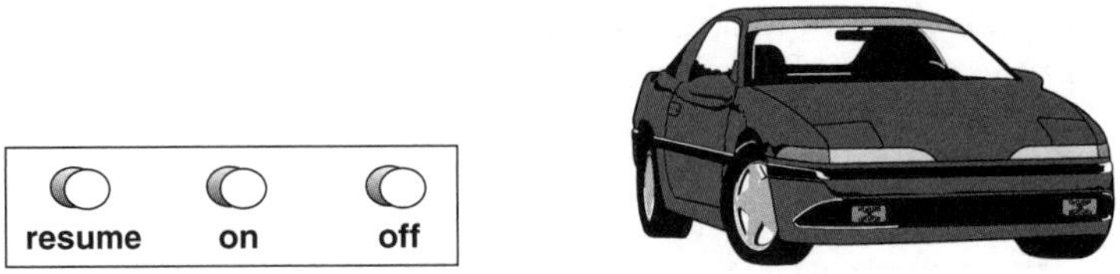

Figure 8.1 Cruise control system.

The hardware that supports the cruise control system is shown in Figure 8.2. It consists of a Parallel Interface Adapter (PIA) which records the actions of the buttons (*on*, *off* and *resume*), the brake (pressed), the accelerator (pressed) and the engine (on or off). The PIA is polled periodically every 100 msec to determine if any of these actions has occurred. A wheel revolution sensor generates interrupts for every wheel revolution in order to enable the system to calculate the current speed of the car. The cruise control system controls the car speed by setting the throttle of the car via a digital-to-analog converter (D/A).

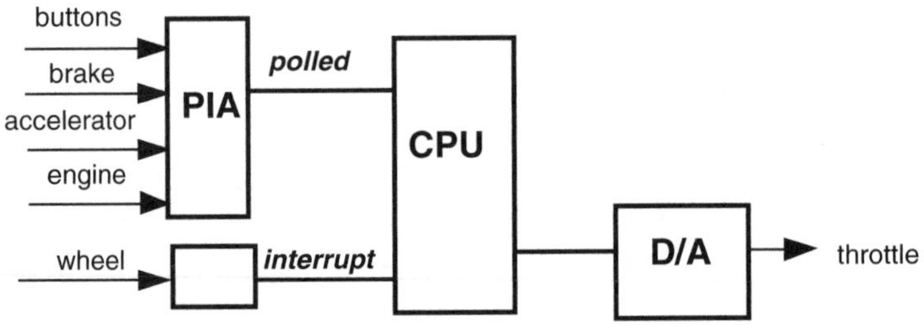

Figure 8.2 Hardware constraints.

8.1.2 Structure of the Model

The structure diagram and actions for the cruise control system shown in Figure 8.3 can be produced using the following design activities:

- Identify the main actions and interactions of the system.
- Identify and define the main processes of the system.
- Identify the main properties of the system.
- Structure the processes into a structure diagram.

These activities correspond to those used in previous chapters and are a refined version of those described above for producing a design architecture. The additional

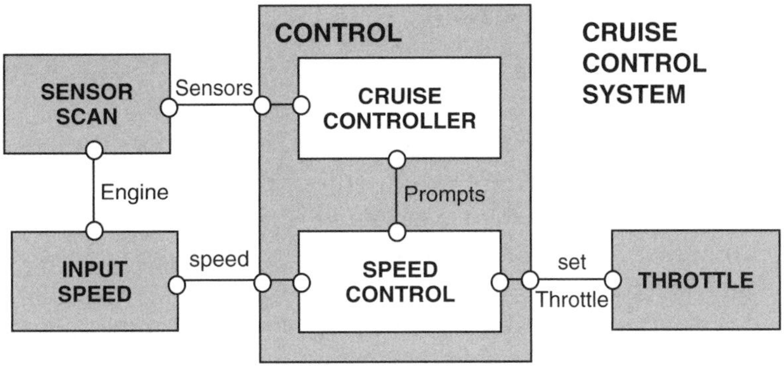

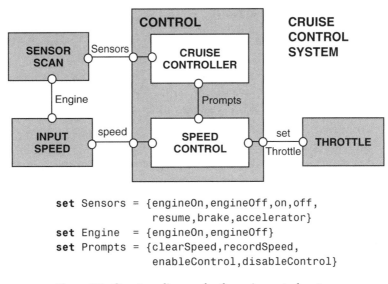

```
set Sensors = {engineOn,engineOff,on,off,
               resume,brake,accelerator}
set Engine  = {engineOn,engineOff}
set Prompts = {clearSpeed,recordSpeed,
               enableControl,disableControl}
```

Figure 8.3 Structure diagram for the cruise control system.

consideration of the properties is to ensure that the model includes those actions necessary for property checking, either as shared actions or actions internal to a process. For instance, we wish to ensure that the cruise control system is disengaged when the brake, accelerator or *off* button is pressed and that the throttle is eventually set. We discuss these properties later in the chapter.

The main internal control for the cruise control system is provided by two processes: the cruise controller and the speed control. The interface to the external sensors and actuators is provided by the other three processes: sensor scan, input speed and throttle. The cruise controller receives the buttons, brake, accelerator and engine events from the sensor scan. The input speed process monitors the speed when the engine is on and provides the current speed readings to the speed control. Depending on the circumstances, cruise controller triggers clear or record the speed, and enable or disable the speed control. The speed control then sets the throttle accordingly. In this way, the sensor scan encapsulates (information hiding) the periodic process of scanning the sensors, the cruise controller encapsulates the decision as to when speed maintenance is activated, and the speed control encapsulates how to record and maintain speed.

As described in earlier chapters, it is beneficial to model and analyze the system design before embarking on implementation. Parallel composition can be used to compose the system from the model processes according to the composition hierarchy. Animation can be used for scenario checking, and automated model checking can be used for verification of safety and progress properties.

8.1.3 Model Elaboration

Each of the processes is defined in Figure 8.4. The sensors are repeatedly scanned; the input speed is repeatedly monitored when the engine is on; and, when the throttle is set, the car "zooms" off! Speed control is initially disabled. It clears and records the current speed setting, and, when it is enabled, it sets the throttle according to the current speed and the recorded speed. The behavior of the cruise controller is as follows. When the engine is switched on, `clearSpeed` is triggered and the cruise controller becomes active. When active, pressing the *on* button triggers recording the current speed and enables the speed control. The system is then cruising. Pressing the *on* button again triggers recording the new current speed and the system remains cruising. Pressing the *off* button, brake or accelerator disables the speed control and sets the system to standby. Switching the engine off at any time makes the system inactive.

```
set Sensors = {engineOn,engineOff,on,off,
               resume,brake,accelerator}
set Engine  = {engineOn,engineOff}
set Prompts = {clearSpeed,recordSpeed,
               enableControl,disableControl}

SENSORSCAN = ({Sensors} -> SENSORSCAN).

INPUTSPEED = (engineOn -> CHECKSPEED),
CHECKSPEED = (speed -> CHECKSPEED
             |engineOff -> INPUTSPEED
             ).

THROTTLE =(setThrottle -> zoom -> THROTTLE).

SPEEDCONTROL = DISABLED,
DISABLED =({speed,clearSpeed,recordSpeed}->DISABLED
          | enableControl -> ENABLED
          ),
ENABLED  =( speed -> setThrottle -> ENABLED
          |{recordSpeed,enableControl} -> ENABLED
          | disableControl -> DISABLED
          ).

set DisableActions = {off,brake,accelerator}
```

Figure 8.4 Model for the cruise control system.

```
CRUISECONTROLLER = INACTIVE,
INACTIVE =(engineOn -> clearSpeed -> ACTIVE
          |DisableActions -> INACTIVE
          ),
ACTIVE   =(engineOff -> INACTIVE
          |on->recordSpeed->enableControl->CRUISING
          |DisableActions -> ACTIVE
          ),
CRUISING =(engineOff -> INACTIVE
          |DisableActions->disableControl->STANDBY
          |on->recordSpeed->enableControl->CRUISING
          ),
STANDBY  =(engineOff -> INACTIVE
          |resume -> enableControl -> CRUISING
          |on->recordSpeed->enableControl->CRUISING
          |DisableActions -> STANDBY
          ).
```

Figure 8.4 (*Continued*).

The corresponding LTS diagram for each of these processes can be inspected to check that the process does indeed model the desired, intuitive behavior. For example, the INPUTSPEED and SPEEDCONTROL LTS diagrams are shown in Figures 8.5 and 8.6 respectively. The LTS diagrams for SPEEDCONTROL and

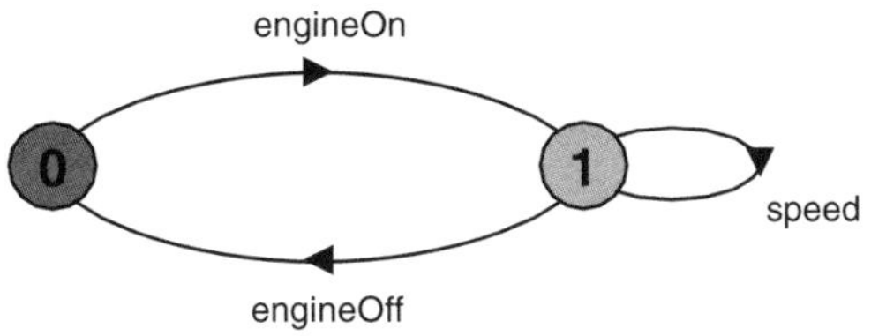

Figure 8.5 LTS diagram for INPUTSPEED.

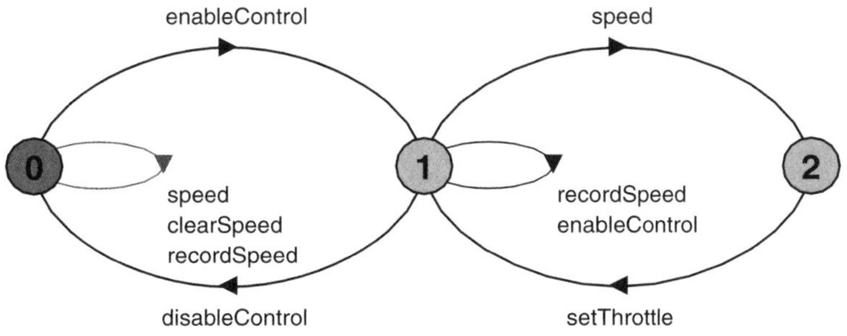

Figure 8.6 LTS diagram for SPEEDCONTROL.

CRUISECONTROLLER are rather complex for easy inspection. At this stage it is often easier to use animation as a means of checking the general process behavior. For instance, the CONTROL subsystem (Figure 8.3) is composed as follows:

```
||CONTROL =(CRUISECONTROLLER||SPEEDCONTROL).
```

It can be animated to produce answers to the following questions:

- Is control enabled after the engine is switched on and the *on* button is pressed?
- Is control disabled when the brake is then pressed?
- Is control enabled when resume is then pressed?

The trace depicted on Figure 8.7 confirms this behavior: Note that the trace also illustrates that, when control is enabled, the speed input causes the throttle to be set, and when disabled, it does not. Although various scenarios help to improve our confidence in the adequacy of the model and its behavior, they do not provide an exhaustive check over all possible execution paths. To this end, we need to specify the safety properties of interest.

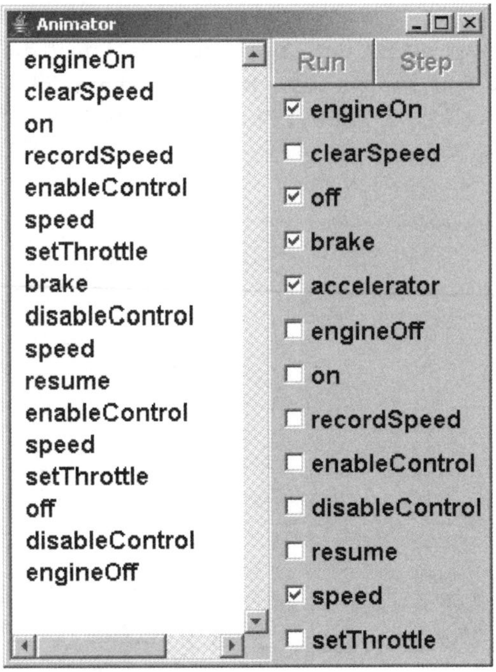

Figure 8.7 CONTROL trace.

8.1.4 Safety Properties

Safety checks are compositional in the sense that, if there is no violation at a subsystem level, then there cannot be a violation when the subsystem is composed with other subsystems. This is because, if the ERROR state of a particular safety property is unreachable in the LTS of the subsystem, it remains unreachable in any subsequent parallel composition which includes the subsystem. Safety checks can therefore be conducted directly on the subsystems which exhibit the behavior to be checked. The following guidelines are used when performing safety checks:

> Safety properties should be composed with the appropriate system or subsystem to which the property refers. In order that the property can check the actions in its alphabet, these actions must not be hidden in the system.

A safety property required of the CONTROL subsystem is as follows:

```
property CRUISESAFETY =
      ({DisableActions,disableControl}
                    -> CRUISESAFETY
      |{on,resume} -> SAFETYCHECK
      ),
SAFETYCHECK =
      ({on,resume} -> SAFETYCHECK
      |DisableActions  -> SAFETYACTION
      |disableControl  -> CRUISESAFETY
      ),
SAFETYACTION =(disableControl->CRUISESAFETY).
```

This property states that, if the CONTROL subsystem is enabled by pressing the on or resume buttons, then pressing the off button, the brake or the accelerator should result in the control system being disabled. The LTS diagram for this property is shown in Figure 8.8. We compose CRUISESAFETY with the CONTROL subsystem processes (Figure 8.3) as follows:

```
||CONTROL =
     (CRUISECONTROLLER||SPEEDCONTROL||CRUISESAFETY).
```

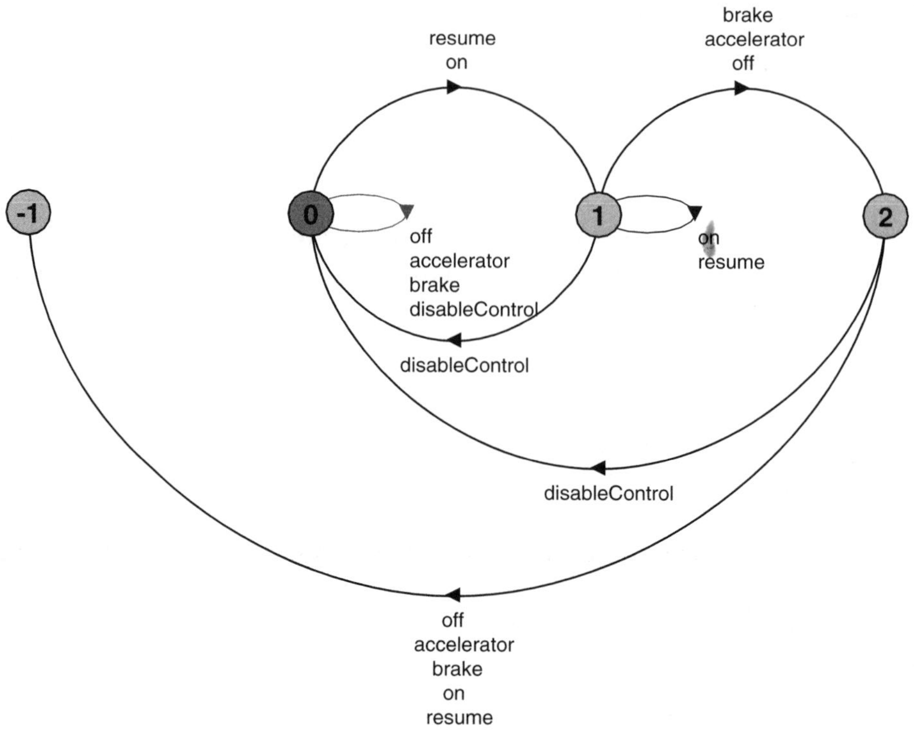

Figure 8.8 LTS diagram for the property `CRUISESAFETY`.

Safety analysis using LTSA produces the following violation:

```
Trace to property violation in CRUISESAFETY:
     engineOn
     clearSpeed
     on
     recordSpeed
     enableControl
     engineOff
     off
     off
```

This indicates a violation of the safety property in rather strange circumstances. If the system is enabled by switching the engine on and pressing the *on* button, and then the engine is switched off, it appears that the control system is not disabled, and disabling actions such as pressing the *off* button can be performed without the system being disabled. What if the engine were switched on again?

To investigate this, we can animate the control system to produce a trace as follows:

```
engineOn
clearSpeed
on
recordSpeed
enableControl
engineOff
engineOn
speed
setThrottle
speed
setThrottle
...
```

If the control system remains enabled, then the car will accelerate and zoom off when the engine is switched on again! This is a highly dangerous situation and one that should definitely be avoided.

To further investigate the circumstances which lead to this violation, we can also examine a minimized LTS diagram of the control system, without the safety property and in which only the `Sensors` and `speed` actions are visible:

```
||CONTROLMINIMIZED =(CRUISECONTROLLER||SPEEDCONTROL)
                    @ {Sensors,speed}.
```

Action hiding and minimization help to reduce the size of the diagram and make it easier to interpret. `CONTROLMINIMIZED` produces the LTS diagram in Figure 8.9 which clearly illustrates the situation where, once the engine is switched on again, the only action which can be performed is `speed`.

8.1.5 Revising the Model

How can this potentially catastrophic situation be avoided? It is clear that control should be disabled when the engine is switched off. This would ensure that control is not enabled when the engine is switched on again. The required change to the `CRUISECONTROLLER` is as follows:

```
...
CRUISING =(engineOff -> disableControl -> INACTIVE
          |DisableActions->disableControl->STANDBY
          |on->recordSpeed->enableControl->CRUISING
          ),
...
```

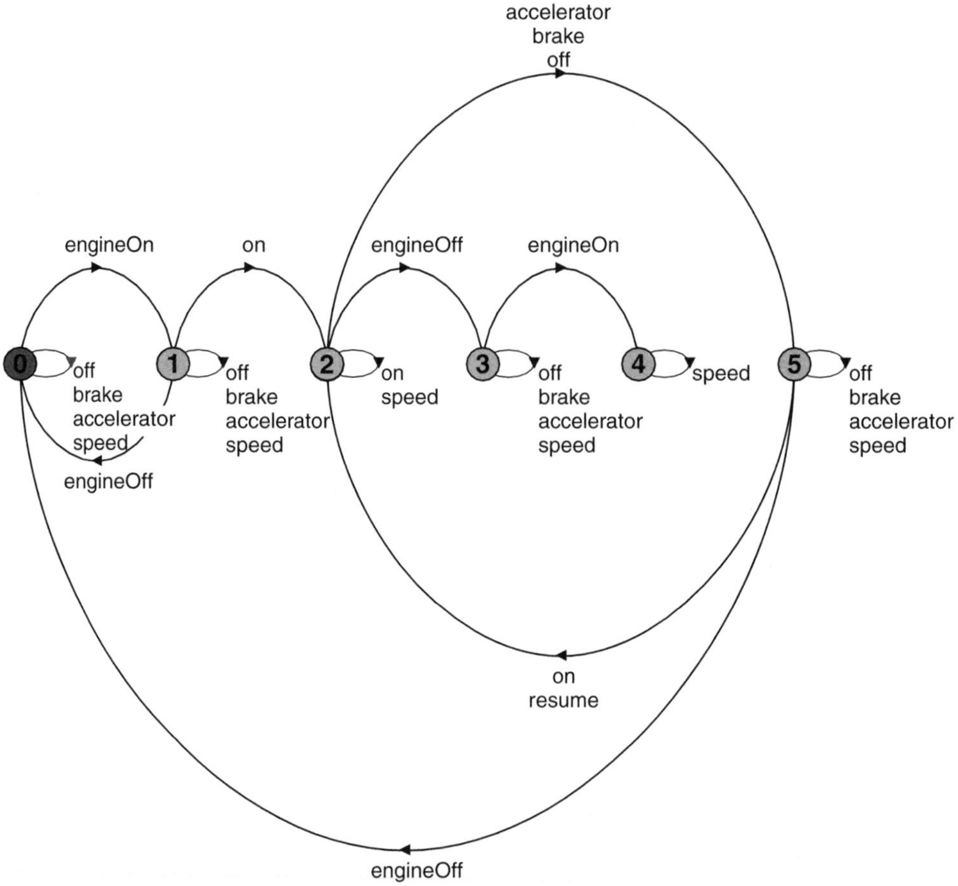

Figure 8.9 Minimized LTS diagram for CONTROLMINIMIZED.

The CRUISESAFETY safety property did not include a check on the engine status. This must now be included to form an improved safety property:

```
property IMPROVEDSAFETY =
      ({DisableActions,disableControl,
           engineOff} -> IMPROVEDSAFETY
      |{on,resume}     -> SAFETYCHECK
      ),
SAFETYCHECK =
      ({on,resume}     -> SAFETYCHECK
      |{DisableActions,engineOff}
                       -> SAFETYACTION
```

```
        |disableControl -> IMPROVEDSAFETY
        ),
   SAFETYACTION =
        (disableControl -> IMPROVEDSAFETY).
```

We can now repeat the analysis process as before. This time there are no safety violations. The minimized control system, as shown in Figure 8.10, is clearly reassuring. It indicates that the control system returns to the initial state when the engine is switched off.

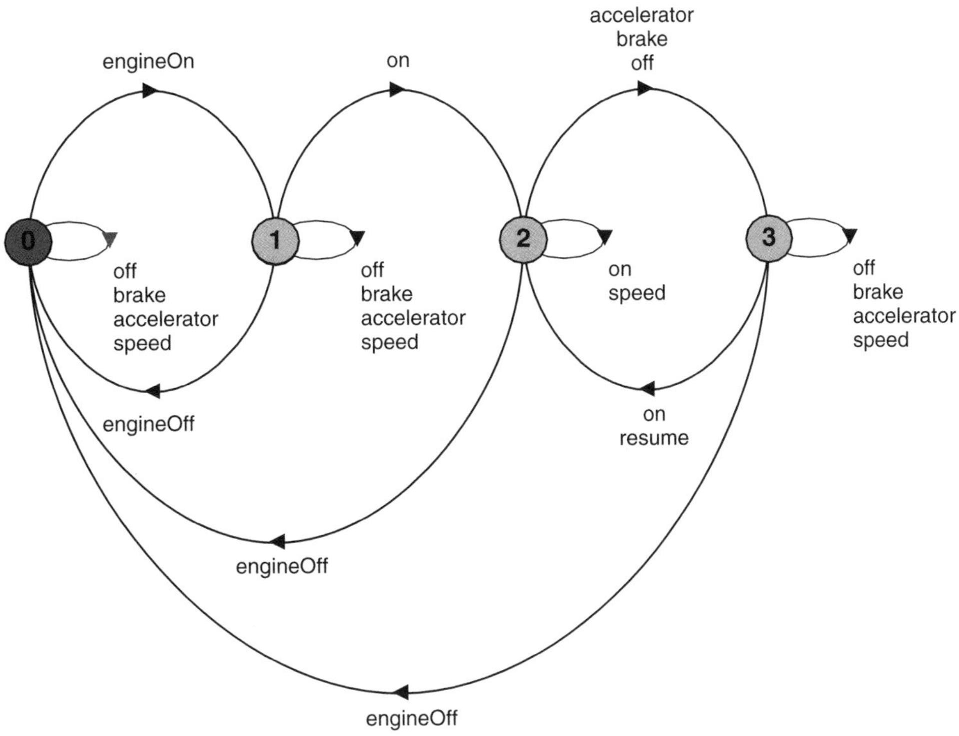

Figure 8.10 Minimized LTS diagram for the revised CONTROLMINIMIZED.

We can now hide internal actions and proceed with the composition of that subsystem to form the complete cruise control system.

```
||CONTROL =
  (CRUISECONTROLLER||SPEEDCONTROL||IMPROVEDSAFETY)
    @ {Sensors,speed,setThrottle}.
```

```
||CRUISECONTROLSYSTEM =
    (CONTROL||SENSORSCAN||INPUTSPEED||THROTTLE).
```

Safety analysis using LTSA verifies that the `CRUISECONTROLSYSTEM` does not deadlock nor violate the revised safety property.

8.1.6 Progress Properties

Progress checks are *not* compositional. Even if there is no violation at a subsystem level, there may still be a violation when the subsystem is composed with other subsystems. This is because an action in the subsystem may satisfy progress yet be unreachable when the subsystem is composed with other subsystems which constrain its behavior. Furthermore, action priority acts to discard lower priority action transitions in preference to higher priority ones. With parallel composition, higher priority actions may become unreachable thereby removing particular choices and requiring the restoration of the lower priority actions. We therefore conduct progress checks on the complete target system.

> Progress checks should be conducted on the complete target system after satisfactory completion of the safety checks.

We can now subject the cruise control system to progress checks, such as that the throttle is eventually set. In fact, the cruise control system is expected to be capable of operating repeatedly whenever the engine is switched on. Hence, we would expect that *no* action suffers starvation and that it is always that case that *every* action can eventually be chosen. We therefore perform a general progress test without specifying particular sets of progress actions. If this general test produces no violations, then we can be certain that there are no violations for any specific progress property. This is the case here, and progress analysis using *LTSA* on the `CRUISECONTROLSYSTEM` produces no violations.

However, progress analysis on the original, unrevised `CRUISECONTROLSYSTEM`, without the safety property, produces the following interesting progress violation:

```
Progress violation for actions:
{accelerator, brake, clearSpeed,
disableControl, enableControl, engineOff,
```

```
engineOn, off, on, recordSpeed, resume}
Trace to terminal set of states:
     engineOn
     clearSpeed
     on
     recordSpeed
     enableControl
     engineOff
     engineOn
Cycle in terminal set:
     speed
     setThrottle
     zoom
Actions in terminal set:
     {setThrottle, speed, zoom}
```

The trace confirms the interpretation that control is not disabled when the engine is switched off. Switching the engine on again leads to the terminal set in which the only actions permitted are speed input, the setting of the throttle and the resulting car `zoom` action. This can be clearly seen in Figure 8.9, except that there the actions `setThrottle` and `zoom` are hidden.

Further analysis of the model could be conducted to investigate system behavior under particular adverse conditions. For instance, we could employ action priorities to check progress when sensors are given high priority.

```
||SENSORSHIGH = CRUISECONTROLSYSTEM << {Sensors}.
```

No progress violations are detected. However, if the sensors are given a low priority:

```
||SENSORSLOW = CRUISECONTROLSYSTEM >> {Sensors}.
```

then the `speed` action dominates and, on analysis, we obtain the following violation:

```
Progress violation for actions:
{engineOn, engineOff, on, off, brake,
accelerator, resume, setThrottle, zoom}
Path to terminal set of states:
     engineOn
     tau
Actions in terminal set:
{speed}
```

This seems to indicate that the system may be sensitive to the priority of the action `speed`. This can be confirmed since, making `speed` a high priority is similar to making `Sensors` low, and making `speed` a low priority results in the following violation:

```
Progress violation for actions:
{speed, setThrottle, zoom}
Path to terminal set of states:
Actions in terminal set:
{engineOn, engineOff, on, off, brake,
accelerator, resume}
```

Thus, models such as this can be used to indicate system sensitivities. If it is possible that erroneous situations detected in the model may occur in the implemented system, then the model should be revised to find a design which ensures that those violations are avoided. However, if it is considered that the real system will not exhibit this behavior, then no further model revisions are necessary. In this way, model interpretation and correspondence to the implementation are important in determining the relevance and adequacy of the model design and its analysis.

In the cruise control system, `speed` monitoring needs to be carefully controlled so that it neither dominates nor suffers from starvation. If we are confident that this can indeed be achieved in our implementation, then we need perform no further modeling. We now turn our attention to an implementation of the cruise control system, based on the model.

8.2 From Models to Implementations

As mentioned, a design architecture describes the gross organization and global structure of the system in terms of its constituent components. In order to support behavior modeling and analysis, the architecture supports an elaborated *view* of its structure and the behavior of its components. We have used structure diagrams and *FSP* for this purpose. However, there are other forms of model and analysis that might be of interest (Figure 8.11). These too can be considered as views on the underlying structure, the elaboration adding those particular details of concern. For instance, another example of a view is a performance model, such as a queuing network.

Our particular concern after modeling is implementation. Note that even the implementation of the system should be considered as an elaboration of the underlying design architecture. Here the detail is the implementation of the component processes as threads and monitors. Maintaining consistency between these views is facilitated by the fact that the architectural structure is common to the different model views and the implementation.

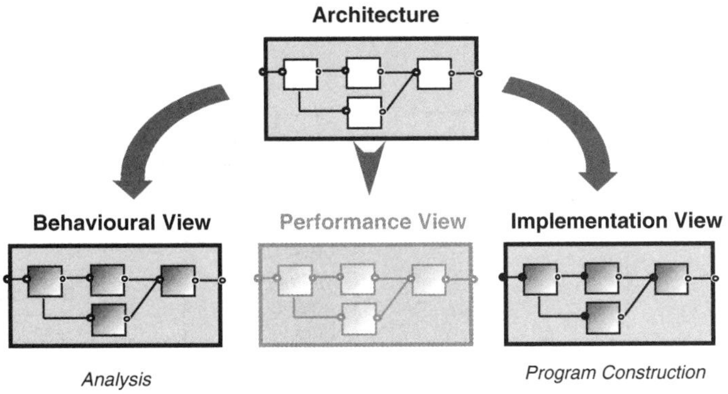

Figure 8.11 Design architecture, behavior model and other models.

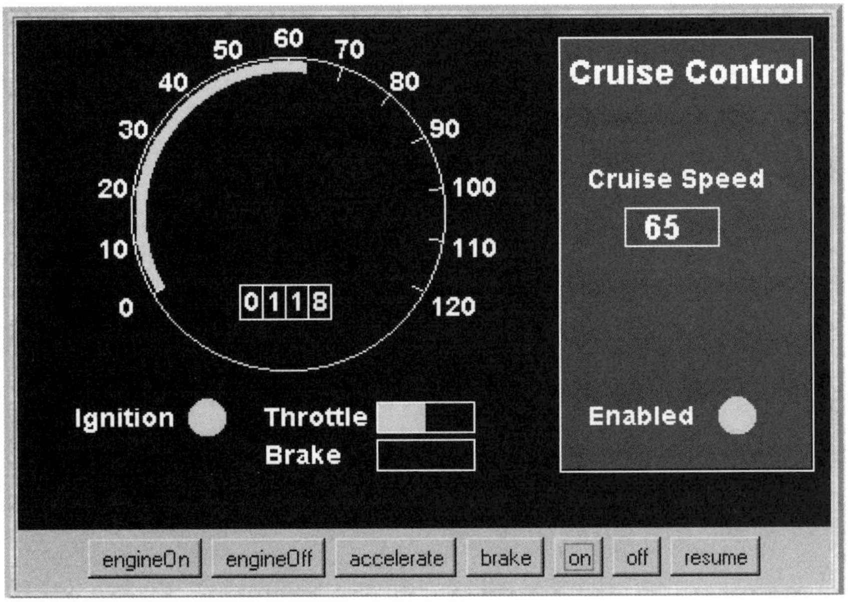

Figure 8.12 Cruise control applet display.

The program described in this section provides a simulation for the environment in which the cruise control implementation executes. Our simulation is a Java applet that provides buttons to simulate the actions of accelerating, braking and turning on and off both the engine and the cruise control system. Car speed is displayed on a simulated speedometer, which includes an odometer that registers the distance the car has progressed. A screen shot of the cruise control applet is depicted in Figure 8.12. The display shows the situation in which cruise control

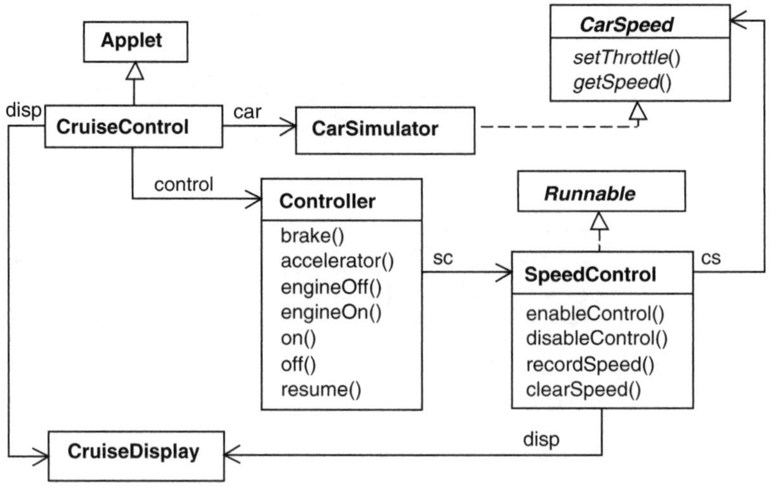

Figure 8.13 Cruise control class diagram.

has been enabled to maintain the car at a steady speed of 65 miles per hour. The car has moved 1.18 miles since it was started.

The class diagram for the cruise control program is shown in Figure 8.13. The classes `Controller` and `SpeedControl` implement the model processes `CRUISECONTROLLER` and `SPEEDCONTROL`. `SpeedControl` interacts with the car simulation provided by the class `CarSimulator` via the interface `CarSpeed`. This interface provides methods to set the throttle and to get the current speed at which the car is traveling. We have introduced this interface so that the classes implementing control are insulated from all the details of the simulation. The interface is listed in Program 8.1.

```
public interface CarSpeed {

    public int getSpeed();

    public void setThrottle(double val);

}
```

Program 8.1 `CarSpeed` interface.

When a button is pressed, this event is passed by the `Applet` class to both the car simulator and the cruise controller using a method call. Thus, the `Controller` class provides a method corresponding to each button.

The implementation of Controller follows directly from the model process CRUISECONTROLLER. Each method modifies the control state and invokes speed control actions. The implementation is listed in Program 8.2. Controller is a passive entity; it always reacts to events and does not instigate them. It is implemented as a monitor with each model action becoming a synchronized method.

In contrast, SpeedControl, listed in Program 8.3, is an active entity. When it is enabled, a thread is created which periodically obtains the current car speed from the car simulator and sets the throttle so that the target cruising speed is maintained. The thread terminates when speed control is disabled. The run() method is also **synchronized** to prevent interference with the other methods of the class, and uses a wait with timeout to provide periodic execution. The wait(long) method of Java can be used to put the current thread to sleep until it is notified or the specified timeout period (in milliseconds) elapses.

```
class Controller {
  final static int INACTIVE  = 0;  // cruise controller states
  final static int ACTIVE    = 1;
  final static int CRUISING  = 2;
  final static int STANDBY   = 3;
  private int controlState  = INACTIVE;  // initial state
  private SpeedControl sc;
  Controller(CarSpeed cs, CruiseDisplay disp)
    {sc=new SpeedControl(cs,disp);}

  synchronized void brake(){
    if (controlState==CRUISING )
      {sc.disableControl(); controlState=STANDBY; }
  }

  synchronized void accelerator(){
    if (controlState==CRUISING )
      {sc.disableControl(); controlState=STANDBY; }
  }

  synchronized void engineOff(){
    if(controlState!=INACTIVE) {
      if (controlState==CRUISING) sc.disableControl();
      controlState=INACTIVE;
    }
  }
```

Program 8.2 Controller class.

```
    synchronized void engineOn(){
      if(controlState==INACTIVE)
        {sc.clearSpeed(); controlState=ACTIVE;}
    }

    synchronized void on(){
      if(controlState!=INACTIVE){
        sc.recordSpeed(); sc.enableControl();
        controlState=CRUISING;
      }
    }

    synchronized void off(){
      if(controlState==CRUISING )
        {sc.disableControl(); controlState=STANDBY;}
    }

    synchronized void resume(){
      if(controlState==STANDBY)
       {sc.enableControl(); controlState=CRUISING;}
    }
  }
```

Program 8.2 *(Continued)*.

`SpeedControl` is the first example we have met of a class that combines both synchronized access methods and a thread. We could have implemented it as two classes, a purely passive entity which encapsulated the `state` and `setSpeed` variables and an active entity with only a `run()` method. However, this would have been unnecessarily complex and would lead to additional methods to set and get the variables. As implemented, the class satisfactorily encapsulates the thread and the methods that control its execution.

Summary

This chapter has consolidated the model-based approach used in previous chapters. It has described the process of progressing from system requirements through modeling to programming. The main activities were identified, including system decomposition into a model structure and model elaboration, analysis and revision, if necessary. The stage at which properties are checked was also discussed. Safety properties can be checked on system or subsystem models as

```
class SpeedControl implements Runnable {
  final static int DISABLED = 0; //speed control states
  final static int ENABLED  = 1;
  private int state = DISABLED;  //initial state
  private int setSpeed = 0;      //target cruise control speed
  private Thread speedController;
  private CarSpeed cs;           //interface to control speed of engine
  private CruiseDisplay disp;

  SpeedControl(CarSpeed cs, CruiseDisplay disp){
    this.cs=cs; this.disp=disp;
    disp.disable(); disp.record(0);
  }

  synchronized void recordSpeed(){
    setSpeed=cs.getSpeed(); disp.record(setSpeed);
  }

  synchronized void clearSpeed(){
    if (state==DISABLED) {setSpeed=0;disp.record(setSpeed);}
  }

  synchronized void enableControl(){
    if (state==DISABLED) {
      disp.enable(); speedController= new Thread(this);
      speedController.start(); state=ENABLED;
    }
  }

  synchronized void disableControl(){
    if (state==ENABLED)  {disp.disable(); state=DISABLED;}
  }

  synchronized public void run() {  //the speed controller thread
    try {
      while (state==ENABLED) {
        double error = (float)(setSpeed-cs.getSpeed())/6.0;
        double steady = (double)setSpeed/12.0;
        cs.setThrottle(steady+error); //simplified feed back control
        wait(500);
       }
    } catch (InterruptedException e) {}
    speedController=null;
 }
```

Program 8.3 `SpeedControl` class.

appropriate. Progress checks need to be performed on the overall system model. The mapping of a model structure into an implementation was also described. No particular design method is imposed. We advocate modeling in association with every design method. Modeling complements program design and is particularly useful when constructing concurrent programs.

A cruise control system for a car was used to illustrate the model-based design approach. This system was briefly introduced in Chapter 1 to motivate model-based design; it was dealt with in detail in this chapter, giving both the model details and an implementation in Java.

Notes and Further Reading

There are numerous books that describe software design methods and techniques, most of which include some form of informal modeling and reasoning to help in the design process. However, few use modeling in a rigorous fashion. One of the exceptions is Giorgio Bruno's book, *Model-Based Software Engineering* (1995), which uses Petri Net models. Another technique of interest is ROOM (Real-Time Object-Oriented Modeling) which combines a language for system structure with state machine models and is supported by the ObjecTime toolset for model execution (Selic, Gullekson and Ward, 1994). Statecharts (Harel, 1987) are supported by the STATEMATE (Harel, Lachover, Naamad, *et al.*, 1990) software tool and are used for the design of reactive systems. A form of statecharts is also incorporated in the UML approach (Fowler and Scott, 1997; Booch, Rumbaugh and Jacobson, 1998), which recognizes the importance of modeling and provides a basketful of modeling notations and techniques. See http://www.uml.org/.

The car cruise control system used in this chapter is a simplified version of a real system. Actual systems do not disengage when the accelerator is pressed, but retain the speed setting and return the car to that speed when the accelerator is released.

The example of the car cruise control system is originally due to Grady Booch (1986) who adapted it from an exercise provided by P. Ward at the Rocky Mountain Institute for Software Engineering. Since then, it has been widely used as an example for the design of concurrent and real-time systems. For instance, Hassan Gomaa uses it as a case study in his book, *Software Design Methods for Concurrent and Real-Time Systems* (1993). Mary Shaw uses it as a common example for *Comparing architectural design styles* (1995).

The process of moving from requirements to models is recognized as far from easy. One approach to facilitate early model construction is to synthesize the behavior model using scenarios, such as Message Sequence Charts (MSCs; ITU, 1996). Each scenario is a partial story, describing how system components, the environment and users work concurrently and interact in order to provide system-level functionality. Synthesis is required to combine these so as to provide meaningful behavior. There are a number of approaches that generate statechart models from MSCs such as that of Koskimies, Männistö, Systä, *et al.* (1998) and Whittle and Schumann (2000). Harel and Kugler (2000) generate state-based behavior models using Live Sequence Charts, an extension to MSCs. Uchitel, Kramer and Magee (2003) have provided an approach to synthesize *FSP* models from MSCs and an approach to help perform model elaboration (Uchitel, Kramer and Magee, 2004). Extensions to the *LTSA* support this work.

The constructed models (whether by design or by synthesis) are intended to provide behavior that represents reality and the user requirements. In much the same way as the simulations are used to demonstrate the behavior of the Java implementations, so graphic animation of model behavior can be useful to help users understand and check model behavior before implementation. Magee, Pryce, Giannakopoulou, *et al.* (2000) have provided a technique in which *LTS* behavior models can drive graphical animations. An XML document maps between the model and the animation, implemented as a set of JavaBeans. An extension to *LTSA* supports this work. Another interesting approach is proposed by Harel and Marelly who propose the use of a mock user as a means for playing in scenarios into an LSC interpreter called the Play-Engine (Harel and Marelly, 2003).

Exercises

8.1 Each of the rooms in a building has a control station for monitoring and controlling the environment. Each control station measures and displays the current temperature and humidity. For each room, the desired temperature and humidity is set by a pair of dials. If the current readings are outside the desired setting by more than 1%, then the station can control the heating or ventilation accordingly. A central operator station is able to request the current readings from any control station.

Outline the design structure of a room control station given that it is decomposed into the following processes: sensors, dials, heater – ventilator, display and controller. Provide a model for each process and check that the control station satisfies appropriate safety and progress properties.

Provide an implementation for the room control station.

8.2 A self-service gas station has a number of pumps for delivering gas to customers for their vehicles. Customers are expected to prepay a cashier for their gas. The cashier activates the pump to deliver gas.

Provide a model for a simple system with two customers and a gas station with one pump and a cashier. Include in the model a range for the different amounts of payment and that a customer is not satisfied (`ERROR`) if the incorrect amount of gas is delivered:

```
range A = 1..3
CUSTOMER = (prepay[a:A]->gas[x:A]->
                if (x==a) then CUSTOMER
                          else ERROR
           ).
```

Check the safety and progress properties for this system.
Provide a simple Java implementation for the gas station system.

8.3 Extend the gas station model in exercise 8.2 to cater for *N* customers and *M* pumps. Specify and check a safety property, FIFO, which ensures that customers are served in the order in which they pay.

9
Dynamic Systems

In the programs we have described so far, threads are created during initialization and they run until program termination. The organization of threads, and the monitors through which they interact in these programs, has been static during program execution. This chapter examines systems in which thread creation and termination occur dynamically during program execution. The number of active threads thus varies as execution progresses. This sort of behavior occurs in operating systems where processes are created dynamically in response to user commands. For example, when a user clicks on the word processor icon, a process is created to run the word processor program; when the user exits the word processor program, the process terminates.

To illustrate some of the issues involved in modeling and programming dynamic systems, we consider the problem of resource allocation in which dynamically created threads need variable amounts of a resource to proceed. To make the problem less abstract, we simulate a golf club with players simulated by threads and golf balls representing the resources they require.

A specific problem addressed in this chapter is the relevance of finite state models to dynamic systems. Briefly stated, the problem is that the models we construct must be static with a fixed number of processes to permit analysis, while a dynamic system has a variable number of processes. To see how this is handled, we proceed by developing the program first and then developing a model. We examine how much of the behavior of the dynamic system is captured in the static model and whether this static model is helpful in analyzing the behavior of the dynamic system.

Finally, the chapter looks at the use of the Java `join()` method, which permits a thread to wait for the termination of another thread, which it has usually created dynamically.

9.1 Golf Club Program

A golf club has a limited number of golf balls available for hire. Players can hire golf balls for their game from the club and return them to the club after use. Expert players, who tend not to lose any of their golf balls, only hire one or two. Novice players hire more balls, so that they have spares during the game in case of loss. However, they are required to buy replacements for lost balls so that they return the same number that they originally hired. To simulate the golf club as a Java program, we create a new thread for each player arriving at the golf club and use a monitor to control the hiring of golf balls to players. The display for the program is shown in Figure 9.1.

Figure 9.1 Golf Club applet display.

New players, with their golf ball requirements indicated in parentheses, are created by clicking the buttons at the bottom of the display. Each newly created player is given a name consisting of a letter, allocated consecutively in alphabetic order, and the number of golf balls the player requires. A newly created player appears briefly in the "new" window and then appears in the "wait golf balls" window if there are not enough golf balls available for the player to start playing. When the player acquires golf balls and starts playing, its identity appears in the "playing" window. When finished playing, the player's identity appears briefly in the "end" window. The "SimpleAllocator" window displays the state of the monitor controlling golf ball allocation. The maximum number of golf balls available is set to five.

Figure 9.1 depicts the situation in which there are currently no golf balls available for hire since all five are in use by players **c2, f1, e1** and **g1**. The novice player

d4 who requires four golf balls to start playing is thus waiting. Note that the expert players **e1, f1** and **g1** were created after **d4**. They have started playing before **d4** since at the time they requested golf balls, there were enough to satisfy their requirements but not enough to satisfy **d4**. In fact, if we keep creating new expert golfers that only require one or two golf balls, then the novice **d4** will continue waiting. A continuous stream of expert players arriving at the golf club can cause novices to wait forever. In other words, the program has a liveness problem in which novice players may experience *starvation*. Before examining this problem in more detail using a model, we describe the program that drives the display of Figure 9.1. The classes involved are depicted in the UML class diagram of Figure 9.2.

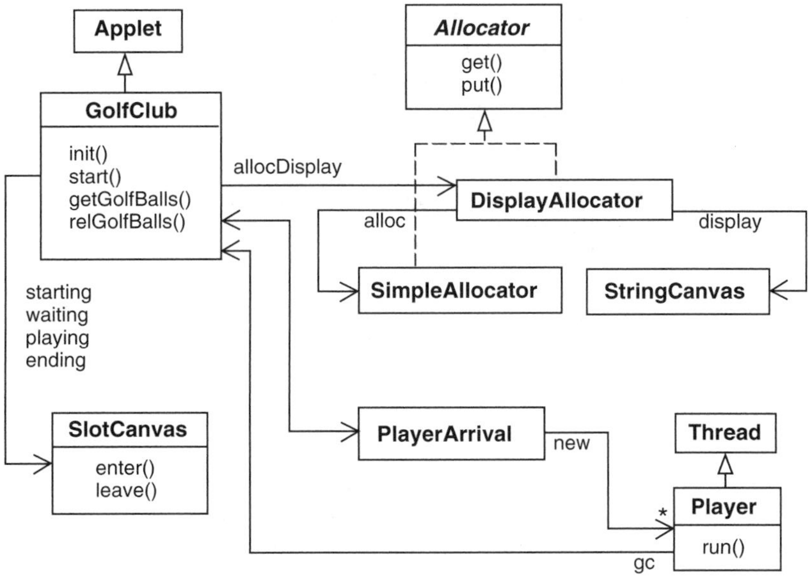

Figure 9.2 Golf Club class diagram.

We are going to develop a number of implementations of the golf ball allocator. To allow us to substitute these implementations without modifying the rest of the program, we define the Java interface `Allocator` as listed in Program 9.1. The `DisplayAllocator` class implements this interface and delegates calls to `get` and `put` golf balls to `SimpleAllocator` which actually implements the allocation monitor. In addition, `DisplayAllocator` displays the state of the monitor using the `StringCanvas` class we have used in previous chapters. The code for the `SimpleAllocator` monitor is also listed in Program 9.1.

From Program 9.1, it can be seen that a call to get n golf balls will block a calling thread until enough balls become available. When a thread returns golf balls, all

```
public interface Allocator {
  //get n golf balls
  public void get(int n) throws InterruptedException;
  //put back n golfballs
  public void put(int n);
}

public class SimpleAllocator implements Allocator {
  private int available;

  public SimpleAllocator(int n)
    { available = n; }

  synchronized public void get(int n)
           throws InterruptedException {
    while (n>available) wait();
    available -= n;
  }

  synchronized public void put(int n) {
    available += n;
    notifyAll();
  }
}
```

Program 9.1 `Allocator` interface and `SimpleAllocator` class.

blocked threads are awakened so that they can see if there are now sufficient for them to proceed. Notice that this allows a thread trying to get a large number of golf balls to remain blocked while a thread requiring fewer can proceed.

The `PlayerArrival` class creates new `Player` threads in response to button presses. Each newly created thread is passed a reference to the applet class `GolfClub`. The thread needs this reference since it calls the golf ball allocator monitor indirectly via the `GolfClub` methods `getGolfBalls()` and `relGolfBalls()`. The program has been organized this way to avoid passing all the display objects to every newly created thread. The code for the `Player` class is listed in Program 9.2.

Notice that, in contrast to the threads we have defined in previous chapters, the `run()` method of the `Player` class does not involve a loop. After it has been started, the player gets the golf balls it requires by calling `getGolfBalls()`, sleeps for a period of time to simulate playing and then releases the golf balls using `relGolfBalls()`. The `run()` method then terminates. Rather than listing the entire code for the class `GolfClub`, since it is rather lengthy, we have listed below the two methods used by `Player`:

```
class Player extends Thread {
  private GolfClub gc;
  private String name;
  private int nballs;

  Player(GolfClub g, int n, String s) {
     gc = g; name = s; nballs =n;
  }

  public void run() {
    try {
      gc.getGolfBalls(nballs,name);
      Thread.sleep(gc.playTime);
      gc.relGolfBalls(nballs,name);
    } catch (InterruptedException e){}
  }
}
```

Program 9.2 `Player` class.

```
void getGolfBalls(int n, String name)
         throws InterruptedException {
  String s = name+n;
  starting.enter(s);
  Thread.sleep(500);
  starting.leave(s);
  waiting.enter(s);
  alloc.get(n);
  waiting.leave(s);
  playing.enter(s);
}

void relGolfBalls(int n, String name)
          throws InterruptedException {
  String s = name+n;
  alloc.put(n);
  playing.leave(s);
  ending.enter(s);
  Thread.sleep(500);
  ending.leave(s);
}
```

These methods access the allocator monitor using `alloc` which references the `DisplayAllocator` object which in turn calls `SimpleAllocator` as previously explained. The references `starting`, `waiting`, `playing` and `ending` refer to instances of the `SlotCanvas` class. This is the first time we have used this display class. An outline of the methods it provides is listed in Program 9.3.

```
public class SlotCanvas extends Canvas {
  ...
  //create display with slots boxes
  public SlotCanvas
    (String title, Color c, int slots) {...}

  //enter the string name in an empty box
  public synchronized void enter(String name){...}

  //clear the box containing name
  public synchronized void leave(String name) {...}
  ...
}
```

Program 9.3 `SlotCanvas` class.

This completes the description of the golf club program. As discussed previously, it has the problem that novices can wait forever to play while they are continuously overtaken by expert players. In the next section, we investigate a solution to this liveness problem by modeling the golf club.

9.2 Golf Club Model

In modeling the golf club program, we need only be concerned with the player threads and the allocator monitor that embody the concurrent behavior of the golf club. We can abstract away from the details of how the program's display interface is constructed. We first model the allocator monitor and then examine the problem of modeling dynamically created threads. The model for the allocator is listed below:

```
const N=5      //maximum #golf balls
range B=0..N //available range

ALLOCATOR = BALL[N],
BALL[b:B] = (when (b>0) get[i:1..b]->BALL[b-i]
            | put[j:1..N]         ->BALL[b+j]
            ).
```

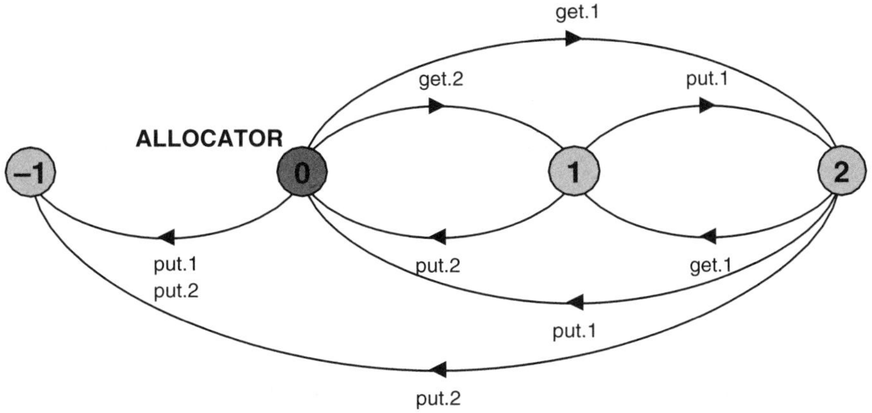

Figure 9.3 ALLOCATOR *LTS* for $N = 2$.

The ALLOCATOR process initially has N golf balls to allocate. In the state with b golf balls, the process accepts requests for $1..b$. In other words, the process blocks requests to get more than b golf balls. The process moves into an ERROR state if more golf balls are put back than were previously requested (i.e. $b + j > N$). The behavior of ALLOCATOR can be clearly seen in Figure 9.3 where $N = 2$ to reduce the complexity of the diagram.

How do we model the potentially infinite stream of dynamically created player threads? The straightforward answer is that we cannot since this would involve an infinite state space. However, while we cannot model infinite state spaces, we can model infinite behaviors that are repetitive. In the golf club example, we do not need to model the fact that each player thread is distinct. Instead, we model a fixed population of golfers who continuously repeat the actions involved in playing golf – a situation not too far removed from real life! Effectively, our model constrains the maximum number of golfers who are concurrently trying to play golf. The maximum number of active player threads in the program is only constrained by the available storage. Our model generates an infinite stream of requests from a fixed set of golfers while the program generates a stream of requests with each request originating from a new player.

A player is modeled by a process that initially decides the number of golf balls it needs to play golf. Subsequently, the process continuously attempts to get and then put back that number of golf balls. The model for a player process is:

```
range R=1..N //request range

PLAYER      = (need[b:R]->PLAYER[b]),
PLAYER[b:R] = (get[b]->put[b]->PLAYER[b]).
```

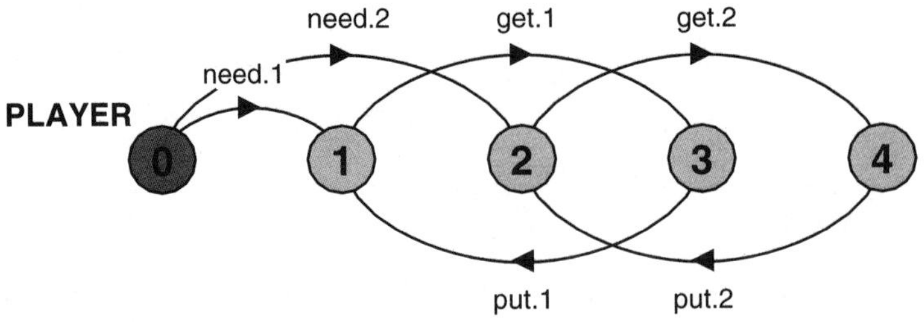

Figure 9.4 PLAYER *LTS* for $N = 2$.

The behavior of PLAYER can be seen in Figure 9.4 where we have again set $N = 2$ to reduce the complexity of the diagram.

We now need to distinguish between expert players and novices. The difference is, of course, that novices require more golf balls than experts. We define an additional process to constrain the numbers of golf balls requested by both novices and experts. We use named label sets to declare the names of players. Sets of labels were first used explicitly in Chapter 4. *FSP* also allows named sets to be declared as below:

```
set Experts = {alice,bob,chris}
set Novices = {dave,eve}
set Players = {Experts,Novices}
```

FSP does not support sets of sets, simply sets of labels. Consequently, the set named `Players` is the union of the sets `Experts` and `Novices`. With these declarations, we can define the constraint that distinguishes experts from novices as:

```
HANDICAP =
  ({Novices.{need[3..N]},Experts.need[1..2]}
           -> HANDICAP)
  +{Players.need[R]}.
```

The alphabet of the process HANDICAP consists of all the `need` actions that can be performed by all players. However, it only engages in actions in which experts need one or two golf balls and novices need between three and N golf balls. When composed with the PLAYER processes, HANDICAP inhibits these processes from performing any other `need` actions. The composition of players, allocator and constraint is described in Figure 9.5.

Analysis of the GOLFCLUB model of Figure 9.5 reveals no safety violations. The system is well-behaved in the sense that players return the same number of golf balls they get and consequently the allocator cannot get into the ERROR state. The problem with this system is not safety but liveness. The following progress

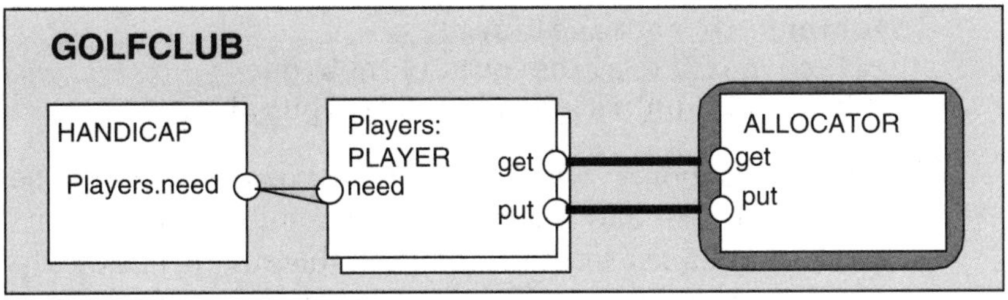

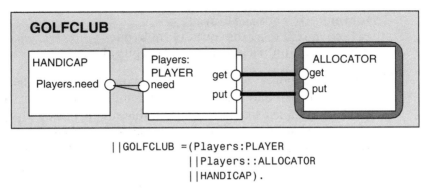

```
||GOLFCLUB =(Players:PLAYER
           ||Players::ALLOCATOR
           ||HANDICAP).
```

Figure 9.5 GOLFCLUB composition.

properties assert for experts and novices that they make progress with respect to getting golf balls.

```
progress NOVICE = {Novices.get[R]}
progress EXPERT = {Experts.get[R]}
```

Notice that we have not specified any particular number of golf balls. Getting any number satisfies the property. Similarly, we have not specified a specific novice or expert. Consequently, if any novice regularly gets any number of golf balls, the property NOVICE is satisfied and similarly for experts. A progress check against these properties reveals no violations. To reveal the problem that occurred in the program, we must set up adverse scheduling conditions using the technique described in Chapter 7. We make the put action, which releases golf balls, low priority:

```
||ProgressCheck = GOLFCLUB >>{Players.put[R]}.
```

Progress analysis of this system detects a violation of the progress property NOVICE. One of the violating traces produced by the analyzer is listed below:

```
Progress violation: NOVICE
Path to terminal set of states:
     alice.need.1
     alice.get.1
     bob.need.1
     bob.get.1
     chris.need.1
     chris.get.1
     dave.need.4
     eve.need.4
```

```
Actions in terminal set:
{alice.get.1, alice.put.1, bob.get.1,
bob.put.1, chris.get.1, chris.put.1}
```

This is the situation in which each of the expert players `alice`, `bob` and `chris` needs a single ball and the novices `dave` and `eve` need four. The terminal set indicates an infinite execution, in which the experts repeatedly `get` and `put` the golf balls they need. However, novices do not get access because the situation does not occur in which two experts `put` their golf balls without an intermediate `get`. Consequently, the allocator never has four golf balls to give to a novice. As in the Java program, experts continuously overtake novices and consequently, the novices make no progress.

9.3 Fair Allocation

Having successfully detected the liveness problem in the model, the next step is to look at ways of solving the problem and to check that they work correctly in the model. We can then change the program to reflect the updated model. In the model, we could simply increase the number of golf balls with which the allocator is initialized. Since we have a fixed population of golfers, we can easily increase the number such that there is no contention. This would not be a general solution since it would always be possible for expert players to arrive at a faster rate and, as a result, novices would starve. Instead, we arrange it such that players wait in an orderly line for golf balls such that experts cannot overtake novices.

Rather than make players line up in first-in-first-out (FIFO) order, we use a ticketing scheme. New tickets are generated in ascending numerical order. Players take a new ticket from a dispenser when they arrive at the golf club and they are subsequently served with golf balls in ticket order. In the model, we do not require an infinite number of tickets since, as long as we have at least as many tickets as players, we can restart the numbering sequence when the last ticket has been handed out.

The ticket dispenser is modeled by the following process:

```
const TM = 5      // maximum ticket
range T = 1..TM // ticket values

TICKET     = NEXT[1],
NEXT[t:T] = (ticket[t]->NEXT[t%TM+1]).
```

We must modify the `PLAYER` process to get tickets and modify the `ALLOCATOR` to only accept requests in ticket order. The modified processes are shown below.

```
PLAYER      = (need[b:R]->PLAYER[b]),
PLAYER[b:R]= (ticket[t:T]
               ->get[b][t]->put[b]->PLAYER[b]).

ALLOCATOR      = BALL[N][1],
BALL[b:B][t:T] =
  (when (b>0) get[i:1..b][t]->BALL[b-i][t%TM+1]
  |put[j:1..N]              ->BALL[b+j][t]
  ).
```

The revised PLAYER process requests a ticket and uses it when requesting golf balls i.e. get[b][t]. The revised ALLOCATOR accepts get actions in ticket order starting with ticket number 1. The ticket scheme increases the size of the model considerably. To compensate for the increase, we modify the HANDICAP constraint such that expert players always request a single golf ball and novices request four:

```
HANDICAP =
     ({Novices.{need[4]},Experts.need[1]}
          -> HANDICAP)
     +{Players.need[R]}.
```

The golf club system is now modeled as follows:

```
||GOLFCLUB =(Players:PLAYER
            ||Players::(ALLOCATOR||TICKET)
            ||HANDICAP
            ).
```

To analyze progress for this system, the progress properties must be slightly revised to take into account the addition of the ticket value in the get action.

```
progress NOVICE = {Novices.get[R][T]}
progress EXPERT = {Experts.get[R][T]}
```

Using ProgressCheck, as defined before, no progress violations are detected. The next section discusses the implementation of the revised allocator.

9.4 Revised Golf Ball Allocator

Fortunately, we can encapsulate the ticketing scheme described in the previous section in a revised implementation of the allocator monitor. Other than using this revised implementation in place of SimpleAllocator, no other changes are required to the program. The new implementation, called FairAllocator, is listed in Program 9.4.

```
public class FairAllocator implements Allocator {
  private int available;
  private long turn = 0; //next ticket to be dispensed
  private long next = 0; //next ticket to be served

  public FairAllocator(int n) { available = n; }

  synchronized public void get(int n)
          throws InterruptedException {
    long myturn = turn; ++turn;
    while (n>available || myturn != next) wait();
    ++next; available -= n;
    notifyAll();
  }

  synchronized public void put(int n) {
    available += n;
    notifyAll();
  }
}
```

Program 9.4 `FairAllocator` class.

We have added two instance variables to implement the ticketing scheme: `next` records the value of the next ticket to be served, and `turn` records the value of the next ticket to be dispensed. A thread gets a ticket by recording it in the local variable `myturn`. Remember that each time a thread calls the method `get`, a new activation record is created. Consequently, a new copy of `myturn` is also created which is only used by the calling thread. A thread is now blocked until there are sufficient golf balls and its ticket is the next one to be served. To keep the code simple, we have not dealt with resetting the ticket when the maximum ticket value is reached. However, by using 64-bit ticket values, we have ensured that, with a player arrival rate of one per second, the program will run for 300 billion years before ticket overflow becomes a problem!

Figure 9.6 shows a screen dump of the revised golf club applet. The changed behavior can clearly be seen. Although two golf balls are available, players **g1** and **h1** are waiting because they cannot overtake **f4** due to the FIFO ordering enforced by the ticketing scheme.

9.5 Bounded Overtaking

The ticketing scheme ensures that starvation does not occur. However, it does not use the available golf ball resources efficiently. Expert players are kept waiting by

Figure 9.6 Golf Club applet with fair allocation.

novices even though the golf balls they require are available. A modified scheme allows experts to overtake novices but denies starvation by setting an upper bound on the number of times a novice can be overtaken. Once that bound is reached, the novice can no longer be overtaken by an expert and must receive his/her allocation next.

The allocator algorithm for bounded overtaking was implemented but not modeled in the first edition of this book. One of our insightful readers pointed out that adverse scheduling by the Java Virtual Machine could result in the bound being violated. The lesson is clear: models are essential in helping to eliminate errors. Below is a new algorithm which has been carefully modeled to support analysis.

In the algorithm, we need to keep track of those players who have overtaken others. This can be modeled as a set, as shown below. Elements of the set are of type T and can be added, removed and checked for set membership. The set is modeled as the parallel composition of elements which preserve the property that an element is only added if it is not already a member of the set, and only removed if it is a member.

```
const False = 0
const True  = 1
range Bool  = 0..1

ELEMENT(Id=0) = IN[False],
IN[b:Bool]    = ( add[Id]          -> IN[True]
                | remove[Id]       -> IN[False]
```

```
                  | contains[Id][b] -> IN[b]
                  ).

property
  ONEADD(Id=0) = (add[Id]->remove[Id]->ONEADD).

||SET = (forall[i:T] (ELEMENT(i) ||  ONEADD(i))).
```

We model bounded overtaking using tickets as in the fair FIFO allocator, where ticket numbers are used to indicate the order in which players make their requests. The allocator records which ticket number is `next`. Overtaking occurs when we allocate balls to a player whose `turn` – indicated by his/her ticket number – is subsequent to a waiting player with the `next` ticket. The overtaking player is added to the overtaking set, and a count `ot` is incremented to indicate the number of times `next` has been overtaken. When the count equals the bound, we allow allocation to the `next` player only. When allocation is made to the `next` player, we need to update `next` to indicate the next (waiting) player. We skip the ticket numbers of those overtaking players who have already received their allocation, remove each of these intervening players from the overtaking set and decrement the overtaking count accordingly. This is achieved in the local process, `WHILE`, in the `ALLOCATOR` given below. Note that the maximum ticket value must not be less than the sum of the number of players and the bound so as to avoid ambiguity when the sequence of ticket numbers restarts.

```
const N  =  5       // maximum #golf balls
const Bd =  2       // bound on overtaking
range B  =  0..N    // available range

const TM = 5 + Bd // maximum ticket
range T  = 1..TM  // ticket values

TICKET     = TURN[1],
TURN[t:T] = (ticket[t]->TURN[t%TM+1]).

ALLOCATOR   = BALL[N][1][0],
BALL[b:B][next:T][ot:0..Bd] =
     (when (b>0 && ot<Bd) get[i:1..b][turn:T] ->
          if (turn!=next) then
             (add[turn] -> BALL[b-i][next][ot+1])
```

```
            else
                WHILE[b-i][next%TM+1][ot]
        |when (b>0 && ot==Bd) get[i:1..b][next] ->
                WHILE[b-i][next%TM+1][ot]
        |put[j:1..N] -> BALL[b+j][next][ot]
        ),
WHILE[b:B][next:T][ot:0..Bd] =
        (contains[next][yes:Bool] ->
            if (yes) then
            (remove[next] ->
                WHILE[b][next%TM+1][ot-1])
            else
                BALL[b][next][ot]
        )+{add[T],remove[T]}.
```

The golf club system is now modeled as follows:

```
||GOLFCLUB = (Players:PLAYER
             || ALLOCATOR||TICKET||SET
             || HANDICAP
             )/ {Players.get/get,
                 Players.put/put,
                 Players.ticket/ticket}.
```

Using `ProgressCheck`, as defined before, no progress violations are detected for this bounded overtaking golf club. Using animation, we can step through to produce a trace which illustrates the bounded allocation algorithm:

`eve.need.4`	*Novices Eve and Dave*
`dave.need.4`	
`chris.need.1`	*Experts Alice, Bob and Chris*
`alice.need.1`	
`bob.need.1`	
`alice.ticket.1`	
`alice.get.1.1`	*Alice gets 1 ball, ticket 1*
`contains.2.0`	*Ticket 2 is next*
`bob.ticket.2`	
`bob.get.1.2`	*Two allocated, three available*
`contains.3.0`	*Ticket 3 is next*
`dave.ticket.3`	***Dave needs four balls: waits***
`chris.ticket.4`	
`chris.get.1.4`	***Chris overtakes***

```
add.4
eve.ticket.5          Eve needs four balls: waits
alice.put.1
alice.ticket.6
alice.get.1.6         Alice overtakes
add.6
bob.put.1
bob.ticket.7
bob.get.1.7           Bob overtakes: bound reached
add.7
chris.put.1
chris.ticket.8        Chris waits: three available
alice.put.1
alice.ticket.1        Alice waits: four available
dave.get.4.3          Dave gets four balls
contains.4.1          remove intervening overtaker
remove.4
contains.5.0          Ticket 5 (Eve) is next
dave.put.4
dave.ticket.2
alice.get.1.1         Alice overtakes: bound reached
add.1
bob.put.1
bob.ticket.3
eve.get.4.5           Eve gets four balls
contains.6.1          remove intervening overtakers
remove.6
contains.7.1
remove.7
contains.8.0          Ticket 8 (Chris) is next
. . .
```

We can easily add a safety property BALLS to check that players return the same number of balls as allocated. This is shown below.

```
property
  BALLS = BALLS[N],
  BALLS[b:0..N] =
    (when b>0
         Players.get[i:1..b][turn:T] -> BALLS[b-i]
    |Players.put[j:1..N] -> BALLS[b+j]
    ).
```

Can we also specify the bounded nature of this allocator as a safety property? This requires more ingenuity in which we check, for each player, that he/she is not overtaken more than bound times. Overtaking is indicated by an allocation to another player whose ticket `t` lies between the `turn` of the player and the `latest` ticket issued.

```
property
   BOUND(P='alice) =
     ({Players {[P]}}.ticket[T] -> BOUND
     |[P].ticket[t:T]   -> WAITING[t][t][0]
     |[Players].get[R][T]        -> BOUND
    ),
   WAITING[turn:T][latest:T][overtaken:0..Bd] =
     ([P].get[b:R][turn] -> BOUND
     |{Players\{[P]}}.get[b:R][t:T] ->
        if ((t>turn && (t<=latest ||  latest<turn))
         || (t<turn && (t<=latest && latest<turn)))
          then WAITING[turn][latest][overtaken+1]
          else WAITING[turn][latest][overtaken]
     |Players.ticket[last:T] ->
                WAITING[turn][last][overtaken]
     ).
```

The golf club system is now modeled as below, where the property is checked for all players. This is a large model of over 4 million states and 10 million transitions. No safety (or progress) violations are found for `CHECKGOLFCLUB`.

```
||CHECKGOLFCLUB = (GOLFCLUB
                  || BALLS
                  || forall [p:Players] BOUND(p)
                  ).
```

However, if we check for an overtaken bound `of 2` in the property `BOUND and` leave the allocator with `Bd` set to `3`, then we quickly get the violation below in which Alice is overtaken three times, twice by Bob and once by Chris. This confirms that the property `BOUND` does indeed detect violations in the overtaking bound.

```
Trace to property violation in BOUND(alice):
     alice.need.1
     alice.ticket.1
     bob.need.1
```

```
bob.ticket.2
bob.get.1.2
chris.need.1
chris.ticket.3
add.2
bob.put.1
bob.ticket.4
bob.get.1.4
add.4
chris.get.1.3
```

9.6 Bounded Overtaking Golf Ball Allocator

Bounded overtaking is implemented in the allocator of Program 9.5. The program follows the algorithm used in our model. Each thread waits if there are insufficient balls available or if the bound has been reached and the player is not next. Overtaking players are added to the `overtakers` set and removed as necessary when `next` is updated; the count of those `overtaken` is incremented and decremented on addition and removal respectively.

The operation of the bounded overtaking allocator can be seen in the applet display shown in Figure 9.7. This captures the situation in which player **f4** has been overtaken by players **g1**, **h1** and **i1**. Since the overtaking bound, which has been set to three, has been exceeded, players **j1** and **k1** are blocked although there are two golf balls available. They will remain blocked until **f4** has been served.

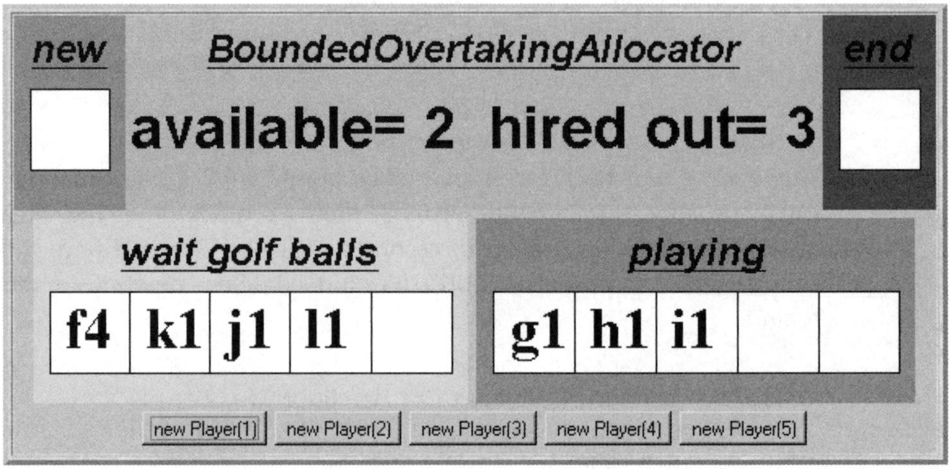

Figure 9.7 Golf Club with bounded overtaking allocator (bound = 3).

```
public class BoundedOvertakingAllocator
                        implements Allocator{
  private int TM;
     //must be maximum active threads + bound
  private int available;
  private int bound;
  private int turn = 1;
  private int next = 1;
  private int overtaken =0;
  private BitSet overtakers;

  public BoundedOvertakingAllocator(int n, int b)
    { available = n; bound = b; TM = 10000+b;
      overtakers = new BitSet(TM+1);}

  synchronized public void get(int n)
           throws InterruptedException{
    int myturn = turn; turn = turn%TM + 1;
    while (n>available ||
          (myturn!=next && overtaken>=bound)) {
      wait();
    }
     if (myturn!=next)  {
          overtakers.set(myturn); ++overtaken;
     }
     else  {
          next =  next%TM + 1;
          while (overtakers.get(next)) {
               overtakers.clear(next);
               --overtaken;
               next =  next%TM + 1;
          }
     }
    available -= n;
    notifyAll();
  }

  synchronized public void put(int n) {
    available += n;
    notifyAll();
  }
}
```

Program 9.5 `BoundedOvertakingAllocator` class.

9.7 Master-Slave Program

In the golf club example, when a player thread finished playing and returned its golf balls, it simply terminated. In some concurrent programming situations, we may want to determine a result that is computed by a dynamically created thread. Usually, a *slave* thread is created to perform some input/output (I/O) activity while the *master* thread that created it continues with some other activity. At some point, the master must synchronize with the slave to retrieve the result of the I/O activity. This *master–slave* arrangement is frequently used to allow the master thread to continue executing while the slave waits for a remote communication to complete. When the remote communication completes, the slave thread terminates and the master must obtain the result of the remote communication. We could use a monitor to allow the slave to signal when it is about to terminate. Alternatively, the master could continuously test the status of the slave thread using the `isAlive()` method. This method returns false when the thread to which it is applied terminates. However, this busy wait would consume CPU cycles that could be put to better use by another thread. To avoid this busy wait, the Java `Thread` class provides a method to allow one thread to await the termination of another:

> **public final** `void join()` **throws** `InterruptedException`
> Waits for this thread to die, e.g. by returning from `run()` or as a result of `stop()`.

Figure 9.8 is the display of an applet that demonstrates the operation of `join()`. The upper display shows the master executing concurrently with the slave. The slave was created at the point the master's segment changed color. The bottom display shows the point at which the slave has terminated and the master has obtained the result of its computation. In the demonstration, the result is the amount the slave rotates its display before terminating. The amount of slave rotation can be adjusted by the slider control positioned below its rotating segment. The amount that the master rotates before waiting for the slave to terminate is adjusted using the other slider.

By adjusting the sliders, it is possible to arrange for the master to wait for the slave to terminate or for the slave to terminate before the master gets the result. The code for both `Master` and `Slave` threads is depicted in Program 9.6.

The `Slave` thread is created and started using the `start()` method provided by `ThreadPanel`. This returns a reference to the new thread. The result is obtained from the `Slave` thread by calling the `result()` method after the `Slave` thread has terminated. Note that `result()` need not be **`synchronized`** since, as long as

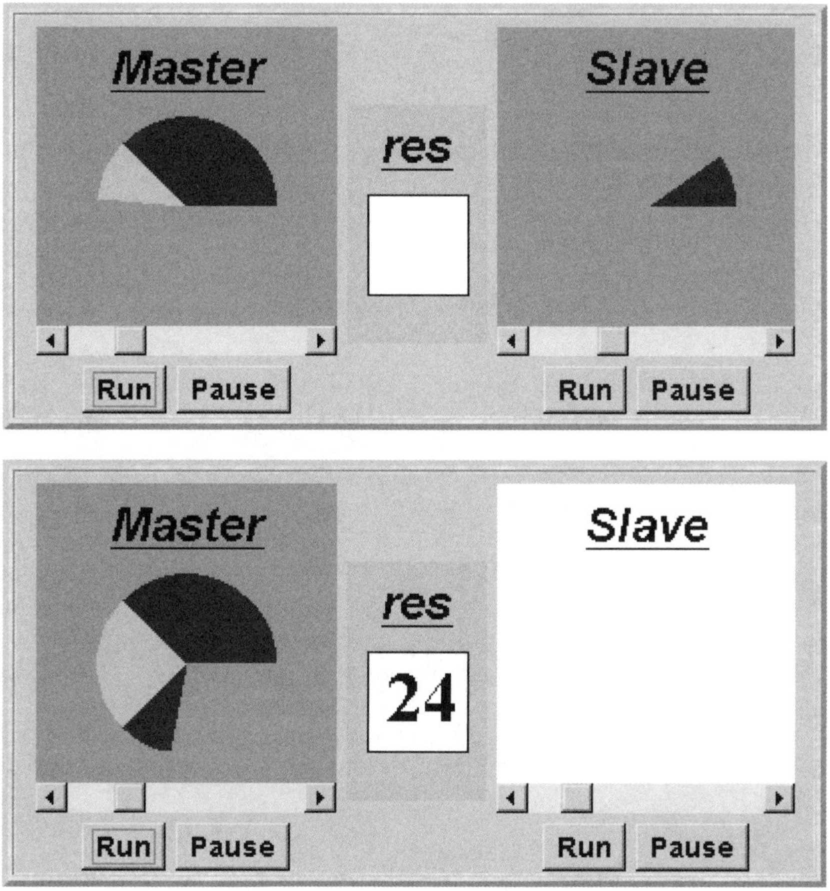

Figure 9.8 `join()` demonstration applet.

it is only called after termination, there can be no interference between `Master` and `Slave` threads.

9.8 Master–Slave Model

We can construct a satisfactory model of the master–slave program by observing that, although it creates a sequence of new slave processes, only a single slave thread is active at any one time. Consequently, we use a single slave process, which after it terminates, immediately becomes available to be started again:

```
SLAVE = (start->rotate->join->SLAVE).
```

```
class Master implements Runnable {
  ThreadPanel slaveDisplay;
  SlotCanvas resultDisplay;

  Master(ThreadPanel tp, SlotCanvas sc)
    {slaveDisplay=tp; resultDisplay=sc;}

  public void run() {
    try {
      String res=null;
      while(true) {
        while (!ThreadPanel.rotate());
        if (res!=null) resultDisplay.leave(res);
        // create new slave thread
        Slave s = new Slave();
        Thread st = slaveDisplay.start(s,false);
        // continue execution
        while (ThreadPanel.rotate());
        // wait for slave termination
        st.join();
        // get and display result from slave
        res = String.valueOf(s.result());
        resultDisplay.enter(res);
      }
    } catch (InterruptedException e){}
  }
}

class Slave implements Runnable {
  int rotations = 0;

  public void run() {
    try {
      while (!ThreadPanel.rotate()) ++rotations;
    } catch (InterruptedException e){}
  }

  int result(){
    return rotations;
  }
}
```

Program 9.6 `Master` and `Slave` classes.

The master thread is modeled by the following process:

```
MASTER = (slave.start->rotate
          ->slave.join->rotate->MASTER).
```

The master–slave program can now be modeled as the composition:

```
||MASTER_SLAVE = (MASTER || slave:SLAVE).
```

The behavior of this model is depicted in the *LTS* of Figure 9.9.

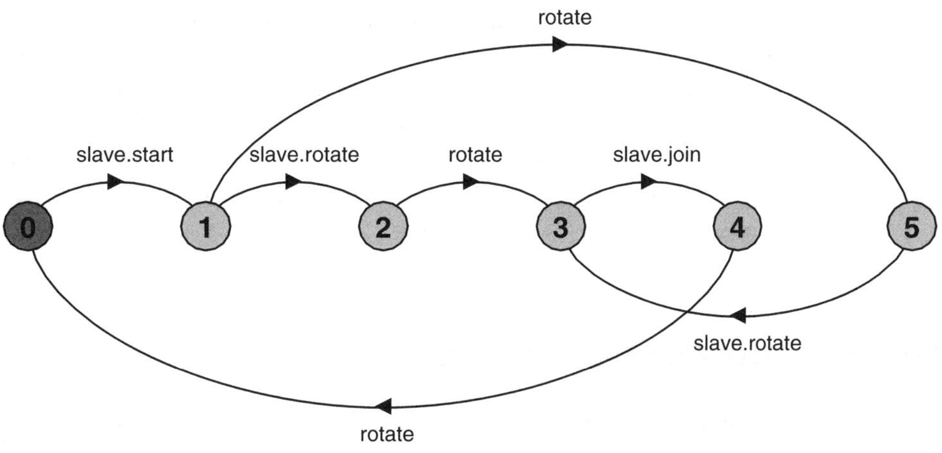

Figure 9.9 MASTER_SLAVE *LTS*.

From the *LTS*, it can be seen that the slave rotation action, `slave.rotate`, and the master rotation action, `rotate`, are concurrent since they can occur in any order. However, after the `slave.join` action only the master rotation action can take place, as in the applet. The model can easily be generalized to a system in which two or more slave processes are active concurrently.

Summary

In this chapter, we have looked at programs in which threads both start and terminate dynamically during program execution. We have shown that it is possible to construct satisfactory finite state models for this sort of program by using a static population of processes with cyclic behavior. The model fixes the maximum number of concurrently active processes while concurrent thread activation in the program is only limited by available storage. We regard a model as satisfactory if it exhibits the same behavior as the program it is modeling with respect to safety and liveness properties. We were able to use the golf club model to investigate and correct a liveness problem and subsequently to implement that correction in the program.

The main example concerned a resource allocator that managed a pool of identical reusable resources. Threads competed for access to these resources. In our example, the resources were golf balls. In computing systems, this form of allocation is required for resources such as memory pages and message buffers.

The results of this chapter show that the models we constructed in previous chapters for resource access also apply to programs in which threads are created dynamically. For example, the Readers–Writers program of Chapter 7 had a fixed number of Reader and Writer threads with cyclic behavior. However, the monitor that controlled read/write access would work equally well in a program with a dynamically varying number of Reader and Writer threads.

Finally, this chapter demonstrated the use of the Java `join()` method which allows one thread to await the termination of another. The example was a master–slave arrangement in which the master thread obtained the result of the slave computation.

Notes and Further Reading

One of the first proposals for thread creation was the **fork** *L* command, which transfers control to the statement labeled *L* and also allows control to pass to the statement after **fork**. In this way, two concurrently executing threads of control are created. A **join** command was provided to allow the two threads to rejoin execution. The first thread to reach **join** blocks until the second thread also executes the command. Only a single thread executes after the join. Unstructured use of fork and join leads to extremely complex multi-threaded programs. The UNIX operating system has a version of the fork command with no label. The fork operating system call creates a complete copy of the calling process and starts it executing. The fork call returns a result, which lets a process determine whether it is the *parent* or *child*.

To resolve the problems caused by unstructured use of fork and join, Dijkstra (1965) proposed what later became the **cobegin..coend** construct:

cobegin *P*; *Q* **coend**

P and *Q* are executed concurrently as separate threads until both have terminated. The construct can easily be generalized to more than two threads. It was proposed for use in block-structured languages such as Algol. In these languages, the main structuring tools are procedures and procedure activations rather than classes and objects. Storage for procedure activations is managed as a stack in these languages and the addition of threads created using the **cobegin..coend** construct requires a tree of stacks, sometimes called a "cactus" stack.

The Java thread model does not enforce this degree of structure on thread execution. A thread can continue executing after the thread that created it has terminated. This is more appropriate in an object-oriented language where we are generally less concerned with the lifetime of objects. Storage is managed by a heap structure. Objects exist until they are garbage collected and threads exist until they terminate, at which point their storage can also be garbage collected. Java provides the `ThreadGroup` class to manage collections of threads and to enforce security policies by dynamically restricting access to `Thread` operations. For example, a thread may only `stop()` another thread if both are in the same group. By default, each thread is created in the same `ThreadGroup` as its creator. We have been able to ignore `ThreadGroups` in the examples since all threads are created in the default group provided by browsers for applet execution.

In this chapter, we have dealt with programs where dynamic thread creation and termination can be modeled by a fixed set of cyclic processes. The more general problem is to model programs in which the configuration of threads and monitors evolves as execution proceeds. For this sort of program, using *FSP*, each configuration must be enumerated. The program can then be modeled as the composition of its possible configurations. To address the problem of describing concurrent systems in which configuration changes dynamically, Robin Milner introduced the π-calculus (Milner, Parrow and Walker, 1992). This permits an elegant and concise description of dynamic systems. However, in general, these π-calculus descriptions are not amenable to the form of state exploration analysis that we use for *FSP* descriptions.

The idea of bounded delays to provide a class of resource allocation strategies is due to Dijkstra (1972a). These strategies can be characterized as satisfying a set of safe scheduling rules for resource allocation to a *fixed* pool of m processes from a pool of n reusable resources:

1. No process should wait for resources unless some other process is using resources.
2. If process i has requested resources, not more than k other processes can be given their requested resources before satisfying process i (for some bound $k \geq m - 2$).
3. The number of resources in the pool plus the sum of the number allocated to processes equals n.

The first two rules avoid resource starvation for an individual process and the third rule preserves resource integrity. Allocation from a pool of reusable resources was used as an exercise in rigorous program design at Imperial College in the late 1970s. Students were required to design, verify and implement a resource allocator in SIMULA (Birtwistle, Dahl, Myhrhaug, *et al.*, 1973). The rules were used by Cunningham and Kramer (1978) as an invariant to guide the development and verification of the program. Rule two was subsequently modified as follows to permit simpler implementations and to cater for dynamic systems where there is no bound on the number of processes (Kramer and Cunningham, 1979):

2′. If process i has requested resources, not more than k' *subsequently arriving* requests can be serviced before i (for some bound $k' \geq 0$).

The golf club problem and the particular formulation described in this book evolved from that experience.

We are grateful to Alexander Höher for his insight into potential problems with the implementation given in the first edition of this book.

Exercises

9.1 The cheese counter in a supermarket is continuously mobbed by hungry customers. There are two sorts of customer: bold customers who push their way to the front of the mob and demand service; and meek customers who wait patiently for service. Request for service is denoted by the action `getcheese` and service completion is signaled by the action `cheese`. Assuming that there is always cheese available, model the system for a fixed population of two bold customers and two meek customers. Show that meek customers may never be served when their requests to get cheese have lower priority than those of bold customers.

9.2 To restore order, the management installs a ticket machine that issues tickets to customers. Tickets are numbered in the range 1..*MT*. When ticket *MT* has been issued, the next ticket to be issued is ticket number 1, i.e. the management install a new ticket roll. The cheese counter has a display that indicates the ticket number of the customer currently being served. The customer with the ticket with the same number as the counter display then goes to the counter and is served. When the service is finished, the number is incremented (modulo *MT*). Model this system and show that, even when their requests have low priority, meek customers are now served.

9.3 Translate the model of the cheese counter from exercise 9.2 into a Java program. Each customer should be implemented by a dynamically created thread that obtains a ticket, is served cheese and then terminates.

9.4 Extend the master–slave model of section 9.8 to cater for two slave processes. Now generalize this model to describe systems with N slave processes.

9.5 Modify the demonstration applet of section 9.7 to create two slave processes.

10 Message Passing

In previous chapters, we have seen that when threads interact through shared variables, these variables must be encapsulated in monitor objects to ensure correct behavior. An alternative way of organizing concurrent programs which does not require shared variables is to use message passing. In message-passing programs, processes interact by sending and receiving messages. Processes that interact solely by message exchange do not need to access shared memory and consequently can be located on different computers connected by a communication network. However, message passing is also frequently used when processes are intended to run within a single computer.

Fundamental to message passing are the operations to *send* and *receive* a message. There are a surprising number of different definitions for these operations in message-passing systems. We examine the two basic models for message passing: *synchronous* message passing, in which the sender of a message waits until it has been received; and *asynchronous* message passing, in which the sender does not wait and messages which have been sent but not yet received are buffered. These are both one-way forms of communication: the messages are transmitted in one direction only, from sender to receiver. In addition, we examine the *rendezvous*, a two-way message-passing protocol used for client–server interaction.

10.1 Synchronous Message Passing

An important design decision in a message-passing scheme is how to designate the sources and destinations of messages. Messages can be addressed directly to the destination process or indirectly to some intermediate entity. In discussing synchronous message passing, we adopt the scheme used in OCCAM (INMOS Ltd., 1988a), in which messages are sent to and received from *channels*. We will see that it is possible, in some message-passing schemes, for many senders to communicate with a receiver through a single communication entity. However, as in OCCAM, we specify that a channel connects two and only two processes. A single process can send to the channel and a single process can receive from the channel as shown in Figure 10.1. Communication is said to be *one-to-one*.

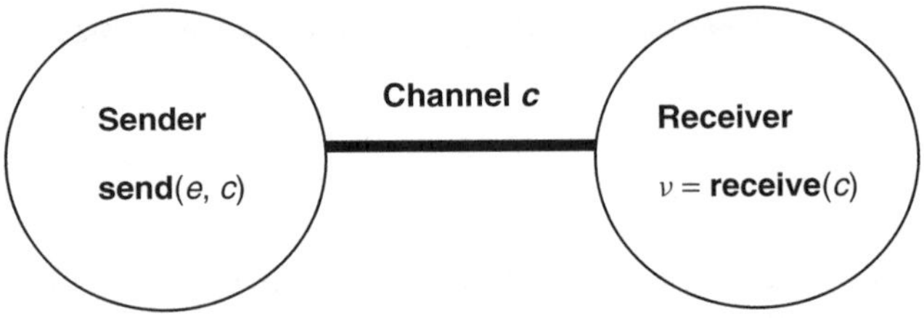

Figure 10.1 Synchronous message-passing channel.

The send and receive operations on channels are:

> **send**(e, c)–send the value of the expression e to channel c. The process calling the send operation is blocked until the message is received from the channel.
> v = **receive**(c)–receive a value into local variable v from channel c. The calling process is blocked waiting until a message is sent to the channel.

The first process, whether sender or receiver, to perform a channel operation is blocked until its partner performs the complementary action. After a communication occurs, sender and receiver can proceed independently. This form of message passing is termed synchronous, since the sender and receiver must be exactly synchronized for communication to occur. Another way of thinking of synchronous communication is that it implements a distributed assignment in which the sender's expression is assigned to the receiver's local variable ($v = e$). In the language OCCAM and the CSP formalism (Hoare, 1985) which inspired it, the notation for send is $c!e$ and for receive is $c?v$.

Synchronous message operations do not require messages to be buffered. If the sender process is running on the same computer as the receiver then the message can be copied directly from the sender into the receiver's local variable. This simplicity enabled the OCCAM send and receive operations to be implemented directly as Transputer (INMOS Ltd., 1988b) machine instructions.

10.1.1 Selective Receive

We have seen that choice between actions is important in both modeling and implementing concurrent programs. In Java, choice is implemented within a monitor. The monitor lock effectively selects a single synchronized method activation to execute from the set of possible activations. The synchronous, message receive operation blocks waiting on a single channel. How do we choose between receiving messages from a set of channels? The solution provided by languages such as OCCAM and Ada is to use a **select** statement. The general form of a select statement is as shown below:

select
  when G_1 **and** v_1 =**receive**($chan_1$) => S_1;
or
  when G_2 **and** v_2 =**receive**($chan_2$) => S_2;
or
  ...
or
  when G_n **and** v_n =**receive**($chan_n$) => S_n;
end

G_1 ..G_n are boolean expressions known as guards. A receive is eligible if the guard associated with it evaluates to true. The select statement chooses an eligible receive operation for which there is a sender waiting to send. The statement S_i is executed after a successful receive on a channel $chan_i$. The select statement then terminates. If none of the channels have waiting sends then the select statement blocks. The reader should immediately see the correspondence between this select construct and choice over guarded actions in *FSP*. Indeed, we will see later that this is exactly the way selective receive is modeled in *FSP*. As in *FSP*, guards are usually optional in select statements such that an omitted guard is equivalent to **when** *true* **and**. Some select statements allow *non-blocking* semantics by providing an **else** alternative as follows:

select
  v=**receive**($chan$) => S;
else
  $S_{elsepart}$;
end

If a sender is not waiting on the channel then the **else** part is immediately chosen. Another variation is to permit a timeout as an alternative. If no message arrives within the timeout period then the statements associated with the timeout part are executed and the select terminates.

The send and receive operations are symmetrical in synchronous message passing in that the send blocks if there is no corresponding receive and vice versa. Consequently, it is reasonable to suggest that send operations should be allowed as select alternatives in addition to receive operations. However, because of the resulting implementation complexity, only experimental message-passing languages have included both send and receive select alternatives.

10.1.2 Synchronous Message Passing in Java

We have seen in the preceding chapters that Java supports thread interaction through monitors. How do we write message-passing programs in Java? The answer is to use Java's object-oriented programming facilities to implement and encapsulate message-passing abstractions. We can implement the synchronous message-passing channel as a class. The outline of the Java class that implements the channel abstraction is defined in Program 10.1.

```
public class Channel<T> extends Selectable{
    public synchronized void send(T v)
            throws InterruptedException {. . .}
    public synchronized T receive()
            throws InterruptedException {. . .}

}
```

Program 10.1 `Channel` class.

The implementation of `Channel` is a monitor that has synchronized access methods for send and receive. (The code may be found on the website that accompanies this book.) The class extends the `Selectable` base class to support the Java selective receive implementation, described later.

To demonstrate the operation of the Channel implemented in Java, we develop a simple program in which a sender thread communicates with a receiver thread using a single channel. The display for this program is depicted in Figure 10.2. The display depicts the situation where the sender thread is blocked waiting to send the value in e. The receiver has not yet executed the receive operation to copy the value into its local variable v. The sender simply transmits a sequence of integer values from 0 to 9 and then restarts at 0 again.

The code for both `Sender` and `Receiver` threads is given in Program 10.2. The threads use the display class that we defined in Chapter 9, `SlotCanvas`. The threads and channel are created by the following Java code:

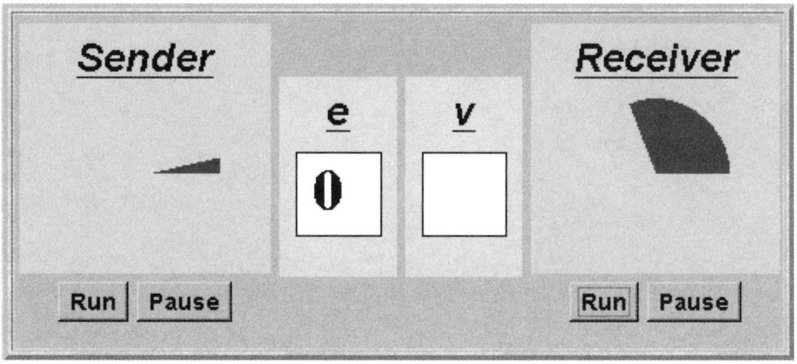

Figure 10.2 Synchronous message-passing applet display.

```
class Sender implements Runnable {
  private Channel<Integer> chan;
  private SlotCanvas display;

  Sender(Channel<Integer> c, SlotCanvas d)
    {chan=c; display=d;}

  public void run() {
    try {
      int ei = 0;
      while(true) {
        display.enter(String.valueOf(ei));
        ThreadPanel.rotate(12);
        chan.send(new Integer(ei));
        display.leave(String.valueOf(ei));
        ei=(ei+1)%10; ThreadPanel.rotate(348);
      }
    } catch (InterruptedException e){}
  }
}

class Receiver implements Runnable {
  private Channel<Integer> chan;
  private SlotCanvas display;

  Receiver(Channel<Integer> c, SlotCanvas d)
    {chan=c; display=d;}
```

Program 10.2 `Sender` and `Receiver` threads.

```
    public void run() {
      try {
        Integer v=null;
        while(true) {
          ThreadPanel.rotate(180);
          if (v!=null) display.leave(v.toString());
          v = chan.receive();
          display.enter(v.toString());
          ThreadPanel.rotate(180);
        }
      } catch (InterruptedException e){}
    }
  }
```

Program 10.2 (*Continued*).

```
Channel<Integer> chan = new Channel<Integer>();
tx.start(new Sender(chan,senddisp));
rx.start(new Receiver(chan,recvdisp));
```

where `tx` and `rx` are instances of the thread display class, `ThreadPanel`, and `senddisp` and `recvdisp` are instances of `SlotCanvas`.

While the code of Program 10.2 is straightforward, a subtlety can lead to problems if the programmer is not aware of it. Our implementation of channels in Java simply copies the reference to an object from sender to receiver, it does not make a copy of the referenced object. Consequently, it is possible for the receiver to modify an object held by the sender. When messages are passed by reference, the safest discipline to adopt is that a sender should not access an object if it has sent its reference to another thread. If a thread needs to reference the object in the future, it should copy it before sending it. With this discipline, a thread is guaranteed mutually exclusive access to the objects it has received but not sent. The sample program obeys this discipline even though the receiver does not modify the messages it receives.

10.1.3 Modeling Synchronous Message Passing

To illustrate how message-passing programs are modeled, we start with the simple Sender–Receiver example of the previous section. The model of the `Sender` thread is:

```
range M = 0..9
SENDER = SENDER[0],
SENDER[e:M] =(chan.send[e]->SENDER[(e+1)%10]).
```

where `chan.send[e]` models the action of sending a value *e* to a channel *chan*. The model of the `Receiver` thread is:

```
RECEIVER = (chan.receive[v:M]->RECEIVER).
```

where `chan.receive[v:M]` models the action of receiving a value into a local variable *v* of type *M* from channel *chan*. The remaining question is how to model the channel entity. In fact, as sending and receiving are synchronous, they become the same action in the model. Consequently, we do not need a separate process to model a channel; we simply rename send and receive to be the same action. We can thus rename both the action `chan.send` and `chan.receive` to be the action `chan` shown in the structure diagram of Figure 10.3.

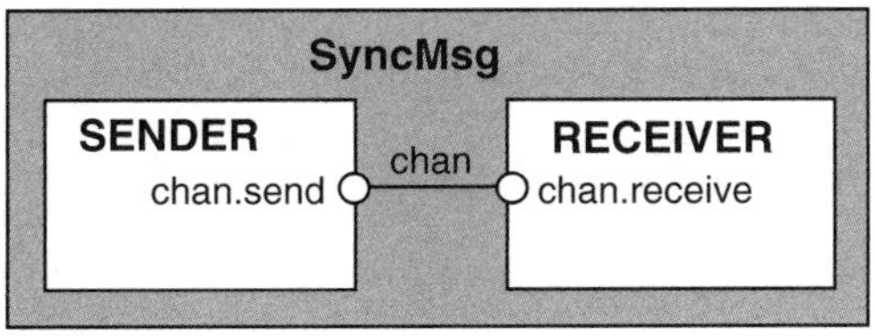

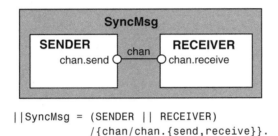

```
||SyncMsg = (SENDER || RECEIVER)
            /{chan/chan.{send,receive}}.
```

Figure 10.3 Modeling synchronous message passing.

To avoid the relabeling, we could have modeled the send action directly as `chan[e]` and the receive action as `chan[v:M]`. In the following, we model synchronous message passing by:

Message Operation	FSP Model
Send(*e*, *chan*)	chan[e]
v = **receive**(*chan*)	chan[e:M]

The only difference between the model for send and receive actions is that **receive** is modeled as a choice between a set of values *M* which can be sent over a channel whereas **send** specifies a specific value *e*. In the example, the values are in the range 0..9. The composite behavior for the example is given by the *LTS* of Figure 10.4.

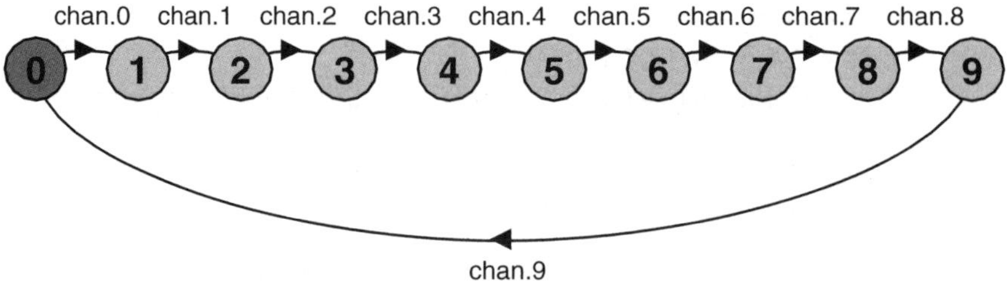

Figure 10.4 SyncMsg labeled transition system.

10.1.4 Modeling and Implementing Selective Receive

To explain how to model and implement selective message reception, we use the car park example from Chapter 5. In this example, an arrivals gate signals the arrival of a car at the car park and the departures gate signals the departure of a car from the car park. The model for the car park is repeated in Figure 10.5.

Instead of implementing the CARPARKCONTROL process as a monitor with arrive and depart access methods, we implement the process as a thread which receives signals from channels called arrive and depart. The behaviors of the ARRIVALS and DEPARTURES processes are implemented by a common MsgGate class as shown in Program 10.3. A thread created from MsgGate sends messages to the channel with which it is initialized. Messages in this example contain no

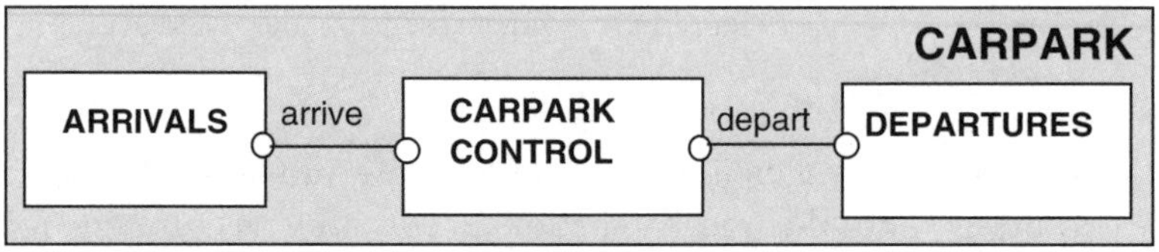

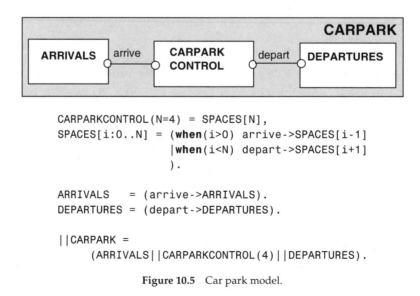

```
CARPARKCONTROL(N=4) = SPACES[N],
SPACES[i:0..N] = (when(i>0) arrive->SPACES[i-1]
                 |when(i<N) depart->SPACES[i+1]
                 ).

ARRIVALS   = (arrive->ARRIVALS).
DEPARTURES = (depart->DEPARTURES).

||CARPARK =
     (ARRIVALS||CARPARKCONTROL(4)||DEPARTURES).
```

Figure 10.5 Car park model.

```
class MsgGate implements Runnable {
  private Channel<Signal> chan;
  private Signal signal = new Signal();

  public MsgGate (Channel<Signal> c) {chan=c;}

  public void run() {
    try {
      while(true)  {
        ThreadPanel.rotate(12);
        chan.send(signal);
        ThreadPanel.rotate(348);
      }
    } catch (InterruptedException e){}
  }
}
```

Program 10.3 `MsgGate` class.

information, and are implemented by a `Signal` class. They signal the arrival or departure of a car from the car park.

The transformation of the CARPARKCONTROL process into a thread using message passing is straightforward since, as we noted earlier, choice and guarded actions express the behavior of selective receive. An outline implementation for the CARPARKCONTROL process using a selective receive is shown below:

MsgCarPark::

```
while(true)
   select
       when spaces>0 and receive(arrive) => ++spaces;
   or
       when spaces< N and receive(depart) => --spaces;
   end
```

We use the object-oriented facilities of Java to implement the selective receive abstraction in the same way that we packaged channels as a class. Channels are derived from the `Selectable` base class, which provides the public method, `guard`. A selective receive is constructed using the `Select` class, which provides the `add` public method to include a `Selectable` object into a selective receive. Using these classes, the outline of the message version of car park control can be translated into Java, as shown in the `MsgCarPark` class of Program 10.4.

A selective receive is executed by invoking the `choose()` method on a `Select` object. This returns the index of a `Selectable` object which is *ready*. A selectable

```
class MsgCarPark implements Runnable {
  private Channel<Signal> arrive,depart;
  private int spaces,N;
  private StringCanvas disp;

  public MsgCarPark(Channel<Signal> a, Channel<Signal> l,
               StringCanvas d,int capacity) {
    depart=l; arrive=a; N=spaces=capacity; disp = d;
    disp.setString("Cars: "+0+"   Spaces: "+spaces);
  }

  private void display(int s) throws InterruptedException {
    disp.setString("Cars: "+(N-s)+"    Spaces: "+s);
    ThreadPanel.rotate(348);
  }

  public void run() {
    try {
     Select sel = new Select();
     sel.add(depart);
     sel.add(arrive);
     while(true) {
       ThreadPanel.rotate(12);
       arrive.guard(spaces>0);
       depart.guard (spaces<N);
       switch (sel.choose()) {
       case 1:depart.receive();display(++spaces);
              break;
       case 2:arrive.receive();display(--spaces);
              break;
       }
     }
    } catch (InterruptedException e){}
  }
}
```

Program 10.4 `MsgCarPark` class.

channel is *ready* if the sender has performed a send operation. The index is allocated to a selectable object based on the order that the object was added to the select object. Thus, in the example, the `depart` channel is allocated index 1 and the `arrive` channel index 2. When receive on the chosen channel is executed, it does not block since the channel is *ready*. If no selectable objects are ready then `choose()` blocks the calling thread waiting, in the example case, for a send on either the leave or the arrive channel.

This rather clumsy coding of a selective receive in Java would normally be done by a compiler if we had used a message-passing language. However, we have used Java so that readers can run message-passing programs in the same environment as the rest of the example programs in the book.

10.2 Asynchronous Message Passing

In asynchronous message passing, the send operation does not block, as in the synchronous scheme, but continues. Messages which have been sent but not received are held in a message queue. Senders add messages to the tail of the queue and a receiver removes messages from the head. The abstraction we use for asynchronous message communication is termed a *port*. As shown in Figure 10.6, many senders may send to a port but only a single receiver may receive messages from it. Communication is said to be *many-to-one*.

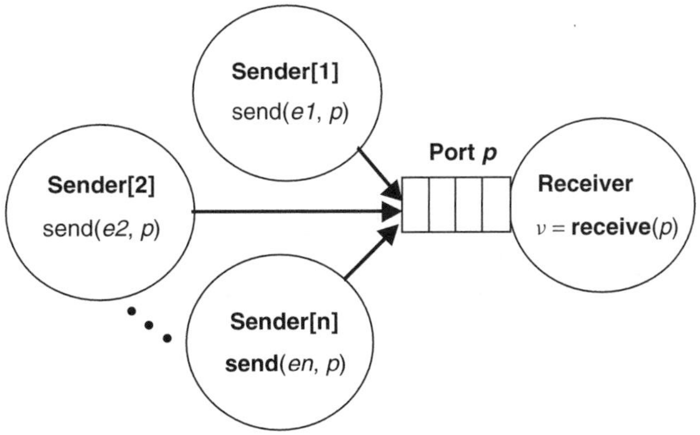

Figure 10.6 Asynchronous message-passing port.

A port is a (conceptually) unbounded first-in-first-out (FIFO) queue of messages. The send and receive operations on ports are defined as follows:

> **send**(e, p)–send the value of the expression e to port p. The process calling the send operation is not blocked. The message e is queued at the port if the receiver is not waiting.
>
> v = **receive**(p)–receive a value into local variable v from port p. The calling process is blocked if there are no messages queued to the port.

This form of communication is termed asynchronous since the sender proceeds independently of the receiver. Synchronization only occurs when the receiver waits for a sender if the queue of messages at the port is empty. If send operations can occur more frequently than receive, then there is no upper bound on the length of queue required and consequently no upper bound on the amount of store required to buffer messages. Obviously, in a real computer system there is a fixed bound on the buffer space available. It is the responsibility of the designer to ensure that a message-passing program does not exceed this bound.

A process may selectively wait for messages from a set of ports using exactly the same select construct described earlier for synchronous message passing.

10.2.1 Asynchronous Message Passing in Java

We can implement asynchronous message passing in Java in the same way as we implemented channels. The outline of the Java class that implements the port abstraction is described in Program 10.5.

```
class Port<T> extends Selectable{
  . . .
  public synchronized void send(T v) {. . .}
  public synchronized T receive()
           throws InterruptedException {. . .}
}
```

Program 10.5 Port class.

The `Port` class extends the `Selectable` base class so that receive operations on ports can be combined in selective receive operations as described in section 10.1.4 for channel receives. In fact, the implementation permits channels and ports to be combined in the same `Select` object since they are both derived from the same `Selectable` base class.

The operation of asynchronous message communication can be observed using the applet depicted in Figure 10.7. The demonstration program has two sender threads which each send a sequence of messages with values 0..9 to the receiver thread via a port. The receiver thread receives a sequence of values, which is a merge of the two sequences sent. The display depicts the situation in which

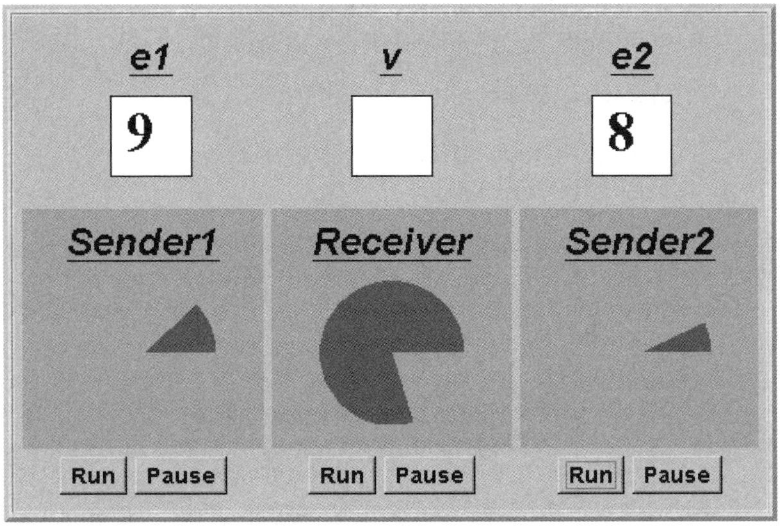

Figure 10.7 Asynchronous message-passing applet display.

`Sender1` is about to send the value 9 and `Sender2` is about to send the value 8. The port is currently empty and the receiver blocked. The receiver thread performs four receive operations on every revolution of its display while the senders perform a single send on each revolution. Consequently, if all three threads are running, the port will have a maximum of two messages queued and for most of the time it will be empty. However, if the receiver thread is suspended using the **Pause** button then the senders continue to run queuing messages in the port. In this situation, the applet will eventually terminate with a Java `OutOfMemory` runtime error. The code for sender and receiver threads is given in Program 10.6.

The threads and port are created by the Java code:

```
Port<Integer> port = new Port<Integer>();
tx1.start(new Asender(port,send1disp));
tx2.start(new Asender(port,send2disp));
rx.start(new Areceiver(port,recvdisp));
```

where `tx1`, `tx2` and `rx` are instances of `ThreadPanel` and `send1disp`, `send2disp` and `recvdisp` are instances of `SlotCanvas`.

10.2.2 Modeling Asynchronous Message Passing

We modeled synchronous communication directly as actions shared between two processes. A channel was modeled as the name of a shared action. Modeling

```
class Asender implements Runnable {
  private Port<Integer> port;
  private SlotCanvas display;

  Asender(Port<Integer> p, SlotCanvas d)
  {port=p; display =d;}

  public void run() {
    try {
      int ei = 0;
      while(true) {
        display.enter(String.valueOf(ei));
        ThreadPanel.rotate(90);
        port.send(new Integer(ei));
        display.leave(String.valueOf(ei));
        ei=(ei+1)%10; ThreadPanel.rotate(270);
      }
    } catch (InterruptedException e){}
  }
}

class Areceiver implements Runnable {
  private Port<Integer> port;
  private SlotCanvas display;

  Areceiver(Port<Integer> p, SlotCanvas d)
    {port=p; display =d;}

  public void run() {
    try {
    Integer v=null;
    while(true) {
      ThreadPanel.rotate(45);
      if (v!=null) display.leave(v.toString());
      ThreadPanel.rotate(45);
      v = port.receive();
      display.enter(v.toString());
    }
    } catch (InterruptedException e){}
  }
}
```

Program 10.6 `Asender` and `Areceiver` classes.

asynchronous communication is considerably more difficult. The first difficulty arises because of the potentially unbounded size of port queues. As discussed earlier, models must be finite so that we can carry out analysis. Consequently, we cannot model a port with an unbounded queue. Instead, we use the solution we adopted in modeling semaphores in Chapter 5 and model a finite entity that causes an error when it overflows. The model for a port that can queue up to three messages is:

```
range M = 0..9
set   S = {[M],[M][M]}

PORT                 // empty state, only send permitted
  = (send[x:M] ->PORT[x]),
PORT[h:M]            // one message queued to port
  = (send[x:M] ->PORT[x][h]
    |receive[h]->PORT
    ),
PORT[t:S][h:M]       // two or more messages queued to port
  = (send[x:M] ->PORT[x][t][h]
    |receive[h]->PORT[t]
    ).
```

The set S defines the set of values that can be taken by the tail of the queue when the queue contains two or more messages. However, care must be taken when modeling queues since the port described above, for a queue of up to three messages, generates a labeled transition system with 1111 states. A port to queue up to four messages can be produced by redefining the set S to be {[M],[M][M],[M][M][M]}. Extending the model to queue up to four messages would generate an *LTS* with 11111 states. In general, the model of a queue with n places for messages which can take up to x distinct values requires $(x^{n+1} - 1)/(x - 1)$ states. In modeling asynchronous message-passing programs, care must be taken to restrict both the range of data values that a message can take and the size of queues. Otherwise, intractably large models are produced. The port model with 1111 states is clearly too large to view as a graph. To check that the model describes the correct behavior, we can abstract from the value of messages and examine only send and receive actions. To do this, we relabel the send and receive actions as shown below:

```
||APORT = PORT
          /{send/send[M],receive/receive[M]}.
```

The minimized *LTS* for this abstracted port, called APORT, consists of only four states and is depicted in Figure 10.8.

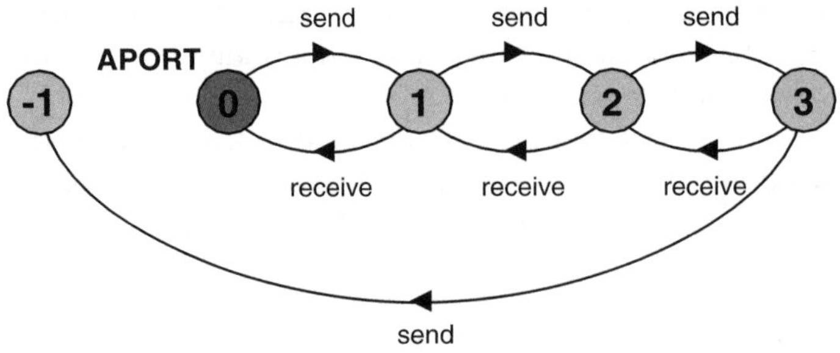

Figure 10.8 APORT labeled transition system.

Figure 10.8 clearly shows that the port accepts up to three consecutive sends. A fourth send causes the port queue to overflow and the port to move to the ERROR state.

With the model for a port, we can now provide a complete model for the example program of the previous section. The Sender and Receiver threads are modeled as:

```
ASENDER        = ASENDER[0],
ASENDER[e:M]   = (port.send[e]->ASENDER[(e+1)%10]).

ARECEIVER      = (port.receive[v:M]->ARECEIVER).
```

The composition of two SENDER processes and a RECEIVER process communicating by a port is described in Figure 10.9.

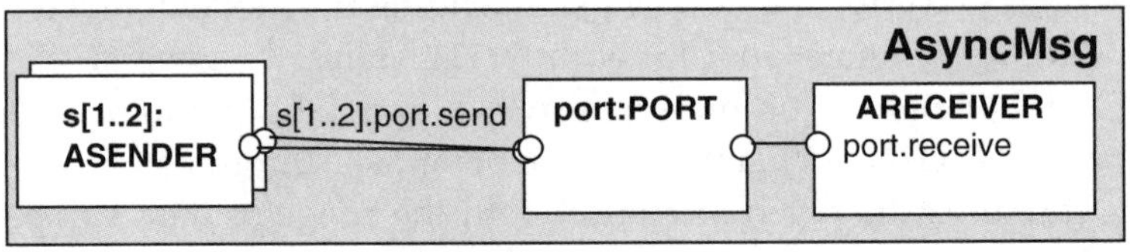

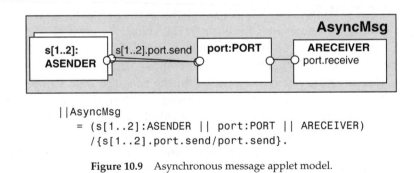

```
||AsyncMsg
   = (s[1..2]:ASENDER || port:PORT || ARECEIVER)
     /{s[1..2].port.send/port.send}.
```

Figure 10.9 Asynchronous message applet model.

A safety analysis of AsyncMsg produces the following output:

```
Trace to property violation in port:PORT:
     s.1.port.send.0
```

```
s.1.port.send.1
s.1.port.send.2
s.1.port.send.3
```

This is the situation where a fourth consecutive send causes the port queue to overflow. Since the model abstracts from time, it takes no account of the fact that in the implementation, we have made the receiver run faster than the senders. However, queue overflow (or rather memory overflow) can occur in the implementation if we slow the receiver by suspending it. The demonstration applet is inherently unsafe since, no matter how large the port queue, it can eventually overflow.

10.3 Rendezvous

Rendezvous, sometimes called *request-reply*, is a message-passing protocol used to support client–server interaction. Client processes send request messages to a server process requesting the server to perform some service. These request messages are queued to an *entry* in FIFO order. The server accepts requests from the *entry* and on completion of the requested service sends a reply message to the client that made the request. The client blocks waiting for the reply message. Rendezvous involves *many-to-one* communication in that many clients may request service from a single server. The reply to a request is a *one-to-one* communication from the server process to the client that requested the service. The protocol is depicted in Figure 10.10.

The abstraction that supports rendezvous is termed an *entry*. The operations on entries are defined as follows:

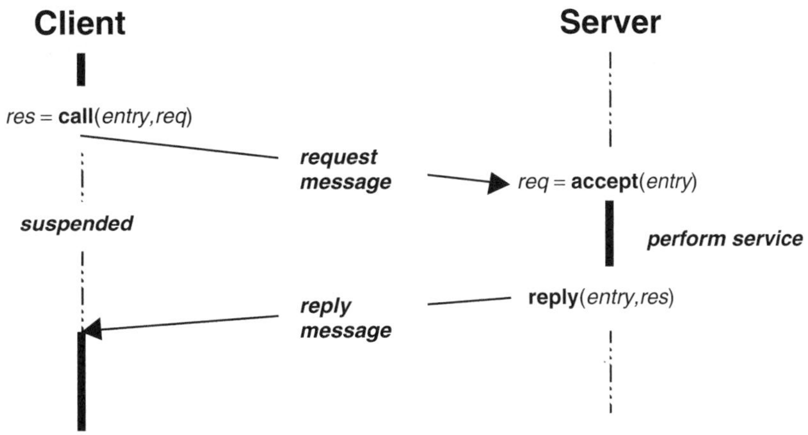

Figure 10.10 Rendezvous message-passing protocol.

> *res* = **call**(*e*, *req*)– send the value *req* as a request message which is queued to the entry *e*. The calling process is blocked until a reply message is received into the local variable *res*.
> *req* = **accept**(*e*)–receive the value of the request message from the entry *e* into the local variable *req*. If there are no request messages queued to the entry, then the server process is blocked.
> **reply**(*e*,*res*)–send the value *res* as a reply message to entry *e*.

The term ''rendezvous'' for this form of interaction was coined by the designers of the Ada programming language (Department of Defense, 1983) in which it is the main process interaction mechanism. *Rendezvous* captures the essence of the interaction since client and server meet and synchronize when the server performs a service for the client.

As with channels and ports, a server process may selectively wait for messages from a set of entries using the select construct described in section 10.1.1.

10.3.1 Rendezvous in Java

We implement the rendezvous entry abstraction using the port and channel abstractions defined in the previous sections. Remembering that request communication is many-to-one, we use a port to implement it. Since reply communication is one-to-one, we can use a channel. Each client that communicates with a server via an entry requires its own channel to receive replies. The entry implementation is depicted in Program 10.7.

The `Entry` class extends `Port`, which in turn extends `Selectable`. Consequently, `Entry` objects can be added to a `Select` object in the same way as `Channels` and `Ports`. The `call` method creates a channel object on which to receive the reply message. It then constructs a message, using the `CallMsg` class, consisting of a reference to this channel and a reference to the `req` object. After the `Client` thread has queued this message using `send`, it is suspended by a `receive` on the channel. The server calls `accept` to get a message from the entry. The `accept` method keeps a copy of the channel reference on which to reply in the local variable `cm`. The `reply` method sends the reply message to this channel. Note that although the `reply` method performs a synchronous `send` operation, this does not suspend the server since the client must always be blocked waiting on the reply channel. `Call`, `accept` and `reply` are not **`synchronized`** methods since `Client` and `Server` threads do not share any variables within `Entry`. The

```
class Entry<R,P> extends Port<R> {
  private CallMsg<R,P> cm;
  private Port<CallMsg<R,P>> cp = new Port<CallMsg<R,P>>();

  public P call(R req) throws InterruptedException {
    Channel<P> clientChan = new Channel<P>();
    cp.send(new CallMsg<R,P>(req,clientChan));
    return clientChan.receive();
  }

  public R accept() throws InterruptedException {
    cm = cp.receive();
    return cm.request;
  }

  public void reply(P res) throws InterruptedException {
    cm.replychan.send(res);
  }

  private class CallMsg<R,P> {
    R  request;
    Channel<P> replychan;
    CallMsg(R m, Channel<P> c)
      {request=m; replychan=c;}
  }

}
```

Program 10.7 `Entry` class.

`cm` variable is only accessed by the `Server` thread. `Client` and `Server` threads interact via `Port` and `Channel` objects, which are thread-safe.

Runtime systems for Ada have much more efficient implementations of rendezvous than the implementation described here. They exploit the fact that, since the client is blocked during a rendezvous, when client and server are on the same computer messages can be copied directly between client memory and server memory without buffering.

The applet display of Figure 10.11 demonstrates the operation of rendezvous using the `Entry` class. The display depicts the situation where both clients have called the server and are waiting for a reply. The server is currently servicing the request from Client A. The color of the rotating segment of the server is set to the same color as the client it is servicing.

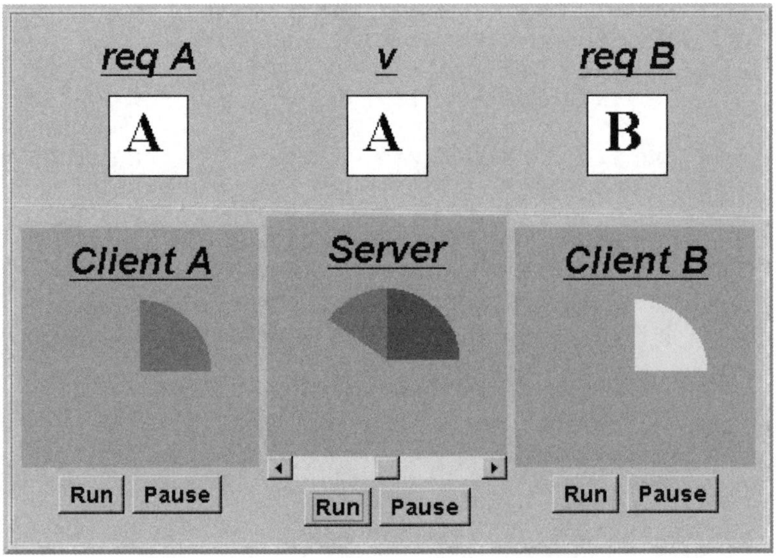

Figure 10.11 Rendezvous message-passing applet display.

The code for `Client` and `Server` threads is given in Program 10.8. The threads and entry for the demonstration program are created by the following Java code:

```
Entry<String,String> entry = new Entry<String,String>();
clA.start(new Client(entry,clientAdisp,"A"));
clB.start(new Client(entry,clientBdisp,"B"));
sv.start(new Server(entry,serverdisp));
```

where `clA`, `clB` and `sv` are instances of `ThreadPanel`, and `clientAdisp`, `clientBdisp` and `serverdisp` are instances of `SlotCanvas`.

10.3.2 Modeling Rendezvous

To model rendezvous communication, we can reuse the models for ports and channels in the same way as we reused the implementation classes `Port` and `Channel` in implementing the `Entry` class. In modeling the demonstration program, we ignore the message data values and concentrate on interaction. Consequently, the message that is sent by a client to the server consists of only the reply channel. This message is defined by:

```
set M = {replyA,replyB}
```

```
class Client implements Runnable {
  private Entry<String,String> entry;
  private SlotCanvas display;
  private String id;
  Client(Entry<String,String> e, SlotCanvas d, String s)
    {entry=e; display =d; id=s;}

  public void run() {
    try {
      while(true) {
        ThreadPanel.rotate(90);
        display.enter(id);
        String result = entry.call(id);
        display.leave(id); display.enter(result);
        ThreadPanel.rotate(90);
        display.leave(result);
        ThreadPanel.rotate(180);
      }
    } catch (InterruptedException e){}
  }
}
class Server implements Runnable {
  private Entry<String,String> entry;
  private SlotCanvas display;
  Server(Entry<String,String> e, SlotCanvas d)
    {entry=e; display =d;}

  public void run() {
    try {
      while(true) {
        while(!ThreadPanel.rotate());
        String request = entry.accept();
        display.enter(request);
        if (request.equals("A"))
           ThreadPanel.setSegmentColor(Color.magenta);
        else
           ThreadPanel.setSegmentColor(Color.yellow);
        while(ThreadPanel.rotate());
        display.leave(request);
        entry.reply("R");
      }
    } catch (InterruptedException e){}
  }
}
```

Program 10.8 `Client` and `Server` threads.

The PORT process queues messages of this type. An entry is modeled by:

```
||ENTRY = PORT/{call/send, accept/receive}.
```

This reuses the PORT definition from the previous section and relabels send to be call and receive to be accept. The Server thread is modeled by:

```
SERVER = (entry.accept[ch:M]->[ch]->SERVER).
```

The server accepts a message from the entry consisting of the name of the reply channel and then replies using this channel name. Remember that we model synchronous communication by a single shared action which is the name of the channel. The client is modeled by:

```
CLIENT(CH='reply) = (entry.call[CH]
                    ->[CH]->CLIENT).
```

where CH is a parameter initialized to the action label reply. In *FSP*, action labels used as parameter values or in expressions must be prefixed with a single quote to distinguish them from variables. The CLIENT process sends this parameter, which names the reply channel, to the entry and then waits for the reply. The composite model describing the demonstration program is shown in Figure 10.12.

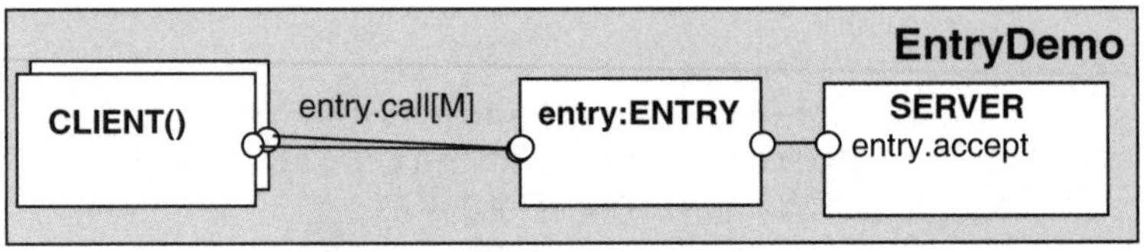

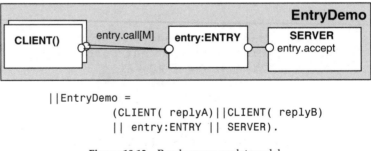

```
||EntryDemo =
        (CLIENT('replyA)||CLIENT('replyB)
        || entry:ENTRY || SERVER).
```

Figure 10.12 Rendezvous applet model.

We do not need to prefix the CLIENT processes since their parameter values lead to each having a distinct alphabet. For example, the alphabet of CLIENT('replyA) is {entry.call.replyA, replyA}. The following trace is the scenario in which both clients request service and the server has accepted the request for client A and replied:

```
entry.call.replyA
entry.call.replyB
entry.accept.replyA
replyA
```

A safety analysis of `EntryDemo` reveals no deadlocks or errors. Rendezvous communication means that each client can only have one outstanding request queued to the server entry at any one time. Consequently, in our demonstration program with two clients, the maximum entry queue length is two. In the model, we have used a port capable of queuing three messages. We can redefine this to be a queue with maximum capacity two by redefining the set `S` to be `{[M]}`. A safety analysis of this system reveals that the entry queue does not overflow.

10.3.3 Rendezvous and Monitor Method Invocation

From the viewpoint of a client, apart from syntactic differences, a call on an entry is the same as calling a monitor access method. The difference between rendezvous and monitor method invocation is to do with how the call from the client is handled. In the case of a rendezvous, the call is handled by a server thread that accepts the call from an entry. In the case of method invocation, the call is serviced by execution of the body of the method. The method body is executed by the client thread when it acquires the monitor lock. We saw how a bounded buffer can be implemented by a monitor in Chapter 5. The same buffer semantics from the viewpoint of the client can be implemented using rendezvous communication as sketched in outline below:

```
Buffer::
  entry put, get;
  int count = 0;        //number of items in buffer

  while(true)
    select
    when (count<size) and o =accept(put) =>
      ++count;   //insert item o into buffer

  reply(put,signal)
  or
  when (count>0) and accept(get)=>
      --count;   //get item o from buffer

  reply(put,o);
  end
```

Mutual exclusion is ensured by the fact that the buffer state is encapsulated in the server thread. Since the server thread processes only one request at a time, mutual exclusion is guaranteed. Which implementation is more efficient, monitor or rendezvous? In considering this question, we should compare rendezvous as implemented in Ada rather than the example implementation presented in this chapter. However, even with an efficient implementation, in a local context, where the client is located on the same computer as the server, the monitor implementation is more efficient since the rendezvous implementation always involves two context switches. For each rendezvous, there is a switch from client thread to server thread and then back from server to client. A method call to a monitor may require no context switch: for example, a get from a non-empty buffer when the producer does not currently have the monitor lock. However, the situation is not so clear-cut when the client is located on a different computer to the server. In this situation, the rendezvous may be better for the following reasons. If the client is remote from the monitor, then a protocol such as Java's Remote Method Invocation (RMI) must be used to transfer the client's invocation to the remote computer on which the monitor is located. At this location, RMI creates a new thread to perform the invocation on the monitor on behalf of the client. This thread creation is not required by a remote rendezvous.

We have used the issue of efficiency to focus on the differences in implementation between rendezvous and monitor method invocation. However, we can model programs at a sufficiently abstract level that the model can be implemented by either mechanism. For example, the model for the bounded buffer presented in Chapter 5 captures the behavior of both the monitor implementation and the rendezvous implementation we have outlined in this section. This illustrates a more general point. The modeling techniques we are using to describe and analyze concurrent programs are not restricted to programs implemented in Java. They can be used to model message-passing programs with equal facility.

Summary

This chapter has described three different kinds of message-passing mechanism. In *synchronous* message passing, the sender of a message is blocked until it is received. In *asynchronous* message passing, the sender continues after sending. Messages that have been sent and not received must be buffered. The buffering requirement of asynchronous message communication is potentially unbounded. In *rendezvous*, a two-way message-passing protocol provides for client–server interaction. Selective receive provides a way of implementing guarded actions in message-passing systems.

To illustrate message-passing programs, we developed three different abstractions: the `Channel` for synchronous message passing, the `Port` for asynchronous message passing and the `Entry` for rendezvous communication. The implementation relationship between these classes is summarized in the class diagram of Figure 10.13. In constructing `Entry` directly from `Port` we have deliberately ignored good object-oriented programming practice in the interests of simplicity. The problem we have ignored is that it is possible to invoke both `send()` and `receive()` methods on `Entry` objects. A more robust implementation would introduce a port implementation class with protected send and receive methods which would be used by both `Port` and `Entry` to implement their public interfaces.

Notes and Further Reading

Synchronous communication was introduced by C.A.R. Hoare (1978) in his paper on communicating sequential processes. The ideas in this paper led both to the CSP formalism (Hoare, 1985) and to the OCCAM programming language (INMOS Ltd., 1988a) designed by David May. OCCAM was used to program the Transputer (INMOS Ltd., 1988b), which supported both intra- and inter-processor synchronous communication in hardware.

Asynchronous message passing originated in operating systems in the late 1960s. Brinch-Hansen (1970) describes a set of message-passing primitives for the Danish RC4000 computer. Bob Balzer (1971) introduced the notion of a communication port. Asynchronous message-passing operations can now be found in all operating systems which allow processes to communicate with other machines on

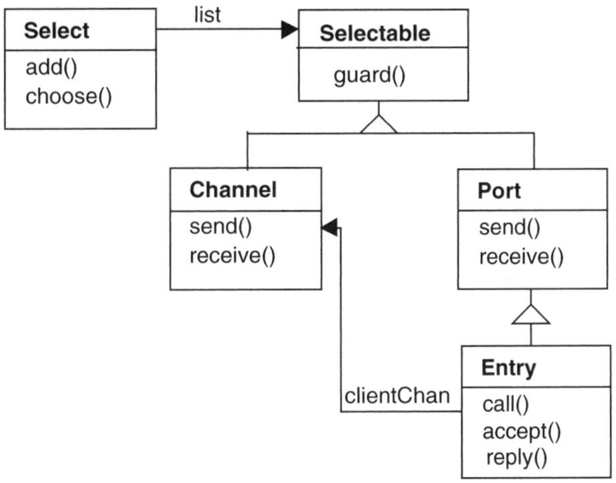

Figure 10.13 Message-passing classes.

a network. For example, UNIX provides a port-like abstraction called a socket and a variety of calls for sending and receiving messages. Asynchronous message passing has been included in a number of experimental programming languages and in the telecommunications language CHILL (CCITT, 1993). However, neither synchronous nor asynchronous message-passing primitives have found their way into a widely accepted general-purpose programming language. Consequently, message passing in concurrent programs remains at the level of operating system calls.

The name "rendezvous" is primarily associated with the Ada programming language (Department of Defense, 1983). We have described only the basic Ada rendezvous scheme in this chapter and omitted details concerned with timeouts on calls and accepts, conditional call and conditional accept, terminate alternative in a select, and so on. These additions make the semantics of Ada inter-process communication quite complex. In particular, they make extending the Ada rendezvous from a local interaction mechanism to a remote interaction mechanism difficult. The use of rendezvous-style communication is, of course, not restricted to Ada. Many operating system message-passing primitives support request–reply message passing reasonably directly. For example, `recvfrom()` on a UNIX datagram socket returns an address which can be used to send a reply message. In conclusion, the use of request–reply message protocols for client–server interaction is pervasive.

In his book, Vijay Garg (2004) provides further information on message passing and implementation of a number of distributed algorithms in Java.

Exercises

10.1 Ignoring the feature that allows objects of the `Channel` class to be used in a select, program a monitor in Java that implements the send and receive operations on channels (i.e. consider that `Channel` is not derived from `Selectable`).

Optional: Test your implementation by using it, instead of the provided `Channel` class, in the synchronous message-passing demonstration applet.

10.2 Modify your implementation of the previous exercise such that the receive operation can time out. The receive becomes:

```
synchronized Object receive(int timeout);
```

If the timeout period expires before a message is sent to the channel, the receive operation returns the value `null`.

10.3 Design a message-passing protocol which allows a producer process communicating with a consumer process by *asynchronous* messaging to send only a bounded number of messages, N, before it is blocked waiting for the consumer to receive a message. Construct a model which can be used to verify that your protocol prevents queue overflow if ports are correctly dimensioned.

Optional: Design and implement an applet which demonstrates the operation of your protocol.

10.4 Translate the bounded buffer outline of section 10.3.3 into Java using the `Entry` and `Select` classes.

Optional: Modify the bounded buffer applet of Chapter 5 to use this implementation rather than the monitor.

11 Concurrent Architectures

The term *architecture* is used in this chapter to mean the process structure of a concurrent program together with the way in which the elements of the program interact. For example, the client–server architecture of Chapter 10 is a structure consisting of one or more client processes interacting with a single server process. The interaction is bi-directional consisting of a request from a client to the server and a reply from the server to the client. This organization is at the heart of many distributed computing applications. The client–server architecture can be described independently of the detailed operation of client and server processes. We do not need to consider the service provided by the server or indeed the use the client makes of the result obtained from requesting the service. In describing the concurrent architecture of a program, we can ignore many of the details concerned with the application that the program is designed to implement. The advantage of studying architecture is that we can examine concurrent program structures that can be used in many different situations and applications. In the following, we look at some architectures that commonly occur in concurrent programs.

11.1 Filter Pipeline

A *filter* is a process that receives a stream of input values, performs some computation on these values and sends a stream of results as its output. In general, a filter can have more than one input stream and produce results on more than one output stream. Filters can easily be combined into larger computations by connecting the output stream from one filter to the input stream of another. Where filters have more than one input and output, they can be arranged into networks with complex topologies. In this section, we restrict the discussion to filters that have a single input and a single output. Such filters can be combined into *pipeline* networks. Many of the user-level commands in the UNIX operating system are filter processes, for example the text formatting programs *tbl, eqn* and *troff*. In UNIX, filter processes can be combined using pipes. A UNIX *pipe* is essentially a bounded buffer that buffers bytes of data output by one filter until they are input to the next filter. We will see in the following that the pipes that interconnect filters do not always need to include buffering.

To illustrate the use of filter pipelines, we develop a program with this architecture that computes prime numbers. The program is a concurrent implementation of a classic algorithm known as the Primes Sieve of Eratosthenes, after the Greek mathematician who developed it. The algorithm to determine all the primes between 2 and n proceeds as follows. First, write down a list of all the numbers between 2 and n:

2 3 4 5 6 7 . . . n

Then, starting with the first uncrossed-out number in the list, 2, cross out each number in the list which is a multiple of 2:

2 3 ~~4~~ 5 ~~6~~ 7 . . . n

Now move to the next uncrossed-out number, 3, and repeat the above by crossing out multiples of 3. Repeat the procedure until the end of the list is reached. When finished, all the uncrossed-out numbers are primes. The primes form a sieve which prevents their multiples falling through into the final list.

11.1.1 Primes Sieve Model

The concurrent version of the primes sieve algorithm operates by generating a stream of numbers. The multiples are removed by filter processes. The outline architecture of the program is depicted in Figure 11.1. It is essentially a process structure diagram from which we have omitted the details of action and process labels.

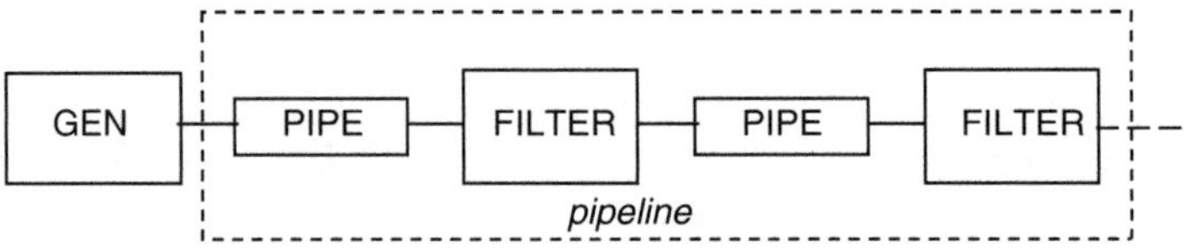

Figure 11.1 Primes Sieve process architecture.

The diagram describes the high-level structure of the program. The process `GEN` generates the stream of numbers from which multiples are filtered by the `FILTER` processes. To fully capture the architecture of the program, we must also consider how the application-specific processes interact. Interaction between these elements in the example is described by the `PIPE` processes. In the terminology of Software Architecture, these processes are termed *connectors*. Connectors encapsulate the interaction between the components of the architecture. Connectors and components are both modeled as processes. The distinction with respect to modeling is thus essentially methodological. We model the pipe connectors in the example as one-slot buffers as shown below:

```
const MAX = 9
range NUM = 2..MAX
set S = {[NUM],eos}
PIPE = (put[x:S]->get[x]->PIPE).
```

The `PIPE` process buffers elements from the set `S` which consist of the numbers `2..MAX` and the label `eos`, which is used to signal the end of a stream of numbers. This end of stream signal is required to correctly terminate the program.

To simplify modeling of the `GEN` and `FILTER` processes, we introduce an additional *FSP* construct – the conditional process. The construct can be used in the definition of both primitive and composite processes.

> The process **`if`** B **then** `P` **else** `Q` behaves as the process `P` if the condition `B` is true otherwise it behaves as `Q`. If the **else** `Q` is omitted and `B` is false, then the process behaves as `STOP`.

The definition of `GEN` using the conditional process construct is given below:

```
GEN         = GEN[2],
GEN[x:NUM]  = (out.put[x] ->
                  if x<MAX then
                  GEN[x+1]
                  else
                  (out.put.eos->end->GEN)
               ).
```

The `GEN` process outputs the numbers 2 to `MAX`, followed by the signal `eos`. The action `end` is used to synchronize termination of the `GEN` process and the filters. After `end` occurs, the model re-initializes rather than terminates. This is done so that, if deadlock is detected during analysis, it will be an error and not because of correct termination. The `FILTER` process records the first value it gets and subsequently filters out multiples of that value from the numbers it receives and forwards to the next filter in the pipeline.

```
FILTER = (in.get[p:NUM]->prime[p]->FILTER[p]
         |in.get.eos->ENDFILTER
         ),
FILTER[p:NUM] = (in.get[x:NUM] ->
                  if x%p!=0 then
                    (out.put[x]->FILTER[p])
                  else
                    FILTER[p]
                |in.get.eos->ENDFILTER
                ),
ENDFILTER     = (out.put.eos->end->FILTER).
```

The composite process that conforms to the structure given in Figure 11.1 can now be defined as:

```
||PRIMES(N=4) =
   ( gen:GEN
   ||pipe[0..N-1]:PIPE
   ||filter[0..N-1]:FILTER
   )/{ pipe[0]/gen.out,
       pipe[i:0..N-1]/filter[i].in,
       pipe[i:1..N-1]/filter[i-1].out,
       end/{filter[0..N-1].end,gen.end}
     }@{filter[0..N-1].prime,end}.
```

Safety analysis of this model detects no deadlocks or errors. The minimized *LTS* for the model is depicted in Figure 11.2. This confirms that the model computes the primes between 2 and 9 and that the program terminates correctly.

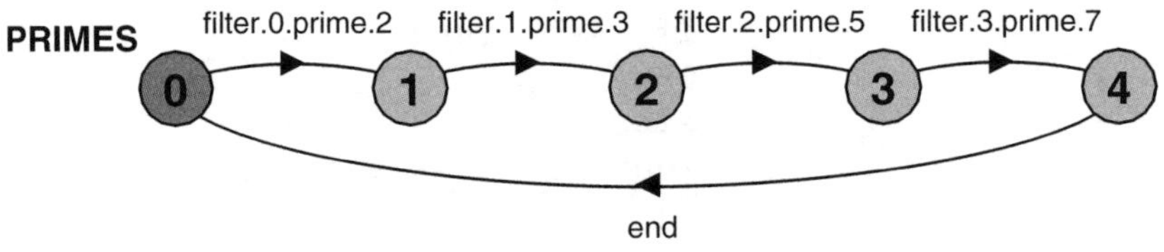

Figure 11.2 Minimized PRIMES *LTS*.

In fact, the concurrent version of the primes sieve algorithm does not ensure that all the primes between 2 and MAX are computed: it computes the first *N* primes where N is the number of filters in the pipeline. This can easily be confirmed by changing MAX to 11 and re-computing the minimized *LTS*, which is the same as Figure 11.2. To compute all the primes in the range 2 to 11, five filters are required.

Unbuffered Pipes

We have modeled the filter pipeline using single-slot buffers as the pipes connecting filters. Would the behavior of the overall program change if we used unbuffered pipes? This question can easily be answered by constructing a model in which the PIPE processes are omitted and instead, filters communicate directly by shared actions. This model is listed below. The action pipe[i] relabels the out.put action of filter[i-1] and the in.get action of filter[i].

```
||PRIMESUNBUF(N=4) =
  (gen:GEN || filter[0..N-1]:FILTER)
    /{ pipe[0]/gen.out.put,
      pipe[i:0..N-1]/filter[i].in.get,
      pipe[i:1..N-1]/filter[i-1].out.put,
      end/{filter[0..N-1].end,gen.end}
    }@{filter[0..N-1].prime,end}.
```

The minimized *LTS* for the above model is depicted in Figure 11.3.

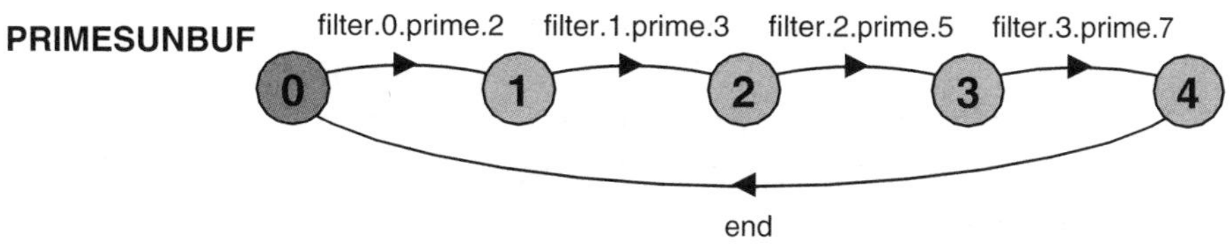

Figure 11.3 Minimized PRIMESUNBUF *LTS*.

The reader can see that the *LTS* of Figure 11.3 is identical to that of Figure 11.2. The behavior of the program with respect to generating primes and termination has not changed with the removal of buffers. Roscoe (1998) describes a program as being *buffer tolerant* if its required behavior does not change with the introduction of buffers. We have shown here that the primes sieve program is buffer tolerant to the introduction of a single buffer in each pipe. Buffer tolerance is an important property in the situation where we wish to distribute a concurrent program and, for example, locate filters on different machines. In this situation, buffering may be unavoidable if introduced by the communication system.

Abstracting from Application Detail

We showed above that the primes sieve program is tolerant to the introduction of a single buffer in each pipe. The usual problem of state space explosion arises if we try to analyze a model with more buffers. To overcome this problem, we can abstract from the detailed operation of the primes sieve program. Instead of modeling how primes are computed, we concentrate on how the components of the program interact, independently of the data values that they process. The abstract versions of components can be generated mechanically by relabeling the range of values NUM to be a single value. This is exactly the same technique that we used in section 10.2.2 to generate an abstract model of an asynchronous message port. The abstract versions of `GEN`, `FILTER` and `PIPE` are listed below.

```
||AGEN    = GEN/{out.put/out.put[NUM]}.

||AFILTER = FILTER/{out.put/out.put[NUM],
                    in.get /in.get.[NUM],
                    prime /prime[NUM]
                   }.

||APIPE   = PIPE/{put/put[NUM],get/get[NUM]}.
```

The *LTS* for the abstract version of a filter process is shown in Figure 11.4. In the detailed version of the filter, the decision to output a value depends on the computation as to whether the value is a multiple of the filter's prime. In the abstract version, this computation has been abstracted to the non-deterministic choice as to whether, in *state* (4), after an `in.get` action, the *LTS* moves to *state* (5) and does an `out.put` action or remains in *state* (4). This is a good example of how non-deterministic choice is used to abstract from computation. We could, of course, have written the abstract versions of the elements of the primes sieve program directly, rather than writing detailed versions and abstracting mechanically as we have done here. In fact, since *FSP*, as a design choice, has extremely limited facilities for describing and manipulating data, for complex programs abstraction is usually the best way to proceed.

To analyze the primes sieve program with multi-slot pipes, we can use a pipeline of `APIPE` processes defined recursively as follows:

```
||MPIPE(B=4) =
  if B==1 then
    APIPE
  else
    (APIPE/{mid/get} || MPIPE(B-1)/{mid/put})
  @{put,get}.
```

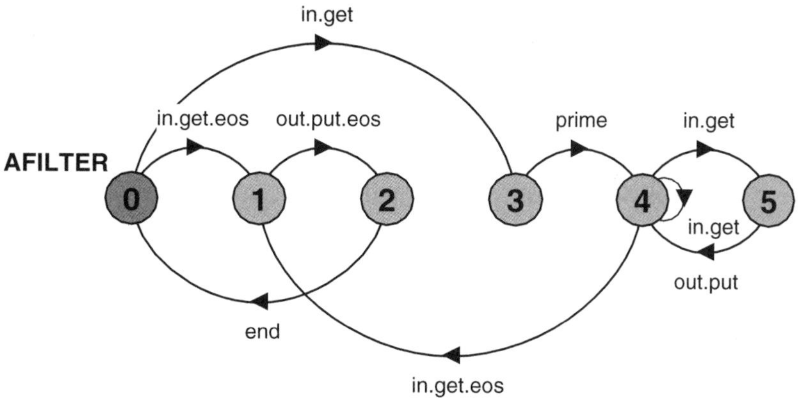

Figure 11.4 Minimized AFILTER *LTS*.

The abstract model for the primes program, with exactly the architecture of Figure 11.1, can now be defined as:

```
||APRIMES(N=4,B=3) =
   (gen:AGEN || PRIMEP(N)
   || pipe[0..N-1]:MPIPE(B)
   || filter[0..N-1]:AFILTER)
   /{ pipe[0]/gen.out,
      pipe[i:0..N-1]/filter[i].in,
      pipe[i:1..N-1]/filter[i-1].out,
      end/{filter[0..N-1].end,gen.end}
    }.
```

where PRIMEP is a safety property which we define in the following discussion.

Architectural Property Analysis

We refer to the properties that we can assert for the abstract model of the primes sieve program as architectural properties since they are concerned with the concurrent architecture of the program – structure and interaction – rather than its detailed operation. The general properties we wish to assert at this level are absence of deadlock and eventual termination (absence of livelock). Eventual termination is checked by the progress property END, which asserts that, in all executions of the program, the terminating action end must always occur.

```
progress END = {end}
```

The property specific to the application is that the prime from `filter[0]` should be produced before the prime from `filter[1]` and so on. The following safety property asserts this:

```
property
PRIMEP(N=4)    = PRIMEP[0],
PRIMEP[i:0..N]= (when (i<N)
                   filter[i].prime->PRIMEP[i+1]
                 |end -> PRIMEP
                 ).
```

The property does not assert that all the filters must produce primes before `end` occurs since the model can no longer determine that there are four primes between 2 and 9.

Analysis of `APRIME` using *LTSA* determines that there are no deadlocks, safety violations or progress violations for four filters and three slot pipes. The reader should verify that the safety and progress properties hold for other combinations of filters and buffering. When building this model, it is important that the *LTSA* option **`Minimize during composition`** is set, otherwise the minimized models for the abstracted elements are not built and consequently, the reduction in state space is not realized.

11.1.2 Primes Sieve Implementation

Figure 11.5 is a screen shot of the Primes Sieve applet display. The implementation supports both a buffered and unbuffered implementation of the pipe connector. The figure depicts a run using unbuffered pipes. The box in the top left hand of the display depicts the latest number generated by the thread that implements `GEN`. The rest of the boxes, at the top, display the latest number received by a filter. The boxes below display the prime used by that filter to remove multiples.

The implementation follows in a straightforward way from the model developed in the previous section. The number generator and filter processes are implemented as threads. As mentioned above, we have provided two implementations for the pipe connector. The classes involved in the program and their inter-relationships are depicted in the class diagram of Figure 11.6. The display is handled by a single class, `PrimesCanvas`. The methods provided by this class, together with a description of their functions, are listed in Program 11.1.

The code for the `Generator` and `Filter` threads is listed in Programs 11.2 and 11.3. The implementation of these threads corresponds closely to the detailed models for `GEN` and `FILTER` developed in the previous section. Additional code has been added only to display the values generated and processed. To simplify

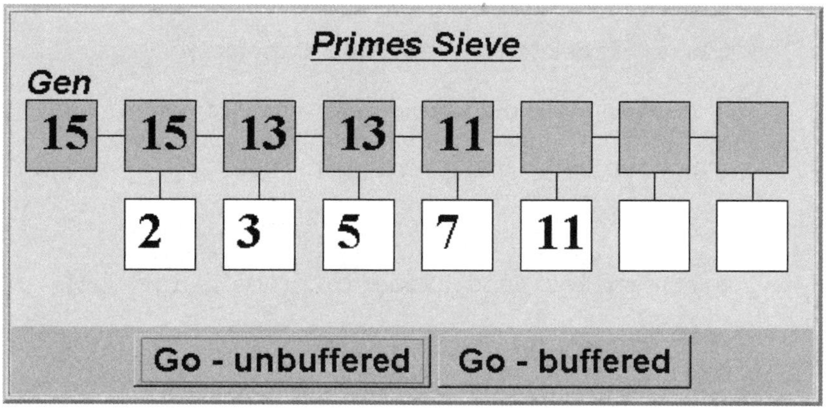

Figure 11.5 Primes Sieve applet display.

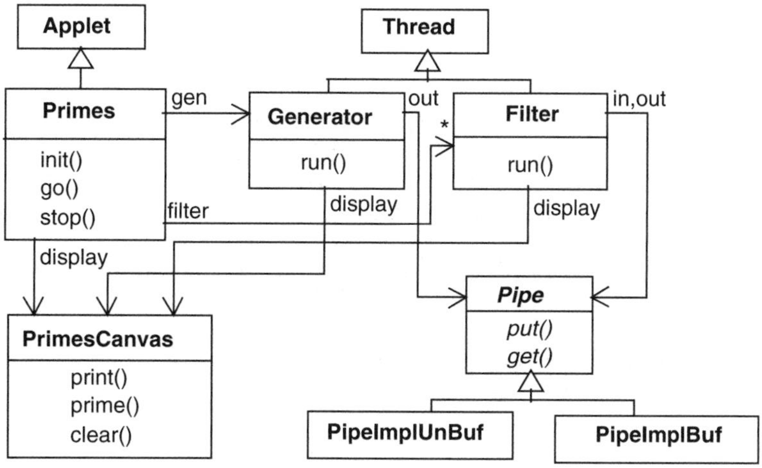

Figure 11.6 Primes class diagram.

the display and the pipe implementations, the end-of-stream signal is an integer value that does not occur in the set of generated numbers. The obvious values to use are `0`, `1`, `-1` or `MAX+1`. In the applet class, `Primes.EOS` is defined to be `-1`.

Instead of implementing buffered and unbuffered pipes from scratch, we have reused classes developed in earlier chapters. The synchronous message-passing class, `Channel`, from Chapter 10 is used to implement an unbuffered pipe and the bounded buffer class, `BufferImpl`, from Chapter 5 is used to implement buffered pipes. The `Pipe` interface and its implementations are listed in Program 11.4.

```
class PrimesCanvas extends Canvas {

   // display val in an upper box numbered index
   // boxes are numbered from the left
synchronized void print(int index, int val){...}

   // display val in a lower box numbered index
   // the lower box indexed by 0 is not displayed
synchronized void prime(int index, int val){...}

   // clear all boxes
synchronized void clear(){...}

}
```

Program 11.1 `PrimesCanvas` class.

```
class Generator extends Thread {
  private PrimesCanvas display;
  private Pipe<Integer> out;
  static int MAX = 50;

  Generator(Pipe<Integer> c, PrimesCanvas d)
    {out=c; display = d;}

  public void run() {
    try {
      for (int i=2;i<=MAX;++i) {
        display.print(0,i);
        out.put(i);
        sleep(500);
      }
      display.print(0,Primes.EOS);
      out.put(Primes.EOS);
    } catch (InterruptedException e){}
  }

}
```

Program 11.2 `Generator` class.

```
class Filter extends Thread {
  private PrimesCanvas display;
  private Pipe<Integer> in,out;
  private int index;

  Filter(Pipe<Integer> i, Pipe<Integer> o,
    int id, PrimesCanvas d)
    {in = i; out=o;display = d; index = id;}

  public void run() {
    int i,p;
    try {
      p = in.get();
      display.prime(index,p);
      if (p==Primes.EOS && out!=null) {
        out.put(p); return;
      }
      while(true) {
        i= in.get();
        display.print(index,i);
        sleep(1000);
        if (i==Primes.EOS) {
          if (out!=null) out.put(i); break;
        } else if (i%p!=0 && out!=null)
          out.put(i);
      }
    } catch (InterruptedException e){}
  }
}
```

Program 11.3 `Filter` class.

The structure of a generator thread and N filter threads connected by pipes is constructed by the `go()` method of the `Primes` applet class. The code is listed below:

```
public interface Pipe<T> {

  public void put(T o)
     throws InterruptedException; // put object into buffer

  public T get()
     throws InterruptedException; // get object from buffer
}

// Unbuffered pipe implementation
public class PipeImplUnBuf<T> implements Pipe<T> {
  Channel<T> chan = new Channel<T>();

  public void put(T o)
    throws InterruptedException {
    chan.send(o);
  }

  public T get()
    throws InterruptedException {
    return chan.receive();
  }
}

// Buffered pipe implementation
public class PipeImplBuf<T> implements Pipe<T> {
  Buffer<T> buf = new BufferImpl<T>(10);

  public void put(T o)
    throws InterruptedException {
    buf.put(o);
  }

  public T get()
    throws InterruptedException {
    return buf.get();
  }
}
```

Program 11.4 `Pipe`, `PipeImplUnBuf` and `PipeImplBuf` classes.

```
private void go(boolean buffered) {
    display.clear();

    //create channels
    ArrayList<Pipe<Integer>> pipes =
      new ArrayList<Pipe<Integer>>();
```

```
    for (int i=0; i<N; ++i)
      if (buffered)
        pipes.add(new PipeImplBuf<Integer>());
      else
        pipes.add(new PipeImplUnBuf<Integer>());

    //create threads
    gen = new Generator(pipes.get(0),display);
    for (int i=0; i<N; ++i)
      filter[i] = new Filter(pipes.get(i),
             i<N-1?pipes.get(i+1):null,i+1,display);
      gen.start();
      for (int i=0; i<N; ++i) filter[i].start();
  }
```

Why Use Buffering?

We saw from modeling the primes sieve program that it computed the correct result, whether or not the pipes connecting filter processes were buffered. In line with the model, the implementation also works correctly with and without buffers. Why then should we ever use buffering in this sort of architecture when the logical behavior is independent of buffering? The answer is concerned with the execution efficiency of the program.

When a process or thread suspends itself and another is scheduled, the operating system performs a context switch which, as discussed in Chapter 3, involves saving the registers of the suspended process and loading the registers for the newly scheduled process. Context switching consumes CPU cycles and, although the time for a thread switch is much less than that for an operating system process, it is nevertheless an overhead. A concurrent program runs faster if we can reduce the amount of context switching. With no buffering, the generator and filter threads are suspended every time they produce an item until that item is consumed by the next thread in the pipeline. With buffers, a thread can run until the buffer is full. Consequently, in a filter pipeline, buffering can reduce the amount of context switching. In our implementation, this benefit is not actually realized since we have introduced delays for display purposes. However, it is generally the case that a pipeline architecture performs better with buffered pipes.

If filters are located on physically distributed processors, buffering has an additional advantage. When a message is sent over a communication link, there is a fixed processing and transmission overhead that is independent of message size. Consequently, when transmitting a lot of data, it is better to transmit a few large messages rather than many small messages. With buffering in the filter pipeline, it is easy to arrange that a sequence of items be sent in the same message.

11.2 Supervisor–Worker

Supervisor–Worker is a concurrent architecture that can be used to speed up the execution of some computational problems by exploiting parallel execution on multiple processors. The architecture applies when a computational problem can be split up into a number of independent sub-problems. These independent sub-problems are referred to as *tasks* in the following discussion. The process architecture of a Supervisor–Worker program is depicted in Figure 11.7.

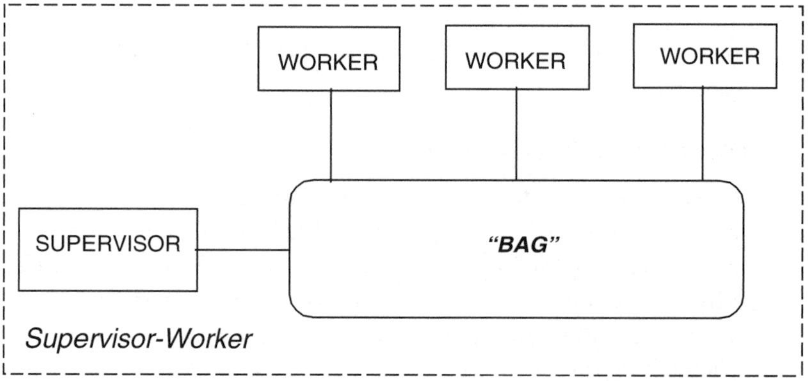

Figure 11.7 Supervisor–Worker process architecture.

Supervisor and worker processes interact by a connector that we refer to, for the moment, as a "bag". The supervisor process is responsible for generating an initial set of tasks and placing them in the bag. Additionally, the supervisor collects results from the bag and determines when the computation has finished. Each worker repetitively takes a task from the bag, computes the result for that task, and places the result in the bag. This process is repeated until the supervisor signals that the computation has finished. The architecture can be used to parallelize divide-and-conquer problems since workers can put new tasks into the bag as well as results. Another way of thinking of this is that the result computed by a worker can be a new set of tasks. Thus, in a divide-and-conquer computation, the supervisor places an initial task in the bag and this is split into two further problems by a worker and so on. We can use any number of worker processes in the Supervisor–Worker architecture. Usually, it is best to have one worker process per physical processor. First, we examine an interaction mechanism suitable for implementing the *bag* connector.

11.2.1 Linda Tuple Space

Linda is the collective name given by Carriero and Gelernter (1989a) to a set of primitive operations used to access a data structure called a *tuple space*. A tuple space is a shared associative memory consisting of a collection of tagged data records called tuples. Each data tuple in a tuple space has the form:

(''tag'', $value_1, \ldots, value_n$)

The tag is a literal string used to distinguish between tuples representing different classes of data. $value_i$ are zero or more data values: integers, floats and so on.

There are three basic Linda operations for manipulating data tuples: **out, in** and **rd**. A process deposits a tuple in a tuple space using:

out (''tag'', $expr_1, \ldots, expr_n$)

Execution of **out** completes when the expressions have been evaluated and the resulting tuple has been deposited in the tuple space. The operation is similar to an asynchronous message **send** except that the tuple is stored in an unordered tuple space rather than appended to the queue associated with a specific **port**. A process removes a tuple from the tuple space by executing:

in (''tag'', $field_1, \ldots, field_n$)

Each $field_i$ is either an expression or a formal parameter of the form ?*var* where *var* is a local variable in the executing process. The arguments to **in** are called a template; the process executing **in** blocks until the tuple space contains a tuple that matches the template and then removes it. A template matches a data tuple in the following circumstances: the tags are identical, the template and tuple have the same number of fields, the expressions in the template are equal to the corresponding values in the tuple, and the variables in the template have the same type as the corresponding values in the tuple. When the matching tuple is removed from the tuple space, the formal parameters in the template are assigned the corresponding values from the tuple. The **in** operation is similar to a message **receive** operation with the tag and values in the template serving to identify the port.

The third basic operation is **rd**, which functions in exactly the same way as **in** except that the tuple matching the template is not removed from the tuple space. The operation is used to examine the contents of a tuple space without modifying it. Linda also provides non-blocking versions of **in** and **rd** called **inp** and **rdp** which return true if a matching tuple is found and return false otherwise.

Linda has a sixth operation called **eval** that creates an active or process tuple. The **eval** operation is similar to an **out** except that one of the arguments is a procedure that operates on the other arguments. A process is created to evaluate the procedure and the process tuple becomes a passive data tuple when the procedure terminates. This **eval** operation is not necessary when a system has some other mechanism for creating new processes. It is not used in the following examples.

Tuple Space Model

Our modeling approach requires that we construct finite state models. Consequently, we must model a tuple space with a finite set of tuple values. In addition, since a tuple space can contain more than one tuple with the same value, we must fix the number of copies of each value that are allowed. We define this number to be the constant *N* and the allowed values to be the set *Tuples*.

```
const N = ...
set Tuples = {...}
```

The precise definition of `N` and `Tuples` depends on the context in which we use the tuple space model. Each tuple value is modeled by an *FSP* label of the form $tag.val_1 \ldots val_n$. We define a process to manage each tuple value and the tuple space is then modeled by the parallel composition of these processes:

```
const False = 0
const True = 1
range Bool = False..True

TUPLE(T='any) = TUPLE[0],
TUPLE[i:0..N]
  = (out[T]                       -> TUPLE[i+1]
    |when (i>0) in[T]             -> TUPLE[i-1]
    |when (i>0) inp[True][T]      -> TUPLE[i-1]
    |when (i==0)inp[False][T]     -> TUPLE[i]
    |when (i>0) rd[T]             -> TUPLE[i]
    |rdp[i>0][T]                  -> TUPLE[i]
    ).

||TUPLESPACE = forall [t:Tuples] TUPLE(t).
```

The *LTS* for `TUPLE` value `any` with `N=2` is depicted in Figure 11.8. Exceeding the capacity by performing more than two `out` operations leads to an `ERROR`.

An example of a conditional operation on the tuple space would be:

```
inp[b:Bool][t:Tuples]
```

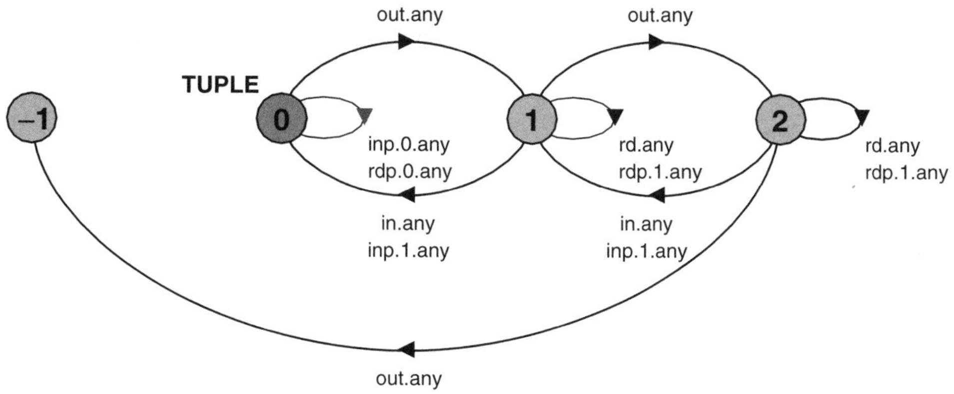

Figure 11.8 TUPLE *LTS.*

The value of the local variable t is only valid when b is true. Each TUPLE process has in its alphabet the operations on one specific tuple value. The alphabet of TUPLESPACE is defined by the set TupleAlpha:

```
set TupleAlpha
  = {{in,out,rd,rdp[Bool],inp[Bool]}.Tuples}
```

A process that shares access to the tuple space must include all the actions of this set in its alphabet.

Tuple Space Implementation

Linda tuple space can be distributed over many processors connected by a network. However, for demonstration purposes we describe a simple centralized implementation that allows matching of templates only on the tag field of a tuple. The interface to our Java implementation of a tuple space is listed in Program 11.5.

```
public interface TupleSpace {

  // deposits data in tuple space
  public void out (String tag, Object data);

  // extracts object with tag from tuple space, blocks if not available
  public Object in (String tag)
                        throws InterruptedException;
  // reads object with tag from tuple space, blocks if not available
  public Object rd (String tag)
```

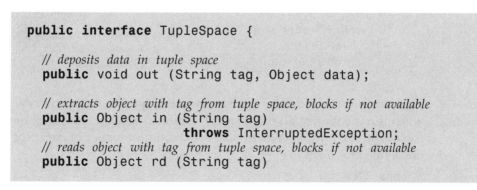

Program 11.5 TupleSpace interface.

```
                          throws InterruptedException;
    // extracts object if available, return null if not available
    public Object inp (String tag);

    // reads object if available, return null if not available
    public Object rdp (String tag);

}
```

Program 11.5 *(Continued)*.

We use a hash table of vectors to implement the tuple space (Program 11.6). Although the tuple space is defined to be unordered, for simplicity, we have chosen to store the tuples under a particular tag in FIFO order. New tuples are appended to the end of a vector for a tag and removed from its head. For simplicity, a naive synchronization scheme is used which wakes up all threads whenever a new tuple is added. A more efficient scheme would wake up only those threads waiting for a tuple with the same tag as the new tuple.

11.2.2 Supervisor-Worker Model

We model a simple Supervisor–Worker system in which the supervisor initially outputs a set of tasks to the tuple space and then collects results. Each worker repetitively gets a task and computes the result. The algorithms for the supervisor and each worker process are sketched below:

```
Supervisor::
   forall tasks: out("task",...)
   forall results: in("result",...)
   out("stop")
Worker::
   while not rdp("stop") do
      in("task",...)
      compute result
      out("result",...)
```

To terminate the program, the supervisor outputs a tuple with the tag "stop" when it has collected all the results it requires. Workers run until they read this tuple. The set of tuple values and the maximum number of copies of each value are defined for the model as:

```
const N      = 2
set   Tuples = {task,result,stop}
```

```
class TupleSpaceImpl implements TupleSpace {
  private Hashtable tuples = new Hashtable();

  public synchronized void out(String tag,Object data){
    Vector v = (Vector) tuples.get(tag);
    if (v == null) {
      v = new Vector();
      tuples.put(tag,v);
    }
    v.addElement(data);
    notifyAll();
  }

  private Object get(String tag, boolean remove) {
    Vector v = (Vector) tuples.get(tag);
    if (v == null) return null;
    if (v.size() == 0) return null;
    Object o = v.firstElement();
    if (remove) v.removeElementAt(0);
    return o;
  }

  public synchronized Object in (String tag)
                  throws InterruptedException {
    Object o;
    while ((o = get(tag,true)) == null) wait();
    return o;
  }

  public Object rd (String tag)
                  throws InterruptedException {
    Object o;
    while ((o = get(tag,false)) == null) wait();
    return o;
  }

  public synchronized Object inp (String tag) {
    return get(tag,true);
  }

  public synchronized Object rdp (String tag) {
    return get(tag,false);
  }
}
```

Program 11.6 `TupleSpaceImpl` class.

The supervisor outputs *N* tasks to the tuple space, collects *N* results and then outputs the "stop" tuple and terminates.

```
SUPERVISOR    = TASK[1],
TASK[i:1..N] =
  (out.task   ->
     if i<N then TASK[i+1] else RESULT[1]),
RESULT[i:1..N] =
  (in.result ->
     if i<N then RESULT[i+1] else FINISH),
FINISH =
  (out.stop   -> end -> STOP) + TupleAlpha.
```

The worker checks for the "stop" tuple before getting a task and outputting the result. The worker terminates when it reads "stop" successfully.

```
WORKER =
  (rdp[b:Bool].stop->
    if (!b) then
      (in.task -> out.result -> WORKER)
    else
      (end -> STOP)
  )+TupleAlpha.
```

The *LTS* for both SUPERVISOR and WORKER with N=2 is depicted in Figure 11.9.

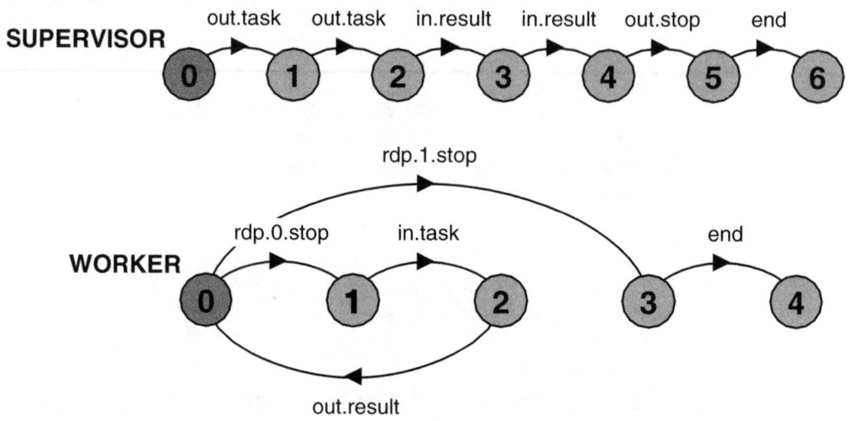

Figure 11.9 SUPERVISOR and WORKER *LTS*.

In the primes sieve example, we arranged that the behavior was cyclic to avoid detecting a deadlock in the case of correct termination. An alternative way of avoiding this situation is to provide a process that can still engage in actions after the end action has occurred. We use this technique here and define an ATEND process that engages in the action ended after the correct termination action end occurs.

```
ATEND   = (end->ENDED),
ENDED = (ended->ENDED).
```

A Supervisor–Worker model with two workers called redWork and blueWork, which conforms to the architecture of Figure 11.7, can now be defined by:

```
||SUPERVISOR_WORKER
    = ( supervisor:SUPERVISOR
      || {redWork,blueWork}:WORKER
      || {supervisor,redWork,blueWork}::TUPLESPACE
      || ATEND
      )/{end/{supervisor,redWork,blueWork}.end}.
```

Analysis

Safety analysis of this model using *LTSA* reveals the following deadlock:

```
Trace to DEADLOCK:
    supervisor.out.task
    supervisor.out.task
    redWork.rdp.0.stop            – rdp returns false
    redWork.in.task
    redWork.out.result
    supervisor.in.result
    redWork.rdp.0.stop            – rdp returns false
    redWork.in.task
    redWork.out.result
    supervisor.in.result
    redWork.rdp.0.stop            – rdp returns false
    supervisor.out.stop
    blueWork.rdp.1.stop           – rdp returns true
```

This trace is for an execution in which the red worker computes the results for the two tasks put into tuple space by the supervisor. This is quite legitimate behavior for a real system since workers can run at different speeds and take different amounts of time to start. The deadlock occurs because the supervisor only outputs the "stop" tuple *after* the red worker attempts to read it. When the red worker tries to read, the "stop" tuple has not yet been put into the tuple space and, consequently, the worker does not terminate but blocks waiting for another task. Since the supervisor has finished, no more tuples will be put into the tuple space and consequently, the worker will never terminate.

This deadlock, which can be repeated for different numbers of tasks and workers, indicates that the termination scheme we have adopted is incorrect. Although the supervisor completes the computation, workers may not terminate. It relies on a worker being able to input tuples until it reads the "stop" tuple. As the model demonstrates, this may not happen. This would be a difficult error to observe in an implementation since the program would produce the correct computational result. However, after an execution, worker processes would be blocked and consequently retain execution resources such as memory and system resources such as control blocks. Only after a number of executions might the user observe a system crash due to many hung processes. Nevertheless, this technique of using a "stop" tuple appears in an example Linda program in a standard textbook on concurrent programming!

A simple way of implementing termination correctly would be to make a worker wait for either inputting a "task" tuple or reading a "stop" tuple. Unfortunately, while this is easy to model, it cannot easily be implemented since Linda does not have an equivalent to the selective receive described in Chapter 10. Instead, we adopt a scheme in which the supervisor outputs a "task" tuple with a special stop value. When a worker inputs this value, it outputs it again and then terminates. Because a worker outputs the stop task before terminating, each worker will eventually input it and terminate. This termination technique appears in algorithms published by the designers of Linda (Carriero and Gelernter, 1989b). The revised algorithms for supervisor and worker are sketched below:

Supervisor::
    forall tasks:- **out**("task",...)
    forall results:- **in**("result",...)
    out("task",*stop*)
Worker::
    while true do
        in("task",...)
        if value is *stop* then **out**("task",*stop*); exit
        compute result
        out("result",...)

The tuple definitions and models for supervisor and worker now become:

```
set Tuples   = {task,task.stop,result}

SUPERVISOR    = TASK[1],
TASK[i:1..N] =
  (out.task ->
```

```
      if i<N then TASK[i+1] else RESULT[1]),
  RESULT[i:1..N] =
    (in.result ->
      if i<N then RESULT[i+1] else FINISH),
  FINISH =
    (out.task.stop -> end -> STOP)
    + TupleAlpha.

  WORKER =
    (in.task -> out.result -> WORKER
    |in.task.stop -> out.task.stop -> end ->STOP
    ) + TupleAlpha.
```

The revised model does not deadlock and satisfies the progress property:

```
progress END = {ended}
```

A sample trace from this model, which again has the red worker computing both tasks, is shown in Figure 11.10.

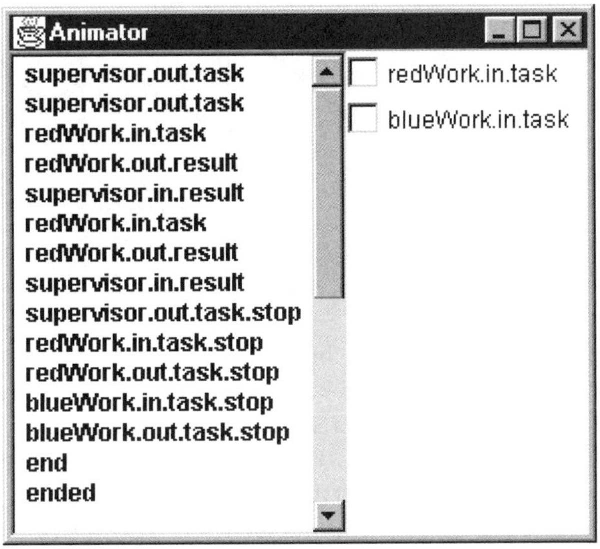

Figure 11.10 Trace of Supervisor–Worker model.

In the first section of this chapter, the primes sieve application was modeled in some detail. We then abstracted from the application to investigate the concurrent properties of the Filter Pipeline architecture. In this section, we have modeled the

Supervisor–Worker architecture directly without reference to an application. We were able to discover a problem with termination and provide a general solution that can be used in any application implemented within the framework of the architecture.

11.2.3 Supervisor-Worker Implementation

To illustrate the implementation and operation of Supervisor–Worker architectures, we develop a program that computes an approximate value of the area under a curve using the *rectangle method*. More precisely, the program computes an approximate value for the integral:

$$\int_{0}^{1.0} f(x)dx$$

The rectangle method involves summing the areas of small rectangles that nearly fit under the curve as shown in Figure 11.11.

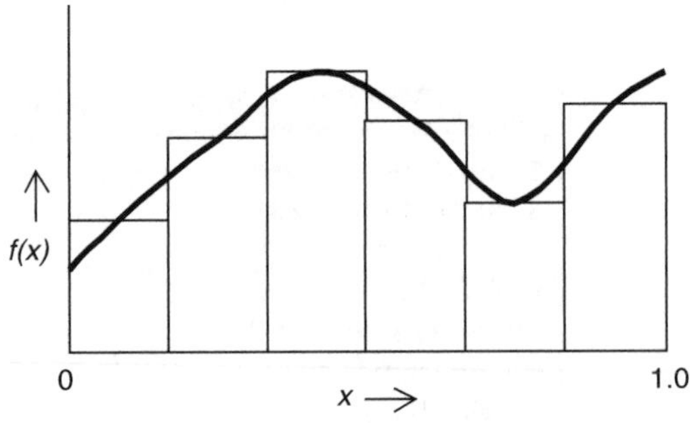

Figure 11.11 Rectangle method.

In the Supervisor–Worker implementation, the supervisor determines how many rectangles to compute and hands the task of computing the area of the rectangles to the workers. The demonstration program has four worker threads each with a different color attribute. When the supervisor inputs a result, it displays the rectangle corresponding to that result with the color of the worker. The display of a completed computation is depicted in Figure 11.12.

Each worker is made to run at a different speed by performing a delay before outputting the result to the tuple space. The value of this delay is chosen at random when the worker is created. Consequently, each run behaves differently. The display of Figure 11.12 depicts a run in which some workers compute more results than others. During a run, the number of the task that each worker thread is currently computing is displayed. The last task that the worker completed is

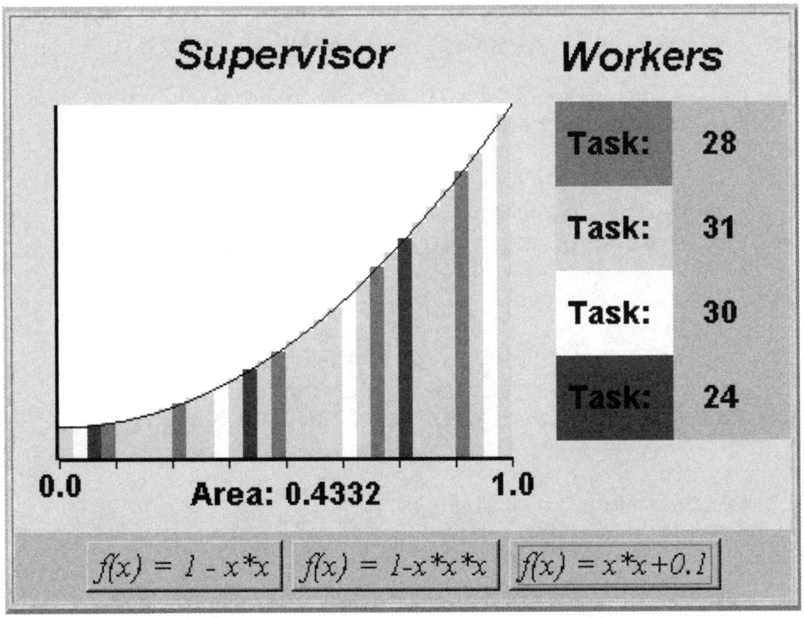

Figure 11.12 Supervisor–Worker applet.

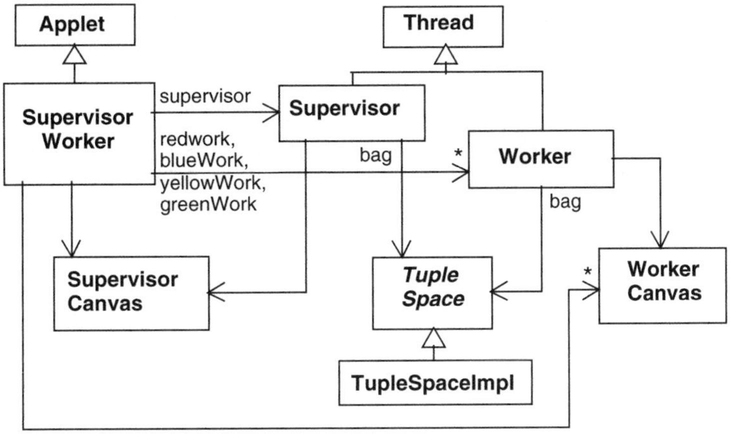

Figure 11.13 Supervisor–Worker class diagram.

displayed at the end of a run. The class diagram for the demonstration program is shown in Figure 11.13.

The displays for the supervisor and worker threads are handled, respectively, by the classes `SupervisorCanvas` and `WorkerCanvas`. The methods provided by these classes, together with a description of what they do, are listed in Program 11.7.

```
class SupervisorCanvas extends Canvas {

  // display rectangle slice i with color c, add a to area field
  synchronized void setSlice(
              int i,double a,Color c) {...}

  // reset display to clear rectangle slices and draw curve for f
  synchronized void reset(Function f) {...}

}

class WorkerCanvas extends Panel {
  // display current task number val
  synchronized void setTask(int val) {...}
}

interface Function {
  double fn(double x);
}

class OneMinusXsquared implements Function {
  public double fn (double x) {return 1-x*x;}
}

class OneMinusXcubed implements Function {
  public double fn (double x) {return 1-x*x*x;}
}

class XsquaredPlusPoint1 implements Function {
  public double fn (double x) {return x*x+0.1;}
}
```

Program 11.7 `SupervisorCanvas`, `WorkerCanvas` and `Function` classes.

The interface for the function *f(x)* together with three implementations are also included in Program 11.7.

A task that is output to the tuple space by the supervisor thread is represented by a single integer value. This value identifies the rectangle for which the worker computes the area. A result requires a more complex data structure since, for display purposes, the result includes the rectangle number and the worker color attribute in addition to the computed area of the rectangle. The definition of the `Result` and the `Supervisor` classes is listed in Program 11.8.

The supervisor thread is a direct translation from the model. It outputs the set of rectangle tasks to the tuple space and then collects the results. Stop is encoded

```
class Result {
  int task;
  Color worker;
  double area;
  Result(int s, double a, Color c)
    {task =s; worker=c; area=a;}
}

class Supervisor extends Thread {
  SupervisorCanvas display;
  TupleSpace bag;
  Integer stop = new Integer(-1);

  Supervisor(SupervisorCanvas d, TupleSpace b)
    { display = d; bag = b; }

  public void run () {
    try {
      // output tasks to tuplespace
      for (int i=0; i<SupervisorCanvas.Nslice; ++i)
        bag.out("task",new Integer(i));
      // collect results
      for (int i=0; i<display.Nslice; ++i) {
        Result r = (Result)bag.in("result");
        display.setSlice(r.task,r.area,r.worker);
      }
      // output stop tuple
      bag.out("task",stop);
    } catch (InterruptedException e){}
  }
}
```

Program 11.8 `Result` and `Supervisor` classes.

as a "task" tuple with the value −1, which falls outside the range of rectangle identifiers. The `Worker` thread class is listed in Program 11.9.

The choice in the worker model between a task tuple to compute and a stop task is implemented as a test on the value of the task. The worker thread terminates when it receives a negative task value. The worker thread is able to compute the area given only a single integer since this integer indicates which "slice" of the range of x from 0 to 1.0 for which it is to compute the rectangle. The worker is initialized with a function object.

The structure of supervisor, worker and tuple space is constructed by the `go()` method of the `SupervisorWorker` applet class. The code is listed below:

```
class Worker extends Thread {
  WorkerCanvas display;
  Function func;
  TupleSpace bag;
  int processingTime = (int)(6000*Math.random());

  Worker(WorkerCanvas d, TupleSpace b, Function f)
    { display = d; bag = b; func = f; }

  public void run () {
    double deltaX = 1.0/SupervisorCanvas.Nslice;
    try {
      while(true){
        // get new task from tuple space
        Integer task = (Integer)bag.in("task");
        int slice = task.intValue();
        if (slice <0) {   // stop if negative
            bag.out("task",task);
            break;
        }
        display.setTask(slice);
        sleep(processingTime);
        double area
          = deltaX*func.fn(deltaX*slice+deltaX/2);
        // output result to tuple space
        bag.out( "result",
           new Result(slice,area,display.worker));
      }
    } catch (InterruptedException e){}
  }
}
```

Program 11.9 `Worker` class.

```
private void go(Function fn) {
  display.reset(fn);
  TupleSpace bag = new TupleSpaceImpl();
  redWork = new Worker(red,bag,fn);
  greenWork = new Worker(green,bag,fn);
  yellowWork = new Worker(yellow,bag,fn);
  blueWork = new Worker(blue,bag,fn);
  supervisor = new Supervisor(display,bag);
  redWork.start();
  greenWork.start();
```

```
    yellowWork.start();
    blueWork.start();
    supervisor.start();
  }
```

where `display` is an instance of `SupervisorCanvas` and red, green, yellow and blue are instances of `WorkerCanvas`.

Speedup and Efficiency

The *speedup* of a parallel program is defined to be the time that a sequential program takes to compute a given problem divided by the time that the parallel program takes to compute the same problem on N processors. The *efficiency* is the speedup divided by the number of processors N. For example, if a problem takes 12 seconds to compute sequentially and 4 seconds to compute on six processors, then the speedup is 3 and the efficiency 0.5 or 50%.

Unfortunately, the demonstration Supervisor–Worker program would not exhibit any speedup if executed on a multiprocessor with a Java runtime that scheduled threads on different processors. The most obvious reason for this is that we have introduced delays in the worker threads for display purposes. However, there is a reason that provides a more general lesson.

The amount of CPU time to compute each task in the example is very small, since each task requires only a few arithmetic operations. The supervisor uses more CPU time putting the task into tuple space and retrieving the result than it would if it computed the task locally. Speedup of greater than unity is only achieved in Supervisor–Worker programs if the tasks require significantly more computation time than the time required for communication with the workers.

The advantage of the Supervisor–Worker architecture is that it is easy to develop a parallel version of an existing sequential program in which sub-problems are independent. Often the sub-problem solution code from the sequential program can be reused directly in the parallel version. In practice, the architecture has been successfully applied to computation-intensive problems such as image rendering using ray-tracing techniques.

11.3 Announcer–Listener

Announcer–Listener is an example of an event-based architecture. The announcer process announces that some event has occurred and disseminates it to all those listener processes that are interested in the event. The communication pattern is one (announcer) to zero or more (listeners). Listener processes indicate their interest in a particular event by registering for that event. In the architecture diagram of

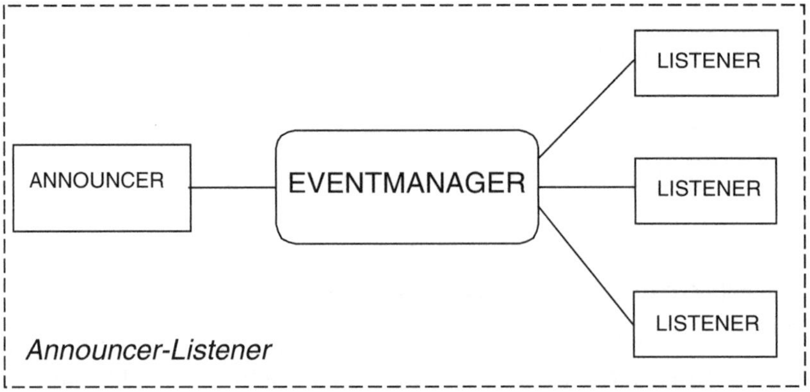

Figure 11.14 Announcer–Listener process architecture.

Figure 11.14, we have termed the connector that handles event dissemination an "event manager".

Listeners can choose to receive only a subset of the events announced by registering a "pattern" with the event manager. Only events that match the pattern are forwarded to the listener. The architecture can be applied recursively so that listeners also announce events to another set of listeners. In this way, an event dissemination "tree" can be constructed.

An important property of this architecture is that the announcer is insulated from knowledge of how many listeners there are and from which listeners are affected by a particular event. Listeners do not have to be processes; they may simply be objects in which a method is invoked as a result of an event. This mechanism is sometimes called *implicit invocation* since the announcer does not invoke listener methods explicitly. Listener methods are invoked implicitly as a result of an event announcement.

The Announcer–Listener architecture is widely used in user interface frameworks, and the Java Abstract Windowing Toolkit (AWT) is no exception. In section 11.3.2, we use the AWT event mechanism in an example program. In AWT, listeners are usually ordinary objects. Events, such as mouse clicks and button presses, cause methods to be invoked on objects. Our example uses events to control the execution of thread objects.

11.3.1 Announcer-Listener Model

The model is defined for a fixed set of listeners and a fixed set of event patterns:

```
set Listeners = {a,b,c,d}
set Pattern   = {pat1,pat2}
```

The event manager is modeled by a set of **REGISTER** processes, each of which controls the registration and event propagation for a single, particular listener.

```
REGISTER = IDLE,
IDLE = (register[p:Pattern] -> MATCH[p]
       |announce[Pattern]    -> IDLE
       ),

MATCH[p:Pattern] =
       (announce[a:Pattern] ->
           if (a==p) then
              (event[a] -> MATCH[p]
              |deregister -> IDLE)
           else
              MATCH[p]
       |deregister -> IDLE
       ).

||EVENTMANAGER = (Listeners:REGISTER)
                 /{announce/Listeners.announce}.
```

The REGISTER process ensures that the event action for a listener only occurs if the listener has previously registered, has not yet unregistered, and if the event pattern matches the pattern with which the listener registered. Figure 11.15 depicts the *LTS* for a:REGISTER for listener a.

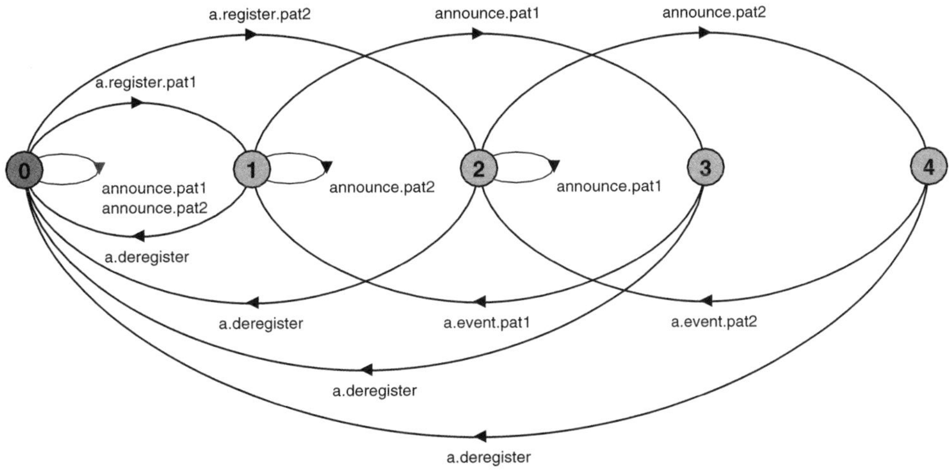

Figure 11.15 *LTS* for a:REGISTER.

The announcer is modeled as repeatedly announcing an event for one of the patterns defined by the Pattern set:

```
ANNOUNCER = (announce[Pattern] -> ANNOUNCER).
```

The listener initially registers for events of a particular pattern and then either performs local computation, modeled by the action compute, or receives an event. On receiving an event, the process either continues computing or deregisters and stops.

```
LISTENER(P='pattern) =
  (register[P] -> LISTENING),
LISTENING =
  (compute   -> LISTENING
  |event[P]  -> LISTENING
  |event[P]  -> deregister -> STOP
  )+{register[Pattern]}.
```

ANNOUNCER_LISTENER describes a system with four listeners a, b, c, d, in which a and c register for events with pattern pat1 and b and d register for pat2.

```
||ANNOUNCER_LISTENER
          = ( a:LISTENER('pat1)
            ||b:LISTENER('pat2)
            ||c:LISTENER('pat1)
            ||d:LISTENER('pat2)
            ||EVENTMANAGER
            ||ANNOUNCER
            ||Listeners:SAFE).
```

Analysis

The safety property, SAFE, included in the composite process ANNOUNCER_LISTENER, asserts that each listener only receives events while it is registered and only those events with the pattern for which it registered. The property is defined below:

```
property
  SAFE = (register[p:Pattern]  -> SAFE[p]),
  SAFE[p:Pattern]= (event[p]    -> SAFE[p]
                   |deregister -> SAFE
                   ).
```

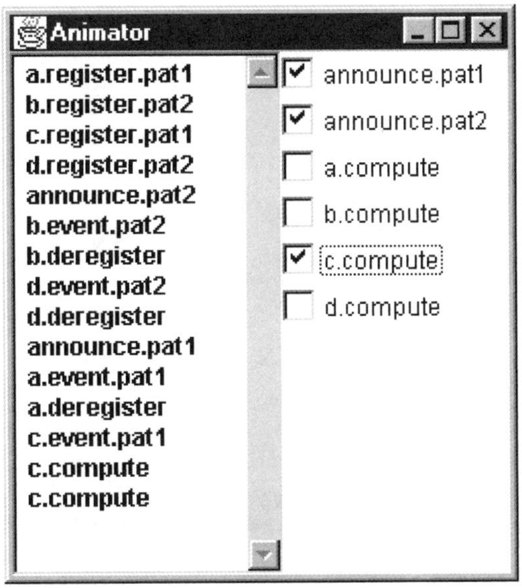

Figure 11.16 ANNOUNCER_LISTENER trace.

Safety analysis reveals that the system has no deadlocks or safety violations. A sample execution trace is shown in Figure 11.16.

The important progress property for this system is that the announcer should be able to announce events independently of the state of listeners, i.e. whether or not listeners are registered and whether or not listeners have stopped. We can assert this using the following set of progress properties:

```
progress ANNOUNCE[p:Pattern] = {announce[p]}
```

Progress analysis using *LTSA* verifies that these properties hold for ANNOUNCER_LISTENER.

11.3.2 Announcer - Listener Implementation

To illustrate the use of the Announcer – Listener architecture, we implement the simple game depicted in Figure 11.17. The objective of the game is to hit all the moving colored blocks with the minimum number of mouse presses. A moving block is hit by pressing the mouse button when the mouse pointer is on top of the block. When a block is hit, it turns black and stops moving.

Each block is controlled by a separate thread that causes the block it controls to jump about the display at random. The threads also listen for mouse events that

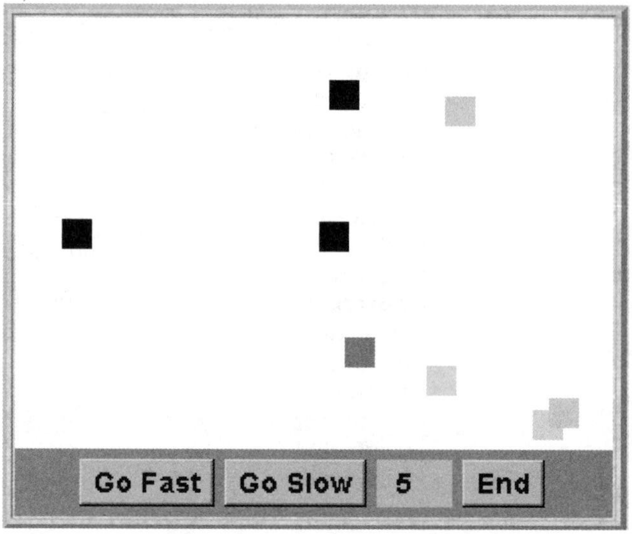

Figure 11.17 EventDemo applet display.

```
class BoxCanvas extends Canvas {

  // clear all boxes
  synchronized void reset(){...}

  // draw colored box id at position x,y
  synchronized void moveBox(int id, int x, int y){...}

  // draw black box id at position x,y
  synchronized void blackBox(int id, int x, int y){...}
}
```

Program 11.10 BoxCanvas class.

are announced by the display canvas in which the blocks move. These events are generated by the AWT and the program uses the AWT classes provided for event handling. The class diagram for the program is depicted in Figure 11.18.

The display for the `EventDemo` applet is provided by the `BoxCanvas` class described in outline by Program 11.10.

The AWT interface `MouseListener` describes a set of methods that are invoked as a result of mouse actions. To avoid implementing all these methods, since

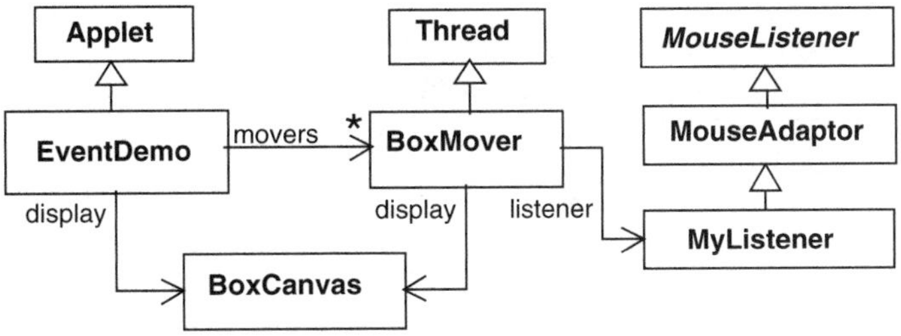

Figure 11.18 EventDemo class diagram.

we are only interested in the mouse-pressed event, we use the adapter class MouseAdapter which provides null implementations for all the methods in the MouseListener interface. MyClass extends MouseAdapter and provides an implementation for the mousePressed method. MyClass is an inner class of the BoxMover thread class; consequently, it can directly call private BoxMover methods. The code for BoxMover and MyListener is listed in Program 11.11.

The run() method of BoxMover repeatedly computes a random position and displays a box at that position. After displaying the box, waitHit() is called. This uses a timed wait() and returns for two reasons: either the wait delay expires and the value false is returned or isHit() computes that a hit has occurred and calls notify() in which case true is returned. Because MyListener is registered as a listener for events generated by the display, whenever the display announces a mouse-pressed event, MyListener.mousePressed() is invoked. This in turn calls isHit() with the mouse coordinates contained in the MouseEvent parameter.

If we compare the run() method with the LISTENER process from the model, the difference in behavior is the addition of a timeout action which ensures that after a delay, if no mouse event occurs, a new box position is computed and displayed. A model specific to the BoxMover thread is described by:

```
BOXMOVER(P='pattern) =
  (register[P] -> LISTENING),
LISTENING =
  (compute->          // compute and display position
    (timeout -> LISTENING       // no mouse event
    |event[P] -> timeout -> LISTENING // miss
    |event[P] -> deregister -> STOP    // hit
    )
  )+{register[Pattern]}.
```

```
import java.awt.event.*;
class BoxMover extends Thread {
  private BoxCanvas display;
  private int id, delay, MaxX, MaxY, x, y;
  private boolean hit=false;
  private MyListener listener = new MyListener();

  BoxMover(BoxCanvas d, int id, int delay) {
    display = d; this.id = id; this.delay=delay;
    display.addMouseListener(listener); // register
    MaxX = d.getSize().width; MaxY = d.getSize().height;
  }

  private synchronized void isHit(int mx, int my) {
    hit = (mx>x && mx<x+display.BOXSIZE
        && my>y && my<y+display.BOXSIZE);
    if (hit) notify();
  }

  private synchronized boolean waitHit()
    throws InterruptedException {
    wait(delay);
    return hit;
  }

  public void run() {
    try {
      while (true) {
          x = (int)(MaxX*Math.random());
          y = (int)(MaxY*Math.random());
          display.moveBox(id,x,y);
          if (waitHit()) break;
      }
    } catch (InterruptedException e){}
    display.blackBox(id,x,y);
    display.removeMouseListener(listener); // deregister
  }

  class MyListener extends MouseAdapter {
    public void mousePressed(MouseEvent e) {
      isHit(e.getX(),e.getY());
    }
  }
}
```

Program 11.11 `BoxMover` and `MyListener` classes.

The reader should verify that the safety and progress properties for the ANNOUNCER_LISTENER still hold when BOXMOVER is substituted for LISTENER.

Summary

In this chapter, we have described three different concurrent architectures: Filter Pipeline, Supervisor – Worker and Announcer – Listener. A model was developed for each architecture and analyzed with respect to general properties such as absence of deadlock and correct termination. Guided by the models, we developed example programs to demonstrate how the components of each architecture interact during execution.

Each of the architectures uses a different type of connector to coordinate the communication between the components of the architecture. The Filter Pipeline uses *pipes*, which are essentially communication channels with zero or more buffers. We showed that the behavior of our primes sieve application, organized as a Filter Pipeline, was independent of the buffering provided in pipes. The components of the Supervisor – Worker architecture interact via a Linda *tuple space*, which is an unordered collection of data tuples. We provided a model of Linda tuple space and used it to investigate termination strategies for Supervisor – Worker systems. The Announcer – Listener components interact by event dissemination. We presented a general model of event dissemination and then used Java AWT events to implement the example program.

Pipes support *one-to-one* communication, tuple space supports *any-to-any* communication and event dissemination is *one-to-many*. These connectors were chosen as the most natural match with the topology of the architecture to which they were applied. However, it is possible, if not very natural, to use tuple space to implement a set of pipes and, more reasonably, to use rendezvous (section 10.3) instead of tuple space in the Supervisor – Worker architecture. In other words, for each architecture we have described one technique for organizing the communication between participating components. However, many variants of these architectures can be found in the literature, differing in the mechanisms used to support communication, how termination is managed and, of course, in the applications they support. A particular concurrent program may incorporate a combination of the basic architectures we have described here and in the rest of the book. For example, the filter processes in a pipeline may also be the clients of a server process.

Notes and Further Reading

As mentioned earlier, Filter Pipeline is the basic architecture used in the UNIX operating system to combine programs. The architecture is also used extensively in multimedia applications to process streams of video and audio information. An example of this sort of program can be found in Kleiman, Shah and Smaalders (1996). A discussion of the properties of more general pipe and filter networks may be found in Shaw and Garlan's book on *Software Architecture* (1996).

The Supervisor – Worker architecture appears in many guises in books and papers on concurrent programming. Andrews (1991) calls the architecture "replicated worker", Burns and Davies (1993) call it "process farm", while Carriero and Gelernter (1989b) characterize the form of parallelism supported by the architecture as "agenda parallelism". A paper by Cheung and Magee (1991) presents a simple way of assessing the likely performance of a sequential algorithm when parallelized using the Supervisor – Worker architecture. The paper also describes a technique for making the architecture fault-tolerant with respect to worker failure. The Supervisor – Worker architecture has been used extensively in exploiting the computational power of clusters of workstations.

A large literature exists on Linda (Gelernter, 1985; Carriero and Gelernter, 1989a, 1989b) and its derivatives. The proceedings of the "Coordination" series of conferences describe some of the current work on tuple-space-based models for concurrent programming, starting from the early conferences (Ciancarini and Hankin, 1996; Garlan and Le Metayer, 1997) and including more recent events (Nicola, Ferari and Meredith, 2004; Jacquet and Picco, 2005). The Linda tuple space paradigm clearly influenced the work on JavaSpaces™ (Freeman, Hupfer and Arnold, 1999).

Event-based architectures have been used to connect tools in software development environments (Reiss, 1990). As discussed in the chapter, windowing environments are usually event-based, as Smalltalk (Goldberg and Robson, 1983). In a distributed context, event processing forms an important part of network management systems (Sloman, 1994). Shaw and Garlan (1996) discuss some of the general properties of event-based systems.

Exercises

11.1 *N* processes are required to synchronize their execution at some point before proceeding. Describe a scheme for implementing this *barrier* synchronization using Linda tuple space. Model the scheme using `TUPLESPACE` and generate a trace to show the correct operation of your scheme.

11.2 Describe a scheme for implementing the Supervisor – Worker architecture using rendezvous message-passing communication rather than tuple space.
(Hint: Make the Supervisor a server and the Workers clients.)
Model this scheme and show absence of deadlock and successful termination. Modify the Java example program to use `Entry` rather than `TupleSpace`.

11.3 A process needs to wait for an event from either announcer *A* or announcer *B*, for example events indicating that button A or button B has been pressed, i.e.

```
(buttonA -> P[1] | buttonB -> P[2]).
```

Sketch the implementation of a Java thread that can block waiting for either of two events to occur. Assume initially that the Java events are handled by the same listener interface. Now extend the scheme such that events with different listener interfaces can be accommodated.

11.4 Provide a Java class which implements the following interface and has the behavior of EVENTMANAGER:

```
class Listener {
   public action(int event);
}

interface EventManager {
   void announce(int event);
   void register(Listener x);
   void deregister(Listener x):
   }
```

11.5 Each filter in a pipeline examines the stream of symbols it receives for a particular pattern. When one of the filters matches the pattern it is looking for the entire pipeline terminates. Develop a model for this system and show absence of deadlock and correct termination. Outline how your model might be implemented in Java, paying particular attention to termination.

11.6 A *token ring* is an architecture which is commonly used for allocating some privilege, such as access to a shared resource, to one of a set of processes at a time. The architecture works as follows:

A token is passed round the ring. Possession of the token indicates that that process has exclusive access to the resource. Each process holds on to the token while using the resource and then passes it on to its successor in the ring, or passes on the token directly if it does not require access.

Develop a model for this system and show absence of deadlock, exclusive access to the resource and access progress for every process. Is the system ''buffer tolerant''? Outline how your model might be implemented in Java.

11.7 Consider a ring of nodes, each of which acts as a simplified replicated database (Roscoe, 1998). Each node can autonomously update its local copy. Updates are circulated round the ring to update other copies. It is possible that two nodes perform local updates at similar times and propagate their respective updates. This would lead to the situation where nodes receive updates in different orders, leading to inconsistent copies even after all the updates have propagated round the ring. Although we are prepared to tolerate copy inconsistency while updates are circulating, we cannot accept inconsistency that persists. To ensure consistent updates in the presence of node autonomy and concurrency, we require that, when quiescent (no updates are circulating and no node is updating its copy), all copies should have the same value.

In order to achieve this, we assign a priority to each update according to an (arbitrary) ordering of the originating node. Thus, in the case of clashes due to two simultaneous updates by different nodes, node i has priority over node j if i<j. Simultaneity is recognized by a node receiving an update while still having an outstanding update.

Develop a model for this system and show absence of deadlock and consistent values when quiescent.

(*Hint*: In order to keep the problem simple, let each node deal with only a single value. Updates are passed round the ring in the form: [j][x] where j=originator and x=update value. Nodes should be connected by channels which can be modeled as follows.)

```
const N = 3                    // number of nodes
range Nodes = 0..N-1
const Max = 2                  // update values
range Value = 0..Max-1
CHANNEL =
(in[j:Nodes][x:Value]->out[j][x]->CHANNEL).
```

12 Timed Systems

The programs we have developed in the previous chapters of this book are not explicitly concerned with the passage of time. We have used delays to make the execution of example programs viewable in a convenient way, however the correct operation of these programs is independent of time. Correctness depends on performing actions in a certain order and not on performing an action by a certain time. This has the advantage that the programs work safely, independently of processor speed and thread scheduling.

In this chapter, we develop programs that *are* concerned with the passage of time and in which correctness *does* depend on performing actions by specific times. In general, we deal with the relationship between the time at which program actions are executed and the time that events occur in the real world. We make the simplifying assumption that program execution proceeds sufficiently quickly such that, when related to the time between external events, it can be ignored. For example, consider a program that detects double mouse clicks. The program notes the time that passes between successive mouse clicks and causes a double-click action to be executed when this is less than some specified period. The inter-click time for such a program would be specified in tenths of a second, while the instructions necessary to recognize clicks and measure the inter-click time would require tenths of a millisecond. In modeling and developing such a program, it is reasonable to ignore the execution time of actions. We can assume that the execution of an action takes zero time, although we do not assume that executing an infinite number of actions takes zero time. A much more difficult approach to action execution time is to specify and subsequently guarantee an upper bound to execution time. This falls into a specialized area of concurrent software design termed *real-time* and it is beyond the scope of this book.

In the following, we first examine how we can incorporate time into models and then how the behavior exhibited by these models can be implemented in Java.

12.1 Modeling Timed Systems

In Chapter 3, we stated that our model of concurrent execution was *asynchronous*; processes proceed at arbitrary relative speeds. Consequently, the delay between two successive actions of a process can take an arbitrarily long time. How then do we make processes aware of the passage of time and, in particular, how can we synchronize their execution with time? The answer is to adopt a discrete model of time in which the passage of time is signaled by successive ticks of a clock. Processes become aware of the passage of time by sharing a global tick action. Time is measured as a positive integer value. To illustrate the use of this model of time, we return to the double-click program described in the introduction to the chapter. Figure 12.1 depicts the relationship between discrete time and mouse clicks.

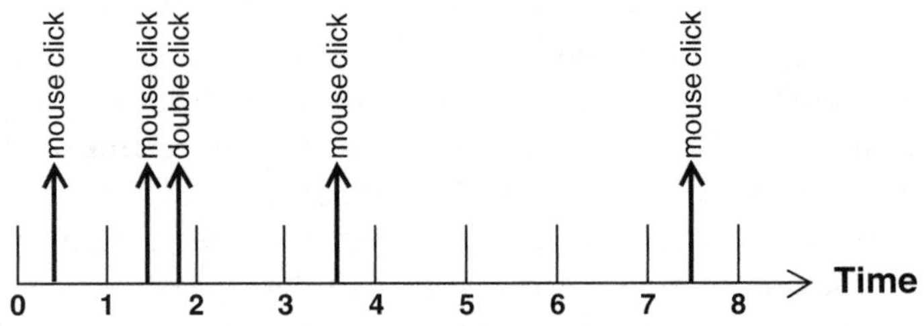

Figure 12.1 Discrete time and mouse clicks.

To make the discussion concrete, assume that the unit of time represented in Figure 12.1 is a second. We specify that a double-click should be recognized when the time between two successive mouse clicks is less than, say, three seconds. We can easily see that the click during period 0 and the click during period 1 constitute a double-click since the interval between these clicks must be less than two seconds. The click during period 3 and the click during period 7 do not form a double-click since there is an interval between these clicks of at least three seconds. The use of discrete time means that we cannot determine precisely when an event occurs, we can only say that it occurs within some period delimited by two ticks of the clock. This gives rise to some *timing uncertainty*. For example, if the last mouse click happened in period 6, would a double-click have occurred or not? The most we could say is that the last two mouse clicks were separated by at least two seconds and not more than four seconds. We can increase the accuracy by having more ticks per second, however some uncertainty remains. For example, with two ticks per second, we could say that two clicks were separated by at least 2.5 seconds and not more than 3.5 seconds. In fact, this uncertainty also exists in implementations since time is measured in computer systems using a clock that ticks with a fixed periodicity, usually in the order of milliseconds. An implementation can only detect that two events are separated by time $(n \pm 1) * T$, where T is the periodicity of the clock and n the number of clock ticks between the two events. In general, despite the limitations we have discussed above, discrete time is sufficient to model many timed systems since it is also the way time is represented in implementations.

In the example above, if we want to ensure that the clicks which form a double-click are never more than three seconds apart, the last click would have to happen in period 5. Consequently, after the first mouse click occurs, the clock must not tick more than two times before the second click of a double-click occurs. To capture the behavior of the double-click program as a model in *FSP*, we use the `tick` action to signal the beginning (and end) of each period. A `doubleclick` action occurs if less than three `tick` actions occur between successive mouse `clicks`. The behavior of the double-click program is modeled as follows:

```
DOUBLECLICK(D=3) =
  (tick -> DOUBLECLICK | click -> PERIOD[1]),
PERIOD[t:1..D] =
  (when (t==D) tick -> DOUBLECLICK
  |when (t<D)   tick -> PERIOD[t+1]
  |click -> doubleclick -> DOUBLECLICK
  ).
```

The `DOUBLECLICK` process accepts a `click` action at any time, since, initially, there is a choice between `click` and `tick`. When a `click` occurs, the process starts counting the `tick` s that follow. If a `click` occurs before the third succeeding `tick`, then a `doubleclick` action is output, otherwise the process resets. Figure 12.2 shows the *LTS* for `DOUBLECLICK` and two possible traces of the model; in (a) a `doubleclick` is output after two clicks and in (b) it is not.

In discussing the double-click program, we assumed that clock ticks occur every second. However, this is simply an interpretation of the model. We choose an interpretation for a tick that is appropriate to the problem at hand. For example, in modeling hardware circuits, ticks would delimit periods measured in nanoseconds. However, within a particular time frame, the more accurately we represent time, the larger the model. For example, if we wanted to increase the accuracy of the double-click model while retaining the same time frame, we could decide to have two ticks per second and, consequently, the parameter `D` would become 6 rather than 3. This would double the number of states in `DOUBLECLICK`.

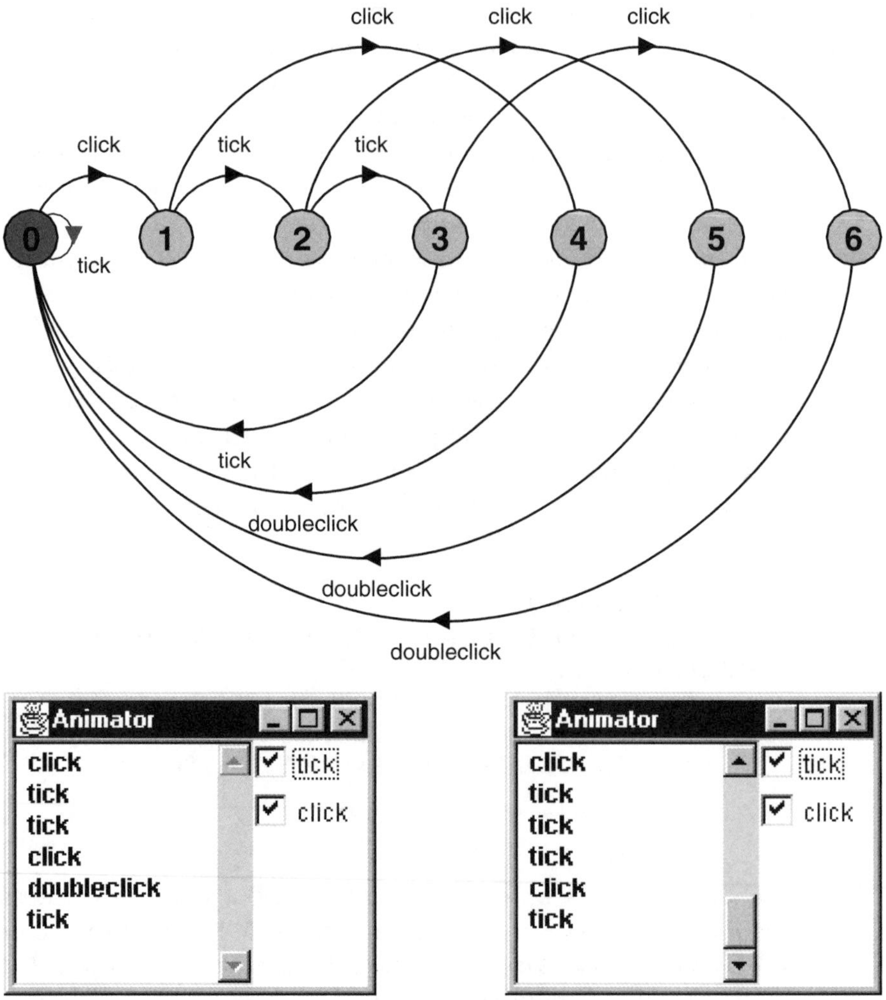

Figure 12.2 DOUBLECLICK *LTS* and traces.

12.1.1 Timing Consistency

The previous example dealt with how a process is made aware of the passage of time. We now examine the implications of time in models with multiple processes. We look at a simple producer – consumer system in which the PRODUCER process produces an item every *Tp* seconds and the CONSUMER process takes *Tc* seconds to consume an item. The models for the PRODUCER and CONSUMER processes are listed below:

```
CONSUMER(Tc=3) =
  (item -> DELAY[1] | tick -> CONSUMER),
DELAY[t:1..Tc] =
  (when(t==Tc) tick -> CONSUMER
  |when(t<Tc)  tick -> DELAY[t+1]
  ).

PRODUCER(Tp=3) =
  (item -> DELAY[1]),
DELAY[t:1..Tp] =
  (when(t==Tp) tick -> PRODUCER
  |when(t<Tp)  tick -> DELAY[t+1]
  ).
```

Note that the consumer initially has a choice between getting an `item` and a `tick` action. This models waiting for an action to happen while allowing time to pass. We can model the three possible situations that can occur when the PRODUCER and CONSUMER processes are combined. Firstly, the situation where items are produced at the *same* rate that they are consumed:

```
||SAME = (PRODUCER(2) || CONSUMER(2)).
```

Analysis of this system does not detect any safety problems. Similarly, analysis detects no problems in the system in which items are produced at a *slower* rate that they are consumed:

```
||SLOWER = (PRODUCER(3) || CONSUMER(2)).
```

However, analysis of the system in which the producer is *faster* than the consumer detects the deadlock depicted in Figure 12.3.

```
||FASTER = (PRODUCER(2) || CONSUMER(3)).
```

The deadlock occurs because after the first item is produced and accepted by the consumer, the producer tries to produce another item after two clock ticks, while the consumer must accept a third clock tick before it can accept another item. The deadlock is caused by the timing inconsistency between producer and consumer. The producer is required to produce an item every two seconds while the consumer can only consume an item every three seconds. This kind of deadlock, caused by timing inconsistencies, is termed a *time-stop*. If we combine processes into a system and time-stop does not occur, we can say that the timing assumptions built into these processes are consistent.

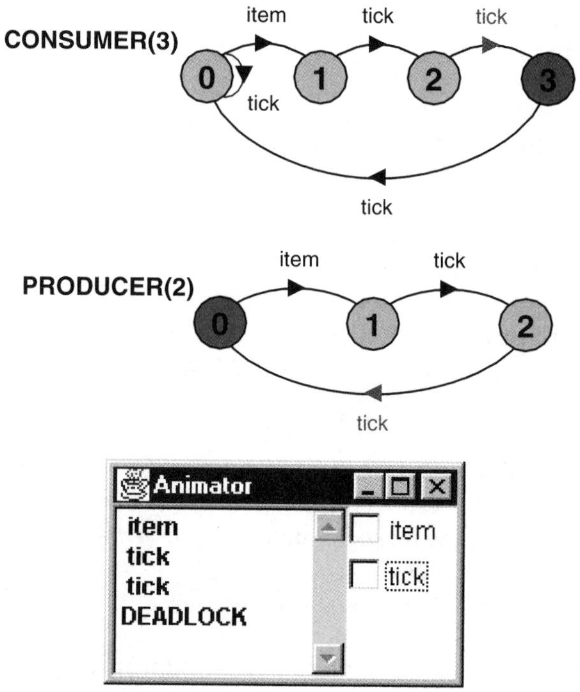

Figure 12.3 Timed Producer – Consumer deadlock.

12.1.2 Maximal Progress

Consider a system that connects the PRODUCER and CONSUMER processes of the previous section by a store for items as shown below:

```
STORE(N=3) = STORE[0],
STORE[i:0..N] = (put -> STORE[i+1]
               |when(i>0) get -> STORE[i-1]
               ).

||SYS = ( PRODUCER(1)/{put/item}
        ||CONSUMER(1)/{get/item}
        ||STORE
        ).
```

We would reasonably expect that if we specify that items are consumed at the same rate that they are produced then the store would not overflow. In fact, if a safety analysis is performed then the following violation is reported:

```
Trace to property violation in STORE:
       put
       tick
       put
       tick
       put
       tick
       put
```

This violation occurs because the consumer has a choice between getting an item from the store, by engaging in the `get` action, and engaging in the `tick` action. If the consumer always chooses to let time pass, then the store fills up and overflows. To avoid this form of spurious violation in timed models, we must ensure that an action occurs as soon as all participants are ready to perform it. This is known as ensuring *maximal progress* of actions. We can incorporate maximal progress into our timed models by making the `tick` action low priority. For the example, a system that ensures maximal progress is described by:

```
||NEW_SYS = SYS>>{tick}.
```

Safety analysis of this system reveals no violations. Maximal progress means that after a tick, all actions that can occur will happen before the next tick. However, even though we assume that actions take a negligible amount of time, it would be unrealistic to allow an infinite number of actions to occur between ticks. We can easily check for this problem in a model using the following progress property, which asserts that a `tick` action must occur regularly in any infinite execution (see Chapter 7).

```
progress TIME = {tick}
```

The following process violates the `TIME` progress property because it permits an infinite number of `compute` actions to occur between `tick` actions:

```
PROG = (start   -> LOOP | tick -> PROG),
LOOP = (compute -> LOOP | tick -> LOOP).

||CHECK = PROG>>{tick}.
```

The progress violation is reported by the analyzer as:

```
Progress violation: TIME
Path to terminal set of states:
    start
Actions in terminal set:
{compute}
```

If we include an action that terminates the loop and then engages in a `tick` action, the progress property is not violated:

```
PROG = (start   -> LOOP | tick -> PROG),
LOOP = (compute -> LOOP | tick -> LOOP
       |end -> tick -> PROG
       ).
```

This may seem strange since the loop still exists in the process. However, the `end` and `compute` actions are the same priority and consequently, with the fair choice assumption of Chapter 7, the `compute` action cannot be chosen an infinite number of times without the `end` action being chosen. The revised `LOOP` now models a finite number of iterations. The `tick` action following `end` means that the `PROG` process can only execute this finite `LOOP` once every clock tick. Consequently, the `TIME` progress property is not violated.

12.1.3 Modeling Techniques

Incorporating time in models by the simple expedient of a global `tick` action is surprisingly powerful. In the following, we look at modeling techniques for situations that occur frequently in timed systems.

Output in an Interval

The examples we have seen so far produce an output or accept an input at a precise time, within the limitations of the discrete model of time. The `INTERVAL` process below produces an output at any time after `Min` ticks and before `Max` ticks. The *LTS* for the process is depicted in Figure 12.4.

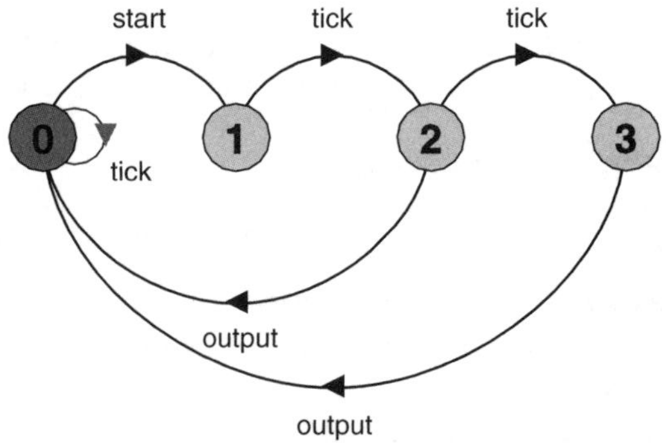

Figure 12.4 *LTS* for `OUTPUT (1,3)`.

```
OUTPUT(Min=1,Max=3) =
  (start -> OUTPUT[1] | tick -> OUTPUT),
OUTPUT[t:1..Max] =
  (when (t>Min && t<=Max) output ->OUTPUT
  |when (t<Max)           tick ->OUTPUT[t+1]
  ).
```

The technique of using choice with respect to the `tick` action allows us to model processes in which the completion time is variable, for example, due to loading or congestion.

Jitter

A variation on the previous technique is a process that periodically produces an output at a predictable rate. However, the output may be produced at any time within the period. In communication systems, this kind of timing uncertainty is termed *jitter*. The `JITTER` process defined below is an example of how jitter can be modeled. Figure 12.5 depicts the *LTS* for the `JITTER` process.

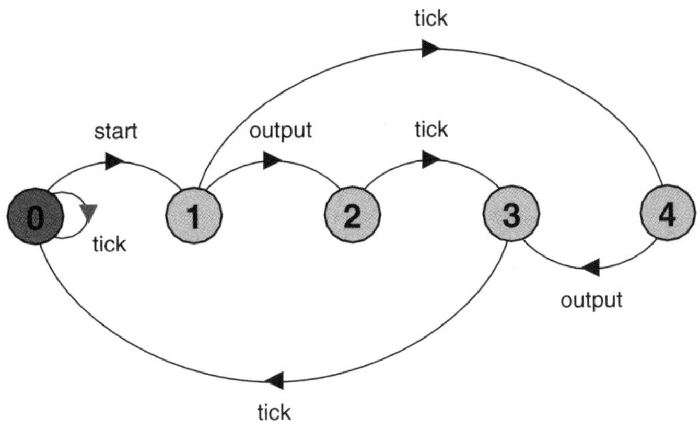

Figure 12.5 *LTS* for `JITTER(2)`.

```
JITTER(Max=2) =
  (start -> JITTER[1] | tick -> JITTER),
JITTER[t:1..Max] =
  (output -> FINISH[t]
  |when (t<Max)   tick  -> JITTER[t+1]
  ),
```

```
FINISH[t:1..Max] =
  (when (t<Max)  tick -> FINISH[t+1]
  |when (t==Max) tick -> JITTER
  ).
```

Timeout

Timeouts are frequently used to detect the loss of messages in communication systems or the failure of processes in distributed systems. Java provides a version of the `wait()` synchronization primitive that takes a timeout parameter – a `wait()` invocation returns either when notified or when the timeout period expires. The most elegant way to model a timeout mechanism is to use a separate process to manage the timeout, as shown below for a receive operation with a timeout. The timeout and receive processes are combined into a `RECEIVER` process.

```
TIMEOUT(D=1)
  = (setTO          -> TIMEOUT[0]
    |{tick,resetTO} -> TIMEOUT
    ),
TIMEOUT[t:0..D]
  = (when (t<D) tick      -> TIMEOUT[t+1]
    |when (t==D)timeout   -> TIMEOUT
    |resetTO              -> TIMEOUT
    ).

RECEIVE = (start   -> setTO -> WAIT),
WAIT    = (timeout -> RECEIVE
          |receive -> resetTO -> RECEIVE
          ).

||RECEIVER(D=2) = (RECEIVE || TIMEOUT(D))
                  >>{receive,timeout,start,tick}
                  @{receive,tick,timeout,start}.
```

In addition to `tick`, the `start`, `receive` and `timeout` actions are declared as low priority in the `RECEIVER` composite process. This is because maximal progress requires that an action take place when all the participants in that action are ready. However, the participants in interface actions depend on the system into which `RECEIVER` is placed, so we should not apply maximal progress to these actions within the `RECEIVER` process but later at the system level. Consequently, we give interface actions the same priority as the `tick` action. All internal actions have a

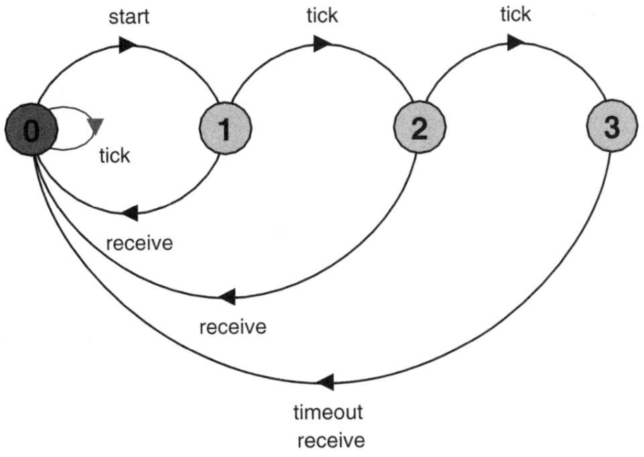

Figure 12.6 *LTS* for `RECEIVER(2)`.

higher priority. The minimized *LTS* for `RECEIVER`, which hides the internal actions concerned with setting and resetting the timeout, is depicted in Figure 12.6.

12.2 Implementing Timed Systems

Timed concurrent systems can be implemented in Java by a set of threads which use `sleep()` and timed `wait()` to synchronize with time. We can characterize this as a *thread-based* approach since active entities in the model are translated into threads in an implementation. This approach to translating models into programs was used in the preceding chapters for non-timed systems. In this chapter, we exploit the time-driven nature of the models and use an *event-based* approach in which active entities are translated into objects that respond to timing events. Essentially, the `tick` action in the model becomes a set of events broadcast by a time manager to all the program entities that need to be aware of the passage of time. The organization of a timed system implementation conforms to the Announcer – Listener architecture described in Chapter 11, with the time manager acting as the announcer and timed objects as the listeners. We have chosen this event-based approach for two reasons. First, the translation from timed model to timed implementation is reasonably direct; and secondly, for timed systems with many activities the resulting implementation is more efficient than the thread-based approach since it avoids context-switching overheads. However, as discussed in the following, the approach also has some limitations when compared with a thread-based approach.

12.2.1 Timed Objects

Each process in a timed model that has `tick` in its alphabet becomes a *timed* object in an implementation. A timed object is created from a class that implements the `Timed` interface listed in Program 12.1.

Each timed object is registered with the time manager, which implements a two-phase event broadcast. In phase 1, the `pretick()` method of each timed object is invoked and, in phase 2, the `tick()` method is invoked. The behavior of a timed object is provided by the implementation of these two methods. In the *pre-tick* phase, the object performs all output actions that are enabled in its current state. These may modify the state of other timed objects. In the *tick* phase, the object updates its state with respect to inputs and the passage of time. Two phases are needed to ensure that communication between timed objects completes within a single clock cycle. We clarify the translation from model processes into timed objects, with `pretick()` and `tick()` methods and the use of the `TimeStop` exception, in the examples that follow.

```
public interface Timed {
  void pretick() throws TimeStop;
  void tick();
}
```

Program 12.1 `Timed` interface.

CountDown Timer

A version of the countdown timer model introduced in Chapter 2 is given below.

```
COUNTDOWN (N=3)   = COUNTDOWN[N],
COUNTDOWN[i:0..N] =
  (when(i>0)  tick -> COUNTDOWN[i-1]
  |when(i==0) beep -> STOP
  ).
```

The `COUNTDOWN` process outputs a `beep` action after *N* ticks and then stops. The implementation is given in Program 12.2. The translation from the model is straightforward. Each invocation of the `tick()` method decrements the integer variable `i`. When `i` reaches zero, the next invocation of `pretick()` performs the `beep` action and the timer stops by removing itself from the time manager. The operation of `TimeManager` is described in the next section.

```
class TimedCountDown implements Timed {
  int i; TimeManager clock;

  TimedCountDown(int N, TimeManager clock) {
    i = N; this.clock = clock;
    clock.addTimed(this); // register with time manager
  }

  public void pretick() throws TimeStop {
    if (i==0) {
        // do beep action
        clock.removeTimed(this); // unregister = STOP
    }
  }

  public void tick(){ --i; }
}
```

Program 12.2 `TimedCountDown` class.

Timed Producer-Consumer

The next example implements the producer – consumer model of section 12.1.1. To keep the code succinct, the timed class definitions are nested inside the `ProducerConsumer` class of Program 12.3. The class creates the required instances of the `Producer`, `Consumer` and `TimeManager` classes.

```
class ProducerConsumer {
  TimeManager clock = new TimeManager(1000);
  Producer producer = new Producer(2);
  Consumer consumer = new Consumer(2);
  ProducerConsumer() {clock.start();}

  class Consumer implements Timed {...}
  class Producer implements Timed {...}
}
```

Program 12.3 `ProducerConsumer` class.

For convenience, the `PRODUCER` process is listed below:

```
PRODUCER(Tp=3) =
  (item -> DELAY[1]),
```

```
DELAY[t:1..Tp] =
  (when(t==Tp) tick -> PRODUCER
  |when(t<Tp) tick -> DELAY[t+1]
  ).
```

Initially, the producer outputs an item and then waits for *Tp* clock ticks before outputting another item. The timed class that implements this behavior is listed in Program 12.4.

```
class Producer implements Timed {
  int Tp,t;

  Producer(int Tp) {
    this.Tp = Tp; t = 1;
    clock.addTimed(this);
  }

  public void pretick() throws TimeStop {
    if (t==1) consumer.item(new Object());
  }

  public void tick() {
    if (t<Tp) { ++t; return; }
    if (t==Tp) { t = 1; }
  }
}
```

Program 12.4 `Producer` class.

An instance of the `Producer` class is created with `t = 1` and the `consumer.item()` method is invoked on the first pre-tick clock phase after creation. Each subsequent tick increments `t` until a state is reached when another item is output. The behavior corresponds directly with `PRODUCER`.

Now let us examine how the `item()` method is handled by the consumer. The timed model for the consumer is shown below. The consumer waits for an item and then delays *Tc* ticks before offering to accept another item.

```
CONSUMER(Tc=3) =
  (item -> DELAY[1] | tick -> CONSUMER),
DELAY[t:1..Tc] =
```

```
(when(t==Tc) tick -> CONSUMER
|when(t<Tc) tick -> DELAY[t+1]
).
```

The implementation of CONSUMER is listed in Program 12.5.

```
class Consumer implements Timed {
  int Tc,t; Object consuming = null;

  Consumer(int Tc) {
    this.Tc = Tc; t = 1;
    clock.addTimed(this);
  }

  void item(Object x) throws TimeStop {
    if (consuming!=null) throw new TimeStop();
    consuming = x;
  }

  public void pretick() {}

  public void tick() {
    if (consuming==null) return;
    if (t<Tc) { ++t; return;}
    if (t==Tc) {consuming = null; t = 1;}
  }
}
```

Program 12.5 Consumer class.

In the Consumer class, the tick() method returns immediately if the consuming field has the value null, implementing the behavior of waiting for an item. The item() method sets this field when invoked by the producer. When consuming is not null, the tick() method increments t until Tc is reached and then resets consuming to null indicating that the item has been consumed and that another item can be accepted. Effectively, consuming represents the DELAY states in the model. If the producer tries to set consuming when it is not null then a TimeStop exception is thrown. This signals a timing inconsistency in exactly the same way that a *time-stop* deadlock in the model is the result of a timing inconsistency. TimeStop is thrown if the producer tries to output an item when the previous item has not yet been consumed. As we see in the next section, a `TimeStop` exception stops the time manager and consequently, no further actions are executed. The implementation of producer – consumer has exactly the same property as the model. For correct execution, *Tc* must be less than or equal to *Tp*. Note that, in the `Consumer` class, the method `pretick()` has no implementation because the class has no outputs.

The Two-Phase Clock

The operation of the two-phase clock cycle should now be clear. Methods on other objects are invoked during the pre-tick phase and the changes in state caused by these invocations are recognized in the tick phase. This ensures that actions complete in a single clock cycle. However, this scheme only approximates the maximal progress property of timed models. Maximal progress ensures that all actions that can occur happen before the next tick. Our implementation scheme only gives each timed object one opportunity to perform an action, when its `pretick()` method is executed. A multi-way interaction between timed objects thus requires multiple clock cycles. An example of a multi-way interaction would be a request action followed by a reply followed by an acknowledgment (three-way). Maximal progress in the model ensures that such a multi-way interaction would occur within a single clock cycle if no intervening tick events were specified. We could implement a multi-phase clock scheme to allow multi-way interaction in a single clock cycle, however this complexity might be better dealt with by reverting to a thread-based implementation scheme. In fact, the examples later in the chapter show that the two-phase scheme is sufficiently powerful to implement quite complex systems that exhibit the same behavior as their models. We take care that multi-way interaction within a single clock cycle is not required. This usually means that we introduce an intervening tick in the model, for example between a request and a reply.

In addition to the ease with which models can be translated into implementations, the event-based implementation scheme has the advantage, when compared to the thread-based scheme, that we do not have to synchronize access to shared objects. The activations of the `tick()` and `pretick()` methods of a timed object are indivisible with respect to other a ctivations of these methods. This is because the methods are dispatched sequentially by the time manager. Method dispatch incurs much less overhead than context switching between threads. Consequently, the event-based scheme is more efficient in systems with large numbers of time-driven concurrent activities. An example of such a system is presented in the final section of the chapter.

12.2.2 Time Manager

The `TimeManager` class (Program 12.6) maintains a list of all those timed objects which have registered with it using `addTimed()`. The `pretick()` and `tick()` methods are invoked on all `Timed` objects in this list by the `TimeManager` thread every `delay` milliseconds. The value of `delay` can be adjusted by an external control, such as a slider through the `AdjustmentListener` interface that the class implements.

The data structure used to hold the list of timed objects must be designed with some care. A `pretick()` or `tick()` method may cause a timed object to remove itself from the list. To ensure that such a removal does not destroy the integrity of the list data structure, we use an immutable list that does not change during an enumeration off it. If a removal occurs during a broadcast, this removal generates a new list which is used for the next broadcast. The class implementing the immutable list is given in Program 12.7.

```
public class TimeManager extends Thread
                      implements AdjustmentListener{
  volatile int delay;
  volatile ImmutableList<Timed> clocked = null;

  public TimeManager(int d) {delay = d;}

  public void addTimed(Timed el) {
    clocked = ImmutableList.add(clocked,el);
  }

  public void removeTimed(Timed el) {
    clocked = ImmutableList.remove(clocked,el);
  }

  public void
    adjustmentValueChanged(AdjustmentEvent e) {
    delay = e.getValue();
  }
  public void run () {
    try {
      while(true) {
        try {
          for (Timed e: clocked) e.pretick(); //pretick broadcast
                for (Timed e :clocked) e.tick(); //tick broadcast
        } catch (TimeStop s) {
```

Program 12.6 `TimeManager` class.

```
            System.out.println("*** TimeStop");
            return;
        }
        Thread.sleep(delay);
      }
    } catch (InterruptedException e){}
  }
}
```

Program 12.6 (*Continued*).

```
public class ImmutableList<T> implements Iterable<T> {
  ImmutableList<T> next;
  T item;

  private ImmutableList
        (ImmutableList<T> next, T item) {
    this.next = next; this.item=item;
  }

  public static<T> ImmutableList<T> add
          (ImmutableList<T> list, T item) {
    return new ImmutableList<T>(list, item);
  }

  public static<T> ImmutableList<T> remove
          (ImmutableList<T> list, T target) {
    if (list == null) return null;
    return list.remove(target);
  }

  private ImmutableList<T> remove(T target) {
    if (item == target) {
      return next;
    } else {
      ImmutableList<T> new_next = remove(next,target);
      if (new_next == next ) return this;
      return new ImmutableList<T>(new_next,item);
    }
  }
}
```

Program 12.7 `ImmutableList` class.

The `delay` and `clocked` `TimeManager` fields (Program 12.6) are declared to be **`volatile`** since they can be changed by external threads. The keyword **`volatile`** ensures that the `run()` method reads the actual value of these fields before every broadcast. It prevents a compiler optimizing access by storing the fields in local variables or machine registers. If such an optimization occurred, the values would be read only once, when the `run()` method started, and it would not see subsequent updates.

The `pretick()` method allows a timed object to throw a `TimeStop` exception if it detects a timing inconsistency. This exception terminates the `TimeManager` thread. Consequently, a timing inconsistency in an implementation has the same behavior as a model with timing inconsistency – no further actions can be executed.

12.3 Parcel Router Problem

The parcel router problem is concerned with the simple parcel-sorting device depicted in Figure 12.7.

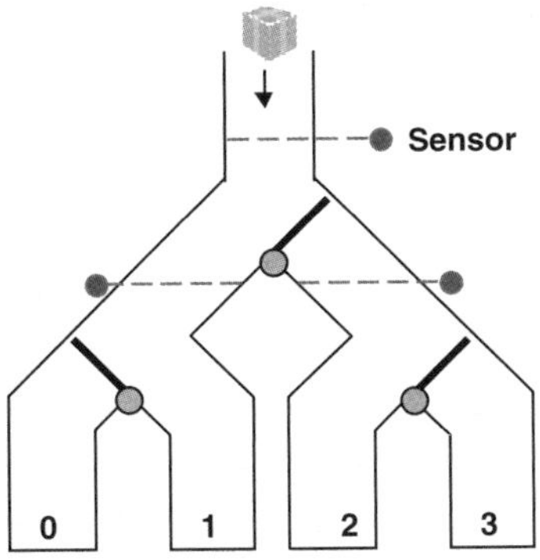

Figure 12.7 Parcel router device.

Parcels are dropped into the top of the router and fall by gravity through the chutes. Each parcel has a destination code that can be read by sensors. When a parcel passes a sensor, its code is read and the switch following the sensor is set to route the parcel to the correct destination bin. In this simple router, there are only four possible destinations numbered from zero to three. The switches can only be moved when there is no parcel in the way. The problem was originally formulated as a simple case study to show that specifications are not independent of implementation bias (Swartout and Balzer, 1982). It was called the *Package Router* problem. We have renamed packages to parcels to avoid possible confusion with Java packages.

In the following, we develop a timed model of the parcel router and then implement a simulation based on the model. We ignore gravity and friction and assume that parcels fall at a constant rate through chutes and switches.

12.3.1 Parcel Router Model

The overall structure of the parcel router model is depicted in Figure 12.8. Parcels are fed into the routing network by a generator process and emerge from the network into one of four destination bins.

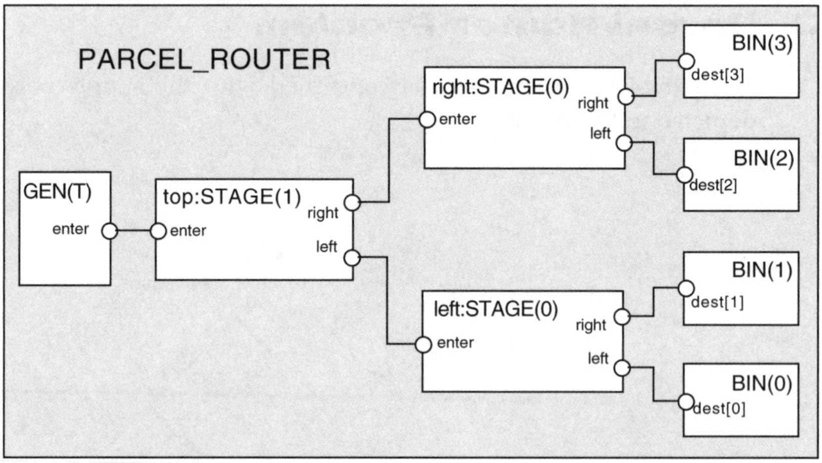


```
||PARCEL_ROUTER(T=4) =
  (top:STAGE(1) || left:STAGE(0)|| right:STAGE(0)
  || GEN(T) || forall[d:0..3] BIN(d)
  )/{ enter/top.enter,
      top.left/left.enter, top.right/right.enter,
      dest[0]/left.left,   dest[1]/left.right,
      dest[2]/right.left,  dest[3]/right.right,
      tick/{top,left,right}.tick
    }>>{tick}@{enter,dest,tick}.
```

Figure 12.8 Parcel router model structure.

GEN

The generator process GEN, defined below, generates a parcel every T units of time. Each parcel contains the number of its destination. The generator picks a destination for a parcel using non-deterministic choice.

```
range Dest = 0..3
set Parcel = {parcel[Dest]}

GEN(T=3) =
  (enter[Parcel] -> DELAY[1] | tick -> GEN),
DELAY[t:1..T] =
  (tick -> if (t<T) then DELAY[t+1] else GEN).
```

BIN

The destination bins are property processes that assert that the parcel delivered by the routing network to the bin must have the same destination number as the bin.

```
property
    BIN(D=0) = (dest[D].parcel[D] -> BIN)
               +{dest[D][Parcel]}.
```

STAGE

We have subdivided the routing network into three stages. Each stage has an identical structure. The parameter to a stage determines its level in the routing network. The structure of the STAGE composite process is depicted in Figure 12.9.

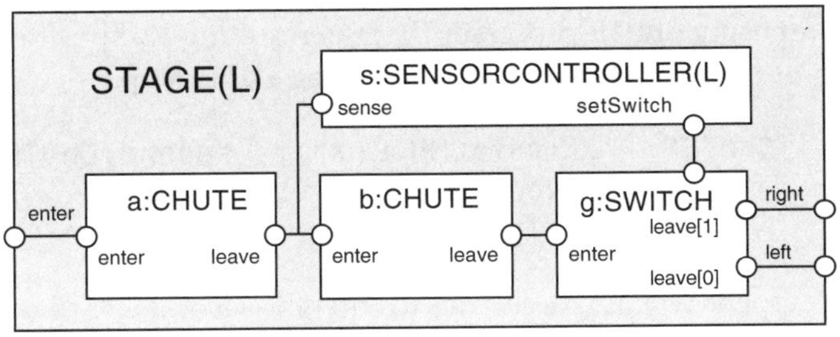

Figure 12.9 STAGE structure.

The composition expression which Figure 12.9 represents graphically is:

```
||STAGE(L=0) =
   ( a:CHUTE || b:CHUTE || g:SWITCH
   || s:SENSORCONTROLLER(L)
   )/{ enter/a.enter,   b.enter/{s.sense,a.leave},
```

```
        g.enter/b.leave, s.setSwitch/g.setSwitch,
        left/g.leave[0], right/g.leave[1],
        tick/{a,b,g}.tick
      } >>{enter,left,right,tick}
         @{enter,left,right,tick}.
```

CHUTE

Each physical chute in the physical device is modeled by a set of CHUTE processes. A CHUTE process models the movement of a single parcel through a segment of a physical chute. To model a chute that can have *n* parcels dropping through it, we need *n* CHUTE processes. In modeling the system, we use two processes and so we are modeling a physical chute that can accommodate only two parcels. The CHUTE process is given below:

```
CHUTE(T=2) =
  (enter[p:Parcel] -> DROP[p][0]
  |tick            -> CHUTE
  ),
DROP[p:Parcel][i:0..T] =
  (when (i<T)  tick      -> DROP[p][i+1]
  |when (i==T) leave[p] -> CHUTE
  ).
```

A parcel enters the chute and leaves after T units of time. We must be careful when composing CHUTE processes that the resulting composition has consistent timing. For example, the following system has a time-stop.

```
||CHUTES = (first:CHUTE(1) || second:CHUTE(2))
           /{second.enter/first.leave,
             tick/{first,second}.tick}.
```

It happens when a parcel tries to enter the second CHUTE before the previous parcel has left. Time-stop in this context can be interpreted as detecting a parcel jam in the physical device. For consistent timing in a pipeline of CHUTE processes, each process must have a delay which is the same or greater than the delay of its successor.

SENSORCONTROLLER

This process detects a parcel by observing the action caused by a parcel passing from one CHUTE to the next. Based on the destination of the parcel, it computes how the switch should be set. This routing function depends on the level of the stage. Because the network is a binary tree, it is simply (*destination*$\gg$*Level*)&1

(in this expression context, $\gg$ is the bit *shift* operator and & the bit-wise *and* operator). The function returns either zero, indicating left, or one, indicating right. SENSORCONTROLLER is not a timed process since we assume that detection of the parcel and computation of the route take negligible time. Each execution occurs within a clock cycle.

```
SENSORCONTROLLER(Level=0)
  = (sense.parcel[d:Dest] -> setSwitch[(d>>Level)&1]
     -> SENSORCONTROLLER).
```

SWITCH

During the time that a parcel takes to pass through the parcel switch, it ignores commands from the SENSORCONTROLLER. This models the physical situation where a parcel is passing through the switch and consequently, the switch gate is obstructed from moving.

```
range Dir = 0..1 //Direction  0  =  left,  1  =  right

SWITCH(T=1)    = SWITCH[0],
SWITCH[s:Dir] =
  (setSwitch[x:Dir] -> SWITCH[x]      //accept switch command
  |enter[p:Parcel]  -> SWITCH[s][p][0]
  |tick             -> SWITCH[s]
  ),
SWITCH[s:Dir][p:Parcel][i:0..T] =
  (setSwitch[Dir]         -> SWITCH[s][p][i]  //ignore
  |when (i<T) tick        -> SWITCH[s][p][i+1]
  |when (i==T)leave[s][p] -> SWITCH[s]
  ).
```

The SWITCH process extends the behavior of the CHUTE process with an additional component of its state to direct output and an extra action to set this state. SWITCH can be implemented by deriving its behavior, using inheritance, from the implementation of CHUTE.

Analysis

Having completed the definition of all the elements of the PARCEL_ROUTER model, we are now in a position to investigate its properties. We first perform a safety analysis of a minimized PARCEL_ROUTER(3). This system feeds a new parcel every three timing units into the routing network. This produces the following property violation:

```
Trace to property violation in BIN(0):
      enter.parcel.0
      tick
      tick
      tick
      enter.parcel.1
      tick
      tick
      tick
      enter.parcel.0
      tick
      tick
      tick
      enter.parcel.0
      tick
      dest.0.parcel.0
      tick
      tick
      enter.parcel.0
      tick
      dest.0.parcel.1
```

The trace clearly shows that a parcel intended for destination one has ended up in `BIN` zero. However, while it may be obvious to the reader why this has occurred, it is not clear from the trace since we have hidden the intermediate events that occur in each stage. We can elicit more information from the model in a number of ways. We can make internal actions visible and rerun the analysis or we can investigate the problem using the animator tool provided by *LTSA*. The second approach has the advantage that we do not need to modify the model in any way. We simply select `STAGE` as the target for analysis (with default level parameter as 0) and run the Animator using the following menu to specify the actions we wish to control.

```
menu TEST = {enter[Parcel],tick}
```

The trace depicted in Figure 12.10 was produced by initially choosing an `enter.parcel.0` action followed by three `tick` actions, then `enter.parcel.1` followed by five `ticks`. This is the trace produced by the safety violation, without the subsequent parcel entries. The Animator trace clearly exposes the reason for the violation. The first parcel is still in the switch when the sensor detects the second parcel and tries to set the switch to direction 1. Since the first parcel is in the switch, the `s.setSwitch.1` action is ignored and the switch does not change. Consequently, the second parcel follows the first in going to the left when it should have been switched to the right.

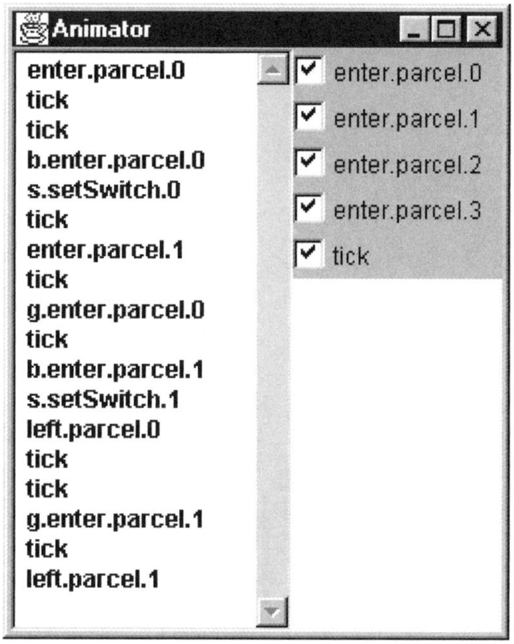

Figure 12.10 Animation trace for `STAGE(0)`.

The physical interpretation of the problem is that parcels are too close together to permit correct routing. We can check this intuition by analyzing a system with a slower parcel arrival rate, `PARCEL_ROUTER(4)`. Safety analysis finds no problems with this system and progress analysis demonstrates that the `TIME` property is satisfied.

In the next section, we describe a simulation of the parcel router based on the model. This implementation faithfully follows the model in allowing parcels that are too close together to be misrouted.

12.3.2 Parcel Router Implementation

The display for the parcel router simulation is shown in Figure 12.11. A new parcel for a particular destination is generated by pressing the button beneath that destination. Parcels that arrive at the wrong destination flash until they are replaced by a correct arrival. The speed of the simulation can be adjusted using the slider control to the right of the display. This controls the `TimeManager` described in section 12.2.2.

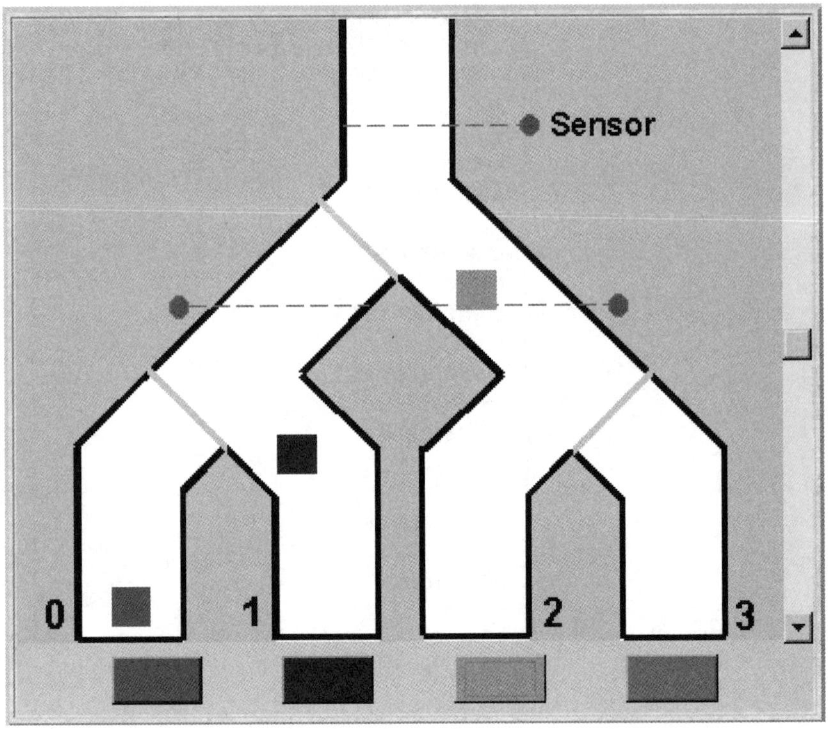

Figure 12.11 Parcel router applet display.

In describing the parcel router implementation, we concentrate on the interfaces and classes shown in Figure 12.12. These classes implement the timed behavior of the simulation. Display is implemented by the `ParcelCanvas` and `Parcel` classes. Each `Parcel` object is registered with the `ParcelCanvas`, which displays the parcel at its current position once per clock cycle. In addition, the `ParcelCanvas` displays the background and the current state of each switch. The `Parcel` and `ParcelCanvas` code can be found on the website that accompanies this book.

To permit flexible interconnection of `Chute`, `Switch`, `SensorController` and `DestinationBin` objects, each class implements the `ParcelMover` and `SwitchControl` interfaces listed in Program 12.8. The latter interface is required to allow switches to be connected to controllers.

The `Chute` class listed in Program 12.9 is a direct translation of the `CHUTE` process defined in the previous section using the method described in section 12.2.1. If the `current` field is not `null` then the chute contains a parcel. After `T` clock cycles this parcel is transferred to the `ParcelMover` object referenced by the `next`

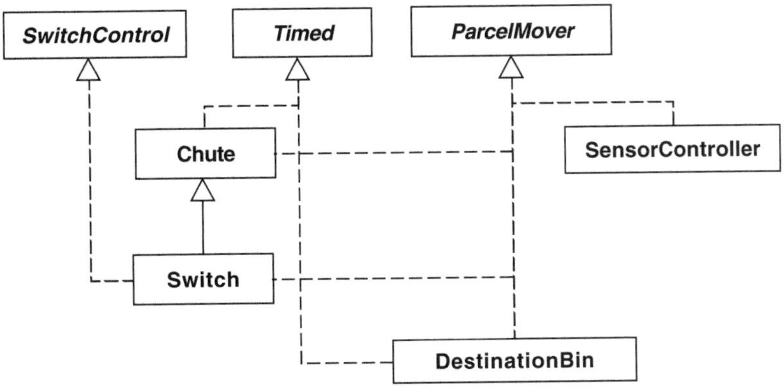

Figure 12.12 Parcel router classes and interfaces.

```
interface ParcelMover {
    void enter(Parcel p) throws TimeStop;
}

interface SwitchControl {
    void setSwitch(int direction);
}
```

Program 12.8 `ParcelMover` and `SwitchControl` interfaces.

field. This field is initialized when the configuration of chutes, switches, etc. is constructed by the `ParcelRouter` applet.

The `Switch` class listed in Program 12.10 is derived from `Chute`. A `Switch` object has references to the `ParcelMover` objects to its `left` and `right`. The `setSwitch` method sets the next field of the super class to one of these if there is no parcel currently occupying the switch. If there is, the command to switch is ignored, as in the model. Setting the `next` field means that when a parcel leaves, it is sent to the `ParcelMover` referenced by either `left` or `right`.

The `SensorController` class is listed in Program 12.11. Parcels pass through within a single clock cycle. The class is not aware of time and does not implement the `Timed` interface. Only model processes that have `tick` in their alphabets need to be implemented as `Timed` classes.

The `ParcelRouter` applet class contains a set of methods that create and "wire together" the parts of the simulation. The method listed below creates an assembly that corresponds to the `STAGE` composite process of the model.

```
class Chute implements ParcelMover, Timed {
  protected int i,T,direction;
  protected Parcel current = null;
  ParcelMover next = null;

  Chute(int len, int dir)
    { T = len; direction = dir;}

  // parcel enters chute
  public void enter(Parcel p) throws TimeStop {
    if (current!=null) throw new TimeStop();
    current = p; i = 0;
  }

  public void pretick() throws TimeStop {
    if (current==null) return;
    if (i == T) {
        next.enter(current); // package leaves chute
        current = null;
    }
  }

  public void tick(){
    if (current==null) return;
            //update display position of parcel
    ++i; current.move(direction);
  }
}
```

Program 12.9 `Chute` class.

```
class Switch extends Chute
        implements SwitchControl {
  ParcelMover left = null;
  ParcelMover right = null;
  private ParcelCanvas display;
  private int gate;

  Switch(int len, int dir, int g, ParcelCanvas d )
    { super(len,dir); display = d; gate = g;}
```

Program 12.10 `Switch` class.

```
    public void setSwitch(int direction) {
      if (current==null) {
        // nothing passing through switch
        display.setGate(gate,direction);
        if (direction==0)
          next = left;
        else
          next = right;
        }
    }
}
```

Program 12.10 (*Continued*).

```
class SensorController implements ParcelMover {
  ParcelMover next;
  SwitchControl controlled;
  protected int level;
  SensorController(int level){this.level=level;}

  // parcel enters and leaves within one clock cycle
  public void enter(Parcel p) throws TimeStop {
    route(p.destination);
    next.enter(p);
  }

  protected void route(int destination) {
    int dir = (destination>>level) & 1;
    controlled.setSwitch(dir);
  }
}
```

Program 12.11 `SensorController` class.

```
ParcelMover makeStage
    (ParcelMover left, ParcelMover right,
     int fallDir, // movement direction for parcel display
     int level,   // 0 or 1 as in the model
     int gate     // identity of gate for display purposes
    )
```

```
{
  // create parts and register each with TimeManager ticker
  Chute a = new Chute(16,fallDir);
  ticker.addTimed(a);
  SensorController s = new SensorController(level);
  Chute b = new Chute(15,fallDir);
  ticker.addTimed(b);
  Switch g = new Switch(12,fallDir,gate,display);
  ticker.addTimed(g);
  // wire parts together
  a.next = s; s.next = b;    s.controlled = g;
  b.next = g; g.left = left; g.right = right;
  return a;
}
```

The method exhibits a pleasing correspondence with the STAGE model. The model process prefix names become object references and the model relabels become reference assignments.

The DestinationBin class, which may be found on the website that accompanies this book, accepts a Parcel object and displays it in a fixed position. When a new parcel arrives, the old parcel is removed from the display. Parcels that arrive at the wrong destination are flashed by hiding and revealing them on alternate clock cycles.

The reader is encouraged to run the PackageRouter applet and observe that its behavior is as predicted by the model. The restriction that only one-way interactions can be supported by the clocking scheme has not caused a problem in this example. Even though the interaction between Chute, SensorController and Switch requires more than one method call in a clock cycle, it is still a uni-directional interaction in which a chute output causes an input to another chute and a switch.

12.4 Space Invaders

The final example of a timed system is a simple video arcade game. The display is depicted in Figure 12.13. The spaceship can be moved around the screen using the cursor keys. Pressing the space bar on the keyboard launches a missile from the spaceship. Missiles move up the display and appear as white arrows on the display. Aliens, depicted as spheres, drop from the top of the screen and explode when hit by a missile. When an alien collides with the spaceship, an explosion occurs and the shield strength of the spaceship is reduced. The game terminates

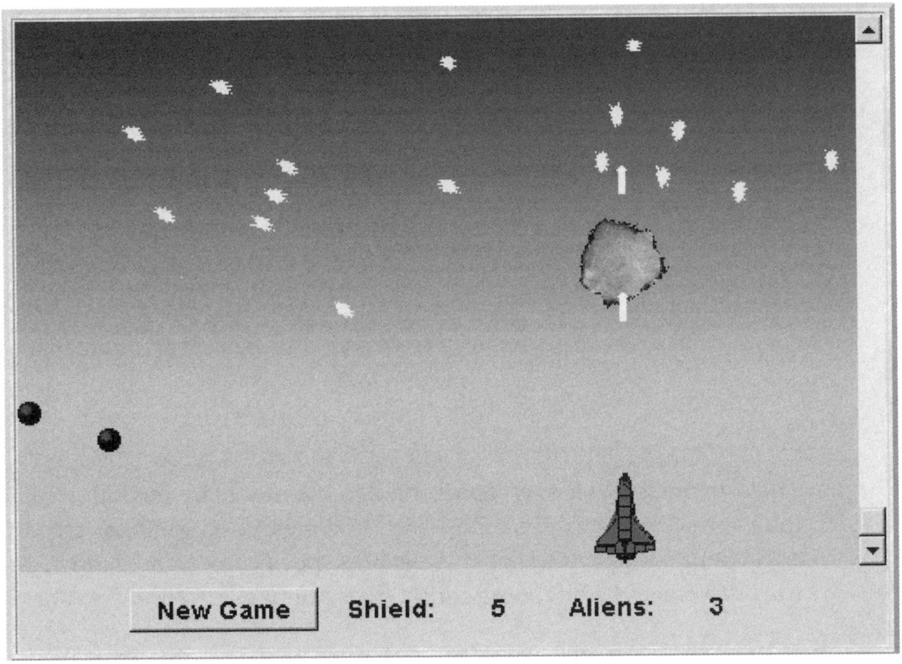

Figure 12.13 Space Invaders applet display.

when the shield strength drops to zero. The objective, as is usual in this style of game, is to shoot as many aliens as possible.

Video games involve many active entities, called *sprites*, which move around independently and concurrently. A sprite has a screen representation and a behavior. Sprites may interact when they collide. In Space Invaders, the sprites are the spaceship, aliens, missiles and explosions. Sprites are essentially concurrent activities, which we could consider implementing as threads. However, this would result in a game with poor performance due to the synchronization and context-switching overheads involved. A much better scheme is to implement sprites as timed objects. Each sprite has an opportunity to move once per clock cycle. This has the advantage that it is simple to synchronize screen updates with sprite activity. We simply repaint the screen once per clock cycle.

12.4.1 Space Invaders Model

Sprites move about in the two-dimensional space depicted in Figure 12.14. In an implementation, the coordinates refer to screen locations. In the model, we use a smaller space to permit analysis.

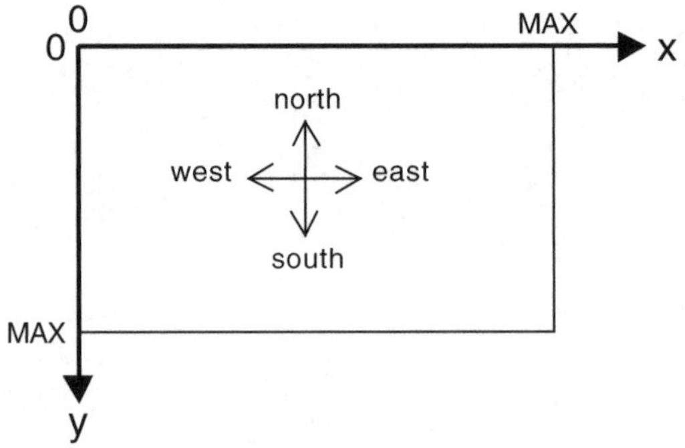

Figure 12.14 Game space.

The coordinate system is represented in the model by the following definitions. In the interests of simplicity, the width of the game space is assumed to be the same as its depth. The `undef` label is used to specify the coordinate of a sprite that has not been created and consequently does not have a defined position on the screen.

```
const MAX = 4
range D   = 0..MAX
set   Coord = {[D][D],undef} //(x,y)
```

Sprite

The entities that comprise the Space Invaders game have behavior in common with respect to the way that they move about in the game space. We model this common behavior as the `SPRITE` process listed below. The behavior of the spaceship, missiles and aliens is defined using this process.

```
SPRITE =
  (create[x:D][y:D] -> SPRITE[x][y]
  |tick -> SPRITE
  |pos.undef -> SPRITE
  ),
SPRITE[x:D][y:D] =
  (pos[x][y] -> SPRITE[x][y]
  |tick ->
   (north -> if y>0   then SPRITE[x][y-1] else END
   |south -> if y<MAX then SPRITE[x][y+1] else END
   |west  -> if x>0   then SPRITE[x-1][y] else END
   |east  -> if x<MAX then SPRITE[x+1][y] else END
```

```
      | {rest,action[x][y]} -> SPRITE[x][y]
      )
    ),
  END = (end -> SPRITE).
```

Before a sprite is created, its location is undefined. A query using the action `pos` will return the `undef` value for its location. After the `create` action, `pos` returns a valid coordinate for the sprite's current location. At each clock tick, a sprite can move in one of four directions, or it can remain in the same position (`rest` action). The sprite implementation described in the next section allows a sprite to move in one of eight directions; however, four directions are sufficient detail for modeling purposes. In addition to moving, a sprite can instigate an `action` during a clock cycle. When a sprite moves out of the game space, it indicates that it has terminated by performing the `end` action. In an implementation, a sprite would then be garbage collected. In the model, the sprite goes back to the state in which it can be created. As described in Chapter 9, we use cyclic behavior to model dynamic creation. The set of actions that the `SPRITE` process can engage in – excluding `tick` and the position query `pos` – is specified by:

```
set Sprite =
   {north,south,west,east,rest,action[D][D],create[D][D]}
```

Alien

An alien is a sprite that moves down the screen. Consequently, we can specify its behavior by constraining the movement of the `SPRITE` process. In the model, an alien starts at the top of the screen and moves vertically down; in the implementation, it can also move diagonally down.

```
ALIEN_CONSTRAINT =
  (create[D][0] -> MOVE),
MOVE =
  (south -> MOVE | end -> ALIEN_CONSTRAINT)
  +Sprite.

||ALIEN = (SPRITE || ALIEN_CONSTRAINT).
```

The constraint permits an alien to be created at any x-position at the top of the screen and only permits it to move `south` and then `end` when it leaves the screen. The `ALIEN` composite process permits only these actions to occur since the constraint has the `Sprite` alphabet.

Missile

The behavior of the missile sprite is defined in exactly the same way. In this case, the missile is only permitted to move `north`, up the screen.

```
MISSILE_CONSTRAINT =
    (create[D][MAX] -> MOVE),
MOVE =
   (north -> MOVE | end -> MISSILE_CONSTRAINT)
   + Sprite.

||MISSILE = (SPRITE || MISSILE_CONSTRAINT).
```

Spaceship

The spaceship has more complex behavior. It is constrained to moving horizontally at the bottom of the screen, either `east` or `west`, or staying in the same position, `rest`. It is created in the center of the screen and is constrained not to move off the screen. The spaceship can perform an `action`, which is used to create a missile, as explained later. In fact, the implementation permits the spaceship to move up and down the screen as well. However, horizontal movement is sufficient detail for us to gain an understanding of the operation of the system from the model.

```
SPACESHIP_CONSTRAINT =
    (create[MAX/2][MAX] -> MOVE[MAX/2]),
MOVE[x:D] =
    ( when (x>0)  west -> MOVE[x-1]
    | when (x<MAX) east -> MOVE[x+1]
    | rest -> MOVE[x]
    | action[x][MAX] -> MOVE[x]
    ) + Sprite.

||SPACESHIP =(SPRITE || SPACESHIP_CONSTRAINT).
```

Collision Detection

Collision detection is modeled by the `COLLIDE` process which, after a `tick`, queries the positions of two sprites and signals a collision through the action `explode` if their positions coincide. Undefined positions are excluded. In the implementation, the detection of a collision results in the creation of an explosion sprite that displays a series of images to create the appropriate graphic appearance. In the model, we omit this detail.

```
COLLIDE(A='a, B='b) =
  (tick -> [A].pos[p1:Coord] -> [B].pos[p2:Coord]
   -> if (p1==p2 && p1!='undef && p2!='undef) then
         ([A][B].explode -> COLLIDE)
      else
         COLLIDE
  ).
```

Space Invaders

The composite process SPACE_INVADERS models a game that, in addition to the spaceship, permits only a single alien and a single missile to appear on the screen. This simplification is required for a model of manageable size. However, we have defined sprites as having cyclic behavior that models recreation. Consequently, the alien can reappear in different start positions and the spaceship can launch another missile as soon as the previous one has left the screen. The model captures all possible behaviors of the combination of spaceship, alien and missile.

To model launching a missile, we have associated the spaceship's action with the missile's create by relabeling. Two collision detectors are included to detect spaceship–alien and alien–missile collisions.

```
||SPACE_INVADERS =
   ( alien    :ALIEN
   || spaceship:SPACESHIP
   || missile :MISSILE
   || COLLIDE('alien,'spaceship)
   || COLLIDE('missile,'alien))
   /{spaceship.action/missile.create,
     tick/{alien,spaceship,missile}.tick}
   >>{tick}.
```

Analysis

Safety analysis of SPACE_INVADERS does not detect a time-stop and progress analysis demonstrates that the TIME progress property is satisfied. Further, the progress properties:

```
progress SHOOT_ALIEN={missile.alien.explode}
progress ALIEN_SHIP ={alien.spaceship.explode}
```

are satisfied, showing that both alien – missile and alien – spaceship collisions can occur. To gain an understanding of the operation of the model, we can animate it to produce example execution traces. An alternative approach to producing sample traces is to use safety properties as follows. Suppose we wish to find a trace that results in a collision between an alien and a missile. We specify a safety property that the action `missile.alien.explode` should not occur and analyze the system with respect to this property:

```
property ALIEN_HIT = STOP + {missile.alien.explode}.
||FIND_ALIEN_HIT = (SPACE_INVADERS || ALIEN_HIT).
```

The trace produced is:

```
Trace to property violation in ALIEN_HIT:
     alien.create.1.0
     spaceship.create.2.4
     tick
     alien.south
     spaceship.west
     missile.pos.undef
     alien.pos.1.1
     spaceship.pos.1.4
     tick
     alien.south
     spaceship.action.1.4  – missile launched
     missile.pos.1.4
     alien.pos.1.2
     spaceship.pos.1.4
     tick
     alien.south
     missile.north
     missile.pos.1.3
     alien.pos.1.3
     missile.alien.explode
```

Exactly the same approach can be used to find a trace leading to a spaceship – alien collision.

The emphasis of the Space Invaders model is not so much on demonstrating that it satisfies specific safety and liveness properties but rather as a means of investigating interactions and architecture. After all, the program is far from a safety-critical application. However, in abstracting from implementation details concerned with the display and concentrating on interaction, the model provides a clear explanation of how the program should operate. In addition, it provides some indication of how the implementation should be structured. For example, it indicates that a `CollisionDetector` class is needed and confirms that a `Sprite` class can be used to implement the common behavior of missiles, aliens and the spaceship.

12.4.2 Space Invaders Implementation

The implementation of the Space Invaders program is large in comparison to the example programs presented previously. Consequently, we restrict ourselves to describing the structure of the program using class diagrams. The translation from timed processes to timed objects should be clear from examples presented in earlier sections of this chapter. The reader can find the Java code for each of the classes we mention on the website that accompanies this book.

Sprite and SpriteCanvas

The display for the Space Invaders program is handled by the two classes depicted in Figure 12.15. A `Sprite` is created with an initial position and an image. The `SpriteCanvas` maintains a list of sprites. Every clock tick, the `SpriteCanvas` calls the `paint()` method of each sprite on its list. The sprite then draws its image at its current position.

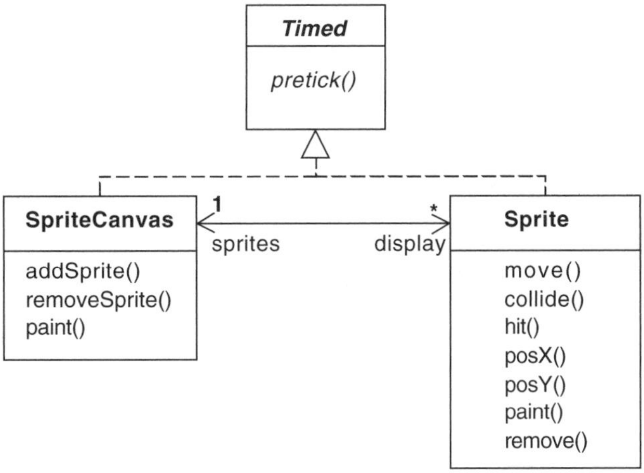

Figure 12.15 `Sprite` and `SpriteCanvas` classes.

The `move()` method has a direction parameter that specifies one of eight directions in which the sprite can move. It is called by a subclass each clock cycle to change the position of the sprite. The `collide()` method tests whether the sprite's bounding rectangle intersects with the sprite passed as a parameter. The `hit()` method is called by the collision detector when a collision is detected. `PosX()` and `PosY()` return the current x and y coordinates of the sprite.

CollisionDetector

The collision detector maintains a list of the alien sprites and missile sprites and a reference to the spaceship sprite as shown in Figure 12.16. Every clock cycle, the detector determines whether each alien has collided with either a missile or the spaceship. If a collision is detected, the `hit()` methods of the sprites involved in the collision are invoked.

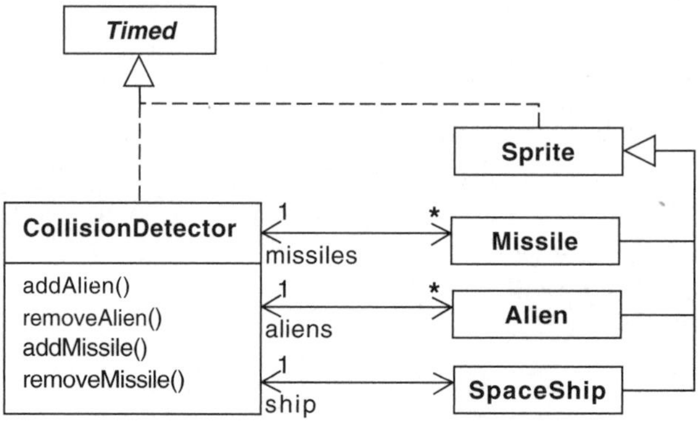

Figure 12.16 `CollisionDetector` class diagram.

The method listed below is the implementation provided for the `hit()` method in the `Alien` class.

```
public void hit() {
  new Explosion(this);
  SpaceInvaders.score.alienHit();
  SpaceInvaders.detector.removeAlien(this);
  remove(); // remove from SpriteCanvas
}
```

The method creates a new explosion sprite at the same location as the alien, records an alien hit on the scoreboard and removes the alien from the collision detector and the display. The `CollisionDetector`, `Alien`, `Missile` and `Spaceship` classes implement the essential behavior of the game. These classes correspond to the `COLLIDE`, `ALIEN`, `MISSILE` and `SPACESHIP` model processes.

SpaceInvaders

The `SpaceInvaders` applet class creates the spaceship, the alien generator, the missile launcher and the score board in addition to the display, time manager and collision detector as shown in Figure 12.17.

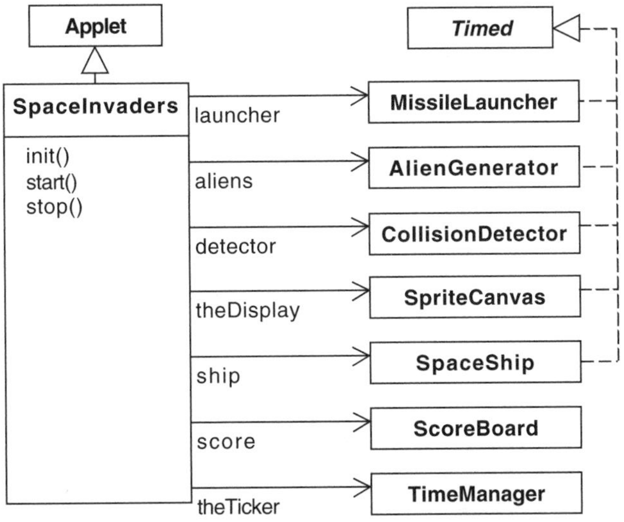

Figure 12.17 `SpaceInvaders` class diagram.

The `AlienGenerator` waits for a random number of clock cycles and then creates a new alien with a randomly chosen start position and a random downward direction. The `MissileLauncher` creates a new missile when the space bar is pressed. The x-coordinate of the new missile is the current position of the spaceship. The classes included in Figure 12.17 provide the infrastructure for scoring and the creation and display of sprites.

The collision detector and display run during the pre-tick clock phase; the remaining program actions, such as sprite movement, occur during the tick phase. This permits the display to render a consistent set of positions and for the effect of hits to be computed during tick processing. However, in reality, we could implement this sort of program using only a single-phase clock. This is because the clock ticks rapidly and, since the screen is updated every cycle, any inconsistencies which resulted from an action happening over two clock cycles rather than one would not be visible to a user.

Summary

This chapter has presented a discrete approach to modeling and implementing timed systems. The passage of time is signaled by regular successive ticks of a clock. In models, this tick appears as an action that is shared by the processes for which behavior depends on the passage of time. In implementations, the tick is an event broadcast by a time manager.

In discrete time models, we saw that the composition of processes with inconsistent timing resulted in a deadlock. This sort of deadlock is termed a *time-stop*. The order in which actions can occur in a timed model is restricted by making a *maximal progress* assumption. This ensures that an action occurs as soon as all participants are ready to perform it. Maximal progress is true for a model when we make the `tick` action low priority. This ensures that all ready actions occur within a clock cycle. Maximal progress thus reflects the implementation assumption that actions take negligible time to execute.

We described an implementation approach for timed systems that is *event-based* rather than *thread-based*. In this approach, each model process that has `tick` in its alphabet is translated into a timed object. Timed objects are invoked regularly by a time manager that dispatches timing events. We use a two-phase scheme that requires a pre-tick and tick event dispatch. Timed objects produce outputs during the pre-tick phase and compute the next state based on received inputs during the tick phase. This scheme permits one-way communication interactions to occur atomically within a single clock cycle. It was pointed out that multi-way interactions within a single clock cycle are not supported by this scheme. However, this did not cause problems in the example programs. The advantage of using timed objects rather than threads to implement timed processes is concerned with runtime efficiency. Timed objects are activated by method invocation, which has a lower overhead than context-switching threads. Further, since the pre-tick and tick methods run sequentially, there is no synchronization overhead to ensure mutual exclusion. Lastly, for programs largely concerned with display, the approach naturally synchronizes screen updates from multiple activities.

We should also point out some of the disadvantages of the event-based approach or the reader might wonder why we have devoted the main part of the book to a thread-based approach. Threads abstract from the detail of how activities should be scheduled to organize interaction. We saw that the timed approach was limited to uni-directional interactions in a single clock cycle. More complex interaction needs to be explicitly scheduled with either a multi-phase clock or, alternatively, over multiple clock cycles. This rapidly becomes unmanageable for complex interactions. Further, the event-based scheme required a timed object to examine its state every clock cycle to determine whether an event has occurred. A thread-based implementation may incur lower overhead for systems in which activities do not perform some action every clock cycle. The thread scheduler dispatches a thread only when there is some work for it to do.

Finally, we note that the model-based approach to concurrent programming permits a designer the flexibility to use either an event-based or thread-based implementation scheme or indeed a hybrid. We use the same modeling and analysis techniques for both implementation approaches.

Notes and Further Reading

A comprehensive treatment of using discrete time in the context of CSP may be found in Roscoe's book (1998). We have adapted the approach presented there to fit with the modeling tools and techniques used in this book. However, our approach is essentially the same and much credit is due to Roscoe for providing the first generally accessible introduction to this style of modeling time.

It was explicitly stated in the introduction that the timed systems we deal with are not real-time in the sense of guaranteeing deadlines. The interested reader will find that there is a vast literature on the specification, verification and analysis of real-time systems. A good starting point is a book edited by Mathai Joseph which presents a number of techniques with respect to the same case study (1996). One of the techniques presented is Timed CSP, which uses a dense continuous model of time in contrast to the discrete model we present. Continuous time is more expressive but leads to difficulties in automated analysis.

Exercises

12.1 Define a process that models a timed single-slot buffer. The buffer should both wait to accept input and wait to produce output. The buffer requires a minimum of T time units to transfer an item from its input to its output.

12.2 Using the process defined in exercise 12.1, define a two-slot timed buffer and explore its properties. Determine the timing consistency relationship between the delays for the two buffers. Explore the effect of applying maximal progress by making `tick` low priority.

12.3 Implement the timed buffer process of exercise 12.1 as a timed object and explore the runtime behavior of a system composed of these objects with producer and consumer timed objects. (*Note*: Waiting to produce an output is implemented in timed systems by *balking* rather than throwing a time-stop. By balking, we mean that the method performing the output returns a boolean indicating whether or not the output was possible. If it fails, it is retried on the next clock cycle.)

12.4 An electric window in a car is controlled by two press-button switches: **up** and **down**. When the up button is pressed, then the window starts closing. If the up button is pressed for less than T seconds then the window closes completely. If the up button is pressed for more than T seconds then when the button is released, the window stops closing. The down button works in exactly the same way, except that the window opens rather than closes. A mechanical interlock prevents both buttons being pressed at the same time.
The window is moved by a motor that responds to the commands **start_close, stop_close, start_open** and **stop_open.** Two sensor switches, **closed** and **opened**, detect, respectively, when the window is fully closed and when it is fully open. The window takes R units of time to move from the completely open position to the completely closed position or vice versa.

Define a timed model for the electric window system in *FSP*. Specify safety properties that assert that the motor is not active when the window is fully closed or fully opened.

12.5 Translate the model of the electric window system into a Java implementation using timed objects.

13 Program Verification

Up to this point, we have taken a modeling approach to the design of concurrent programs. Models are constructed, so that we can focus on actions, interaction and concurrency before proceeding to implementation and adding the details concerned with data representation, resource usage and user interface. We use the model as a basis for program construction by identifying a mapping from model processes to Java threads and monitor objects. However, we do not demonstrate other than by testing and observation that the behavior of the implementation corresponds to the behavior predicted by the model. Essentially, we rely on a systematic translation of the model into Java to ensure that the program satisfies the same safety and progress properties as the model.

In this chapter, we address the problem of verifying implementations, using *FSP* and its supporting *LTSA* tool. In doing verification, we translate Java programs into a set of *FSP* processes and show that the resulting *FSP implementation* model satisfies the same safety and progress properties that the design model satisfied. In this way, we can show that the program is a satisfactory implementation of its design model.

Chapter 4 of the book took exactly this approach of translating a Java program into an *FSP* model to investigate the problem of interference. To perform verification, we need to model the Java program at the level of variables, monitor locks and condition synchronization. In Chapter 4, we showed how to model variables and monitor locks. This chapter develops a model for condition synchronization so that we can verify Java programs that use `wait()`, `notify()` and `notifyAll()`. This implementation model is used in verifying the bounded buffer and Readers–Writers Java programs from Chapters 5 and 7. To allow us to structure the more complex sequences of actions that arise in verification of implementations, we first introduce sequential composition of *FSP* processes.

13.1 Sequential Processes

Although abstractly a process always means the same thing, for pragmatic implementation reasons *FSP* divides processes into three types: local processes that define a state within a primitive process, primitive processes defined by a set of local processes and composite processes that use parallel composition, relabeling and hiding to compose primitive processes. A local process is defined using STOP, ERROR, action prefix and choice. We now extend our definition of processes to include sequential processes.

> A sequential process is a process that can terminate. A process can terminate if the local process END is reachable from its start state.

13.1.1 Local Process END

The local process END denotes the state in which a process successfully terminates. A process engages in no further actions after END. In this respect it has the same semantics as STOP. However, STOP denotes a state in which a process has halted prematurely, usually due to communication deadlock. In earlier chapters, to simplify presentation, we used STOP to indicate termination of a process. It would be more precise to replace these uses of STOP with END. With the introduction of a state describing successful termination, the need to use STOP explicitly in process description largely disappears. Figure 13.1 depicts an example of a sequential process together with its *LTS*, where E is used to denote END.

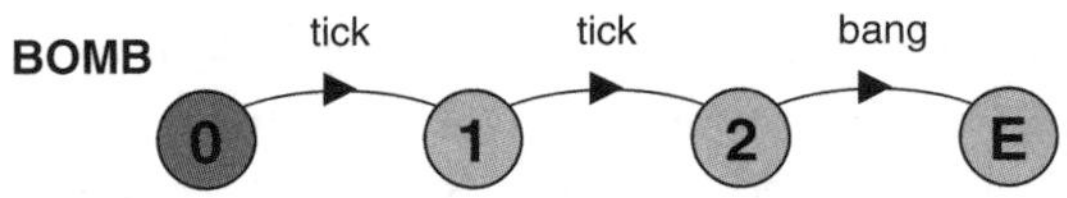


```
BOMB = (tick -> tick -> bang -> END).
```

Figure 13.1 Sequential process BOMB.

13.1.2 Sequential Composition;

> If P is a sequential process and Q is a local process, then P;Q represents the sequential composition such that when P terminates, P;Q becomes the process Q.

If we define a process SKIP = END then P;SKIP ≡ P and SKIP;P ≡ P. A sequential composition in *FSP* always takes the form:

SP1;SP2;..SPn;LP

where SP1,..,SPn are sequential processes and LP is a local process. A sequential composition can appear anywhere in the definition of a primitive process that a local process reference can appear (for example, processes P123 and LOOP in Figure 13.2).

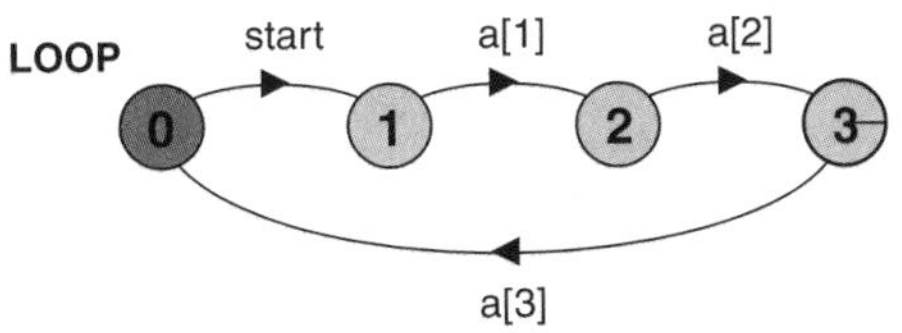

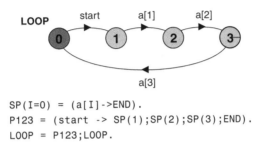

```
SP(I=0) = (a[I]->END).
P123 = (start -> SP(1);SP(2);SP(3);END).
LOOP = P123;LOOP.
```

Figure 13.2 Sequential composition LOOP.

Sequential composition can be used in a recursive context as in Figure 13.3, where process R is defined as the sequential composition of sequential processes R(I) for values of I from 0 to 2 and the local process END when I=3.

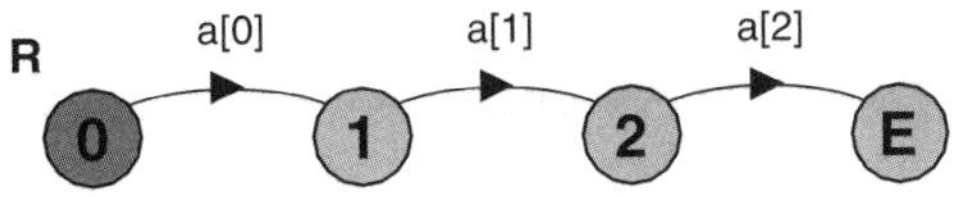

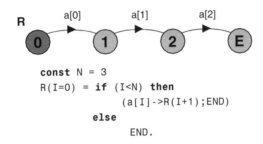

```
const N = 3
R(I=0) = if (I<N) then
                (a[I]->R(I+1);END)
          else
                END.
```

Figure 13.3 Sequential composition and recursion.

13.1.3 Parallel Composition and Sequential Processes

> The parallel composition SP1||SP2 of two sequential processes SP1 and SP2 terminates when both of these processes terminate. If termination is reachable in SP1||SP2 then it is a sequential process.

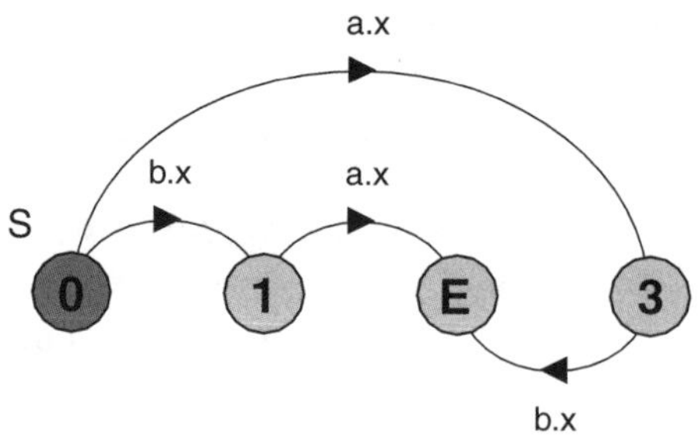


```
P = (x -> END).
||S = (a:P || b:P).
```

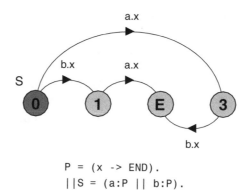

Figure 13.4 Parallel composition of sequential processes.

Figure 13.4 gives an example of parallel composition of sequential processes. Note that a composite process that terminates can appear in the definition of a primitive process.

13.1.4 Sequential Processes and Analysis

While a reachable STOP state is a safety violation resulting in the *LTSA* generating a counter example trace, a reachable END state is not a safety violation. However, a trace to a reachable END state will be generated during progress analysis since the END state violates all progress properties.

13.2 Modeling Condition Synchronization

In Chapter 5, we explained how a guarded action in a design model can be translated into a synchronized method as shown below:

```
FSP:   when cond act -> NEWSTAT

Java:  public synchronized void act()
                throws InterruptedException
       {
         while (!cond) wait();
         // modify monitor data
         notifyAll()
       }
```

We noted that if an action modifies the data of the monitor, it can call `notifyAll()` to awaken all other threads that may be waiting for a particular condition to hold with respect to this data. We also noted that if it is not certain that only a single thread needs to be awakened, it is safer to call `notifyAll()` than `notify()` to make sure that threads are not kept waiting unnecessarily. We use an implementation model to investigate this particular aspect further in the rest of this chapter.

13.2.1 Wait, Notify and NotifyAll

To verify that a program using this translation satisfies the required safety and progress properties, we must model the behavior of `wait()`, `notify()` and `notifyAll()`. We can then rigorously check the use of `notify()` versus `notifyAll()`. A model for the interaction of these methods is developed in the following. Firstly, we define a process `ELEMENT` to manage the `BLOCKED` state of each thread that accesses a monitor.

```
ELEMENT
  = (wait -> BLOCKED | unblockAll -> ELEMENT),
BLOCKED
  = ({unblock,unblockAll} -> UNBLOCK),
UNBLOCK
  = (endwait -> ELEMENT).
```

The `wait` action, representing a call to `wait()`, puts the process into the `BLOCKED` state. Then either an `unblock` action caused by a `notify()` or an `unblockAll` action caused by a `notifyAll()` causes the process to move to `UNBLOCK` and signal the return of the `wait()` method by the `endwait` action. We will deal with the way that the monitor lock is released and acquired by `wait()` later.

The `CONTROL` process manages how `notify` and `notifyAll` actions, representing the eponymous Java methods, cause `unblock` and `unblockAll` actions:

```
CONTROL = EMPTY,
EMPTY   = (wait -> WAIT[1]

          | {notifyAll,notify} -> EMPTY
          ),
WAIT[i:1..Nthread]
        = (when (i<Nthread)  wait -> WAIT[i+1]
          |notifyAll -> unblockAll -> EMPTY

          |notify -> unblock ->
           if (i==1) then EMPTY else WAIT[i-1]
          ).
```

Since we can only check systems with a finite set of states, we must define a static set of identifiers `Threads` to represent the set of threads that can potentially access a monitor object. The cardinality of this set is defined by the constant `Nthread`. The `CONTROL` process maintains a count of the number of processes in the `BLOCKED` state. If there are no blocked processes then `notify` and `notifyAll` have no effect. If there are many blocked processes then a `notify` action unblocks any one of them. The set of threads waiting on a monitor and the effect of the `wait()`, `notify()` and `notifyAll()` methods are modeled by the composition:

```
const Nthread   = 3          //cardinality of Threads
set   Threads   = {a,b,c} //set of thread indentifiers
set   SyncOps   = {notify,notifyAll,wait}

||WAITSET
      = (Threads:ELEMENT || Threads::CONTROL)
        /{unblockAll/Threads.unblockAll}.
```

The composition defines an `ELEMENT` process for each thread identifier in the set `Threads`. The `CONTROL` process is shared by all the threads in this set. The relabeling ensures that when any thread calls `notifyAll()`, then all waiting threads are unblocked. The behavior of `WAITSET` is best illustrated using the animation facilities of *LTSA*.

Figure 13.5 shows a trace in which thread **b** calls `wait`, then thread **a** calls `wait`. A call by thread **c** to `notify` unblocks thread **a**. Note that while thread **b** was blocked before **a**, it is **a** that is unblocked first. In other words, the model does not assume that blocked threads are held in a FIFO queue, although many Java Virtual

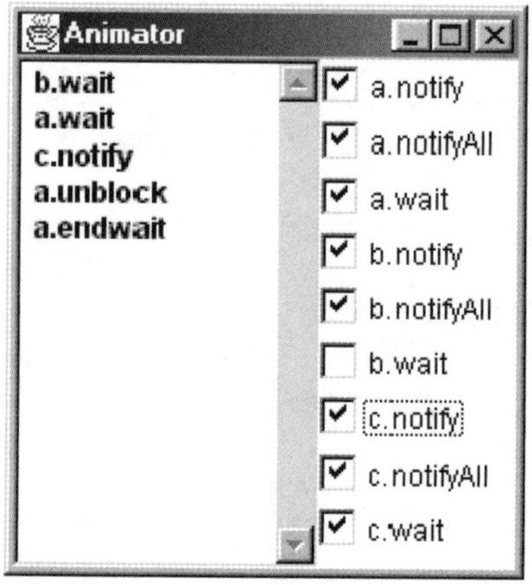

Figure 13.5 `WAITSET` trace for `notify`.

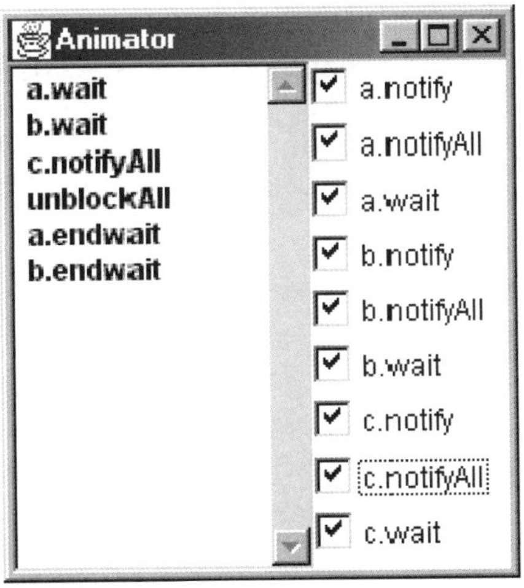

Figure 13.6 `WAITSET` trace for `notifyAll`.

Machines implement thread blocking this way. The Java Language Specification specifies only that blocked threads are held in a set and consequently may be unblocked in any order by a sequence of notifications. An implementation that assumes FIFO blocking may not work correctly on a LIFO implementation. The `WAITSET` model permits all possible unblocking orders and consequently, when we use it in verification, it ensures that if an implementation model is correct, it is correct for all possible orders of blocking/unblocking actions.

Figure 13.6 illustrates the behavior for `notifyAll` when threads **a** and **b** are blocked.

13.3 Modeling Variables and Synchronized Methods

13.3.1 Variables

Variables are modeled in exactly the same way as presented in Chapter 4. However, for convenience, we add actions to model incrementing and decrementing integer variables. An integer variable is modeled as follows:

```
const Imax = 5  // a maximum value that variable can take
range Int  = 0..Imax
set   VarAlpha = {read[Int],write[Int],inc,dec}
```

```
VAR(Init=0)= VAR[Init],
VAR[v:Int] = (read[v]       ->VAR[v]         // v
             |inc           ->VAR[v+1]       // ++v
             |dec           ->VAR[v-1]       // --v
             |write[c:Int]->VAR[c]           // v = c
             ).
```

A boolean variable is modeled by:

```
const False = 0
const True  = 1
range Bool  = False..True
set   BoolAlpha = {read[Bool],write[Bool]}

BOOLVAR(Init=False) = BOOLVAR[Init],
BOOLVAR[b:Bool]     = (read[b]         ->BOOLVAR[b]   // b
                      |write[c:Bool]->BOOLVAR[c]      // b = c
                      ).
```

13.3.2 Monitor Exit and Entry

In Chapter 4, we noted that synchronized methods acquire the monitor lock before accessing the variables of a monitor object and release the lock on exit. We will use the same simple model of a lock used in Chapter 4, ignoring the detail that locks in Java support recursive locking:

```
set LockOps = {acquire,release}
LOCK = (acquire -> release ->LOCK).
```

We can now model the state of a monitor by the set of processes that represent its wait set, lock and variables. For example, the state for a monitor *M* that encapsulates a single boolean variable *cond* is modeled as follows:

```
||Mstate = (Threads::LOCK   || WAITSET
           || Threads::(cond:BOOLVAR)
           ).
```

The definition of the Java `wait()` operation in Chapter 5 requires that a waiting thread releases the synchronization lock. We model this as a sequential process that releases the lock when it blocks and acquires it again when it unblocks and finishes waiting.

```
WAIT = (wait ->release ->endwait ->acquire ->END).
```

In Java, the notification and waiting operations are only valid when the thread calling these operations holds the lock for the monitor object on which the operations are invoked. The following safety property checks that this is the case in the implementation models we construct:

```
property SAFEMON
   = ([t:Threads].acquire -> HELDBY[t]),
HELDBY[t:Threads]
   = ([t].{notify,notifyAll,wait} -> HELDBY[t]
     |[t].release -> SAFEMON
     ).
```

13.3.3 Synchronized Methods

A synchronized method of the form:

```
synchronized void act()throws InterruptedException {
      while (!cond) wait();
      // modify monitor data
      notifyAll()
}
```

can now be modeled by the following *FSP* sequential process. As in Chapter 4, alphabet extension ensures that only intended interactions occur since it is usually the case that a process modeling a synchronized method will only use a subset of the data access actions (in this case only `read` is used on the boolean condition) and synchronization actions (in this case only `notifyAll` is used).

```
ACT    // act()
  = (acquire -> WHILE),        // monitor entry- acquire lock
WHILE
  = (cond.read[b:Bool] ->      // while (!cond) wait();
    if !b then WAIT;WHILE else CONTINUE
    ),

CONTINUE
  = (                          // modify monitor data
    notifyAll                  // notifyAll()
    -> release                 // monitor exit- release lock
    -> END
  ) + {SyncOps, LockOps, cond.BoolAlpha}.
```

Note that with the above constructions, while we can now model monitors in some detail, we are still ignoring the effect of InterruptException occurrence and handling. In the book, we have only used this mechanism to terminate all the threads that constitute the concurrent Java program. At the end of this chapter we discuss the problems that can arise if only a subset of threads is terminated in this way.

13.4 Bounded Buffer Example

Program 13.1 below reproduces the bounded buffer implementation from Chapter 5, Program 5.6 published in the first printing and first edition of this book. In this section, we develop a detailed model of the synchronization of this program and investigate its properties. As usual, we abstract from the details of what items are stored in the buffer and how these items are stored. Consequently, the only variable that we need to consider modeling is the variable *count* that stores the number of items currently stored in the buffer. The state of the buffer monitor implementation is as follows with the count variable initialized to zero:

```
const Size = 2 // number of buffer slots
||BUFFERMON  = ( Threads::LOCK || WAITSET || SAFEMON
               ||Threads::(count:VAR(0))
               ).
```

The alphabet for each thread is defined by:

```
set BufferAlpha = {count.VarAlpha, LockOps, SyncOps}
```

13.4.1 put() and get() Methods

We can now translate the `put()` and `get()` methods of Program 13.1 into *FSP* into a reasonably straightforward way. Since we have abstracted from the details of storing items in the buffer, we replace the actions to place an item in the buffer with the action `put` and the actions to remove an item with the action `get`.

```
  public void put(Object o)
     throws InterruptedException; //put object into buffer
  public Object get()
     throws InterruptedException; //get object from buffer
}

class BufferImpl implements Buffer {
  protected Object[] buf;
```

Program 13.1 `Buffer` interface and `BufferImpl` class.

```
    protected int in = 0;
    protected int out= 0;
    protected int count= 0;
    protected int size;

    BufferImpl(int size) {
      this.size = size; buf = new Object[size];
    }

    public synchronized void put(Object o)
              throws InterruptedException {
      while (count==size) wait();
      buf[in] = o;
      ++count;
      in=(in+1) %size;
      notify();
    }

    public synchronized Object get()
              throws InterruptedException {
      while (count==0) wait();
      Object o =buf[out];
      buf[out]=null;
      --count;
      out=(out+1) %size;
      notify();
      return (o);
      }
  }
```

Program 13.1 *(Continued).*

```
/*  put method */
PUT
  = (acquire -> WHILE),
WHILE
  = (count.read[v:Int] ->     // while (count == size) wait();
     if v==Size then WAIT;WHILE else CONTINUE
    ),
CONTINUE
  = (put                      // buf[in] = o; in=(in+1) %size;
     -> count.inc             // ++count;
     -> notify -> release -> END
    ) + BufferAlpha.
```

```
/* get method */
GET
  = (acquire -> WHILE),
WHILE
  = (count.read[v:Int] ->    // while (count == 0 ) wait()
      if v==0 then WAIT;WHILE else CONTINUE
    ),
CONTINUE
    = (get                    // Object[o] = buf[out]; buf[out]=null;
     -> count.dec             // --count;
     -> notify -> release -> END
     ) + BufferAlpha.
```

13.4.2 Producer and Consumer Threads

To investigate the properties of the bounded buffer implementation, we model systems consisting of one or more producer threads and one or more consumer threads. The producer threads call `put()` and the consumer threads call `get` () as shown below.

```
PRODUCER = PUT;PRODUCER.
CONSUMER = GET;CONSUMER.
```

We noted in section 13.2.1 that we must explicitly define the set of threads that will access the monitor being modeled. For the bounded buffer example, we have a set of producer threads, which put items into the buffer, and a set of consumer threads, which take items out of the buffer, identified as follows:

```
const Nprod = 2                  // #producers
const Ncons = 2                  // #consumers
set   Prod  = {prod[1..Nprod]}   // producer threads
set   Cons  = {cons[1..Ncons]}   // consumer threads

const Nthread  = Nprod + Ncons
set   Threads  = {Prod,Cons}
```

The producer and consumer processes are composed with the processes modeling the buffer monitor by:

```
||ProdCons = (Prod:PRODUCER || Cons:CONSUMER
             || BUFFERMON).
```

13.4.3 Analysis

To verify our implementation model of the bounded buffer, we need to show that it satisfies the same safety and progress properties as the design model. However, the bounded buffer design model was specified in Chapter 5, which preceded the discussion of how to specify properties. Consequently, we simply inspected the *LTS* graph for the model to see that it had the required synchronization behavior. The *LTS* of the implementation model is much too large to verify by inspection. How then do we proceed? The answer with respect to safety is to use the design model itself as a safety property and check that the implementation satisfies this property. In other words, we check that the implementation cannot produce any executions that are not specified by the design. Clearly, this is with respect to actions that are common to the implementation and design models – the `put` and `get` actions. The property below is the same `BUFFER` process shown in Figure 5.11, with the addition of a relabeling part that takes account of multiple producer and consumer processes.

```
property
      BUFFER = COUNT[0],
      COUNT[i:0..Size]
            = (when (i<Size) put->COUNT[i+1]
              |when (i>0)    get->COUNT[i-1]
              )/{Prod.put/put,Cons.get/get}.
```

The *LTS* for this property with two producer processes, two consumer processes and a buffer with two slots (`Size = 2`) is shown in Figure 13.7.

We are now in a position to perform a safety analysis of the bounded buffer implementation model using the composition:

```
||ProdConsSafety = (ProdCons || BUFFER).
```

With two producer processes (`Nprod=2`), two consumer processes (`Ncons=2`) and a buffer with two slots (`Size=2`), safety analysis by the *LTSA* reveals no property violations or deadlocks. In this situation, the implementation satisfies the design. However, safety analysis with two producer processes (`Nprod=2`), two consumer processes (`Ncons=2`) and a buffer with only one slot (`Size=1`) reveals the following deadlock:

```
Trace to DEADLOCK:
  cons.1.acquire
  cons.1.count.read.0
```

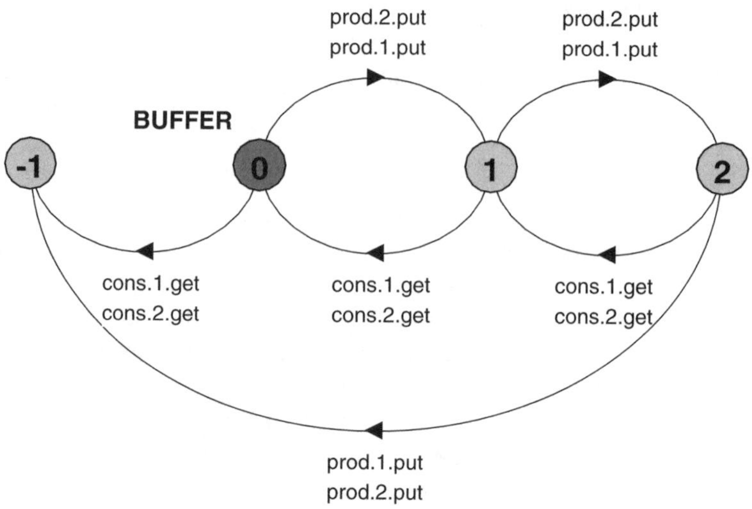

Figure 13.7 *LTS* for `property BUFFER`.

```
cons.1.wait               // consumer 1 blocked
cons.1.release
cons.2.acquire
cons.2.count.read.0
cons.2.wait               // consumer 2 blocked
cons.2.release
prod.1.acquire
prod.1.count.read.0
prod.1.put                // producer 1 inserts item
prod.1.count.inc
prod.1.notify             // producer 1 notifies item available
prod.1.release
prod.1.acquire
prod.1.count.read.1
cons.1.unblock            // consumer 1 unblocked by notify
prod.1.wait               // producer 1 blocks trying to insert 2nd item
prod.1.release
prod.2.acquire
prod.2.count.read.1
prod.2.wait               // producer 2 blocks trying to insert  item
prod.2.release
cons.1.endwait
cons.1.acquire
cons.1.count.read.1
```

```
cons.1.get              // consumer 1 gets item
cons.1.count.dec
cons.1.notify           // consumer 1 notifies space available
cons.1.release
cons.1.acquire
cons.1.count.read.0
cons.2.unblock          // consumer 2 unblocked by notify
cons.1.wait
cons.1.release
cons.2.endwait
cons.2.acquire
cons.2.count.read.0
cons.2.wait             // consumer 2 blocks since buffer is empty
cons.2.release
```

The deadlock occurs because at the point that the consumer process calls `notify` to indicate that a space is available in the buffer, the wait set includes the second consumer process as well as both the producer processes. The consumer is unblocked and finds that the buffer is empty and goes back to waiting. At this point no further progress can be made and the system deadlocks since neither of the producer processes can run. This deadlock occurs if either the number of producer processes or the number of consumer processes is greater than the number of slots in the buffer. Clearly in this situation, the implementation given in the first printing of Chapter 5 was incorrect!

To correct the bounded buffer program of Chapter 5, to handle the situation of a greater number of producer or consumer threads than buffer slots, we need to replace the calls to `notify()` with calls to `notifyAll()`. This unblocks both consumer and the producer threads, allowing an insertion or removal to occur. Replacing the corresponding actions in the implementation model removes the deadlock and verifies that the Java program is now correct.

The lesson here is that it is always safer to use `notifyAll()` unless it can be rigorously shown that `notify()` works correctly. We should have followed our own advice in Chapter 5! The general rule is that `notify()` should only be used if at most one thread can benefit from the change of state being signaled and it can be guaranteed that the notification will go to a thread that is waiting for that particular state change. An implementation model is a good way of doing this.

The corrected model satisfies the following progress properties, which assert lack of starvation for `put` and `get` actions:

```
progress PUT[i:1..Nprod] = {prod[i].put}
progress GET[i:1..Ncons] = {cons[i].get}
```

13.5 Readers-Writers Example

Program 13.2 reproduces the version of the Readers–Writers program from Chapter 7, Program 7.8 that gives Writers priority. This version is again taken from the first printing, first edition of this book.

```
class ReadWritePriority implements ReadWrite{
  private int readers =0;
  private boolean writing = false;
  private int waitingW = 0; // no of waiting Writers.

  public synchronized void acquireRead()
             throws InterruptedException {
    while (writing || waitingW>0) wait();
     ++readers;
  }

  public synchronized void releaseRead() {
    --readers;
    if (readers==0) notify();
  }

  public synchronized void acquireWrite()
             throws InterruptedException {
    ++waitingW;
    while (readers>0 || writing) wait();
    --waitingW;
    writing = true;
  }

  public synchronized void releaseWrite() {
    writing = false;
    notifyAll();
  }
}
```

Program 13.2 Class `ReadWritePriority`.

To verify this program, we proceed as before and translate the Java into *FSP* using the model construction developed in sections 13.2 and 13.3. The first step is to model the state of the monitor. This consists of the wait set, the monitor lock and the variables specific to the `ReadWritePriority` class. The class has three variables – `readers`, `writing` and `waitingW` – which all play a part in synchronization. Consequently, in this example, we model the state of the monitor by:

```
||RWPRIORMON = ( Threads::LOCK || WAITSET || SAFEMON
               ||Threads::( readers:VAR
                          ||writing:BOOLVAR
                          ||waitingW:VAR
                          )
               ).
```

The set `Threads` is defined by:

```
const Nread  = 2                     // #readers
const Nwrite = 2                     // #writers
set   Read   = {reader[1..Nread]}    // reader threads
set   Write  = {writer[1..Nwrite]}   // writer threads

const Nthread =  Nread + Nwrite
set   Threads = {Read,Write}
```

The alphabet that must be added to each monitor method is:

```
set ReadWriteAlpha =
 {{readers,waitingW}.VarAlpha, writing.BoolAlpha,
   LockOps, SyncOps,
   acquireRead,acquireWrite,releaseRead,releaseWrite
 }
```

13.5.1 ReadWritePriority Methods

The next step in verifying an implementation is to derive an *FSP* sequential process for each monitor method. These processes for `acquireRead()`, `releaseRead()`, `acquireWrite()` and `releaseWrite()` are listed below.

```
/*
* acquireRead() method
*/
ACQUIREREAD
  = (acquire -> WHILE),
WHILE                       // while (writing —— waitingW>0) wait();
  = (writing.read[v:Bool] -> waitingW.read[u:Int] ->
```

```
      if (v || u>0) then WAIT;WHILE else CONTINUE
     ),
CONTINUE
  = (acquireRead
      -> readers.inc              // ++readers;
      -> release -> END
      ) + ReadWriteAlpha.

/*
* releaseRead() method
*/
RELEASEREAD
  = (acquire -> releaseRead
     -> readers.dec               // --readers;
     -> readers.read[v:Int] ->    // if (readers==0) notify();
        if (v==0) then (notify -> CONTINUE) else CONTINUE
      ),
CONTINUE
  = (release -> END) + ReadWriteAlpha.

/*
* acquireWrite() method
*/
ACQUIREWRITE                   // ++waitingW;
  = (acquire -> waitingW.inc -> WHILE),
WHILE                          // while (readers>0 —— writing) wait();
  = (writing.read[b:Bool] -> readers.read[v:Int]->
      if (v>0 || b) then WAIT;WHILE else CONTINUE
     ),
CONTINUE
  = (acquireWrite
      -> waitingW.dec          // --waitingW;
      -> writing.write[True]   // writing = true;
      -> release -> END
     )+ ReadWriteAlpha.

/*
* releaseWrite() method
*/
RELEASEWRITE
   = (acquire -> releaseWrite
      -> writing.write[False]  // writing = false;
      -> notifyAll             // notifyAll();
      -> release-> END
      ) + ReadWriteAlpha.
```

We have included the actions `acquireRead`, `acquireWrite`, `releaseRead` and `releaseWrite` in the model, which correspond to the actions in the design model of Chapter 7.

READER and WRITER Processes

Models for READER and WRITER processes are listed below. In this case, we have included actions to represent the calling of the monitor method in addition to modeling the execution of the method. We will see in the next section that these actions are needed to define the required progress property analysis conditions.

```
READER  = (acquireRead.call -> ACQUIREREAD;READING),
READING = (releaseRead.call -> RELEASEREAD;READER).

WRITER  = (acquireWrite.call -> ACQUIREWRITE;WRITING),
WRITING = (releaseWrite.call -> RELEASEWRITE;WRITER).
```

13.5.2 Analysis

To verify that the implementation model satisfies the desired safety properties, we use the safety property RW_SAFE originally specified in section 7.5.1 to check the correct behavior of the design model.

```
property SAFE_RW
  = (acquireRead -> READING[1]
    |acquireWrite->WRITING
    ),
READING[i:1..Nread]
  = (acquireRead -> READING[i+1]
    |when(i>1)  releaseRead -> READING[i-1]
    |when(i==1) releaseRead -> SAFE_RW
    ),
WRITING  = (releaseWrite -> SAFE_RW).
```

The system we perform safety analysis on consists of the reader and writer threads, the monitor state and the safety property as shown below:

```
||RWSYS = (Read:READER || Write:WRITER
          || RWPRIORMON
          || Threads::SAFE_RW
          ).
```

Safety analysis detects the following deadlock:

```
Trace to DEADLOCK:
      reader.1.acquireRead.call
      reader.1.acquire
      reader.1.writing.read.0
      reader.1.waitingW.read.0
      reader.1.acquireRead
      reader.1.readers.inc
      reader.1.release          // reader 1 acquires RW lock
      reader.1.releaseRead.call
      reader.2.acquireRead.call
      writer.1.acquireWrite.call
      writer.1.acquire
      writer.1.waitingW.inc
      writer.1.writing.read.0
      writer.1.readers.read.1
      writer.1.wait  // writer 1 blocked as reader has RW lock
      writer.1.release
      reader.2.acquire
      reader.2.writing.read.0
      reader.2.waitingW.read.1
      reader.2.wait  // reader 2 blocked as writer 1 waiting
      reader.2.release
      writer.2.acquireWrite.call
      writer.2.acquire
      writer.2.waitingW.inc
      writer.2.writing.read.0
      writer.2.readers.read.1
      writer.2.wait     // writer 2 blocked as reader has RW lock
      writer.2.release
      reader.1.acquire
      reader.1.releaseRead
      reader.1.readers.dec
      reader.1.readers.read.0
      reader.1.notify   // reader 1 releases RW lock & notifies
      writer.2.release
      reader.1.release
      reader.1.acquireRead.call
      reader.1.acquire
      reader.1.writing.read.0
      reader.1.waitingW.read.2
      reader.2.unblock  // reader 2 unblocked by notify
      reader.1.wait
```

```
reader.1.release
reader.2.endwait
reader.2.acquire
reader.2.writing.read.0
reader.2.waitingW.read.2
reader.2.wait        // reader 2 blocks as writers waiting
reader.2.release
```

The deadlock happens because the `notify` operation performed by Reader 1 when it releases the read–write lock unblocks another Reader rather than a Writer. This unblocked Reader subsequently blocks again since there are Writers waiting. The solution is again to use a `notifyAll` to awake all waiting threads and thus permit a Writer to run. Changing the `notify` action to `notifyAll` in the `RELEASEREAD` part of the model and rerunning the safety analysis confirms that the deadlock does not occur and that the implementation model satisfies the safety property.

Why did we not observe this deadlock in the actual implementation of `ReadWritePriority` when running the demonstration applet? The reason is quite subtle. In most Java Virtual Machines, the set of threads waiting on notification is implemented as a first-in-first-out (FIFO) queue. With this queuing discipline, the deadlock cannot occur as for the second Reader to block, a Writer must have previously blocked. This Writer will be unblocked by the notification when the first Reader releases the read–write lock and, consequently, the deadlock does not occur. However, although the implementation works for some JVMs, it is not guaranteed to work on all JVMs since, as noted earlier, the Java Language Specification specifies only that blocked threads are held in a set. Our implementation would exhibit the deadlock on a JVM that used a stack for the wait set. Consequently, the implementation is clearly erroneous and the `notify()` in the `releaseRead()` method should be replaced with `notifyAll()`. Again the lesson is that `notify()` should only be used with extreme care! However, it should be noted that the use of `notify()` in the `ReadWriteSafe` version of the read–write lock is correct since it is not possible in that implementation to have both Readers and Writers waiting simultaneously.

Progress Analysis

Having demonstrated that the implementation model satisfies the required safety properties, it now remains to show that it exhibits the same progress properties as the design model. These properties assert lack of starvation for `acquireRead` and `acquireWrite` actions.

```
progress WRITE[i:1..Nwrite] = writer[i].acquireWrite
progress READ [i:1..Nwrite] = reader[i].acquireRead
```

The adverse scheduling conditions needed to check progress in the presence of competition for the read–write lock are arranged by making the actions, representing calls to release read and write access to the lock, low priority:

```
||RWPROGTEST  = RWSYS >> {Read.releaseRead.call,
                          Write.releaseWrite.call}.
```

Progress analysis reveals that the `RWPROGTEST` system satisfies the `WRITE` progress properties but violates the `READ` progress properties. In other words, the Writers priority implementation of the read–write lock satisfies its design goal of avoiding Writer starvation, but, as with the design model, it permits Reader starvation.

Summary

This chapter has presented a way of verifying that Java implementations satisfy the same safety and progress properties as the design models from which they were developed. The approach is to translate the Java program into a detailed *FSP* model that captures all aspects of the Java synchronization mechanisms – in particular, monitor locks and notification. This *implementation* model is then analyzed with respect to the same safety and progress properties used in analyzing the design model. We also showed in the bounded buffer example that the design model itself can be used as a safety property when verifying the implementation model.

Implementation models are considerably more detailed than design models and as such generate much larger state spaces during analysis. It is in general only possible to analyze small parts of an implementation. This is why in the book we have advocated a model-based design approach in which properties are investigated with respect to a design model and then this model is used as a basis for program implementation. Clearly, as we have demonstrated in the examples contained in this chapter, errors can be introduced in going from design model to implementation. Interestingly, the two bugs discovered both arise from the use of `notify()` in place of `notifyAll()`. Perhaps the most important lesson from this supplement is that strict attention must be paid to the rule that `notify()` should only be used if at most one thread can benefit from the change of state being signaled and it can be guaranteed that the notification will go to a thread that is waiting for that particular state change in the monitor class itself or in any subclasses.

Finally, as illustrated in the implementation models, sequential composition can be seen to provide a convenient means for structuring complex sequences of actions from simpler fragments of sequential processes.

Notes and Further Reading

We are indebted to David Holmes for initially pointing out the problems with the bounded buffer and read–write lock that we have exposed in this chapter. He also motivated this chapter by suggesting that we should address the problem of verifying implementations. David is a Senior Research Scientist at the Cooperative Research Centre for Enterprise Distributed Systems Technology (DSTC Pty Ltd.), located in Brisbane, Australia.

We pointed out in this chapter that our model of notification ignores the effect of an interrupt exception. It is possible, for a thread waiting to be notified, to be interrupted before actually returning from the `wait()` call. As a result it returns via an `InterruptedException` not a normal return and essentially, the notification is lost even though other uninterrupted threads may be waiting. This means that programs that use `notify()` and allow `InterruptedException` to be thrown directly are not guaranteed to work correctly. Although we use this technique in the book, it does not result in inconsistencies since in all cases, the interrupt exception is used to terminate all active threads. However, it is another reason for using `notifyAll()` rather than `notify()`. This may sometimes result in a large number of unnecessary thread activations and consequently be inefficient. For example, in the semaphore program of section 5.2.2, a better way to deal with the lost notification problem is to catch the `InterruptedException` and perform an additional `notify()` before rethrowing the exception. Thanks again to David for pointing this out.

The earliest attempt to prove a program correct appears to be that of Turing who presented a paper, *Checking a large routine*, on 24 June 1949 at the inaugural conference of the EDSAC computer at the Mathematical Laboratory, Cambridge. He advocated the use of assertions "about the states that the machine can reach". The formal foundations for techniques for program correctness were laid in the 1960s with contributions by pioneers such as McCarthy, Naur, Floyd, Dijkstra and Hoare (Morris and Jones, 1984). Again, the essence of the approach is to associate logical assertions, pre- and post-conditions, with the statement blocks in a program. Invariants are used to characterize the properties preserved by loops, later extended to characterize objects and monitors (see Chapter 5). This work was initially targeted at proving the correctness of sequential programs, and involved both a proof of satisfaction of the program post-condition and a proof of termination. The correctness of concurrent programs is more complex, requiring that the techniques deal with nonterminating and nondeterministic programs. The foundations were again laid in the 1960s by the insights of researchers such as Dijkstra and Petri, but it was in 1977 that Lamport proposed that correctness of concurrent programs should be argued for two sorts of properties: safety and liveness.

Since those early pioneering days, much research work and experience have been gained. The 1996 state-of-the-art papers on concurrency (Cleaveland, Smolka, *et al.*) and formal methods (Clarke, Wing, *et al.*) provide an excellent overview. All these techniques have had major impact on the design of programming languages and programming methods. However, because of the effort involved, the impact on practice has been limited to a relatively small number of specific circumstances, such as safety-critical software, software which is difficult or impossible to update or software to be used in vast numbers of consumer products. The advance of techniques and technology in theorem proving and model checking over the last ten years has made program verification more accessible and practical.

The approach adopted by many current researchers is to try to extract a model directly from the code. Techniques used vary from code annotation, which provides the mapping between code and model, to various abstraction techniques which hide program detail irrelevant to the particular property or concern. Notable amongst these are the FeaVer Toolset for C programs (Holzmann and Smith, 2002), FLAVERS for Ada programs (Cobleigh, Clarke and Osterweil, 2002), the Java PathFinder tool (Havelund and Pressburger, 2000) and the Bandera toolset (Corbett, Dwyer, Hatcliff, *et al.*, 2000) for Java programs.

Other approaches are attempting to develop verification tools tailored to work directly on a program in a specific programming language. A second version of the Java PathFinder tool (Brat, Havelund, Park, *et al.*, 2000), Microsoft's SLAM project for C (Ball and Rajamani, 2002), and the Blast tool for C (Henzinger, Jhala, Majumdar, *et al.*, 2003) are examples of this work.

Exercises

13.1 Simplify the verification model developed in section 13.5 such that it is a model of the Java program `ReadWriteSafe` (Program 7.7). Show that this model does not violate the property `SAFE_RW` and that it violates the `WRITE` progress property.

13.2 Develop a verification model for the `Semaphore` class (Program 5.3) and use it in verifying that the `SEMADEMO` program of Chapter 5 preserves the mutual exclusion property (section 7.1.2):

```
property MUTEX = (p[i:1..3].enter->p[i].exit->MUTEX).
```

In addition, generate an error trace for the situation in which the semaphore is initialized to 2.

13.3 The following *FSP* specifies the safety property for barrier synchronization. Each process must execute its `before` action before all processes execute the common `sync` action.

```
Pspec = (before -> sync -> Pspec).
property
   ||SAFEBARRIER = (p[1..3]:Pspec)
                   /{sync/p[1..3].sync}\{sync}.
```

Verify that the monitor `Barrier` with a `sync` method that implements barrier synchronization (as required in the solution to Exercise 5.5) satisfies the above property.

13.4 Verify that the `SimpleAllocator` monitor of Program 9.1 satisfies the property `ALLOCATOR` in the system `CHECK`, both shown below:

```
property
  ALLOCATOR(M=3)  = BALL[M],
  BALL[b:0..M]    = (when (b>0) get[i:1..b] -> BALL[b-i]
                    |put[j:1..M]            -> BALL[b+j]
                    ).

PLAYER(I=1) = (get.call -> GET(I);PLAYING),
PLAYING     = (put.call -> PUT(I);PLAYER).


||CHECK = (player[1..3]:PLAYER(1)
          ||player[4..Nthread]:PLAYER(3)
          ||SimpleAllocator(N)
          ||player[1..N]::ALLOCATOR(N)
          ).
```

In addition, determine which of the following progress properties are satisfied by the system `CHECKLIVE` shown below:

```
progress EXPERT = {player[1..3].get[1..N]}
progress NOVICE = {player[4..N].get[1..N]}

||CHECKLIVE = CHECK >> {player[1..N].put.call}.
```

14
Logical Properties

In Chapter 7, we saw that a property is an attribute of a program that is true for every possible execution of that program. We used property processes to specify safety properties and progress properties to express a limited but very common form of liveness property. Here we introduce logical descriptions of properties that capture both safety and liveness.

What do we mean by a logical description? We mean an expression composed out of propositions by logical operators such as *and, or, not*. A proposition is a statement that is either true or false. It can of course be formed from more primitive propositions by the logical operators and so the overall logical description is itself a proposition. Java already uses this form of expression in the **assert** construct. For example, using this construct we can assert that after executing some statements it should be true that variable i has the value 0 and variable j has the value 1: `(assert i==0 && j==1)`.

The Java **assert** construct lets us specify a proposition concerning the state of selected variables that should be true at a particular point in the execution of a program. Of course, if this point is in a loop, it will be visited repeatedly. In our models, we wish to specify propositions that are true for every possible execution of a program without explicit reference to a particular point in the execution of that program. Furthermore, we wish to specify properties independently from models. A logic that permits us to do this is linear temporal logic. A proposition in this logic describes a set of infinite sequences for which the proposition is true. A program execution is essentially a sequence of states and so a program satisfies a linear temporal logic proposition if all its executions belong to the set described by the formula.

How can we refer to states when our *LTS* models are essentially based on actions or events? This chapter introduces fluents as a means of describing abstract states of our models. We show how logical properties for both safety and liveness can be specified in terms of fluents and analyzed using *LTSA*.

14.1 Fluent Propositions

The primitive propositions used to construct assertions in Java are concerned with the values of variables, for example, `i==0`. They are propositions concerning the state of a program as represented by the values of the program's variables. However, our models are focused on interaction and as such they describe sequences of actions and do not explicitly describe state. What should be the primitive propositions that we use in the logical description of properties? One possibility would be to make the occurrence of an action a proposition such that for an action *a*, the synonymous proposition *a* would be true when the action occurred and false at every other time. The problem here is that, as we saw in Chapter 3, we model concurrent execution as an interleaved sequence of actions which we call a trace. Consequently it would always be the case that only one action proposition could be true at any one instant. This makes it difficult to describe quite simple properties. As a result, we have taken an approach which allows us to map an action trace into a sequence of abstract states described by *fluents*.

14.1.1 Fluents

> **fluent** FL = <{s_1,...s_n},{e_1..e_n}> **initially** *B* defines a fluent FL that is initially true if the expression *B* is true and initially false if the expression *B* is false. FL becomes true when any of the initiating actions {s_1,...s_n} occur and false when any of the terminating actions {e_1..e_n} occur. If the term **initially** *B* is omitted then FL is initially false. The same action may not be used as both an initiating and terminating action.

In other words, a fluent holds at a time instant if and only if it holds initially or some initiating action has occurred, and, in both cases, no terminating action has yet occurred. The following fragment defines a fluent `LIGHT` which becomes true when the action `on` occurs and false when the action `off` or `power_cut` occurs.

```
const False = 0
const True  = 1
fluent LIGHT = <{on}, {off, power_cut}> initially False
```

We can think of the above fluent as capturing the state of a light such that when the light is on, the fluent `LIGHT` is true and when the light is off, the fluent `LIGHT` is false. We can define indexed families of fluents in the same way that we define indexed families of processes:

```
fluent LIGHT[i:1..2] = <{on[i]}, {off[i], power_cut}>
```

This is equivalent to defining two fluents:

```
fluent LIGHT_1 = <{on[1]}, {off[1], power_cut}>
fluent LIGHT_2 = <{on[2]}, {off[2], power_cut}>
```

Action Fluents

Fluents are defined by a set of initiating actions and a set of terminating actions. Consequently, given the alphabet α of a system, we can define a fluent for each action a in that alphabet such that the initiating set of actions for the fluent a is $\{a\}$ and the terminating set of actions is $\alpha \cup \{\tau\} - \{a\}$. In other words, the fluent for an action becomes true immediately that action occurs and false immediately the next action occurs. The next action may be the silent action τ. We can also use a set of actions in a fluent expression. The logical value of this is the disjunction (*or*) of each of the actions in the set. We can freely mix action fluents and explicitly defined fluents in fluent expressions. An example is given in the next section.

14.1.2 Fluent Expressions

We can combine fluents with the normal logical operators. If we wished to characterize the state in which two lights are on, this would be the expression `LIGHT[1] && LIGHT[2]`. The state in which either light is on would be `LIGHT[1] || LIGHT[2]`. This latter would also be true if both lights were on. Fluent expressions can be formed using the following logical operators:

&&	conjunction (*and*)
||	disjunction (*or*)
!	negation (*not*)
->	implication ((A->B) ≡ (!A || B))
<->	equivalence ((A<->B) ≡ (A->B)&&(B->A))

For example, given the fluents:

```
fluent POWER  = <power_on, power_off>
fluent LIGHT  = <on, off>
```

the expression `LIGHT->POWER` states our expectation that, for the light to be on, the power must also be on. We do not expect that if the power is on the light need necessarily be on as well.

If we wish to express the proposition that all lights are on, we can use the expression:

```
forall[i:1..2] LIGHT[i]
```

This is exactly the same as `LIGHT[1] && LIGHT[2]`. In a similar way, if we wish to express the proposition that at least one light is on, we can state:

```
exists[i:1..2] LIGHT[i]
```

This is exactly the same as `LIGHT[1] || LIGHT[2]`.

An expression that combines an action fluent and an explicitly defined fluent is `(getkey && LIGHT[1])` which is true when the `getkey` action occurs when the `LIGHT` fluent is true – i.e., the light has previously been turned on.

14.2 Temporal Propositions

Fluents let us express properties about the abstract state of a system at a particular point in time. This state depends on the trace of actions that have occurred up to that point in time. To express propositions with respect to an execution of a model, we need to introduce some temporal operators.

14.2.1 Safety Properties

To illustrate the expression of safety properties using fluents, we return to the mutual exclusion example of section 7.1.2.

```
const N = 2

LOOP = (mutex.down -> enter -> exit -> mutex.up -> LOOP).

||SEMADEMO = (p[1..N]:LOOP
           || {p[1..N]}::mutex:SEMAPHORE(1)).
```

The abstract states of interest here are when each LOOP process enters its critical section. We express these states with fluents:

```
fluent CRITICAL[i:1..N] = <p[i].enter, p[i].exit>
```

We can express the situation in which two processes are in their critical sections at the same time as CRITICAL[1] && CRITICAL[2]. This situation must be avoided at all costs since it violates mutual exclusion. How do we assert that this situation does not occur at any point in the execution of the SEMADEMO system?

> The linear temporal logic formula **[]**F – *always F* – is true if and only if the formula F is true at the current instant and at all instants in the future.

Given this operator, we can now express the property that at all times in any execution of the system, CRITICAL[1] && CRITICAL[2] must not occur. This is:

```
assert MUTEX = []!(CRITICAL[1] && CRITICAL[2])
```

This property is checked by compiling it into a safety property process. As described in Chapter 7, the check is then performed by composing this property with the system and performing an exhaustive search for the ERROR state. The property process compiled from MUTEX above is depicted in Figure 14.1.

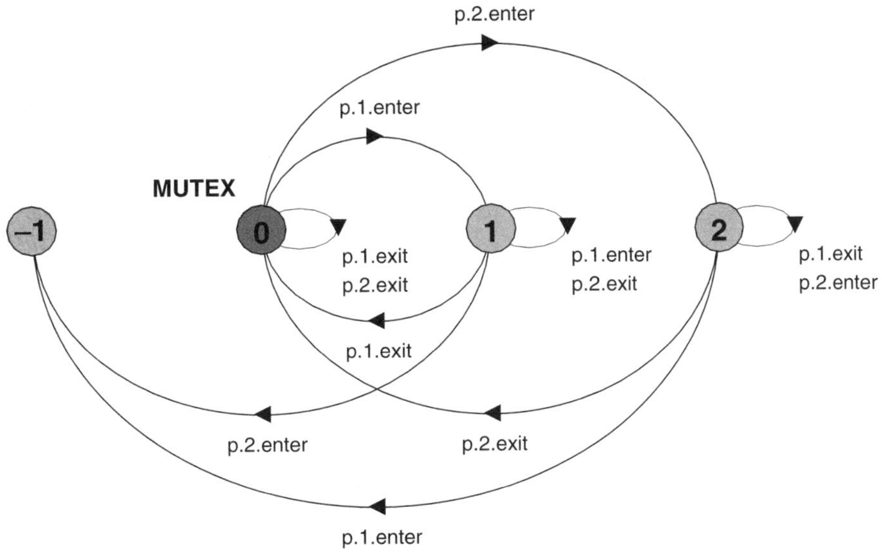

Figure 14.1 MUTEX property process.

The MUTEX property is not violated with the semaphore initialized to one; however if we initialize the semaphore to two (i.e. SEMAPHORE(2)) then a check of the MUTEX property against the SEMADEMO system produces the following trace:

```
Trace to property violation in MUTEX:
      p.1.mutex.down
      p.1.enter              CRITICAL.1
      p.2.mutex.down         CRITICAL.1
      p.2.enter              CRITICAL.1 && CRITICAL.2
```

The *LTSA* annotates the trace with the names of the fluents that are true when the action on the left occurs. So, when the action p.2.enter occurs, both of the CRITICAL fluents are true, violating mutual exclusion. The general expression of the mutual exclusion property for *N* processes is:

```
assert MUTEX_N = []!(exists [i:1..N-1]
                  (CRITICAL[i] && CRITICAL[i+1..N]))
```

This asserts that it is always the case that no pair of processes exist with CRITICAL true. CRITICAL[i+1..N] is a short form for the disjunction **exists** [j:i+1..N] CRITICAL[j].

Single-Lane Bridge Safety Property

The single-lane bridge problem was described in section 7.2. The required safety property was that it should never be the case that a red car (moving from left to right) should be on the bridge at the same time as a blue car (moving from right to left). The following fluents capture the states of red cars and blue cars being on the bridge.

```
const N = 3     // number of each type of car
range ID= 1..N // car identities

fluent RED[i:ID]  = <red[i].enter, red[i].exit>
fluent BLUE[i:ID] = <blue[i].enter, blue[i].exit>
```

The situation in which one or more red cars are on the bridge is described by the fluent expression **exists**[i:ID] RED[i] and similarly for blue cars **exists**[j:ID] BLUE[j]. The required ONEWAY property asserts that these two propositions should never hold at the same time.

```
assert ONEWAY = []!(exists[i:ID] RED[i]
                 && exists[j:ID] BLUE[j])
```

When checked in the context described in section 7.2.1 with no BRIDGE process to constrain car behavior, the following safety violation is produced:

```
Trace to property violation in ONEWAY:
        red.1.enter          RED.1
        blue.1.enter         RED.1 && BLUE.1
```

Since propositions of the form **exists**[i:R] FL[i] can be expressed succinctly as FL[R], we can rewrite ONEWAY above as:

```
assert ONEWAY = []!(RED[ID] && BLUE[ID])
```

This is a considerably more concise description of the required property than that achieved using property processes in section 7.2.1. In addition, it expresses the required property more directly. This is usually the case where a safety property can be expressed as a relationship between abstract states of the system described as fluents. Unsurprisingly where the required property is concerned with the permitted order of actions, direct specification using property processes is usually best.

Finally, safety properties of the form []*P* as we have described here are by far the commonest form of safety properties expressed in temporal logic; however, there are many other forms of safety properties which use additional temporal operators. These operators are described later.

14.2.2 Liveness Properties

A safety property asserts that nothing bad ever happens whereas a liveness property asserts that something good eventually happens. Linear temporal logic provides the *eventually* operator which allows us to directly express the progress properties we introduced in Chapter 7.

> The linear temporal logic formula **<>** ***F*** – *eventually* ***F*** – is true if and only if the formula ***F*** is true at the current instant or at some instant in the future.

We can now assert for the single-lane bridge example that eventually the first red car must enter the bridge:

```
assert FIRSTRED = <>red[1].enter
```

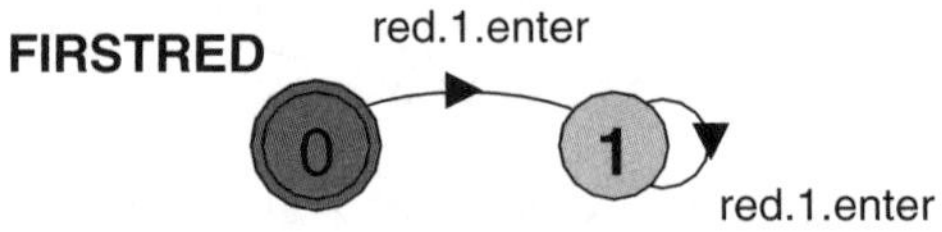

Figure 14.2 Büchi automaton for `FIRSTRED`.

This is compiled into the transition system shown in Figure 14.2. This is a special form of transition system known as a Büchi automaton after its originator. A Büchi automaton recognizes an infinite trace if that trace passes through an acceptance state infinitely often. The example of Figure 14.2 has a single acceptance state marked by two concentric rings. It should be clear that any trace containing the action `red[1].enter` is not accepted by this automaton since the action will move the automaton irretrievably out of the initial acceptance state.

In fact, the Büchi automaton of Figure 14.2 accepts the set of infinite traces represented by the negation of the `FIRSTRED` property – that is, `!<>red[1].enter`. To check whether an assertion holds, the *LTSA* constructs a Büchi automaton for the negation of the assertion and then checks whether there are any infinite traces that are accepted when the automaton is combined with the model. This check can be performed efficiently since it is a search for acceptance states in strongly connected components. If none are found then there is no trace that satisfies the negation of the property and consequently the property holds. We discussed strongly connected components and their relationship to infinite executions in Chapter 7. In checking liveness properties, we make exactly the same fair choice assumption as was made in Chapter 7. The property is satisfied for the basic bridge model but not for the congested model defined by:

```
||CongestedBridge
      = SingleLaneBridge >> {red[ID].exit,blue[ID].exit}.
```

The following property violation is reported for a system with two red cars and two blue cars:

```
Violation of LTL property: @FIRSTRED
Trace to terminal set of states:
      blue.1.enter
Cycle in terminal set:
      blue.2.enter
      blue.1.exit
      blue.1.enter
      blue.2.exit
LTL Property Check in: 10ms
```

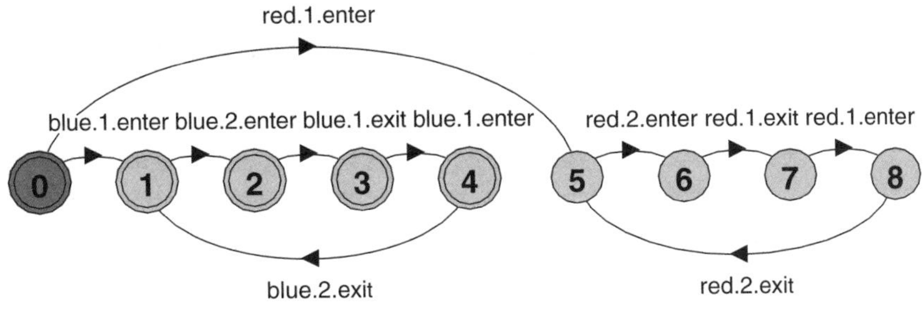

Figure 14.3 `CongestedBridge` showing acceptance states.

The model, combined with the `FIRSTRED` property, is shown in Figure 14.3. The connected component (states 1,2,3,4) containing acceptance states can clearly be seen.

The property `FIRSTRED` is satisfied if the first red car enters the bridge a single time. However, the required liveness property in Chapter 7 is that red cars (and blue cars) get to enter the bridge infinitely often. In other words, it is always the case that a car eventually enters. This is exactly the condition expressed by progress properties. We can now restate those for the single lane bridge in linear temporal logic as:

```
assert REDCROSS  = []<>red[ID].enter
assert BLUECROSS = []<>blue[ID].enter
assert CROSS = (REDCROSS && BLUECROSS)
```

The `CROSS` property is defined as the conjunction of `REDCROSS` and `BLUECROSS` and permits these properties to be checked at the same time. The Büchi automaton for the negation of `REDCROSS` is depicted in Figure 14.4.

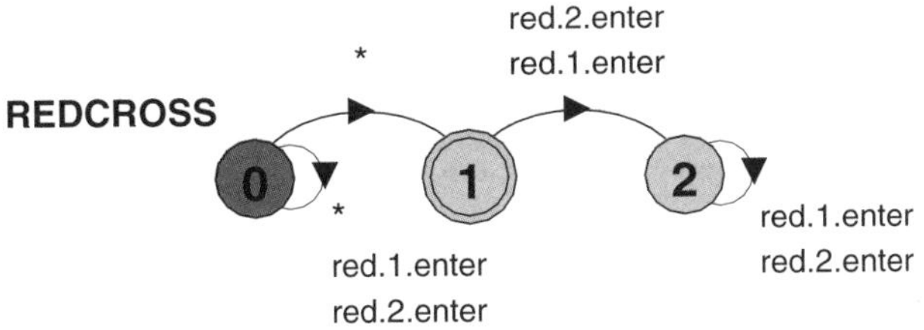

Figure 14.4 REDCROSS Büchi automaton.

In a parallel composition, * synchronizes the transition it labels with all other transitions in the model, i.e. excluding actions `red[1].enter` and `red[2].enter`, but including those labeled by the silent action. It can be seen that the always part of the assertion is captured here by the non-deterministic choice on * which means that at any point in a trace, the automaton can move to state 1.

It could be argued that REDCROSS and BLUECROSS are too weak a specification of the required liveness since they are satisfied if either car 1 or car 2 crosses infinitely often. For example, the properties can be satisfied if car 2 never crosses. This is because, as mentioned previously, a set of actions is treated as a disjunction and so the property REDCROSS is:

```
assert REDCROSS  = []<>(red[1].enter || red[2].enter)
```

A stronger assertion would be:

```
assert STRONGRED =  forall[i:ID] []<>red[i].enter
```

Response Properties

Suppose we wished to assert the liveness property that if a car enters the bridge then it should eventually exit. In other words, it does not stop in the middle or fall over the side! We can specify this property for a car as follows:

```
assert REDEXIT = [](red[1].enter -> <>red[1].exit)
```

The corresponding Büchi automaton (for the negation) is shown in Figure 14.5.

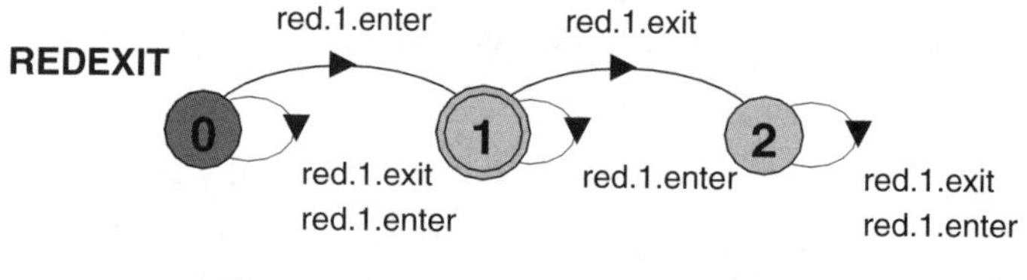

Figure 14.5 REDEXIT Büchi automaton.

The property holds for both SingleLaneBridge and CongestedBridge. Although cars may not ever enter the congested bridge, if they do enter, they also exit. Consequently, the property is not violated. This is an extremely common form of liveness property which is sometimes termed a "response" property since it is of the form [](request -> <>reply). Note that this form of liveness property cannot be specified using the progress properties of Chapter 7.

14.3 Fluent Linear Temporal Logic (FLTL)

In the previous section, we saw the use of the always **[]** operator to express safety properties and the use of the eventually operator **<>** to express liveness properties. These represent by far the most common use of linear temporal logic in expressing properties. In the following, we complete the description of our fluent linear temporal logic (FLTL) by describing the remaining operators – until **U**, weak until **W** and next time **X**.

14.3.1 Until

> The linear temporal logic formula ***p* U *q*** is true if and only if ***q*** is true at the current instant or if ***q*** is true at some instant in the future and ***p*** is true until that instant.

For example, suppose we wish to assert the politeness property of Chapter 7 that we should not enter a room before knocking. We can assert:

```
assert POLITE = (!enter U knock)
```

This asserts both the safety property that we cannot have an `enter` action before a `knock` action, and also that a `knock` action should eventually happen. This can be seen clearly from the Büchi automaton for this property depicted in Figure 14.6. The automaton irretrievably enters the acceptance state 1 if an `enter` action occurs before a `knock` action occurs. However, if a `knock` action never occurs, the property is violated because the automaton remains in state 0 which is also an acceptance state.

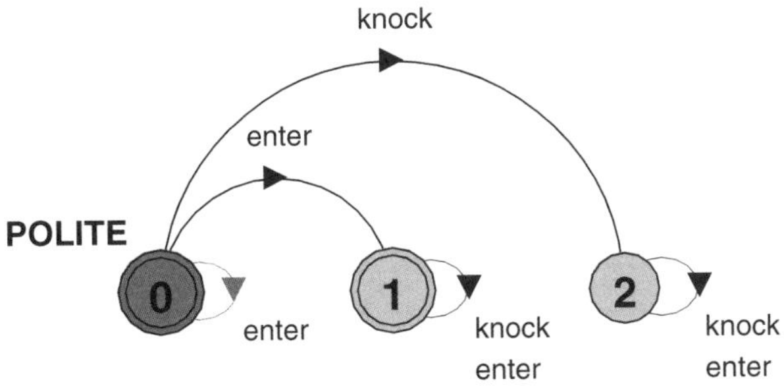

Figure 14.6 `POLITE` Büchi automaton.

Given the until operator, we can state the mutual exclusion property of section 14.2.1 using only action fluents:

```
assert MUTEX_U = []((p[1].enter -> (!p[2].enter U p[1].exit))
                 &&(p[2].enter -> (!p[1].enter U p[2].exit)))
```

This expresses the required mutual exclusion safety property and, in addition, the liveness property that if a process enters the critical section it should eventually exit. However, the property is considerably more complex than that of section 14.2.1 and is difficult to extend to more than two processes.

14.3.2 Weak Until

> The linear temporal logic formula ***p* W *q*** is true if and only if either ***p*** is true indefinitely or if ***p* U *q***.

The difference with the previous definition of until is that this definition does not insist that q eventually happens. The formula also holds if p is true indefinitely. This means that if we use weak until for the `POLITE` property:

```
assert POLITE_W = (!enter W knock)
```

the property becomes a safety property since it no longer requires that `knock` eventually happens. The safety property is depicted in Figure 14.7.

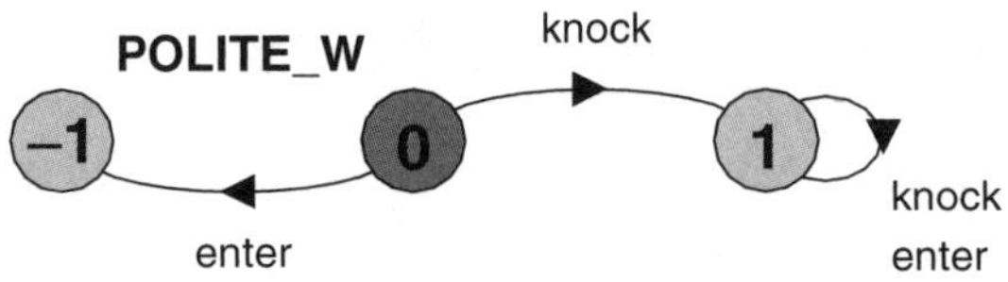

Figure 14.7 `POLITE_W` safety property process.

In the same way, if we replace *until* with *weak until* in the definition of the mutex property, it becomes a safety property which generates exactly the same automaton as that depicted in Figure 14.1.

```
assert MUTEX_W = []((p[1].enter -> (!p[2].enter W p[1].exit))
                 &&(p[2].enter -> (!p[1].enter W p[2].exit)))
```

In general, there is no need to distinguish between safety and liveness properties when using FLTL to specify properties. Since the safety check is more efficient than the connected component search used in checking general FLTL properties, the *LTSA* generates a safety property process if it detects that a property is only a safety property. In fact, determining whether a Büchi automaton can be transformed to a safety property process is non-trivial and the *LTSA* does not guarantee to perform this transformation for all automata that could be reduced.

It should be noted that we could have specified the liveness property that was included in MUTEX_U in the original MUTEX_N property as follows:

```
assert EXIT_N = forall[i:1..N][](p[i].enter -> <>p[i].exit)
assert MUTEX_LIVE = (MUTEX_N && EXIT_N)
```

MUTEX_LIVE expresses the same property for N processes that MUTEX_U does for two. In fact we can parameterize assertions as follows:

```
assert MUTEXP(M=2)
    = []!(exists [i:1..M-1] (CRITICAL[i] && CRITICAL[i+1..M]))
assert EXITP(M=2)
    =  forall[i:1..M] [](p[i].enter -> <>p[i].exit)
assert MUTEX_LIVEP(P=2)
    = (MUTEXP(P) && EXITP(P))
```

Definitions

We can define the temporal operators always **[]**, eventually **<>** and weak until **W** in terms of the until **U** operator as follows:

```
<> p ≡ True U p
[] p ≡ ! <> ! p
p W q≡ []p || (p U q)
```

In fact, FLTL does not have the explicit constants True and False; instead it permits boolean expressions of constants and parameters. These expressions are termed "rigid", since, unlike fluent propositions, they do not change truth value with the passage of time as measured by the occurrence of events. Thus we can define:

```
assert True  = rigid(1)
assert False = rigid(0)
```

Rigid expressions can be used in conjunction with parameters and ranges and are essentially used to introduce boolean expressions into FLTL formulae, e.g.

```
assert Even(V=3) = rigid(V/2 == 0)
```

14.3.3 Next Time

> The linear temporal logic formula **X *p*** is true if and only if ***p*** is true at the next instant.

By "next instant" in the above definition, we mean when the next action occurs – this includes silent actions. For example, the assertion:

```
assert SEQ = (a && X b && X X c)
```

requires that in the initial instant of system execution the action **a** occurs followed by the action **b**, followed by the action **c**. To check for this sequence, the property process shown in Figure 14.8 is generated:

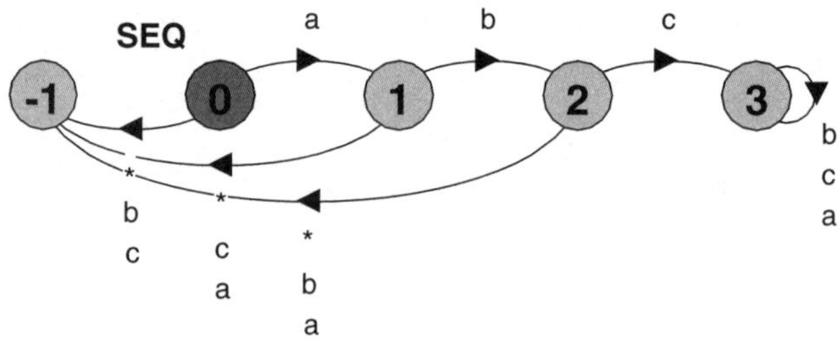

Figure 14.8 SEQ property process.

In fact, this form of property is not very useful. If we were to refine or extend our system (using, say, parallel composition and interleaving) such that actions could occur inbetween **a**, **b** or **c** then the property would no longer hold. This is because next time refers to precisely the time at which the next action occurs, whether silent or not. Consequently, it makes finer distinctions than the observational equivalence that is preserved when we minimize processes. As such, it is rarely used in property specification. In addition, it can prohibit the use of partial order reduction, a technique that can dramatically reduce the time taken to check an FLTL property.

14.4 Database Ring Problem

To illustrate the use of logical properties, let us consider a replicated and distributed database where the database nodes are organized in a ring as depicted

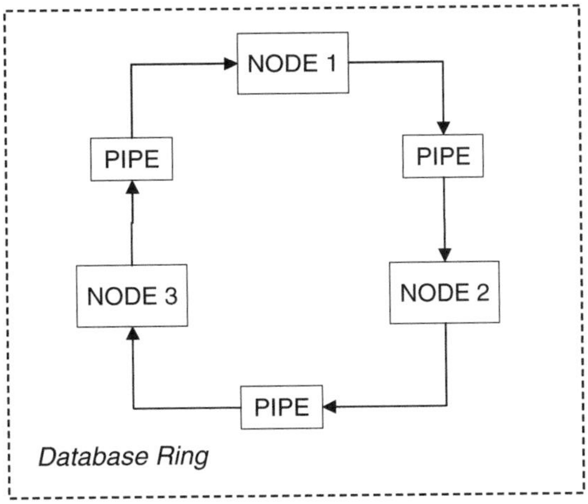

Figure 14.9 Database ring architecture.

in Figure 14.9. Communication is uni-directional, occurring clockwise around the ring such that node 1 can send updates to node 2 and receive them from node 3, via communication pipes. Each node of the database can autonomously update its local copy of the data. Updates are circulated round the ring to update other copies. On completion of a cycle, the originator of an update removes it from the ring. When no updates are in progress the copies should be consistent – i.e., all nodes should hold exactly the same data.

Two nodes may perform local updates at the same time and propagate their updates around the ring. This would lead to the situation where nodes receive updates in different orders, leading to inconsistent copies even after all the updates have propagated round the ring. Although we can tolerate copy inconsistency while updates are circulating, we cannot accept inconsistency that persists.

To avoid inconsistency, an update is given a priority depending on its originating node, node i having priority over node j if i<j. Thus an update from node 1 has a higher priority than an update from node 3. In the case of a conflict due to two simultaneous updates, the update from the lower priority node is discarded. A conflict occurs when a node receives an update while still having an outstanding update, which it originated, circulating around the ring.

14.4.1 Database Ring Model

We can simplify the problem by considering that each database stores only a single data item and by restricting the range of data values that can be stored.

```
const N     = 3              // number of nodes
range Nodes = 1..N
set   Value = {red, green, blue}
```

We model the communication between database nodes using the `PIPE` from section 11.1.1 that models a one-slot buffer:

```
set S = {[Nodes][Value]}
PIPE  = (put[x:S] -> get[x] -> PIPE).
```

The updates that circulate round the ring are pairs consisting of the identity of the originating node and the value of the update. For example, `[1]['red]` is an update from node 1 with the value `red`. The model for each node is as follows:

```
NODE(I=0)
  = NODE['null][False],       // initially null value and not updating
NODE[v:{null,Value}][update:Bool]
  = (when (!update) local[u:Value]        // local update
    -> if (u!=v) then
            (change[u] -> put[I][u] -> NODE[u][True])
        else
            NODE[v][False]
    |get[j:Nodes][u:Value]                 // update [j][u]
    -> if (!update) then
            CHANGE(j,u);NODE[u][False]      // update and pass on
        else if  (I==j ) then
            (passive -> NODE[v][False])     // complete update
        else if (I>j) then
            CHANGE(j,u);NODE[u][False]      // priority update
        else
            NODE[v][update]                 // discard
    ).

CHANGE(J=0,U='null)
  = (change[U] -> put[J][U] -> passive ->END).
```

Whenever a node changes the value of its stored data value, it signals this with the action `change[u]` and whenever an update is complete the node signals `passive`. The constants `True` and `False` are defined in the usual way:

```
const False = 0
const True  = 1
range Bool  = False..True
```

The composite process for the database ring model is:

```
||DATABASE_RING
   = (node[i:Nodes]:NODE(i) || pipe[Nodes]:PIPE)
     /{forall[i:Nodes] {
         node[i].put/pipe[i%N+1].put,
         node[i].get/pipe[i].get}
      }.
```

14.4.2 Database Ring Properties

Overall, the safety property required of the database model is as follows: when there are no updates in progress, the values held at each node should be consistent. A node that is not engaged in an update signals passive. There can be no updates in progress if all nodes are passive, and the system is said to be quiescent. We can capture the state in which a node is passive by means of the following fluent:

```
fluent PASSIVE[i:Nodes]
       = <node[i].passive, node[i].change[Value]>
```

The fluent holds for a node from the time that it signals passive until the time that it signals a change of value. The following assertion captures the quiescent property:

```
assert QUIESCENT = forall[i:Nodes] PASSIVE[i]
```

To describe the consistency property, we need to be able to make propositions about the value held by a node as follows:

```
fluent VALUE[i:Nodes][c:Value]
     = <node[i].change[c],node[i].change[{Value\{[c]}}]>
```

The fluent VALUE is true for a node i and value c if the node has previously changed to the value c and has not yet changed to some other value in the set consisting of Value with c removed. Using this fluent, we can define consistency as the proposition that there exists a value such that each node has that value:

```
assert CONSISTENT
       = exists[c:Value] forall[i:Nodes] VALUE[i][c]
```

The required safety property for the database ring system can now be succinctly expressed by the following assertion, which requires that it is always the case that when the system is quiescent, then it must be consistent.

```
assert SAFE = [](QUIESCENT -> CONSISTENT)
```

The model we have described does indeed satisfy this property. The reader should replace line 14 of the NODE process with:

```
else if (/* I>j */ True) then
```

to obtain an instructive counterexample illustrating the problem of concurrent updates. This modification disables the priority-based conflict resolution in the model.

We have specified the required safety property for the model which ensures that it does not get into a bad state; however, we must also check that the model eventually and repeatedly gets into a good state. The good state for our model is quiescence and the required liveness property is therefore

```
assert LIVE = []<>QUIESCENT
```

which is satisfied by our model.

Witness Executions

When a property is satisfied by a model, no further information is returned by the checking tool. The use of FLTL properties gives us the opportunity to generate examples of model executions (traces) which satisfy the property. Such executions are said to be witness executions since they act as a witness to the truth of the property. To generate a witness execution, we simply assert the negation of the property. If the property is satisfied then its negation cannot be satisfied and the *LTSA* will produce a counterexample trace.

```
assert WITNESS_LIVE = !LIVE
```

The above assertion provides the following witness trace for the LIVE property:

```
Violation of LTL property: @WITNESS_LIVE
Trace to terminal set of states:
      node.1.local.green
      node.1.change.green
      node.1.put.1.green
      node.2.get.1.green
      node.2.change.green
      node.2.put.1.green
       node.2.passive      PASSIVE.2
       node.2.local.red    PASSIVE.2
       node.3.get.1.green  PASSIVE.2
       node.3.change.green PASSIVE.2
       node.3.put.1.green  PASSIVE.2
       node.1.get.1.green  PASSIVE.2
```

```
        node.1.passive    PASSIVE.1 && PASSIVE.2
        node.3.passive    PASSIVE.1 && PASSIVE.2 && PASSIVE.3
  Cycle in terminal set:
        . . . . . . . .
  LTL Property Check in: 281ms
```

Some care needs to be taken with witnesses for properties that contain implication. For example, the negation of the safety property SAFE is the property <>(QUIESCENT && !CONSISTENT). We are expecting a counterexample in which quiescence and consistency hold while the tool produces a counterexample in which neither quiescence nor consistency holds, which also violates the property but is not very useful in explaining the operation of the system.

Finite Executions

Linear temporal logic is defined for infinite sequences. How do we check FLTL properties for finite executions? In fact, we can easily achieve this by a simple trick in which we add an infinite cycle of an action to the final state. For example, suppose we add the constraint to the database ring that it processes only a single local update:

```
ONE_UPDATE = (node[Nodes].local[Value] -> END).
||DATABASE_RING_ONE = (DATABASE_RING || ONE_UPDATE).
```

To permit the FLTL properties to be checked against this modified system, we change the constraint to:

```
ONE_UPDATE = (node[Nodes].local[Value] -> ENDED),
ENDED      = (ended -> ENDED).
```

The properties LIVE and SAFE hold for the systems and the following witness execution can be produced for SAFE:

```
Violation of LTL property: @WITNESS_SAFE
Trace to terminal set of states:
      node.1.local.blue
      node.1.change.blue  VALUE.1.blue
      node.1.put.1.blue   VALUE.1.blue
      node.2.get.1.blue   VALUE.1.blue
      node.2.change.blue  VALUE.1.blue && VALUE.2.blue
      node.2.put.1.blue   VALUE.1.blue && VALUE.2.blue
      node.2.passive      PASSIVE.2
                       && VALUE.1.blue && VALUE.2.blue
      node.3.get.1.blue   PASSIVE.2
                       && VALUE.1.blue && VALUE.2.blue
```

```
        node.3.change.blue   PASSIVE.2
                && VALUE.1.blue && VALUE.2.blue && VALUE.3.blue
        node.3.put.1.blue    PASSIVE.2
                && VALUE.1.blue && VALUE.2.blue && VALUE.3.blue
        node.1.get.1.blue    PASSIVE.2
                && VALUE.1.blue && VALUE.2.blue && VALUE.3.blue
        node.1.passive       PASSIVE.1 && PASSIVE.2
                && VALUE.1.blue && VALUE.2.blue && VALUE.3.blue
        node.3.passive       PASSIVE.1 && PASSIVE.2 && PASSIVE.3
                && VALUE.1.blue && VALUE.2.blue && VALUE.3.blue
    Cycle in terminal set:
        ended       PASSIVE.1 && PASSIVE.2 && PASSIVE.3
                && VALUE.1.blue && VALUE.2.blue && VALUE.3.blue
    LTL Property Check in: 31ms
```

Summary

The primitive propositions of the linear temporal logic we described in this chapter are termed "fluents". A fluent is defined by a set of initiating actions and a set of terminating actions. At a particular instant, a fluent is true if and only if it was initially true or an initiating action has previously occurred and, in both cases, no terminating action has yet occurred. Using fluents, we can map the trace produced by a model into a sequence of sets. Each set in the sequence contains the fluents that are true at the point the corresponding action in the trace occurs. Fluent linear temporal logic (FLTL) is defined with respect to these sequences. For each action, we define a synonymous fluent which holds when the action occurs and becomes false immediately the following action occurs. We termed these actions "fluents" and they can be freely mixed with explicitly defined fluents in expressions. The following table summarizes the temporal operators used in FLTL ("iff" abbreviates "if and only if"):

next time **X F**	iff **F** holds in the next instant.
always **F**	iff **F** holds now and always in the future.
eventually **<>F**	iff **F** holds at some point in the future.
until **P U Q**	iff **Q** holds at some point in the future and **P** holds until then.
weak until **P W Q**	iff **P** holds indefinitely or **P U Q**.

The chapter outlined some typical ways of expressing safety and liveness properties. Using the database ring example, we also explained how to produce witness executions and how to deal with finite executions. In checking liveness properties, we make the same assumptions with respect to fair choice as those made in Chapter 7 and use the same action priority approach to generate adverse scheduling conditions.

Notes and Further Reading

In Chapter 7, we mentioned that the general LTL model-checking procedure – that of translating the negation of the required LTL formula into a Büchi automaton, composing this automaton with the target model and then searching for connected components containing acceptance states – is due to Gribomont and Wolper (1989). We also mentioned that this technique has found widespread usage in the SPIN model checker (Holtzmann, 1991, 1997). Indeed, as far as possible, we have followed the syntax of LTL formulae used in SPIN. The use of fluents in the context of LTL model checking is due to Giannakopoulou and Magee (2003) and the component used in the *LTSA* to translate LTL formulae into Büchi automata is due to Giannakopoulou and Lerda (2002). A version of FLTL for specifying the properties of the timed models of Chapter 12 can be found in Letier, Kramer, Magee, *et al.* (2005). The term "fluent" originally comes from the time-varying quantity in Newton's calculus but has more recently been adopted by the Artificial Intelligence community with a meaning consistent with the one used here (Sandewall, 1995).

Most properties specified in LTL conform to a restricted set of forms or patterns. A set of patterns used in specifying properties has been codified by Dwyer, Avrunin and Corbett (1999). These patterns are coded in a number of formalisms that include linear temporal logic and computation tree logic (CTL). While LTL is defined with respect to infinite execution sequences or linear time, CTL is a temporal logic defined with respect to a branching tree of execution paths or branching time. CTL was used in the model-checking work originated by Clarke, Emerson and Sistla (1986). There has been much academic debate on the relative advantages of LTL and CTL, starting with the classic paper by Lamport (1980) entitled *"Sometime" Is Sometimes "Not Never": On the Temporal Logic of Programs* to the more recent *Branching vs. Linear Time: Final Showdown* by Vardi (2001). Pnueli (1977) was responsible for the original idea of using temporal logic as the logical basis for proving correctness properties of concurrent programs.

Finally, it should be noted that the database ring is due to Bill Roscoe (1998). The example, which was used to illustrate an approach to modeling change in the form of safe node deletion and creation, appears in a paper by Kramer and Magee (1998).

Exercises

14.1 Using FLTL, specify and check the exclusion safety properties for neighbors in the Dining Philosophers problem of Chapter 6. In addition, specify and check the liveness properties, including the response property that ensures that if a philosopher is hungry, he will eventually eat. Use witnesses to provide examples of property satisfaction.

14.2 Using FLTL, specify safety and liveness properties for the Readers–Writers problem of section 7.5. Check that these give the same results as the corresponding properties specified in Chapter 7 and for the same properties used in the verification models of Chapter 13.

14.3 Using FLTL, specify and check the exclusion safety properties for the warring neighbors of exercise 7.6, and for Peterson's Algorithm for two processes of exercise 7.7. In addition, specify and check the liveness properties, including the response property that ensures that if a neighbor wants to enter the field, he will eventually gain exclusive access. Use witnesses to provide examples of property satisfaction.

14.4 Using FLTL, specify safety and liveness properties for the cruise control system of Chapter 8. Check these properties against the model of Chapter 8. (*Hint*: define fluents for each of the abstract states – active, cruising, enabled, etc. – as necessary.)

14.5 Using FLTL, specify a safety property to replace the property SAFE specified in section 11.3.1 for the Announcer–Listener system. (*Hint*: define a fluent which holds when a process registers for a pattern and note that a separate SAFE process is created in Chapter 11 for each listener process.)

Appendix A
FSP Quick Reference

A.1 Processes

A process is defined by one or more local processes separated by commas. The definition is terminated by a full stop. STOP and ERROR are primitive local processes.

Example

```
Process = (a -> Local),
Local   = (b -> STOP).
```

Action Prefix ->	If x is an action and P a process then (x->P) describes a process that initially engages in the action x and then behaves exactly as described by P.
Choice |	If x and y are actions then (x->P|y->Q) describes a process which initially engages in either of the actions x or y. After the first action has occurred, the subsequent behavior is described by P if the first action was x and Q if the first action was y.
Guarded Action **when**	The choice (**when** B x -> P | y -> Q) means that when the guard B is true then the actions x and y are both eligible to be chosen, otherwise if B is false then the action x cannot be chosen.
Alphabet Extension +	The alphabet of a process is the set of actions in which it can engage. P + S extends the alphabet of the process P with the actions in the set S.

Table A.1 Process operators

A.2 Composite Processes

A composite process is the parallel composition of one or more processes. The definition of a composite process is preceded by ||.

Example

```
||Composite = (P || Q).
```

Parallel Composition ||	If P and Q are processes then (P||Q) represents the concurrent execution of P and Q.
Replicator **forall**	**forall** [i:1..N] P(i) is the parallel composition (P(1) || ... || P(N)).
Process Labeling :	a:P prefixes each label in the alphabet of P with a.
Process Sharing ::	{a_1,..,a_x}::P replaces every label n in the alphabet of P with the labels a_1.n,...,a_x.n. Further, every transition (n->Q) in the definition of P is replaced with the transitions ({a_1.n,...,a_x.n}->Q).
Priority High <<	||C =(P||Q)<<{a_1,...,a_n} specifies a composition in which the actions a_1,...,a_n have higher priority than any other action in the alphabet of P||Q including the silent action tau. In any choice in this system which has one or more of the actions a_1,...,a_n labeling a transition, the transitions labeled with lower priority actions are discarded.
Priority Low >>	||C=(P||Q)>>{a_1,...,a_n} specifies a composition in which the actions a_1,...,a_n have lower priority than any other action in the alphabet of P||Q including the silent action tau. In any choice in this system which has one or more transitions not labeled by a_1,...,a_n, the transitions labeled by a_1,...,a_n are discarded.

Table A.2 Composite process operators

A.3 Common Operators

The operators in Table A.3 may be used in the definition of both processes and composite processes.

Conditional **if then else**	The process **if** B **then** P **else** Q behaves as the process P if the condition B is true; otherwise it behaves as Q. If the **else** Q is omitted and B is false, then the process behaves as STOP.
Re-labeling /	Re-labeling is applied to a process to change the names of action labels. The general form of re-labeling is:/{*newlabel_1*/*oldlabel_1*,... *newlabel_n*/*oldlabel_n*}.
Hiding \	When applied to a process P, the hiding operator {a_1..a_x } removes the action names a_1..a_x from the alphabet of P and makes these concealed actions "silent". These silent actions are labeled tau. Silent actions in different processes are not shared.
Interface @	When applied to a process P, the interface operator @{a_1..a_x } hides all actions in the alphabet of P not labeled in the set a_1..a_x.

Table A.3 Common process operators

A.4 Properties

Safety **property**	A safety **property** P defines a deterministic process that asserts that any trace including actions in the alphabet of P is accepted by P.
Progress **progress**	**progress** P = {a_1, a_2..a_n} defines a progress property P which asserts that in an infinite execution of a target system, at least one of the actions a_1, a_2..a_n will be executed infinitely often.

Table A.4 Safety and progress properties

A.5 Fluent Linear Temporal Logic (FLTL)

<table>
<tr><td>Fluent fluent</td><td>fluent FL = <{s_1,...s_n}, {e_1..e_n}> initially B defines a fluent FL that is initially true if the expression B is true and initially false if the expression B is false. FL becomes true immediately any of the initiating actions {s_1,...s_n} occur and false immediately any of the terminating actions {e_1..e_n} occur. If the term initially B is omitted then FL is initially false.</td></tr>
<tr><td>Assertion assert</td><td>assert PF = FLTL_Expression defines an FLTL property.</td></tr>
<tr><td>&&</td><td>conjunction (and)</td></tr>
<tr><td>||</td><td>disjunction (or)</td></tr>
<tr><td>!</td><td>negation (not)</td></tr>
<tr><td>-></td><td>implication ((A->B) ≡ (!A || B))</td></tr>
<tr><td><-></td><td>equivalence ((A<->B) ≡(A->B)&&(B->A))</td></tr>
<tr><td>next time X F</td><td>iff F holds in the next instant.</td></tr>
<tr><td>always []F</td><td>iff F holds now and always in the future.</td></tr>
<tr><td>eventually <>F</td><td>iff F holds at some point in the future.</td></tr>
<tr><td>until P U Q</td><td>iff Q holds at some point in the future and P holds until then.</td></tr>
<tr><td>weak until P W Q</td><td>iff P holds indefinitely or P U Q.</td></tr>
<tr><td>forall</td><td>forall[i:R] FL(i) conjunction of FL(i)</td></tr>
<tr><td>exists</td><td>exists[i:R] FL(i) disjunction of FL(i)</td></tr>
</table>

Table A.5 Fluent Linear Temporal Logic

Appendix B
FSP Language Specification

FSP stands for Finite State Processes. This appendix contains a comprehensive specification of the syntax of *FSP* together with a commentary on features such as variable scope that are not treated explicitly in the body of the book. A formal description of the semantics of the *FSP* process operators may be found in Appendix C.

In specifying the syntax of *FSP*, we have followed the approach used in the Java Language Specification. In particular, the syntax is specified using a context-free grammar that consists of a number of productions. Each production is defined by a non-terminal symbol as its left-hand side and a sequence of one or more terminal and non-terminal symbols as its right-hand side. In the following, non-terminal symbols are shown in italic type and terminal symbols in a fixed width bolded type. The definition of a non-terminal is introduced by its name followed by a colon. One or more alternative right-hand sides for the non-terminal then follow on succeeding lines. For example, the following production specifies the syntax for an *FSP* constant definition.

ConstantDef:
    `const` *ConstantIdent* = *Expression*

The production below specifies an argument list as consisting of either a single expression or a list of expressions separated by commas:

ArgumentList:
    Expression
    ArgumentList **,** *Expression*

The subscripted suffix "*opt*", which may appear after a terminal or non-terminal, indicates an optional symbol.

B.1 *FSP* Description

In addition to definitions for processes and compositions of processes, an *FSP* model description consists of definitions for constants, ranges of integers, sets of action labels, safety properties, progress properties, animation menus, fluents and assertions.

FSPdescription
    FSPdefinition
    FSPdescription FSPdefinition
FSPdefinition
    ConstantDef
    RangeDef
    SetDef
    ProcessDef
    CompositeDef
    PropertyDef
    ProgressDef
    MenuDef
    FluentDef
    AssertDef

B.2 Identifiers

FSP definitions and process parameters are named by identifiers beginning with an uppercase letter. Action label and variable identifiers begin with a lowercase letter.

ConstantIdent:
RangeIdent:
SetIdent:
ParameterIdent:
ProcessIdent:
PropertyIdent:
ProgressIdent:
MenuIdent:
FluentIdent:
AssertIdent:
    UpperCaseIdentifier
Variable:
    LowerCaseIdentifier

Upper- and lowercase identifiers are specified by the following productions in which *UpperCaseLetter* denotes one of the uppercase alphabetical characters and

LowerCaseLetter denotes one of the lowercase alphabetical characters or underscore "_". *Digit* denotes one of the decimal digits.

UpperCaseIdentifier:
  UpperCaseLetter
  UpperCaseIdentifier Letter
  UpperCaseIdentifier Digit
LowerCaseIdentifier:
  LowerCaseLetter
  LowerCaseIdentifier Letter
  LowerCaseIdentifier Digit
Letter:
  UpperCaseLetter
  LowerCaseLetter

B.3 Action Labels

Actions in *FSP* can be labeled either by a lowercase identifier or by a value computed from an expression enclosed by square brackets. Action labels are also formed by concatenating simpler labels with a dot.

ActionLabel:
  LowerCaseIdentifier
  ActionLabel **.** *LowerCaseIdentifier*
  [*Expression* **]**
  ActionLabel **[** *Expression* **]**

Examples

```
in    [43]    in[12]    in[2][i*2]    x[1].y[3]
```

Wherever a single action label can be used in *FSP*, a set of action labels can also be used. The exception is where label values are used in expressions (see section B.10).

ActionLabels:
  ActionLabel
  Set
  [*ActionRange* **]**
  ActionLabels **.** *ActionLabel*
  ActionLabels **.** *Set*
  ActionLabels [*ActionRange*]
  ActionLabels **[** *Expression* **]**

Sets of action labels are defined explicitly by a set or by a range of integer values.

ActionRange:
  Range
  Set
  Variable **:** *Range*
  Variable **:** *Set*
Range:
  RangeIdent
  Expression **..** *Expression*
Set:
  SetIdent
  { *SetElements* **}**
SetElements:
  ActionLabels
  SetElements **,** *ActionLabels*

Examples

```
{a,b,c}  X.a   in[x:1..3]   in[x:T]   a.{x,y,z}
```

Variables can be associated with a set or a range in an *ActionRange*. The variable successively takes on each of the values of the set or range. The scope of variables is discussed in the following with respect to their use in processes, composite processes and re-labeling definitions.

Examples

```
a[i:1..3]   x[v:{a,b,c}]
```

B.4 const, range, set

Named constants, ranges and sets are defined as follows:

ConstantDef:
  const *ConstantIdent* = *SimpleExpression*
RangeDef:
  range *RangeIdent* = *SimpleExpression* **..** *SimpleExpression*
SetDef:
  set *SetIdent* = **{** *setElements* **}**

Examples

```
const N = 3
range R = 0..N
set   S = {a,b,c,d[R]}
```

B.5 Process Definition

A process is defined by one or more local processes. A process can optionally be parameterized and have re-labeling, hiding and alphabet extension parts.

ProcessDef:
  ProcessIdent Param$_{opt}$ **=** *ProcessBody*
    AlphabetExtension$_{opt}$ *Relabel*$_{opt}$ *Hiding*$_{opt}$ **.**
ProcessBody:
  LocalProcess
  LocalProcess **,** *LocalProcessDefs*
LocalProcessDefs:
  LocalProcessDef
  LocalProcessDefs, LocalProcessDef
LocalProcessDef:
  ProcessIdent IndexRanges$_{opt}$ **=** *LocalProcess*
AlphabetExtension:
  + *Set*

The scope of the name for a local process definition is the process in which it is contained. A local process is `END`, `STOP`, `ERROR`, a reference to another local process, a sequential composition, a conditional process or is defined using action prefix and choice.

LocalProcess:
  BaseLocalProcess
  SequentialComposition
  if *Expression* **then** *LocalProcess*
  if *Expression* **then** *LocalProcess* **else** *LocalProcess*
  (*Choice* **)**
BaseLocalProcess:
  END
  STOP
  ERROR
  ProcessIdent Indices$_{opt}$

Choice:
    ActionPrefix
    Choice | *ActionPrefix*
ActionPrefix:
    $Guard_{opt}$ *PrefixActions* -> *LocalProcess*
PrefixActions:
    ActionsLabels
    PrefixActions -> *ActionsLabels*
Guard:
    when *Expression*

Examples

```
TIME = (tick -> TIME).
S = STOP + {a,b,c}.

R = (a -> R | b -> Q),
Q = STOP.

P = (a[i:1..3] ->
        if i==1 then STOP else P).
```

The scope of a variable defined in an action label is the rest of the local process in which it is defined. However, the scope of a variable defined inside a set does not extend beyond that set, e.g. `{a, b, c[i:0..2]}`. Note that variables are a syntactic convenience to permit concise definitions. The example process `P` above can be expanded to an equivalent definition without variables and conditionals:

```
P = (a[1] -> STOP | a[2] -> P | a[3] -> P).
```

In a similar way, processes with guards can be expressed by explicitly enumerating the choices that an action label set represents. For example, the process:

```
P = (a[i:0..3] ->
      ( when i==0 x -> STOP
      | when i!=0 y -> P
      )
      ).
```

is equivalent to:

```
P = (a[0] -> x -> STOP
    |a[1] -> y -> P
```

```
|a[2] -> y -> P
|a[3] -> y -> P
).
```

Index ranges for local processes are also a syntactic convenience. They define a set of local processes.

Indices:
  [*Expression* **]**
  Indices **[** *Expression* **]**
IndexRanges:
  [*Expression* **]**
  [*ActionRange* **]**
  IndexRanges **[** *Expression* **]**
  IndexRanges **[** *ActionRange* **]**

Example

```
P          = S[0],
S[i:0..2]  = (when i<3 a -> S[i+1]),
S[3]       = STOP.
```

The scope of a variable used in a local process definition is the local process, i.e. it extends to the comma that terminates the definition. The example above could be defined without a variable as:

```
P    = S[0],
S[0] = (a -> S[1]),
S[1] = (a -> S[2]),
S[2] = (a -> S[3]),
S[3] = STOP.
```

The reference to a local process can be replaced by substituting its definition, giving:

```
P = (a -> (a -> (a -> STOP))).
```

This is exactly equivalent to:

```
P = (a -> a -> a -> STOP).
```

Variables in *FSP* definitions can always be removed by syntactic transformation. Consequently, in Appendix C, which presents the semantics of *FSP*, variables are not considered.

A sequential composition is always defined within a process. The last process in the sequential composition must be END, STOP, ERROR, or a reference to a local process. The composition essentially concatenates processes with the last (i.e. END) state of a sequential process replaced with the first state of the subsequent process in the composition list.

SequentialComposition:
  SeqProcessList **;** *BaseLocalProcess*
SeqProcessList:
  ProcessRef
  SeqProcessList **;** *ProcessRef*
ProcessRef:
  ProcessIdent $Argument_{opt}$
Argument:
  (*ArgumentList* **)**
ArgumentList:
  Expression
  ArgumentList **,** *Expression*

Examples

```
P(I=1) = (a[I]-> b[I] -> END).

SC = P(1);P(2);SC.
```

The process SC above is defined below without sequential composition and has exactly the same behavior.

```
SC = (a[1] -> b[1] -> a[2] -> b[2] -> SC).
```

B.6 Composite Process

A composite process is distinguished from a primitive process by prefixing its definition with ||. Composite processes are constructed using parallel composition, re-labeling, priority and hiding. Process labeling and sharing are specialized forms of re-labeling. The replication and conditional constructs are purely syntactic conveniences.

CompositeDef:
|| *ProcessIdent* $Param_{opt}$ = *CompositeBody*
  $Priority_{opt}$ $Hiding_{opt}$ **.**

CompositeBody:
  PrefixLabel$_{opt}$ ProcessRef Relabel$_{opt}$
  PrefixLabel$_{opt}$ **(** *ParallelComposition* **)** *Relabel$_{opt}$*
  forall *Ranges CompositeBody* -- replication
  if *Expression* **then** *CompositeBody* -- conditional
  if *Expression* **then** *CompositeBody* **else** *CompositeBody*

PrefixLabel:
  ActionLabels **:** -- process labeling
  ActionLabels **::** -- process sharing
  ActionLabels **::** *ActionLabel***:**

ParallelComposition
  CompositeBody
  ParallelComposition **||** *CompositeBody*

Priority:
  >> *Set*
  << *Set*

Ranges:
  [*ActionRange* **]**
  Ranges **[** *ActionRange* **]**

Examples

```
||S = a[1..3]:P.
||S = {a[1],a[2],a[3]}:P.
||S = forall[i:1..3] a[i]:P.
||S = forall[i:1..3] a:P/{a[i]/a}.
||S = (a[1]:P || a[2]:P || a[3]:P).
```

The composite process definitions above are exactly equivalent and define the same composite process. The syntax for re-labeling is described in section B.8. The scope of a variable in a composite process is the *CompositeBody* in which it is defined together with any other *CompositeBody* contained within that *Composite-Body* definition.

Example

```
||S = forall[i:1..4]
        if (i<=2)then
          (forall[j:1..2] a[i][j]:P)
        else
          (forall[j:1..2] b[i][j]:P).
```

The definitions of the two occurrences of the variable j do not conflict in the above example since they are each defined in a different *CompositeBody*. Neither *CompositeBody* is contained within the other. The replication can be unfolded to give the equivalent definition for S shown below.

```
||S =
  ( a[1][1]:P || a[1][2]:P || a[2][1]:P || a[2][2]:P
  ||b[3][1]:P || b[3][2]:P || b[4][1]:P || b[4][2]:P
  ).
```

B.7 Parameters

Process and composite process parameters must always have a default value. This means that a process can always be compiled into a finite Labeled Transition System (*LTS*). The default parameter value may be changed by an argument when the process, whether composite or primitive, forms part of another composite process.

Param:
  (*ParameterList* **)**
ParameterList:
  Parameter
  ParameterList **,** *Parameter*
Parameter:
  ParameterIdent = *Expression*

Example

```
  P(X=1)   = (a[X] -> STOP).
||S(Y=2)   = (P(Y+1) || P(Y+2)).
```

The scope of a parameter is the process or composite in which it is defined. Parameter substitution creates a new process with each occurrence of the parameter replaced by the argument value. This is simply macro expansion. Substituting the parameters in the example results in the following equivalent definition.

```
P3   = (a[3] -> STOP).
P4   = (a[4] -> STOP).
||S2 = (P3 || P4).
```

B.8 Re-Labeling and Hiding

The re-labeling and hiding operators can be applied to both processes and composite processes.

Relabel:
  /{ *RelabelDefs* **}**
RelabelDefs:
  RelabelDef
  RelabelDefs, RelabelDef
RelabelDef:
  ActionLabels **/** *ActionLabels*
  forall *IndexRanges* **{** *RelabelDefs* **}**

FSP supports relational re-labeling. The re-labeling operator applies a relation to a process, which can result in replacing many labels with a single label and replacing one label with multiple labels. The re-labeling relation is defined by a set of pairs. Each pair takes the form `newlabel/oldlabel`. Sets of labels and the replication construct permit the concise definition of the re-labeling relation. In each of the examples below, both the concise form and the equivalent expanded form of the relation are given.

Examples

```
/* one to one re-labeling */
P/{ forall[i:1..3] {a[i]/x[i]}}
/* equivalent */
P/{ a[1]/x[1], a[2]/x[2], a[3]/x[3] }

/* one to many re-labeling */
P/{ {x,y,z}/a }
/* equivalent */
P/{ x/a, y/a, z/a }

/* many to one re-labeling */
P/{ a/{x,y,z} }
/* equivalent */
P/{ a/x, a/y, a/z }

/* many to many re-labeling */
P/{ {a,b}/{x,y} }
/* equivalent */
P/{ a/x, a/y, b/x , b/y }
```

If the old label does not appear in the alphabet of `P`, then the re-labeling pair `newlabel/oldlabel` has no effect. Re-labeling in *FSP* is always applied before parallel composition such that for a re-labeling relation *R*, `(P||Q)/`*R* is equivalent to `(P/`*R*`||`*Q*`/`*R*`)`.

Hiding:
  \ *Set*
  @ *Set*

There are two forms of the hiding operator: \ applies a set of labels to a process such that the labels that occur in both the alphabet of the process and the set are hidden; @ applies a set of labels to a process such that every label in the alphabet is hidden except those that occur in the set.

Prefix Matching

Action labels in hiding sets, priority sets and on the right-hand side of a re-labeling pair match prefixes of labels in the alphabet of the process to which they are applied. For example, an action label `a` in a hiding set will hide all labels prefixed by `a`, e.g. `a.b`, `a[1]`, `a.x.y`. Similarly, the re-labeling pair `x/a` would replace these labels with `x.b`, `x[1]`, `x.x.y`. Prefix matching permits label details to be ignored when processes are composed.

B.9 property, progress and menu

A safety property is defined by a process prefixed by the keyword **`property`**.

PropertyDef:
  `property` *ProcessDef*

There are two forms of progress property, though we have used only the simpler form in the main text of this book. The first form asserts that at least one action in a set `S` must occur infinitely often. The second form is conditional progress, which takes the form **`if`** `C` **`then`** `S`. This asserts that if one of the actions in the set `C` occurs infinitely often, then so must one of the actions in the set `S`.

ProgressDef:
  `progress` *ProgressIdent* $Ranges_{opt}$ = *Set*
  `progress` *ProgressIdent* $Ranges_{opt}$ = **if** *Set* **then** *Set*

A set of progress properties may be declared using an index range.

Example

```
progress G[i:1..3] = {{a,b}[i]}
```

A menu definition specifies the set of actions that the user can control in an animation.

> *MenuDef:*
> **menu** *MenuIdent* = *Set*

B.10 Expression

Expressions in *FSP* are a subset of expressions in Java. This has the advantage of familiarity; however it has the disadvantage that some of the *FSP* process operators have a different meaning when used in the context of an expression. In particular, the priority operators << and >> mean shift left and shift right when used in an expression, the parallel composition operator || means logical or when used in an expression, the choice operator | means bit-wise or in an expression and the re-label operator / means division. Where confusion might arise, namely in constant and range definitions, expressions with the logical and shift operators must be bracketed. This is the reason why constant and range definitions are defined using *SimpleExpression* rather than *Expression*. The syntax of expressions used in *FSP* is specified by the following expressions.

> *SimpleExpression:*
> *AdditiveExpr*
>
> *Expression:*
> *OrExpr*
>
> *OrExpr:*
> *AndExpr*
> *OrExpr* **||** *AndExpr*
>
> *AndExpr:*
> *BitOrExpr*
> *AndExpr* **&&** *BitOrExpr*
>
> *BitOrExpr:*
> *BitExclOrExpr*
> *BitOrExpr* **|** *BitExclOrExpr*
>
> *BitExclOrExpr:*
> *BitAndExpr*
> *BitExclOrExpr*^ *BitAndExpr*
>
> *BitAndExpr:*
> *EqualityExpr*
> *BitAndExpr* **&** *EqualityExpr*

EqualityExpr:
  RelationalExpr
  EqualityExpr **==** *RelationalExpr*
  EqualityExpr **!=** *RelationalExpr*
RelationalExpr:
  ShiftExpr
  RelationalExpr **<** *ShiftExpr*
  RelationalExpr **<=** *ShiftExpr*
  RelationalExpr **>** *ShiftExpr*
  RelationalExpr **>=** *ShiftExpr*
ShiftExpr:
  AdditiveExpr
  ShiftExpr **>>** *AdditiveExpr*
  ShiftExpr **<<** *AdditiveExpr*
AdditiveExpr:
  MultiplicativeExpr
  AdditiveExpr **+** *MultiplicativeExpr*
  AdditiveExpr **-** *MultiplicativeExpr*
MultiplicativeExpr:
  UnaryExpr
  MultiplicativeExpr ***** *UnaryExpr*
  MultiplicativeExpr **** *UnaryExpr*
  MultiplicativeExpr **%** *UnaryExpr*
UnaryExpr:
  BaseExpr
  + *BaseExpr*
  - *BaseExpr*
  ! *BaseExpr*
BaseExpr:
  IntegerLiteral
  Variable
  ConstantIdent
  'ActionLabel
  # *SetIdent*
  @(*SetIdent* **,** *Expression* **)**
  (*Expression* **)**

FSP supports only integer and label expressions. Variables may take either an integer value or a label value. Label literals are formed by preceding an action label with a quote – this distinguishes a label value from a variable. The only valid operators on label values are equality and inequality.

The expression @(*A*, *e*) returns a label value which is the eth element of the set identified by *A*.

The expression # *A* returns as an integer value the cardinality of the set identified by *A*.

As in the programming language C, the results of boolean expressions in *FSP* are integer values. A false expression has the value 0 and a true expression the value 1.

B.11 Basic *FSP*

In the previous sections, we have indicated that constructs such as guards, replicators, conditionals, variables and index ranges are syntactic conveniences to permit concise descriptions. Models described using these constructs can be syntactically transformed into a more basic form of *FSP*. This basic form of *FSP* uses only the process operators and the primitive local processes `END`, `STOP` and `ERROR`. The syntax of basic *FSP* is described by the following productions:

BProcessDef:
  BProcessBody AlphabetExtension$_{opt}$ Relabel$_{opt}$ Hiding$_{opt}$ **.**
BProcessBody:
  ProcessIdent = *BLocalProcess*
  BProcessBody **,** *ProcessIdent* = *BLocalProcess*
BLocalProcess:
  BBaseProcess
  (*BChoice* **)**
BBaseProcess:
  END
  STOP
  ERROR
  ProcessIdent
  ProcessIdent **;** *BBaseProcess*
BChoice:
  ActionLabel -> *BLocalProcess*
  BChoice **|** *ActionLabel* -> *BLocalProcess*
BCompositeDef:
  || *ProcessIdent* = *BCompositeBody Priority$_{opt}$ Hiding$_{opt}$*.
BCompositeBody:
  ProcessIdent Relabel$_{opt}$
  (*BParallelComposition* **)** *Relabel$_{opt}$*
BParallelComposition:
  BCompositeBody
  BParallelComposition **||** *BCompositeBody*

A formal semantics for basic *FSP* is presented in Appendix C.

B.12 fluent and assert

Fluents used in Linear Temporal Logic expressions are defined by two sets of action labels and an optional initialization expression that determines whether the fluent is initially true or false. The sets may be singletons, in which case a single action label may be defined. If initialization is omitted, by default, the fluent is initially false. A set of fluents may be declared using an index range.

FluentDef:
    fluent *FluentIdent IndexRanges*$_{opt}$
        = < *ActionLabels, ActionLabels* **>** *Initially*$_{opt}$
Initially:
    initially *SimpleExpression*

Example

```
fluent Simple  = <a,b>
fluent Sets    = <{start,begin},{end,finish}>
fluent Indexed[i:1..8]
            = <a[i],b[i]> initially (i%2==0)
```

Assertions define properties expressed in Fluent Linear Temporal Logic (FLTL). Assertions are named FLTL formulae and they may be parameterized and used in the definition of more complex properties.

AssertDef:
    assert *AssertIdent Param*$_{opt}$ **=** *FLTLUnaryExpression*
FLTLOrExpr:
    FLTLBinaryExpr
    FLTLOrExpr **||** *FLTLBinaryExpr*
FLTLBinaryExpr:
    FLTLAndExpr
    FLTLBinaryExpr **U** *FLTLAndExpr* -- until
    FLTLBinaryExpr **W** *FLTLAndExpr* -- weak until
    FLTLBinaryExpr -> *FLTLAndExpr* -- implication
    FLTLBinaryExpr <-> *FLTLAndExpr* -- equivalence
FLTLAndExpr:
    FLTLUnaryExpr
    FLTLAndExpr **&&** *FLTLUnaryExpr*
FLTLUnaryExpr:
    FLTLBaseExpr
    ! *FLTLUnaryExpr* -- negation

X *FLTLUnaryExpr* -- next time
<> *FLTLUnaryExpr* -- eventually
[] *FLTLUnaryExpr* -- always
forall *Ranges FLTLUnaryExpr*
exists *Ranges FLTLUnaryExpr*

FLTLBaseExpr:
FluentIdent Ranges$_{opt}$
ActionLabels
AssertIdent Argument$_{opt}$
rigid *SimpleExpression*
(*FLTLOrExpr* **)**

Uppercase identifiers in FLTL expressions refer either to fluent or assertion definitions. Lowercase identifiers refer to action labels. Where a set of action labels is used, this means the disjunction of the fluents representing each individual action as described in Chapter 14. The simple expression introduced by the keyword **rigid** is a boolean expression that must evaluate to either 0 *false* or 1 *true*.

Appendix C
FSP Semantics

The semantics of basic *FSP* are defined in terms of Labeled Transition Systems (*LTSs*). In the body of the book, we have depicted the *LTS* that corresponds to an *FSP* process as a graph. In the following, we formally define what an *LTS* is and then describe the correspondence between *FSP* process expressions and *LTSs*. This correspondence is defined by the function:

$$lts : Exp \rightarrow \wp$$

where *Exp* is the set of *FSP* process expressions, and $\wp$ the set of *LTSs*. The function *lts* is defined inductively on the structure of *FSP* process expressions.

C.1 Labeled Transition System (LTS)

Let *States* be the universal set of states including π a designated *error* state, L be the universal set of labels, and $Act = L \cup \{\tau\}$, where τ is used to denote an internal action that cannot be observed by the environment of an *LTS*.
A finite *LTS* P is a quadruple $< S, A, \Delta, q >$ where:

- $S \subseteq States$ *is* a finite set of states.
- $A = \alpha P \cup \{\tau\}$, where $\alpha P \subseteq L$ denotes the *alphabet* of P.
- $\Delta \subseteq S - \{\pi\} \times A \times S$, denotes a transition relation that maps from a state and an action onto another state.
- $q \in S$ indicates the initial state of P.

The only *LTS* that is allowed to have the error state π as its initial state is $<\{\pi\}$, Act, $\{\}$, $\pi>$, named Π. The alphabet of this process $\alpha\Pi = L$.

An *LTS* $P = < S, A, \Delta, q >$ *transits* with action $a \in A$ into an *LTS* P', denoted as $P \xrightarrow{a} P'$, if:

- $P' = < S, A, \Delta, q' >$, where $q' \neq \pi$ and $(q, a, q') \in \Delta$, or
- $P' = \Pi$, and $(q, a, \pi) \in \Delta$.

We use $P \xrightarrow{a}$ to mean that $\exists P'$ such that $P \xrightarrow{a} P'$, and $P \stackrel{a}{\not\rightarrow}$ to mean that $\not\exists P'$ such that $P \xrightarrow{a} P'$.

We define a set of designated end states $ES \subseteq States$ such that an LTS $P = < S, A, \Delta, q >$ is terminating if there is a state $e \in S$ and $e \in ES$ and $\not\exists(e, a, q) \in \Delta$ for all $a \in A$.

C.2 Processes

In the following, E ranges over *FSP* process expressions, Q ranges over process identifiers, and A, B range over sets of observable actions (i.e. $A \subseteq L$ and $B \subseteq L$).

Process Definition:

$Q = E$ means that $lts(Q) =_{\text{def}} lts(E)$.

Process Constants:

$lts(\text{END}) = <\{e\}, \{\tau\}, \{\}, e>$ where $e \in ES$
$lts(\text{STOP}) = <\{s\}, \{\tau\}, \{\}, s>$
$lts(\text{ERROR}) = \Pi$

Prefix -> :

If $lts(E) = < S, A, \Delta, q >$ and E is not ERROR
then $lts(a \text{ -> } E) = < S \cup \{p\}, A \cup \{a\}, \Delta \cup \{(p, a, q)\}, p >$, where $p \notin S$.
$lts(a \text{ -> ERROR}) =< \{p, \pi\}, \{a\}, \{(p, a, \pi)\}, p >$, where $p \neq \pi$.

Choice | :

Let $1 \leq i \leq n$, and $lts(E_i) = < S_i, A_i, \Delta_i, q_i >$,
then $lts(a_1 \text{ -> } E_1 \mid \ldots \mid a_n \text{ -> } E_n)$
$= < S \cup \{p\}, A \cup \{a_1 \ldots a_n\}, \Delta \cup \{(p, a_1, q_1) \ldots (p, a_n, q_n)\}, p >$,
where $p \notin S_i$, $S = \bigcup_i Si$, $A = \bigcup_i Ai$, $\Delta = \bigcup_i \Delta i$.
If E_i is ERROR then $A_i = \{\}$.

Alphabet Extension +:

If $lts(E) =< S, A, \Delta, q >$,
then $lts(E + B) =< S, A \cup B, \Delta, q >$.

Recursion:

We represent the *FSP* process defined by the recursive equation $X = E$ as $rec(X = E)$, where X is a variable in E. For example, the process defined by the recursive definition $X = (a \text{ -> } X)$ is represented as $rec(X = (a \text{ -> } X))$.

We use $E[X \leftarrow rec(X = E)]$ to denote the *FSP* expression that is obtained by substituting $rec(X = E)$ for X in E. Then $lts(rec(X = E))$ is the smallest *LTS* that satisfies the following rule:

$$rec(X = (a \text{ -> } X)) \sim lts(E[X \leftarrow rec(X = E)])$$

where "$\sim$" is strong semantic equivalence defined in section C.6.1. Mutually recursive equations can be reduced to the simple form described above. For local processes, all occurrences of process variables are guarded by an action prefix and consequently, recursive definitions are guaranteed to have a fixed-point solution.

Sequential Composition:
If $lts(P) = < S_p, A_p, \Delta_p, q_p >$ is terminating with end state $e_p \in ES$
and $lts(E) = < S_e, A_e, \Delta_e, q_e >$
then $lts(P; E) = < S_p \cup S_e, A_p \cup A_e, \Delta_p \cup \Delta_e, q_p >$ where $q_e = e_p$.

C.3 Composite Processes

Before defining the meaning of composition in *FSP* and of the priority operators on composite processes, we must first describe the meaning of composition and priority in the underlying *LTS* model.

C.3.1 *LTS* Composition

The parallel composition $P||Q$ of two *LTS*s P and Q is defined as follows:

If $P = \Pi$ or $Q = \Pi$, then $P||Q = \Pi$.
For $P = < S_1, A_1, \Delta_1, q_1 >$ and $Q = < S_2, A_2, \Delta_2, q_2 >$, such that $P \neq \Pi$ and $Q \neq \Pi$,
$P||Q = < S_1 \times S_2, A_1 \cup A_2, \Delta, (q_1, q_2) >$,
where Δ is the smallest relation satisfying the rules:

Let $a \in Act$ in

$$\frac{P \xrightarrow{a} P'}{P||Q \xrightarrow{a} P'||Q} a \notin \alpha Q \qquad \frac{Q \xrightarrow{a} Q'}{P||Q \xrightarrow{a} P||Q'} a \notin \alpha P$$

$$\frac{P \xrightarrow{a} P', Q \xrightarrow{a} Q'}{P||Q \xrightarrow{a} P'||Q'} a \neq \tau$$

Parallel composition is both commutative and associative. Consequently, the order in which *LTS*s are composed is not significant.

In addition:
$P \mid\mid lts(\text{END}) = P$, $lts(\text{END}) \mid\mid P = P$ and $lts(\text{END}) \mid\mid lts(\text{END}) = lts(\text{END})$.

C.3.2 *LTS* Priority

The set of actions $B \subseteq Act$ are *high* priority in the *LTS* $P \ll B$, where $P = < S, A, \Delta', q >$.

$P \ll B = < S, A, \Delta, q >$ where Δ is the smallest relation satisfying the rule:
Let $a, b \in Act$ in

$$\frac{P \xrightarrow{a} P'}{P \ll B \xrightarrow{a} P' \ll B} \text{ if}((a \in B) \text{ or } (\forall b \in B, P \overset{b}{\not\rightarrow}))$$

The set of actions $B \subseteq Act$ are *low* priority in the *LTS* $P \gg B$, where $P = < S, A, \Delta', q >$.

$P \gg B = < S, A, \Delta, q >$ where Δ is the smallest relation satisfying the rule:
Let $a, b \in Act$ in

$$\frac{P \xrightarrow{a} P'}{P \gg B \xrightarrow{a} P' \gg B} \text{ if}((a \notin B) \; or \; (\forall b \in (A - B), P \overset{b}{\not\rightarrow}))$$

C.3.3 *FSP* Composition and Priority

Using the definitions for *LTS* composition and priority, we can now simply define the meaning of composition and priority in *FSP*. In the following, *CE* refers to *FSP* composition expressions of the form $(Q_1 \mid\mid \ldots \mid\mid Q_n)$ and Q refers to the identifier of a process or composite process.

Parallel Composition || :
$lts(Q_1 \mid\mid Q_2) = lts(Q_1) \mid\mid lts(Q_2)$.

Priority High << :
$lts(CE << B) = lts(CE) << B$.

Priority Low >> :
$lts(CE >> B) = lts(CE) >> B$.

C.4 Common Operators

To define the *FSP* re-labeling, hiding and interface operators, which can be applied to processes and composite processes, we first describe the meaning of re-labeling and hiding in the underlying *LTS* model.

C.4.1 Re-Labeling

Re-labeling applies a relation over action labels $R \subseteq L \times L$, to an *LTS* $P = < S, A, \Delta, q >$ such that:

$$P/R = < S, (A - B_1) \cup B_2, (\Delta - \Delta_1) \cup \Delta_2, q > .$$

where

$B_1 = \{a \in A | \exists a'.(a, a') \in R\}$,
$B_2 = \{a' | \exists a \in A.(a, a') \in R\}$,
$\Delta_1 = \{(p, a, p') \in \Delta | a \in B_1\}$, and
$\Delta_2 = \{(p, a', p') | (p, a, p') \in \Delta_1 \wedge (a, a') \in R\}$.

C.4.2 Hiding

The set of actions $B \subseteq Act$ are *hidden* in the *LTS* $P\backslash B$, where $P = < S, A, \Delta, q >$.

If $P = \Pi$ then $P\backslash B = \Pi$ otherwise
$P\backslash B = < S, (A - B) \cup \{\tau\}, \Delta, q >$
where Δ is the smallest relation satisfying the rule:

Let $a \in Act$ in

$$\frac{P \xrightarrow{a} P'}{P\backslash B \xrightarrow{\tau} P'\backslash B}\ a \in B \qquad \frac{P \xrightarrow{a} P'}{P\backslash B \xrightarrow{a} P'\ B}\ a \notin B$$

C.4.3 *FSP* Re-Labeling, Hiding and Interface

Re-labeling /:

$lts(E/\,R) = lts(E)/R.$
$lts((Q_1 \,|\,| \ldots |\,|\, Q_n)/\,R) = lts(Q_1)/R \,||\ldots||\, lts(Q_n)/R$

Hiding \\:

$lts(E\backslash B) = lts(E)\backslash B.$

Interface @:

$lts(E@\,I) = lts(E) \backslash B$ where $B = \alpha(lts(E)) - I$.

C.5 Safety Properties

A safety property Q in *FSP* is represented by an *image* of the *LTS* of the process expression that defines the property. The image *LTS* has each state of the original *LTS* and has a transition from each state for every action in the alphabet of the original. Transitions added to the image *LTS* are to the error state.

property $Q = E$:

$lts(Q) =_{\text{def}} image(lts(E))$,

for an *LTS* $P = < S, A, \Delta, p >$, $image(P) = < S \cup \{\pi\}, A, \Delta', q >$, where $\Delta' = \Delta \cup \{(s, a, \pi) | s \in S, a \in A$, and $\nexists s' \in S$: $(s, a, s') \in \Delta\}$.

C.6 Semantic Equivalences

Minimization of the *LTS* corresponding to an *FSP* process definition results in a semantically equivalent *LTS*. The equivalence relations used in performing minimization are defined in the following sections.

C.6.1 Strong Equivalence

Strong semantic equivalence equates *LTS*s that have identical behavior when the occurrence of all their actions can be observed, including that of the silent action τ.

Let $\wp$ be the universal set of *LTS*s. *Strong semantic equivalence* "$\sim$" is the union of all relations $\boldsymbol{R} \subseteq \wp \times \wp$ satisfying that $(P, Q) \in \boldsymbol{R}$ implies:

1. $\alpha P = \alpha Q$;
2. $\forall a \in Act$:
   - $P \xrightarrow{a} P'$ implies $\exists Q'$, $Q \xrightarrow{a} Q'$ and $(P', Q') \in \boldsymbol{R}$.
   - $Q \xrightarrow{a} Q'$ implies $\exists P'$, $P \xrightarrow{a} P'$ and $(P', Q') \in \boldsymbol{R}$.
3. $P = \Pi$ iff $Q = \Pi$.

The *LTSA* tool performs minimization using strong equivalence if an *LTS* contains no silent actions (τ). For an *LTS P*, without τ-actions:

$minimized(P) \sim P$.

C.6.2 Weak Equivalence

Weak semantic equivalence equates systems that exhibit the same behavior to an external observer who cannot detect the occurrence of τ-actions.

Let $P \overset{a}{\Rightarrow} P'$ denote $P \xrightarrow{\tau^* a \tau^*} P'$, where τ^* means a sequence of zero or more τs. Then *weak (or observational) semantic equivalence* "$\approx$" is the union of all relations $\boldsymbol{R} \subseteq \wp \times \wp$ satisfying that $(P, Q) \in \boldsymbol{R}$ implies:

1. $\alpha P = \alpha Q$;
2. $\forall a \in L \cup \{\varepsilon\}$, where $L = Act - \{\tau\}$, and ε is the empty sequence:
   - $P \overset{a}{\Rightarrow} P'$ implies $\exists Q', Q \overset{a}{\Rightarrow} Q'$ and $(P', Q') \in \boldsymbol{R}$.
   - $Q \overset{a}{\Rightarrow} Q'$ implies $\exists P', P \overset{a}{\Rightarrow} P'$ and $(P', Q') \in \boldsymbol{R}$.
3. $P = \Pi$ iff $Q = \Pi$.

The *LTSA* tool performs minimization using weak equivalence if an *LTS* contains silent actions (τ). For an *LTS P*, with τ-actions:

$$minimized(P) \approx P.$$

Both strong and weak equivalence are congruences with respect to the composition, re-labeling, and hiding operators. This means that strongly or weakly equivalent components may substitute one another in any system constructed with these operators, without affecting the behavior of the system with respect to strong or weak equivalence, respectively.

C.7 Fluent Linear Temporal Logic (FLTL)

C.7.1 Linear Temporal Logic

Given a set of atomic propositions $\wp$, a well-formed LTL formula is defined inductively using the standard Boolean operators **!** (not), **||** (or), **&&** (and), and the temporal operators **X** (next) and **U** (strong until) as follows:

- each member of $\wp$ is a formula,
- if φ and ψ are formulae, then so are **!** φ, φ **||** ψ, φ **&&** ψ, **X** φ, φ **U** ψ.

An interpretation for an LTL formula is an infinite word $w = x_0 x_1 x_2 \ldots$ over $2^{\wp}$. In other words, an interpretation maps to each instant of time a set of propositions that hold at that instant. We write w_i for the suffix of w starting at x_i. LTL semantics is then defined inductively as follows:

- $w \models p$ iff $p \in x_0$, for $p \in \wp$
- $w \models$ **!** φ iff not $w \models \varphi$

- $w \mid= \varphi$ **||** ψ iff $(w| = \varphi)$ or $(w| = \psi)$
- $w \mid= \varphi$ **&&** ψ iff $(w| = \varphi)$ and $(w| = \psi)$
- $w \mid=$ **X** φ iff $w_1| = \varphi$
- $w \mid= \varphi$ **U** ψ iff $\exists i \geq 0$, such that: $w_i| = \psi$ and $\forall\, 0 \leq j < i, w_j| = \varphi$

We introduce the abbreviations "true $\equiv \varphi$ **||** **!** φ" and "false $\equiv$ **!** true". Implication **->** and equivalence **<->** are defined as:

$$\varphi \textbf{ -> } \psi \equiv \textbf{!}\, \varphi \textbf{ || } \psi,$$

$$\text{and} \quad \varphi \textbf{ <-> } \psi \equiv (\varphi \textbf{ -> } \psi) \textbf{ \&\& } (\varphi \textbf{ <- } \psi)$$

Temporal operators **<>** (eventually), **[ ]** (always), and **W** (weak until) are defined in terms of the main temporal operators:

$$\textbf{<>}\varphi \equiv \text{ true } \mathbf{U}$$

$$[]\varphi \equiv \textbf{!<>!}\ \varphi,$$

$$\text{and} \quad \varphi \textbf{ W } \psi \equiv ((\varphi \textbf{ U } \psi) \textbf{ || } \textbf{[ ]}\ \varphi).$$

C.7.2 Fluents

We define a fluent *Fl* by a pair of sets, a set of initiating actions I_{Fl} and a set of terminating actions T_{Fl}:

$$Fl \equiv \langle I_{Fl}, T_{Fl} \rangle \text{ where } I_{Fl}, T_{Fl} \subset Act \text{ and } I_{Fl} \cap T_{Fl} = \varnothing$$

In addition, a fluent *Fl* may initially be true or false at time zero as denoted by the attribute $Initially_{Fl}$.

The set of atomic propositions from which FLTL formulae are built is the set of fluents Φ. Therefore, an interpretation in FLTL is an infinite word over 2^{Φ}, which assigns to each time instant the set of fluents that hold at that time instant. An infinite word $< a_0 a_1 a_2 \cdots >$ over *Act* (i.e. an infinite trace of actions) also defines an FLTL interpretation $< f_0 f_1 f_2 \cdots >$ over 2^{Φ} as follows:

$\forall i \in N, \forall\, Fl \in \Phi, Fl \in f_i$ iff either of the following holds

$- Initially_{Fl} \wedge (\forall k \in N \cdot 0 \leq k \leq i, a_k \notin T_{Fl})$

$- \exists j \in N : ((j \leq i) \wedge (a_j \in I_{Fl}) \wedge (\forall k \in N \cdot j < k \leq i, a_k \notin T_{Fl}))$

In other words, a fluent holds at a time instant if and only if it holds initially or some initiating action has occurred, and, in both cases, no terminating action has yet occurred. Note that the interval over which a fluent holds is *closed* on the left and *open* on the right, since actions have immediate effect on the values of fluents. Since the sets of initiating and terminating actions are disjoint, the value of a fluent is always deterministic with respect to a system execution.

Every action a implicitly defines a fluent whose initial set of actions is the singleton $\{a\}$ and whose terminating set contains all other actions in the alphabet of a process $A \subseteq Act$:

$$Fluent(a) \equiv \langle \{a\}, A - \{a\} \rangle \; Initially_a = \text{false}$$

Fluent(a) becomes true the instant a occurs and becomes false with the first occurrence of a different action. It is often more succinct in defining properties to declare a fluent implicitly for a set of actions as in:

$$Fluent(S) \equiv \langle S, A - S \rangle \; Initially_S = \text{false}, \; \text{where } S = \{a_0, a_1, \ldots a_n\}$$

This is equivalent to $a_0 \; || \; a_1 \; || \; \ldots \; || \; a_n$ where a_i represents the implicitly defined *Fluent*(a_i).

Appendix D
UML Class Diagrams

This appendix presents the subset of UML class diagrams used in the book. We have used UML to describe implementations rather than high-level design. Generalization is consistently used to mean inheritance in Java and association with navigability to mean that the source class holds a reference to an object of the target class.

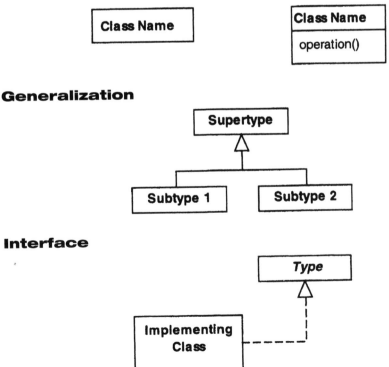

Class

Generalization

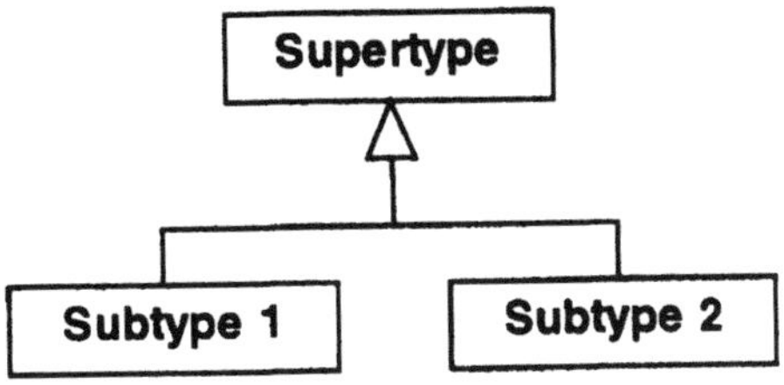

Interface

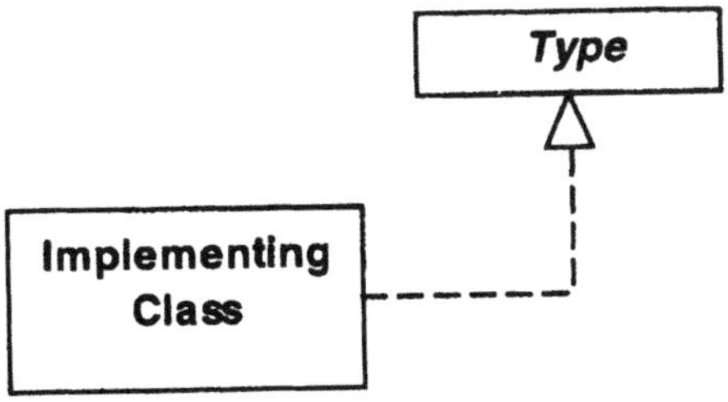

Association

Multiplicities

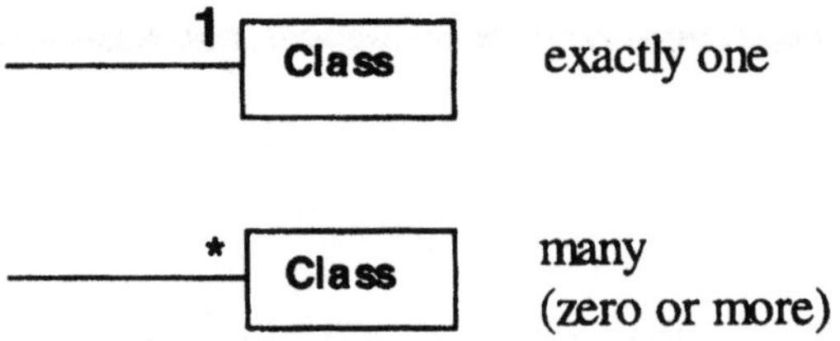

Navigability

Bibliography

Andrews, G.R. (1991). *Concurrent Programming: Principles and Practice*. Redwood City, CA: Benjamin/Cummings Publishing Company.

Ball, T. and Rajamani, S.K. (2002). *The SLAM Project: Debugging System Software via Static Analysis*. POPL 2002, 1–3.

Balzer, R.M. (1971). *PORTS: a method for dynamic interprogram communication and job control*. Proceedings AFIPS SJCC Computer Conference, **39**, 485–489.

Ben-Ari, M. (1990). *Principles of Concurrent and Distributed Programming*. Prentice-Hall International Series in Computer Science.

Birtwistle, G.M., Dahl, O., Myhrhaug, B. and Nygaard, K. (1973). *SIMULA BEGIN*. New York: Van Nostrand Reinhold.

Booch, G. (1986). *Object-oriented development*. IEEE Transactions on Software Engineering **SE-12**, **2** (February), 211–221.

Booch, G., Rumbaugh, J. and Jacobson, I. (1998). *Unified Modeling Language User Guide*. Addison-Wesley Object Technology Series.

Brat, G., Havelund, K., Park, S. and Visser, W. (2000). *Java PathFinder – Second Generation of a Java Model Checker*. Workshop on Advances in Verification.

Brinch-Hansen, P. (1970). *The nucleus of a multiprogramming system*. Communications of the ACM **13**, **4** (April), 238–241.

Brinch-Hansen, P. (1972). *Structured multiprogramming*. Communications of the ACM **15**, **7** (July), 574–578.

Brinch-Hansen, P. (1975). *The programming language Concurrent Pascal*. IEEE Transactions on Software Engineering **SE-1**, **2** (June), 199–206.

Brinch Hansen, Per (2002). *The Origins of Concurrent Programming: From Semaphores to Remote Procedure Calls*. Springer-Verlag.

Bruno, G. (1995). *Model-Based Software Engineering*. London: Chapman & Hall.

Burns, A. and Davies, G.L. (1993). *Concurrent Programming*. Wokingham: Addison-Wesley.

Carriero, N. and Gelernter, D. (1989a). *Linda in context*. Communications of the ACM **32**, **4** (April), 444–458.

Carriero, N. and Gelernter, D. (1989b). *How to write parallel programs: a guide for the perplexed*. ACM Computing Surveys **21**, **3** (September), 323–358.

CCITT (1993). *CCITT High Level Language (CHILL) Recommendation Z200*. Geneva: International Telecommunication Union ITU.

Chandy, K.M. and Misra, J. (1984). *The drinking philosophers problem*. ACM Transactions on Programming Languages and Systems **6**, **4** (October), 632–646.

Cheung, S.C. and Magee, J.N. (1991). *Parallel algorithm design for workstation clusters.* Software: Practice and Experience **21, 3** (March), 235–250.

Cheung, S.C. and Kramer, J. (1999). *Checking safety properties using compositional reachability analysis.* ACM Transactions on Software Engineering and Methodology (TOSEM) **8, 1** (January), 49–78.

Ciancarini, P. and Hankin, C. (eds.) (1996). *Coordination Languages and Models.* Proceedings of Coordination '96, LNCA 1061, Berlin: Springer-Verlag.

Clarke, E.M., Emerson, E.A. and Sistla, A.P. (1986). *Automatic verification of finite state concurrent systems using temporal logic specifications.* ACM Transactions on Programming Languages and Systems **8, 2** (April), 626–643.

Clarke, E.M., Wing, J.M., *et al.* (1996). *Formal methods: state of the art and future directions.* ACM Computing Surveys **28, 4**, 626–643.

Cleaveland, R., Smolka, S.A., *et al.* (1996). *Strategic directions in concurrency research.* ACM Computing Surveys **28, 4**, 607–625.

Cobleigh, J.M., Clarke, L.A. and Osterweil, L.J. (2002). *FLAVERS: a finite state verification technique for software systems.* IBM Systems Journal **41, 1**, 140–165.

Coffman, E.G. Jr., Elphick, M.J. and Shoshani, A. (1971). *System deadlocks.* ACM Computing Surveys **3, 2** (June), 67–78.

Corbett, J., Dwyer, M., Hatcliff, John, *et al.* (2000). *Bandera: Extracting Finite-State Models from Java Source Code.* Proceedings of 22nd IEEE/ACM International Conference on Software Engineering (ICSE-2000), Limerick, Ireland, 439–448.

Cunningham, R.J. and Kramer, J. (1978). *An exercise in program design using SIMULA class invariants.* Software: Practice and Experience **8, 3** (May–June), 355–369.

De Nicola, Rocco, Ferrari, Gianluigi and Meredith, Greg (eds.) (2004). *Coordination Models and Languages.* 6th International Conference, COORDINATION 2004, Pisa, Italy, Proceedings, LNCS 2949, Berlin: Springer-Verlag.

Department of Defense (1983). *Reference Manual for the Ada Programming Language.* New York: Springer-Verlag.

Dijkstra, E.W. (1965). *Solution of a problem in concurrent programming control.* Communications of the ACM **8, 9** (September), 569.

Dijkstra, E.W. (1968a). *Cooperating sequential processes.* In F. Genuys (ed.) *Programming Languages*, 43–112. New York: Academic Press.

Dijkstra, E.W.D. (1968b). *A constructive approach to the problem of program correctness.* BIT **8, 3**, 174–186.

Dijkstra, E.W. (1972a). *A class of allocation strategies inducing bounded delays only.* AFIPS Spring Joint Computer Conference SJCC, 933–936.

Dijkstra, E.W. (1972b). *Hierarchical ordering of sequential processes.* In C.A.R. Hoare and R.H. Perrott (eds.) *Operating System Techniques.* New York: Academic Press.

Dwyer, M.B., Avrunin, G.S. and Corbett, J.C. (1999). *Patterns in Property Specifications for Finite-State Verification.* Proceedings of the 21st International Conference on Software Engineering (ICSE'99), Los Angeles (May).

Floyd, R. (1967). *Assigning Meaning to Programs.* Symposium on Applied Mathematics, New York, 19–32.

Fowler, M. and Scott, K. (1997). *UML Distilled: Applying the Standard Object Modeling Language.* Addison-Wesley Object Technology Series.

Francez, N. (1986). *Fairness.* New York: Springer-Verlag.

Freeman, Eric, Hupfer, Susanne and Arnold, Ken (1999). *JavaSpaces™ Principles, Patterns, and Practice* (1st edition). Pearson Education.

Garg, Vijay K. (2004). *Concurrent and Distributed Computing in Java*. John Wiley and Sons.

Garlan, D. and Le Metayer, D. (eds.) (1997). *Coordination Languages and Models*. Proceedings of the 2nd International Conference, Coordination '97, LNCS 1282, Berlin: Springer-Verlag.

Gelernter, D. (1985). *Generative communication in Linda*. ACM Transactions on Programming Languages and Systems **7**, **1** (January), 80–112.

Giannakopoulou, D., Magee, J.N. and Kramer, J. (1999). *Checking Progress in Concurrent Systems*. 7th ACM SIGSOFT Symposium on the Foundations of Software Engineering/7th European Software Engineering Conference (FSE/ESEC '99), Toulouse, Springer-Verlag, 511–528.

Giannakopoulou, Dimitra and Lerda, Flavio (2002). *From states to transitions: improving translation of LTL formulae to Büchi automata*. FORTE 2002, 308–326.

Giannakopoulou, D. and Magee, J. (2003). *Fluent Model Checking for Event-Based Systems*. Proceedings of the 4th joint meeting of the European Software Engineering Conference and the ACM SIGSOFT Symposium on the Foundations of Software Engineering (ESEC/FSE 2003), Helsinki, Finland (September).

Goldberg, A. and Robson, D. (1983). *Smalltalk-80*. Addison-Wesley.

Gomaa, H. (1993). *Software Design Methods for Concurrent and Real-Time Systems*. Reading, MA: Addison-Wesley.

Gribomont, P. and Wolper, P. (1989). *Temporal logic*. In A. Thayse (ed.) *From Modal Logic to Deductive Databases*. John Wiley and Sons.

Harel, D. (1987). *Statecharts: a visual formalism for complex systems*. Science of Computer Programming **8** (July), 231–274.

Harel, D., Lachover, H., Naamad, A., Pnueli, A., Politi, M., Sherman, R., Shtull-Trauring, A. and Trakhtenbrot, M. (1990). *STATEMATE: a working environment for the development of complex reactive systems*. IEEE Transactions on Software Engineering **SE-16**, **4** (April), 403–414.

Harel, D. and Kugler, H. (2000). *Synthesizing State-Based Object Systems from LSC Specifications*. 5th International Conference on Implementation and Application of Automata (CIAA'2000), Springer-Verlag.

Harel, D. and Marelly, R. (2003). *Come, Let's Play: Scenario-Based Programming Using LSCs and the Play-Engine*. Springer-Verlag.

Havelund, K. and Pressburger, T. (2000). *Model checking Java programs using Java PathFinder*. International Journal on Software Tools for Technology Transfer **2**, **4**, 366–381.

Henzinger, T.A., Jhala, R., Majumdar, R. and Sutre, G. (2003). *Software Verification with Blast*. Proceedings of the Tenth International Workshop on Model Checking of Software (SPIN), LNCS 2648, Berlin: Springer-Verlag, 235–239.

Hoare, C.A.R. (1969). *An axiomatic basis of computer programming*. Communications of the ACM **12**, **10**, 576–580.

Hoare, C.A.R. (1974). *Monitors: an operating system structuring concept*. Communications of the ACM **17**, **10** (October), 549–557.

Hoare, C.A.R. (1978). *Communicating sequential processes*. Communications of the ACM **21**, **8** (August), 666–677.

Hoare, C.A.R. (1985). *Communicating Sequential Processes*. Prentice-Hall International Series in Computer Science.

Holt, R.C. (1983). *Concurrent Euclid, The UNIX System, and Tunis*. Reading, MA: Addison-Wesley.

Holt, R.C. and Cordy, J.R. (1988). *The Turing programming language*. Communications of the ACM **31**, **12** (December), 1410–1423.

Holzmann, G.J. (1991). *Design and Validation of Computer Protocols*. Englewood Cliffs, NJ: Prentice-Hall International.

Holzmann, G.J. (1997). *The model checker SPIN*. IEEE Transactions on Software Engineering **SE-23**, **5** (May), 279–295.

Holzmann, G.J. and Smith, M.H. (2002). *An automated verification method for distributed systems software based on model extraction*. IEEE Transactions on Software Engineering **SE-28**, **4**, 364–377.

INMOS Ltd. (1988a). *OCCAM 2 Reference Manual*. Prentice-Hall International Series in Computer Science.

INMOS Ltd. (1988b). *Transputer Reference Manual*. Englewood Cliffs, NJ: Prentice-Hall International.

ISO/IEC (1988). *LOTOS: Formal description technique based on the temporal ordering of observational behaviour*. International Standard 9074. Geneva: International Organization for Standardization – Information Processing Systems – Open Systems Interconnection.

ITU (1996). *Message Sequence Charts (MSC'96)*. Recommendation Z.120. Telecommunication Standardisation Sector (ITU).

Jacquet, Jean-Marie and Picco, Gian Pietro (eds.) (2005). *Coordination Models and Languages*. 7th International Conference, COORDINATION 2005, Namur, Belgium, Proceedings, LNCS 3454, Berlin: Springer-Verlag.

Joseph, M. (ed.) (1996). *Real-Time Systems: Specification, Verification and Analysis*. Prentice-Hall International Series in Computer Science.

Kanellakis, P.C. and Smolka, S.A. (1990). *CCS expressions, finite state processes, and three problems of equivalence*. Information and Computation **86**, **1** (May), 43–68.

Kleiman, S., Shah, D. and Smaalders, B. (1996). *Programming with Threads*. Upper Saddle River, NJ: SunSoft Press, Prentice-Hall.

Koskimies, K., Männistö, T., Systä, T. and Tuonmi, J. (1998). *Automated support for modeling OO software*. IEEE Software **15**, 87–94.

Kramer, J. and Cunningham, R.J. (1979). *Invariants for Specifications*. Proceedings of 4th IEEE International Conference on Software Engineering (ICSE '79), Munich, 183–193.

Kramer, J. and Magee, J. (1998). *Analysing dynamic change in distributed software architectures*. IEE Proceedings – Software **145**, **5** (October), 146–154.

Lamport, L. (1977). *Proving the correctness of multiprocess programs*. IEEE Transactions on Software Engineering **SE-3**, **2** (March), 125–143.

Lamport, L. (1980). *"Sometime" is Sometimes "Not Never": On the Temporal Logic of Programs*. Proceedings of the 7th ACM SIGPLAN-SIGACT Symposium on Principles of Programming Languages, Las Vegas, 174–185.

Lampson, B.W. and Redell, D.D. (1980). *Experience with processes and monitors in Mesa*. Communications of the ACM **23**, **2** (February), 105–117.

Lea, Doug (1999). *Concurrent Programming in Java™: Design Principles and Patterns* (2nd edition). Addison-Wesley.

Lehman, D. and Rabin, M.O. (1981). *A Symmetric and Fully Distributed Solution to the Dining Philosophers Problem*. Proceedings of the 8th ACM Symposium on Principles of Programming Languages, January, 133–138.

Letier, E., Kramer, J., Magee, J. and Uchitel, S. (2005). *Fluent Temporal Logic for Discrete-Time Event-Based Models*. The Joint 10th European Software Engineering Conference and the

13th ACM SIGSOFT Symposium on the Foundations of Software Engineering (ESEC-FSE 2005), Lisbon, Portugal (September), 70–79.

Leveson, N.G. and Turner, C.S. (1993). *An investigation of the Therac-25 accidents.* IEEE Computer **26**, **7** (July), 18–41.

Lister, A. (1977). *The problem of nested monitor calls.* Operating Systems Review **11**, **3** (July), 5–7.

Lynch, N.A. (1996). *Distributed Algorithms.* San Francisco, CA: Morgan Kaufmann.

McCarthy, J. (1963). *Towards a Mathematical Science of Computation.* IFIP Congress **62**, 21–28.

Magee, J.N., Dulay, N. and Kramer, J. (1994). *Regis: a constructive development environment for distributed programs.* Distributed Systems Engineering Journal **1**, **5**, Special Issue on Configurable Distributed Systems, 304–312.

Magee, J.N., Dulay, N., Eisenbach, S. and Kramer, J. (1995). *Specifying Distributed Software Architectures.* Proceedings of 5th European Software Engineering Conference (ESEC '95), Sitges (September), LNCS 989, Berlin: Springer-Verlag, 137–153.

Magee, J.N., Kramer, J. and Giannakopoulou, D. (1997). *Analysing the Behaviour of Distributed Software Architectures: A Case Study.* Proceedings of 5th IEEE Workshop on Future Trends in Distributed Computing Systems (FTDCS'97), Tunisia (October), 240–247.

Magee, J., Pryce, N., Giannakopoulou, D. and Kramer, J. (2000). *Graphical Animation of Behaviour Models.* Proceedings of 22nd IEEE/ACM International Conference on Software Engineering (ICSE-2000), Limerick, Ireland, 499–508.

Milner, R. (1989). *Communication and Concurrency.* Prentice-Hall International Series in Computer Science.

Milner, R., Parrow, J. and Walker, D. (1992). *A calculus of mobile processes, I and II.* Information and Computation **100**, **1**, 1–77.

Morris, F.L. and Jones, C.B. (1984). *An early program proof by Alan Turing.* Annals of the History of Computing **6**, **2**, 139–143.

Peterson, G.L. (1981). *Myths about the mutual exclusion problem.* Information Processing Letters **12**, **3** (June), 115–116.

Peterson, J.L. (1981). *Petri Net Theory and the Modeling of Systems.* Englewood Cliffs, NJ: Prentice-Hall International.

Pnueli, A. (1977). *The Temporal Logic of Programs.* Proceedings of the 18th IEEE Symposium on the Foundations of Computer Science (FOCS-77), October/November, 46–57.

Reiss, S.P. (1990). *Connecting tools using message passing in the Field Environment.* IEEE Software **7**, **4** (July), 57–66.

Roscoe, A.W. (1998). *The Theory and Practice of Concurrency.* Prentice-Hall International Series in Computer Science.

Rumbaugh, J., Blaha, M., Premerlani, W., Eddy, F. and Lorensen, W. (1991). *Object-Oriented Modeling and Design.* Englewood Cliffs, NJ: Prentice-Hall International.

Sandewall, E. (1995). *Features and Fluents: The Representation of Knowledge about Dynamical Systems.* Oxford University Press.

Schneider, Fred B. (1997). *On Concurrent Programming* (Graduate Texts in Computer Science). Springer-Verlag.

Selic, B., Gullekson, G. and Ward, P.T. (1994). *Real-Time Object Oriented Modeling.* New York: John Wiley and Sons.

Shaw, M. (1995). *Comparing architectural design styles.* IEEE Software **12**, **6** (November), 27–41.

Shaw, M. and Garlan, D. (1996). *Software Architecture: Perspectives on an Emerging Discipline.* Englewood Cliffs, NJ: Prentice-Hall International.

Sloman, M.S. (ed.) (1994). *Network and Distributed Systems Management*. Addison-Wesley.

Swartout, W. and Balzer, R. (1982). *On the inevitable intertwining of specification and implementation*. Communications of the ACM **25**, **7** (July), 438–440.

Turing, A. (1949). *Checking a large routine*. In the Report of a Conference on High Speed Automatic Calculating Machines, pp. 67–69.

Uchitel, S., Kramer, J. and Magee, J. (2003). *Synthesis of behavioral models from scenarios*. IEEE Transactions on Software Engineering **SE-29**, **2** (February), 99–115.

Uchitel, S., Kramer, J. and Magee, J. (2004). *Incremental elaboration of scenario-based specifications and behaviour models using implied scenarios*. ACM Transactions on Software Engineering and Methodology (TOSEM) **13**, **1** (January), 37–85.

Vardi, M. (2001). *Branching vs. Linear Time: Final Showdown*. Proceedings of the 7th International Conference on Tools and Algorithms for the Construction and Analysis of Systems, LNCS 2031, Berlin: Springer-Verlag, 1–22.

Welsh, J. and Bustard, D.W. (1979). *Pascal-Plus: another language for modular multiprogramming*. Software: Practice and Experience **11**, 947–957.

Whittle, J. and Schumann, J. (2000). *Generating Statechart Designs from Scenarios*. Proceedings of 22nd IEEE/ACM International Conference on Software Engineering (ICSE-2000), Limerick, Ireland, 314–323.

Wirth, N. (1977). *Modula: a language for modular multiprogramming*. Software: Practice and Experience **7**, 3–35.

Index